D
R
1812–1888

Lilwen

To remind you of Ionian days
in Chrysolite

Angus 1988

The Royal Academy of Arts
wishes to express its gratitude
to the sponsors of this exhibition

SWAN HELLENIC
A Division of P&O Cruises

Trusthouse Forte

AND

Walker Books Limited

The Royal Academy is also grateful to
Her Majesty's Government for its help
in agreeing to indemnify this exhibition
under the National Heritage Act 1980

EDWARD LEAR

1812–1888

VIVIEN NOAKES

with an introduction by
Sir Steven Runciman
and an essay by
Jeremy Maas

Royal Academy of Arts, London, 1985
Catalogue published in association with
Weidenfeld and Nicolson, London

Opposite: Self-portrait from title page
of *More Nonsense*, 1872 (Cat. 83)

Cover, front: adapted from the cover of the 1888 edition of Lear's
Book of Nonsense; *back*: *Boyhood Silhouette of Edward Lear* (Cat. 4*b*)

House editor Johanna Awdry
Designed by Harry Green for
George Weidenfeld and Nicolson Limited
91 Clapham High Street, London SW4 7TA

ISBN 0 297 786 350 (casebound)
0 297 786 369 (paperback)

Filmset in Garamond
Printed by BAS Printers Limited, Over Wallop, Hampshire
Colour separations by Newsele Litho Limited, Italy
Colour printed in Italy by Printers Srl, Trento, Italy

CONTENTS

List of Lenders

Her Majesty The Queen
Aberdare, Cynon Valley Borough Council
Aldington, The Lord
Bembridge, Ruskin Galleries, Bembridge School, Isle of Wight
Bristol, City of Bristol Museum and Art Gallery
Cambridge, The Syndics of The Fitzwilliam Museum
Cambridge (Mass., USA), The Houghton Library, Harvard University
Davies, Mr Martin R.
D'Oyly Mr N.H.
Ebert, Mr Roger
Edinburgh, Trustees of the National Library of Scotland
Farquharson, Mr J.J.
Farquharson, Mr R.A.
Hollis, Mr H.M.N.
Kenn, Mr Alan
Koe, Mrs M.B.
Lange, Mr Thomas V.
Lincoln, The Tennyson Research Centre, Lincolnshire Library Service
Liverpool, City Libraries
Liverpool, Merseyside County Council, Walker Art Gallery
London, BBC Hulton Picture Library
London, British Library Board
London, The Trustees of the British Museum
London, The Clothworkers' Company
London, The Fine Art Society
London, Islington Libraries
London, The Linnean Society
London, Morton Morris & Company Limited
London, The National Portrait Gallery
London, The Royal Academy of Arts
London, Standard Chartered Bank
London, The Trustees of the Tate Gallery
London, The Trustees of the Victoria and Albert Museum
Mawson, Mr and Mrs David
Michell, Dr David R.
Montreal, Blacker-Wood Library, McGill University, Canada
Morley-Fletcher, Mr Charles
New Haven, Yale Center for British Art
New Haven, The Beinecke Rare Book and Manuscript Library, Yale University
New York, The FORBES Magazine Collection
New York, The Frederick R. Koch Foundation Collection
New York, The Pierpont Morgan Library
Noakes, Vivien
Providence, Museum of Art, Rhode Island School of Design
Runciman, The Hon. Sir Steven, CH
Schiller, Mr Justin G.
Searight Collection
Stileman, Mr David F.M.
Stileman, Mrs R.E.C.
Taunton, Somerset Records Office
Watson, Mr W.P.
Yordan Obegi, Mr Henry

Also many owners who prefer to remain anonymous

Acknowledgements

The Royal Academy of Arts extend their thanks to the following individuals and institutions who have contributed in many ways to the organization and the preparation of the catalogue.

Charles Alabaster
Michael Andrews
Alex Apsis
Jack Baer
Captain Sir Thomas Barlow, Bart.
Bembridge School, Isle of Wight
Judith Bronkhurst
Anne Buddle
Patrick M. Cadell
Herbert Cahoon
Tony Carroll
Jeannie Chapel
Viscount Chewton
Malcolm Cormack
Prof. Pietro Corsi
Gina Douglas
Penelope Eckley
Simon Edsor
J.J. Farquharson
Hugo de Ferranti
The Fine Art Society
Nancy Finlay
Florida State University, Tallahassee, Florida
Henry Ford
Dr Rowena Fowler
Andrea Gall
Donald Gallup
Eleanor M. Garvey
Christopher Gibbs
Glamorgan Record Office
Timothy Goodhue
Evelyn Stern Groom
Hertfordshire County Council Record Office
The late Philip Hofer
Philip Hook
The Staff of the Houghton Library, Harvard University
The Huntington Library, San Marino, California
Fiona Jordan
Edward T. King
Gillian Kyles
Thomas V. Lange
The Library of the University of British Columbia
Lilly Library, University of Indiana, Bloomington, Indiana
Liverpool, The Public Record Office
Rupert Maas
Eleanor MacLean
Robert Manning Strozier Library, Florida State University
Jane Munro
Julie Murphy
Gay Naughton
Michael Noakes
Isabella Oulton
Andrew McIntosh Patrick
L. Candace Pezzara
The Pierpont Morgan Library
Ruth Pitman
Nigel Prescot
Michael Richards
Mr and Mrs Harland Riker
Jane Roberts
Duncan Robinson
John Rogers
J. N. Ross
The John Rylands University Library of Manchester
David Scrace
Rodney Searight
Justin Schiller
Peyton Skipwith
Somerset Record Office, Taunton
Somerville College, Oxford
Anthony Spink
Elizabeth Stevenson
Elyse Topalian
Fani-Maria Tsigakou
Anne Walker
Malcolm Warner
Rowan Watson
David Wickham
Andrew Wilton
R.D. Wise
Christopher Witt
Marjorie Wynne
Iris Young

Photographic Acknowledgements

The exhibition organisers would like to thank the following for making photographs available. All other photographs were provided by the owners of the works.

A.I.C. Photographics, Cat. 62; Derek Balmer, Cat. 52; BBC, Bristol, Cat. 27e; Christie's, Manson and Wood Ltd, Cat. 49; A.C. Cooper Ltd, Cat. 5b, 13a, 15a, c, i, 20b, 21b, 25c, 37a, 41a, 43e, 44b, 64b, 65, 68a, 88, 92b, 93b, 101b, 103, 110b, c, d; Dawes and Billings (Photographics), Howe, Cat. 90b; Delmar Studios, Cat. 96a, c; Elsam, Mann & Cooper Ltd, Cat. 10a–h, 11a, b, d–g; The Fine Art Society, London, Cat. 36, 48, 61; FMR, Milan, Cat. 7a–d, 8a–c, 9b, c, 13f, 14b, 15b, d, g, h, 17c, e, h, 19a, 20c–e, g, 24a–f, 25d, 27c, 29, 32a, b, 33a–c, 34b–k, 35a–c, e, f, 37b, d, 39c; P.J. Gates Photography, Cat. 56; Hazlitt, Gooden and Fox Ltd, Cat. 57, 60; J.P. Photography, Cat. 26; Oxford University Press, Cat. 71a, b, 72a, b, 73b, 78b, 79, 80a, 81d, 83b, 84a, 85, 86, 87b, 95a, 97, 99a; Eric Purchase, Photographer, Cat. 59; Michael Randall, Cat. 55; Tom Scott, Edinburgh, Cat. 20f, 22; Rev. R.W. Smith, LRPS, Cat. 38; Spink and Son Ltd, Cat. 13g, h, 25a, 28

Editorial Note

All quotations from Lear's writings follow the artist's own spelling and punctuation. Titles of works adopt Lear's spelling with the exception of those travel studies where there is a discrepancy between Lear's spelling of a location and the modern spelling; in such cases, the location is given in its modern form.

A single date after a title indicates that the work was executed, or completed, in that year. Two dates separated by a hyphen indicates that the work was definitely executed between these two years, thus: 1855–60. A date preceded by '*c.*' indicates that the work was executed at around this date, thus: *c.* 1855. A date preceded by a question mark indicates that, from external evidence, the work was almost certainly executed within that year, thus: ?1855. A date set within square brackets indicates that, although nowhere indicated on the picture, manuscript or document, the work was definitely executed in that year, thus: [1855].

The medium and support of each work is given; for works on paper, paper is white unless otherwise stated.

Dimensions are given in centimetres and inches, height preceding width.

Inscriptions in ink or paint on the front or back of a work, on the frame or on a label attached to a work are transcribed literally, and their location specified. Colour notes, almost always given in pencil and then washed over in colour, have not been transcribed. Only in exceptional cases are inscriptions in pencil given; in such cases the method adopted follows the one used for inscriptions as outlined above.

The following abbreviations for the locations of signature, date and inscription are used: b: bottom; c: centre; l: left; r: right; t: top.

Provenances have been checked as far as possible. However, many of the works come from private collections where no record of the date and location of acquisition has been preserved.

For works coming from the Houghton Library, Harvard University, no provenance is given beyond Philip Hofer and W. B. Osgood Field. These two collections were begun in 1929. In February and March of that year, the residue of Lear's atelier at San Remo which had been bequeathed to Franklin Lushington was sold through Hodgson's and Sotheby's; three months later, from a London bookseller, Philip Hofer of New York acquired a considerable number of works which had passed through these two sales. On 27 November 1929, Sotheby's also handled the sale of a portion of the Earl of Northbrook's Lear collection. It was from this sale, as well as through dealers such as Craddock and Barnard, that William B. Osgood Field—also of New York—assembled his collection and Hofer continued to extend his own. In 1942, at the opening of the Houghton Library, Harvard University, Hofer and Osgood Field donated their important collections to the Department of Printing and Graphic Arts.

All entries in the catalogue are by Vivien Noakes unless signed with the following initials: B.L. Briony Llewellyn; MA.S. Mary Anne Stevens.

Published and unpublished sources referred to throughout the catalogue have been abbreviated as follows:

MS.	Manuscript
Diary (followed by a date)	An entry from Lear's diary; in manuscript and held by the Houghton Library, Harvard University.
Ann, TS. (followed by a date)	Letter from Edward Lear to his sister, Ann; the original manuscript disappeared in the late 1930s, but a typescript was made.
Surname (followed by a date)	Letter from Edward Lear to the person whose name precedes the date.
LEL 1907	*The Letters of Edward Lear*, ed. Lady Strachey, London, 1907.
LLEL 1911	*The Later Letters of Edward Lear*, ed. Lady Strachey, London, 1911.
I.J., MS. (followed by a date)	Edward Lear's Indian Journal (1873–75); in manuscript and held by the Houghton Library, Harvard University.
J.Alb.	Edward Lear, *Journals of a Landscape Painter in Albania &c.*, London 1851.
J.Cors.	Edward Lear, *Journals of a Landscape Painter in Corsica*, London, 1870.
Davidson 1968 edn	A. Davidson, *Edward Lear: Landscape Painter and Nonsense Poet*, London, 1938, 2nd edn London, 1968.
Fowler 1984	R. Fowler, *Edward Lear: The Cretan Journal*, Athens, 1984.
Hofer 1967	Ph. Hofer, *Edward Lear as a Landscape Draughtsman*, Oxford 1967.
Hyman 1980	S. Hyman, *Edward Lear's Birds*, London, 1980.
Lehmann 1977	J. Lehmann, *Edward Lear and his World*, London, 1977.
Murphey 1953	R. Murphey, *Edward Lear's Indian Journal*, London, 1953.
Noakes 1968 edn	V. Noakes, *Edward Lear, the Life of a Wanderer*, London, 1968.
Noakes 1979 edn	V. Noakes, *Edward Lear, the Life of a Wanderer*, 2nd edn, London, 1979.
Noakes and Lewsen (Birds) 1978	V. Noakes and C. Lewsen, *For Lovers of Birds*, London, 1978.
Noakes and Lewsen (Cats) 1978	V. Noakes, and C. Lewsen, *For Lovers of Cats*, London, 1978.
Osgood Field 1933	W. B. Osgood Field, *Edward Lear on my Shelves*, ed. Bertha C. Slade, New York, 1933.
Reade 1949	B. Reade, *Edward Lear's Parrots*, London, 1949.

Author's note

In addition to the editorial assistants listed below, the author wishes to thank the publisher's editor, Johanna Awdry, for her patience and untiring support during the production of this catalogue.

THE SECRETARY OF THE ROYAL ACADEMY	Piers Rodgers
EXHIBITIONS SECRETARY	Norman Rosenthal
EXHIBITION PLANNING AND SELECTION	Vivien Noakes
EXHIBITION ADMINISTRATION	MaryAnne Stevens Simonetta Fraquelli
CATALOGUE BY	Vivien Noakes
EDITED BY	MaryAnne Stevens
WITH THE ASSISTANCE OF	Suzanne Carter Luci Collings Elizabeth Waters
EXHIBITION DESIGN	Brian Griggs
POSTER AND LEAFLET DESIGN	Ashted Dastor

Edward Lear, *c.* 1864–65

FOREWORD

It is perhaps time, nearly a hundred years after his death, for the Royal Academy to make amends to Edward Lear.

Although he is now best known for his delightful *Nonsense*, Lear had from his youth determined to establish himself as a 'topographical landscape painter'. To this end, he regularly sent his large oil paintings to the Academy's Annual Exhibition, where the Hanging Committee no less persistently 'skyed' them. Ultimately he realised that it was not to be through this institution that he would win the acclaim he sought from fellow artists or from the public.

Lear's desire to paint 'properly' also brought him into contact with the Royal Academy. Largely self-taught, he reached the age of thirty-seven with little knowledge of the handling of oil paints or mastery of figure drawing. On January 16, 1850, he was accepted as a probationer at the Royal Academy Schools and wrote ecstatically to his friend Fortescue:

> 'You will be pleased to hear that the R. Academy have sate on my drawing from the antique, and that I am a 'probationer'—& on my trial until April when the 3 drawings I have made will be again sate on—& I shall be admitted for 10 years as a student—or—rejected.—' (20.i.[1850])

The three drawings passed the test and Lear was duly admitted, on the recommendation of the Librarian of the Royal Academy, Thomas Uwins RA. However, Lear left the Schools after one year spent drawing from the Antique and from life. Ironically he was later to learn the principles of oil painting from one of the young rebels of the Royal Academy, the Pre-Raphaelite, William Holman Hunt!

It is possible for us now to see Lear's paintings in the context of his more familiar literary output—zoological, topographical and Nonsensical—a juxtaposition which would not necessarily have appealed to him. As our visitors survey Lear's ravishing images of exotic parrots, his evocative records of his intrepid travels to the remote corners of Europe, the Near East and India, his innocently humorous Nonsense rhymes and illustrations and his musical settings to the poems of Alfred, Lord Tennyson, they should have no doubt as to his astonishing range. But they will, we trust, also capture from his paintings and drawings as much pleasure and enjoyment as has been engendered in generations of his admirers by his literary work.

Our sincerest gratitude goes to all those institutions and private individuals who have responded most generously, and sometimes at short notice, to our requests to borrow works for the exhibition, and in particular to the Houghton Library at Harvard University, which has allowed us to choose freely from its incomparable collection of works by Lear. It was a sadness to all scholars of Edward Lear that Philip Hofer, formerly Curator of the Houghton Library, should have died while the exhibition was being prepared.

The Royal Academy is most indebted to Vivien Noakes, the biographer of Edward Lear, for her help in reviewing the whole of his artistic and literary work, selecting the elements of the exhibition and contributing a large proportion of the catalogue. Sir Steven Runciman has written a characteristically perceptive introduction, and further important contributions to the catalogue have been made by Jeremy Maas, Briony Llewellyn, Justin Schiller and Derek Wise; research and editorial assistance has been given by Jeannie Chapel and, from the Education Department of the Royal Academy, Luci Collings and Elizabeth Waters. Finally, our thanks must go to the sponsors, Swan Hellenic, Trusthouse Forte and Walker Books Ltd, for responding so readily to our invitation to support this exhibition.

ROGER DE GREY
President, Royal Academy of Arts

INTRODUCTION

Edward Lear was described by one of his contemporaries as 'a man of versatile and original genius.'[1] He was an ornithological draughtsman compared in his own time with Audubon,[2] a superb landscape draughtsman, a traveller and musician, and the creator of a genre of children's writing in which, as Nonsense poet, he stands supreme. Any assessment of his achievement must encompass the whole man.

It is not only his versatility that is extraordinary, but also his productivity. When Lear died he left at least seven thousand watercolours made on his travels, about two thousand studio watercolours including the sets of illustrations to Tennyson's poems, more than three hundred oil paintings which vary in size from six inches to fifteen feet, two books of natural history illustrations and more than a hundred additional published ornithological lithographs, five travel books and five or six travel manuscripts prepared for publication, four books of Nonsense, a dozen published songs, extensive diaries and several thousand delightful letters.

Born in 1812, the twentieth of twenty-one children, Lear was brought up by his sister Ann. Deprived of an inheritance left to him by his maternal grandmother,[3] he began to earn his living at the age of sixteen, making 'uncommon queer shop-sketches—selling them for prices varying from ninepence to four shillings: colouring prints, screens, fans; awhile making morbid disease drawings for hospitals and certain doctors of physic.'[4] In 1828 or 1829 he became an ornithological draughtsman, publishing his first book, *Illustrations of the family of Psittacidae, or Parrots* (Cat. 9*c*), when he was nineteen years old. The format of this book, and Lear's bold style of drawing, set a new pattern of ornithological work which was to be followed with great success by others, particularly John Gould. In 1831 Lear was invited by Lord Stanley, heir to the Earl of Derby, to make drawings of the animals and birds in his menagerie at Knowsley Hall, just outside Liverpool (see Cat. 11). There he mixed with 'half the fine people of the day,'[5] establishing a network of patronage on which he was to depend for the rest of his life.

By the time he was twenty-five he had abandoned his ornithological career to become a landscape painter (see Cat. 13). His next ten years were spent in Rome, a city which at that time still attracted artists from all over Europe, with an English community who were prepared to buy and commission paintings. During these Roman years, between 1837 and 1848 (Cat. 15–19), Lear progressed steadily and found a ready market for his work. He experimented with various styles of drawing, and in this stage of his life we see the greatest variety in his landscape work. He returned to England twice—in 1841, and 1845–46. In 1841 he published a book of lithographs, *Views in Rome and its Environs* (Cat. 64), and in 1846 his first travel book, *Illustrated Excursions in Italy* (Cat. 65). The drawings in this book so impressed Queen Victoria that she invited Lear to give her a series of twelve drawing lessons (see Cat. 66). In 1849 he returned to England, where he planned to settle permanently.

Up to this time Lear had been almost entirely self-taught.[6] Although by now an accomplished landscape draughtsman, he was aware of other limitations, so at the beginning of 1850, and at the age of thirty-seven, he enrolled as a student at the Royal Academy Schools (see Cat. 103). But he was too old and too experienced to be a student, and he stayed for only a year. In 1852 he was introduced to William Holman Hunt,[7] one of the three founding members of the Pre-Raphaelite Brotherhood. For a time he worked with Hunt, seeking his advice both on technique and on the use of colour. During the next few years Lear followed Hunt's methods of working direct from nature (see Cat. 49–51), and although he gradually moved away from these, Hunt's influence remained in Lear's use of colour in his oil paintings.

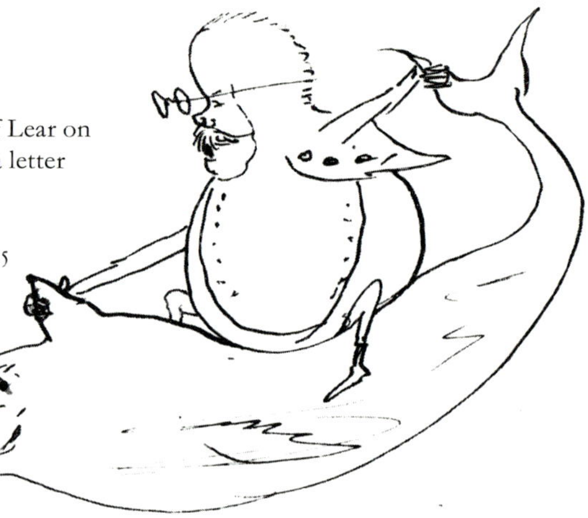

Self-portrait of Lear on a porpoise, in a letter to Chichester Fortescue, 26 September 1875 (Cat. 96*d*)

Throughout the 1850s his work was exhibited in major exhibitions and sold well; but from the early 1860s onwards his reputation steadily declined. A number of factors contributed to this. Ill-health forced him to abandon his plan to settle and work in London: he spent the winter months abroad, returning to London each summer. Whilst a growing reputation could probably survive short periods away from London, Lear's extended travels removed him from the attention of all but a few existing patrons. But more significant was that he misassessed the value of his work. On the one hand he could write to Hunt: 'Coming so late as I did to the light of any kind of truth in painting—when my habits of life were already but too much formed, & my eyes & hands less than ever able to execute what I desired to do, I was never likely to turn out much of a painter.'[8] On the other hand, he overpriced his work at a time when his reputation was not sufficiently well established to justify high prices. In 1861, hearing that Millais had sold his painting *Spring* (*Apple Blossoms*)[9] for 450 guineas Lear decided that his own painting, *The Cedars of Lebanon* (see Cat. 26), was worth 700 guineas. His optimism was misplaced, and the delicate balance of public confidence necessary for the growth of a painter's reputation was destroyed. By the time he eventually sold the painting in 1867 for £200, Lear was no longer sought after as a painter. He attributed this to the whims of fashion dictated by the press that tell the sheep to 'leap where others leap.'[10]

The result was that he came to depend increasingly on the kindness of his friends. In 1877 he wrote:

> 'one of the most curious points in my Artistic Career, is the steadiness with which my friends have relied on my doing them good work, contrasted with the steadiness with which all besides my friends have utterly ignored my power of doing so. Said a foolish Artist to me—"you can hardly be ranked as a Painter—because all you have done, or nearly all,—is merely the result of personal consideration, & you are comparatively if not wholly

> unknown to the public."—Says I to he,—"that don't at all alter the qualities of my pictures—whether they are done to the commissions of Ld N. or Ld A—or Lord C—or Lady W—or Sir F. G.—or F. Lushington, or R. Bright, or F. W. Gibbs—or any other friend,—or whether they are bought in a gallery by Mr. Timothy Timkins or the Duke of Popmuffin:—For the Public, says I, I have no sort of respect not none whatever—for provided pictures are cried up & well hung up—they are safe to be bought—be they by Whistler or anybody else. But the voice of Fashion whether it hissues hout of a Hart Cricket in a Paper, or hout of the mouth of a Duke or Duchess—ain't by no means the voice of Truth. So you see o beloved growler—your ozbervations don't affect me a bit, who haven't got no ambition, nor any sort of Hiss Spree de Kor at all at all.'[11]

But although Lear's ambition had by that time declined, he was less than truthful in saying that he had none at all. He knew the value of his best work, and in 1848 when he was contemplating the possibility of becoming a student so that he might study 'the human figure—which to master alone would enable me to carry out the views & feelings of Landscape I know to exist within me' he wrote, '. . . if I did—*wouldn't* the "Lears" sell in your grandchildren's time!'[12]

In his dislike of the dictates of fashion, however, he remained constant. Though his career had not developed as he had wished, he still believed in the quality of the work he produced, and it was partly this which led to the increasingly brazen overtures he made to those people who thought of buying his work. He would let them know where his work could be seen and how much it cost, suggesting on occasion that they might like to buy pictures by instalments, reminding them unashamedly of his shortage of money. This mistaken approach to potential purchasers hastened the decline of his reputation. In 1880 the 15th Earl of Derby wrote of Lear:

> 'in a world, where nothing succeeds like success, he has done himself much harm by his perpetual neediness. An artist who is always asking his friends to buy a picture, & often to pay for it in advance, makes outsiders believe that he cannot know his business: which in Lear's case is certainly far from the truth. But he has been out at elbows all his life, & so will remain to the last.'[13]

The effects of Lear's misjudgment have lingered until quite recently; it is only within the last few years that his oil paintings have been assessed dispassionately, and the quality of the best of them understood.

But Lear's reputation was affected by more than this. As his respect for the judgment of the buying public declined, so too did his own discernment in what he placed before them; he decided to give them what they deserved. In the winter of 1862–63 he worked on the first group of what he called his Tyrants (see Cat. 39), or mass-produced watercolours which he made simply to sell—they had 'no "upward aspirations" as vorx of hart.'[14] His method of producing these Tyrants was extraordinary. He first chose from his travel drawings a selection of views. He then prepared thirty—or on occasion forty or even sixty—sheets of paper, and moving from one to another he laid in the pencil outlines, then blue washes, then green, then yellow, and so on until he had a collection of completed pictures. These he then framed, exhibited and sold. Writing to Lady Waldegrave in 1863 he said: 'For the present I have done with oil painting, & have collapsed into degredation & small 10 & 12 guinea drawings calculated to attract the attention of small Capitalists.'[15] The immediate result was rewarding, for the sale brought in enough money for him to live. The long-term consequence of this method of working, by which over the years he produced about a thousand Tyrant watercolours, was to lower his reputation still further. Forty years after Lear's death a friend commented that 'if he had exercised a judicious selection of his exhibition pieces, instead of hanging good, bad and indifferent pictures together in Stratford Place and elsewhere, his value at the time would have been considerably enhanced.'[16] But Lear believed that he had given the public the best of his work, and they had spurned it.

In fact, what is now considered by many to be his best work, the freely handled watercolours which he made for his own reference, was not available to his contemporaries. Lear's strength lay particularly in two areas of draughtsmanship: in his ornithological work, and in the best of the many thousand landscape drawings made on his travels. Lear himself said: 'I am certain, whatever good I may get by "colour from nature" I get more by pencil'[17] and it was in his drawing rather than in his use of paint that he built up form. This can be seen most clearly in his travel drawings, but these works were not offered for sale. Lear regarded them as his working capital, the basis of his oil paintings and what he described as his finished watercolours. It was not until the late 1920s that the general public had an opportunity to see and acquire these drawings, and with their appearance there began a reassessment of Lear's contribution as a painter.[18]

Until now it has been customary in exhibiting Lear's work to separate his oil paintings and his illustrations to Tennyson's poems, but to group the rest of his watercolour work merely geographically. In this exhibition Lear's watercolours have, for the first time, been grouped according to the functions they were intended to serve. By far the largest section is

Landoor-Massoorie, 1874 (Cat. 34*b*)

devoted to the watercolours he made on his travels, with their powerful draughtsmanship, their limpid washes and their characteristic notes about colour and form—'rox', 'phiggs', 'bloo ski'. Exhibited separately are the finished watercolours painted either to commission or for exhibition and sale in Lear's studio, and a few of his Tyrants.

Also exhibited with his studio watercolours are his illustrations to Tennyson's poems (see Cat. 42, 43). As with the Tyrants, it is important for these to be seen for what they are. Lear's plan to illustrate Tennyson's poetry dates from 1852 when he and Holman Hunt lived for a short time at Clive Vale Farm. Although he had Tennyson's poetry in mind during his subsequent travels, and recalled lines of his verse when he was painting a number of his oils,[19] Lear did not return to his scheme to make a collection of two hundred Tennyson drawings until after he had settled at San Remo in 1871. The project occupied much of Lear's time during the last years of his life; his plan was to have the work reproduced, on the pattern of J.M.W. Turner's *Liber Studiorum*. He experimented with different forms of reproduction, redrawing the illustrations over and over again as each experiment failed. By now his sight was fading, and his tenacity was greater than his discernment. Many times he contemplated abandoning the project, but in his last, lonely years he struggled on. Until recently two groups, each of two hundred Tennyson drawings prepared for reproduction, survived intact at the Houghton Library and the Tennyson Research Centre at Lincoln. In 1980 those at Lincoln were sold and subsequently dispersed. Despite their charm, these heavy ink drawings by a man with fading sight do little to enhance his reputation.

The re-evaluation of Lear as a painter has happened slowly. It began with the appearance on the market of his travel watercolours; at that time his work was reassessed by Martin Hardie.[20] But in England the momentum was slow, and it was from America that the first real interest came. Two collectors in particular were responsible for this: William B. Osgood Field, whose collection of Lear material was described in *Edward Lear on my Shelves* published in 1933;[21] and Philip Hofer, who died in November 1984 whilst this exhibition was being prepared. In 1968 Philip Hofer published *Edward Lear as a Landscape Draughtsman*,[22] the only study to date of Lear's painting. These two collectors acquired more than three thousand of Lear's travel watercolours, then priced at a few shillings each, mainly those that had previously belonged to Lord Northbrook and which are still housed in the wooden drawers which Lear had made when he moved into Villa Emily. They also bought studies for his bird drawings, Nonsense manuscripts, surviving diaries and many of Lear's own copies of his published books. In 1942 this material was deposited in the Houghton Library, Harvard University, and now forms the most important collection of Lear's work. Much of it has never before been exhibited, and we are particularly grateful to the Houghton Library for its generosity in making so much important Lear material available to us. Their

Civitella, no. 56 of Lear's illustrations to the poems of Alfred Tennyson, 1885 (Cat. 43*b*)

loans extend beyond the watercolours, and include in particular Lear's own drawings for his published Nonsense.

'Nonsense,' wrote Lear, 'is the breath of my nostrils'.[23] It is inseparable from his life and expresses both his merriment and his most deeply held beliefs.

Lear was a man of courage, not only in his travels through remote and difficult countryside, but more particlarly in his constant struggle to overcome the constraints imposed upon him by epilepsy, with the isolation and loneliness this brought. 'Alas! Alas! how fearful a birthright was mine,' he wrote in the last year of his life. 'I wonder if others suffer similarly? Yet I dare not ask or endeavour to know.'[24] Living at a time when sufferers from epilepsy were still considered as social outcasts, Lear told no one of his disease; observing 'a gentle sadness through which his humour shone'[25] they ascribed this to his failure to receive recognition as a painter.

Lear's first epileptic attack came when he was five or six. From the age of seven he also suffered bouts of acute depression. 'The earliest of all the morbidnesses I can recollect must have been about 1819—when my Father took me to a field near Highgate, where was a rural performance of gymnastic clowns &c.—& a band. The music was good,—at least it attracted me:—& the sunset & twilight I remember as if yesterday. And I can recollect crying half the night after all the small gaiety broke up—& also suffering for days at the memory of the past scene.'[26] It was some years before Lear discovered a way in which he could recreate this clownish gaiety himself; he did so through his Nonsense, and in particular his limericks.

Understanding the constraints of his epilepsy, Lear observed in Victorian society other forces which destroyed the fullness of living. The most pervasive of these, one whose influence spread upwards through society as the century progressed, was the Evangelical church of the time, with its inordinate emphasis on sin and damnation. To strict Evangelical Christians life presented many dangers. If they wished to achieve salvation—and the alternative was too terrible to contemplate—they must deny those aspects of their humanity which were sent to beguile them back into their essential sinfulness. Man's will, a demonstration of his pride, must be broken. His body, the unremitting occasion for sin, must be curbed of all excess; the pleasures of food and dress, of song and dance, laughter and play, were vanities of the world which must be denied. Such denial began in earliest childhood; where joy was synonymous with levity, and merriment was a step along the broad road to destruction, there was no place for Godwin's belief that the true object of education, like that of every other moral process, is the generation of happiness.[27]

From this anxious narrowness, where hypocrisy might parade as virtue, there could grow a harsh intolerance. For Lear, aware always of his own shortcomings, man's failures were less to be condemned than to be understood. His ideal of Christianity was 'a plain worship of God, & perpetual endeavour at progress.'[28] 'When will it please God to knock Religion on the head & substitute charity, love & common sense?' he asked.[29] In a world of distorted values he longed to see hypocrisy replaced by honesty, intolerance by charity, ostentation by simplicity, misery by merriment. 'My dear child, I'm sure we shall be allowed to laugh in Heaven!'[30] he reassured a small girl.

At Knowsley he observed other constraints. Alongside the jollity of the 12th Earl, of whom a contemporary wrote, 'Dear old man! his joyous temperament, and his love of society and good cheer, made his guests as happy and merry as himself,'[31] there was the pall of aristocratic ennui. 'The uniform apathetic tone assumed by lofty society irks me *dreadfully*' Lear wrote, 'nothing I long for half so much as to giggle heartily and to hop on one leg down the great gallery—but I dare not.'[32] Different forces operated lower down the social scale, where the newly rich rejected the rougher rural life from which they had come. In the name of gentility the fiddle and the flute gave way to the parlour piano, the traditional ballad to the sentimental song, whilst '"ladies" were not encouraged to exercise their bodies except in dancing.'[33] In an atmosphere of such precarious gentility, reality was subjected to appearances.

In his limericks (see Cat. 72–77), to an extent difficult for us now to imagine, Lear offered children the liberation of unaffected high spirits. In his study, *The Psychology of Laughter*, Boris Sidis suggests: 'In the ludicrous and the comic we let go the earnestness, the seriousness of life. . . . We become free agents. We soar in the air of spiritual freedom, ease, grace, and power of superabundance of energy.'[34] With a simplicity

Title page of *A Book Of Nonsense*
(1st edn) 1846 (Cat. 72*c*)

endorsed by the drawing, the short verse sets the scene and tells the story. The whole—the verse and the drawing—constitute a clownish act, and the two parts are inseparable. Here are grown-ups doing silly things, the kind of things grown-ups never do. They jump and leap and spin, unabashed both by their unseemly abandon and the sheer folly of what they are doing. They play on crude, rustic instruments and dance hornpipes and jigs, they dress in huge bonnets and wigs, they eat and drink vastly, they are immense and immoderate, strange and impulsive. The limericks do not deceive, but share with the children the reality of the human characteristics they display; for all their incongruity, there is in the limericks a truth which is lacking in the improving literature of the time. In an age when children were loaded with shame, Lear attempted to free them from it. By facing both the good and the bad without criticism, he gave them an opportunity of coming affectionately to terms with both themselves and other people.

In Lear's Nonsense songs (see Cat. 78, 82, 84–87), the message of tolerance and understanding was joined by another: the excitement of opening one's eyes and exploring the world around, of discovering undreamt-of lands and wonders not only unseen but scarcely even imagined. Travel was for Lear more than a search for paintable views, important though that was. Brought up as a sickly child, he faced hardships in often harsh and unwelcoming country which drew forth unknown abilities and powers. The strange, more primitive ways of life he observed, and the magnificent grandeur of many remote places scarcely ever visited by foreigners, made him realise the rewards which might come from taking adventurous risks. In a process of self-discovery which greater caution would have made impossible, he demonstrated to himself that his life need not be ruled by his epilepsy; he saw that, for all its suffering, the world was full of beauty and wonder. Above all, he found in these journeys a physical and spiritual freedom he had never imagined possible and which he sought to share in his Nonsense songs.

'. . . the two main obstacles to learning by experience,' wrote Erasmus, 'are a sense of propriety which clouds the judgment and fear which advises against an undertaking once danger is apparent. Folly offers a splendid liberation from both of them. Few mortals realise how many other advantages follow from being free from scruples and ready to venture anything.'[35] Lear does not pretend that the Great Gromboolian Plain and the hills of the Chankly Bore can be reached easily; you have first to face a difficult voyage, as any voyage of real self-discovery must always be. It takes courage to go to sea in a sieve, and it is no easy thing to sail away for a year and a day. As he launched his Jumblies (see Cat. 82*b*), Lear knew that they were embarking on an adventure few had either the vision or the courage to share. Yet 'O Timballo! How happy we are!' they exclaim, and 'how wise we are!' for however ridiculous they may appear with their green heads and their blue hands, and although theirs might seem to be a Ship of Fools, it is the others, with their cautious warnings and anxious fears, who are the fools. It is perhaps all a game, but one with a purpose. 'A true game is one that frees the spirit,' write Peter and Iona Opie. 'It allows of no cares but those fictitious ones engendered by the game itself. When the players commit themselves to the rhythm and incident . . . they opt out of the ordinary world.'[36] In such a game they can take risks, confront dangers and discover their real abilities and limitations. 'Children,' they suggest, 'seem to be instinctively aware that there is more to living than doing what is prudent and permitted.'[37]

In his limericks Lear has taken us to the offshore islands of his Nonsense world; with the songs he carries us to its mainland where the horizons are wide and clear. All his life he sought wide horizons—both the real width of the landscape he explored in his travels and drawings, and the symbolic width of tolerance expressed in the landscape of his Nonsense world. It is Utopian, Hythlodaeus's 'place where every wise man goes',[38] where can be found the Golden Age of Ovid when 'men used to cultivate good faith and virtue spontaneously, without laws. Punishment and fear did not exist, nor were threatening phrases to be read on brazen tablets.'[39] This is the world of the *Roman de la Rose*, where 'people loved one another with a delicate and honest love' and 'danced and disported themselves in sweet idleness, simple quiet people who cared for nothing but to live joyously and in all friendship with one another.'[40] Lear's Nonsense world welcomes anyone, however different. It welcomes nature's oddest creatures—the Pelican (see Cat. 101), the Kangaroo, the Daddy Longlegs—thereby setting an immediate standard of perfectly proper strangeness. To children who knew that they could never attain the unreal perfection demanded of them, such a world—the creation of a man who saw himself as an oddity—must have represented a haven. This was a place where they could be themselves, expressing their freedom in music and dance and ridiculous games. No stranger group can ever have gathered than those who came together on the Quangle Wangle's Hat (see Cat. 85), and yet

'. . . at night by the light of the Mulberry moon
They danced to the Flute of the Blue Baboon,
On the broad green leaves of the Crumpetty Tree,
And all were as happy as happy could be,
With the Quangle Wangle Quee.'

'. . . one finds that constant quiet sympathy is not only one of the most lovable qualities, but one of the very rarest,'[41] Lear had written, but in this Nonsense world it was a commonplace.

It is difficult to say whether Lear's success as the author of the *Book of Nonsense* detracted from his reputation as a painter. He published the first two editions anonymously as Old Derry down Derry (Cat. 72, 73); the third edition bore his name (Cat. 75, 76). This edition appeared in 1861, at the point when he was hoping for his greatest success; its popularity was immediate and widespread, and it may well have confused the serious-minded picture-buying public. If so, that need no longer be the case: we now have the opportunity of judging the full range of this remarkable man's talent.

NOTES

1. Hubert Congreve, LLEL 1911, Preface, p. 37 (see Cat. 38).
2. William Swainson, 26.xi.31, MS., Houghton Library, Harvard University.
3. See the will of Florence Brignell Usher, 1802, Somerset House. Something of Lear's attitude to his patrons can be ascribed to this fact. He was entitled to an inheritance which would have removed him from financial dependence and freed him to do the work he felt capable of achieving. He felt that those who could easily afford to do so should support artists of talent, and that by buying his paintings they received in exchange objects of value from which they would derive pleasure.
4. 'By Way of Preface', *Nonsense Songs and Stories*, 6th edn, 1888.
5. Undated letter, MS., Private Collection; LEL 1907, p. xix.
6. In a letter to Ann of 14.xii.37 Lear talks of attending an evening academy in Rome. He does not appear to have done so for long, however.
7. William Holman Hunt, *Pre-Raphaelitism and the Pre-Raphaelite Brotherhood*, vol. 1, 1905, p. 239.
8. Holman Hunt, 7.ii.57, MS., Houghton Library, Harvard University.
9. Oil on canvas, 110 × 172.7 cm/43½ × 68 in, 1856–59; Viscount Leverhulme.

10. Fortescue, 16.viii.69, LLEL 1911, p. 107.
11. Lord Aberdare, 23.viii.77, MS., Robert Manning Strozier Library, Florida State University.
12. Fortescue, 25.viii.48, LEL 1907, p. 13.
13. Lord Derby's diary, 14.i.80, MS., Private Collection.
14. Diary, 31.xii.62.
15. Lady Waldegrave, 1.i.63, LEL 1907, p. 261.
16. Sir Ian Malcolm, *The Pursuit of Leisure & other essays*, 1929, p. 118.
17. Diary, 18.iv.62.
18. Martin Hardie, 'Edward Lear', *Artwork*, no. 22 (summer 1930), pp. 114–18.
19. Two paintings in this exhibition were related by Lear specifically to Tennyson lines. They are *Philae* (Cat. 52), 'I will see before I die the palms and temples of the south', and *Kasr-es-Saad* (Cat. 62), 'Like the crag that fronts the evening'.
20. See n. 18.
21. Bertha Slade, ed., privately printed, New York, 1933.
22. The Belknap Press of Harvard University Press, and Oxford University Press, 1967.
23. Mrs Bruce, 24.xii.70, MS., Robert Manner Strozier Library, Florida State University.
24. Diary, 2.v.87.
25. Henry Strachey, Introduction to *More Nonsense*, 4th edn, 1888.
26. Diary, 24.iii.77.
27. William Godwin, *The Enquiry Concerning the Principles of Political Justice, and its Influences on General Virtue and Happiness*, 1793.
28. Fortescue, 20.iv.62, LEL 1907, p. 235.
29. Lady Waldegrave, 13.iv.66, LLEL 1911, p. 76.
30. Mrs Hugh Fraser, *A Diplomat's Wife in Many Lands*, vol. II, chapter XX.
31. *The Diary of Frances, Lady Shelley, 1787–1817*, p. 13.
32. Miss Coombe, quoted Angus Davidson, *Edward Lear: Landscape Painter and Nonsense Poet*, 1938, p. 17.
33. G.M. Trevelyan, *Illustrated English Social History*, vol. IV, 1952, p. 24.
34. Boris Sidis, *The Psychology of Laughter*, 1913, pp. 77–78.
35. Erasmus, *The Praise of Folie*, 1549.
36. Iona and Peter Opie, *Children's Games in Street and Playground*, 1969, p. 1.
37. Ibid, p. 263.
38. Thomas More, *Utopia*, 1516.
39. Ovid, *Metamorphoses*.
40. Guillaume de Lorris and Jean de Meung, *Roman de la Rose*, 1480.
41. Quoted in *The Life of Richard Lord Westbury*, T.A. Nash, 1888, p. 51.

'The Daddy Long-legs and the Fly' from *Nonsense Songs, Stories, Botany and Alphabets*, 1871 (Cat. 82)

EDWARD LEAR

Steven Runciman

It is to be hoped that Mr Lear can now and then lean from the gold bar of Heaven and survey the world below. For nothing would delight him more than to find that the Royal Academy had set up an exhibition in his honour. He longed all his life to be recognised as a painter of importance, as the best topographical artist of his time. But it is only now, ninety-seven years after his death, that this accolade, an accolade far beyond his dreams, has been granted to him.

To most of us Edward Lear is best known for his Nonsense Rhymes and Songs. His limericks—he never himself used the term—in the *Book of Nonsense* and *More Nonsense* may lack the punch-line that modern sophisticated taste demands; but the ingenuity of the rhymes and the variety of the situations that he invents, often embarrassing, often ruthless in a form that children enjoy, are still unequalled. His Nonsense Songs are an even more unique achievement; for they contain passages of pure poetry, set off by sudden lapses into the ridiculous. Lear loved and understood children, as did his contemporary Nonsense-writer, Lewis Carroll. But, while Carroll with his mathematical brain used Nonsense as a philosophical commentary on life—and much of it therefore is better appreciated by older readers—Lear's Nonsense is essentially personal. It is not without logic; for Nonsense needs logic to make its effect. But he seems to have realised, perhaps unconsciously, that his own tribulations could be made bearable if they were clothed with fantasies and incongruities. They were written to amuse children. He was, after all, a 'Derry down Derry, who loved to see little folks merry'; and in many ways he remained himself a child. The limericks continuously tell of the cruel fate of innocents and eccentrics. He never forgot overhearing a fellow-traveller describe him as a 'dirty landscape painter'. The Old Man of Thermopylae, who never did anything properly, and so suffered exile, is Lear himself, as is the Old Man of Whitehaven, whom they—public opinion—smashed for dancing a quadrille with a raven.

The Songs are more poignant and more personal. Not all are melancholy. 'The Owl and the Pussy-cat', written to cheer a sick little girl, has a happy ending. The Jumblies returned safely from their voyage in a sieve; and the Pobble was consoled for the loss of his toes. But most of the Songs tell of rejection or desertion. The chorus of 'Calico Pie', which ends: 'They never came back to me!' sets the tone. Even the King and Queen of the Pelicans, who 'think no birds as happy as we,' grieve for their daughter Dell whose marriage has taken her far away. The Dong was deserted by the Jumbly Girl whom he loved. The Yonghy-Bonghy-Bò fails to win the hand of Lady Jingly Jones, just as Lear himself never won the hand of Gussie Bethell. The terrible fate of the Discobbolos family, blown to pieces by their father because the wall on which they lived was no longer suitable, represents Lear's own despair when a hotel was to be built cutting off the view from his villa at San Remo. Most personal and saddest of all is his last poem, 'My Uncle Arly', a brief, transmuted autobiography, its symbols too well disguised for exact interpretation.

It is not only the personal content that makes the Songs hauntingly memorable. They also contain passages of pure poetry. The picture of the Nile in the 'Pelican Chorus' or of the dark night over the Gromboolian Plain are equal to anything written by Tennyson. There are flashes of imagery throughout the songs and a melodiousness—they should be read aloud—that is enhanced by the sudden bumps of Nonsense. Lear was a real poet. Yet, when he tried to write serious verse, the result lacks distinction, probably because he strove too hard for perfection. In his Nonsense works he could let himself go.

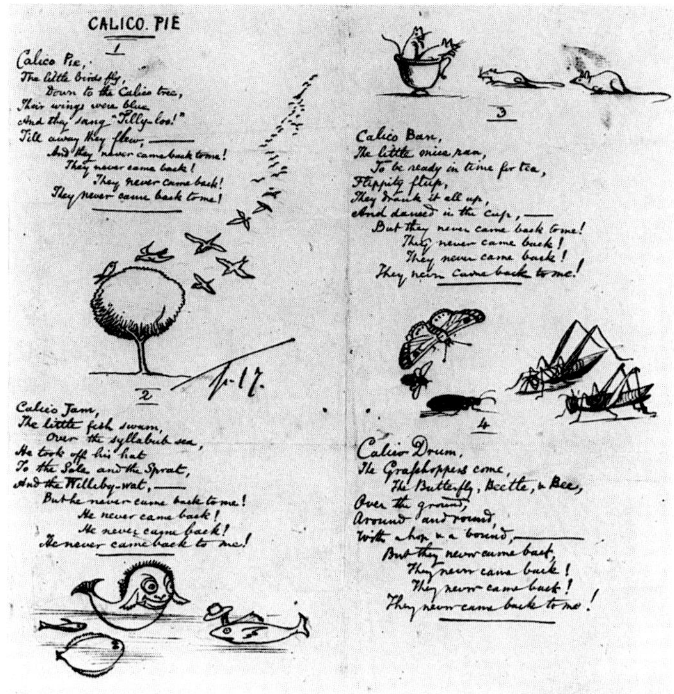

Manuscript for 'Calico Pie' [1870] (Cat. 78*d*)

His short comic pieces have his special charm; and his comic prose stories still can enchant children. His more serious prose works are his books of travel, which are supreme in their genre, with their sensitive descriptions of scenery, their honesty about discomfort and the occasional surliness of his involuntary hosts—he especially disliked the monks of Mount Athos—and the humour that keeps bubbling through. His unedited journals on which the travels books were based are even more interesting; for there he is completely frank about his miseries of illness and depresssion. Indeed, in his Indian Journal he seems at times atrociously ungrateful to Lord Northbrook, whose guest he was; but on the next day he will express his delight at something lovely that he has seen. He was a wonderful letter-writer. He loved to send and to receive letters; and his own glow with affection and delicious fantasy.

He was a musician too, an untrained but eager pianist, and a composer: though his surviving settings of his own and of Tennyson's poems can best be described as pleasantly banal.

Much as he loved to have his verse praised by men such as Ruskin or Kingsley and even his music by Archbishop Tait, yet it was as a painter that he sought to make his name and earn his living. He was a superb draughtsman, as his early drawings of birds made clear; and Queen Victoria showed good sense in employing him as a drawing-master: though, curiously, he never was very good at the human figure. Maybe his happy facility in drawing grotesque personages to illustrate his Nonsense somehow inhibited him. But when he sat down to paint his great oil landscapes that Victorian search for perfection made him over-finish the work. Lady Waldegrave shrewdly said of him that his father was a poet and his mother was a photographer. The photographer shows in his finished landscapes, which are meticulous in their detail and therein very valuable in providing historical evidence. The poet shows in his landscape drawings and sketches. Several thousand survive. When on his travels, he would go out and draw as many as three in a day, recording the date and often the hour. Then at his leisure he would lightly colour them, relying on notes that he had scribbled on them. Only a few more finished examples were intended for sale. Others might be used for lithographs, to illustrate his books, or for the basis of an oil painting which he hoped some patron would order. The charm of the sketches lies largely in their spontaneity. He amused himself with them, spelling the notes in his own phonetical way, often in rather inaccurate Greek, or inserting himself sitting on a rock, or, when drawing Cythera, the island where Aphrodite was born, adding a little nude goddess emerging from the sea. The system did not work so well when he had to depict tropical secenery, as in Ceylon, but it suited the scenery of Mediterranean lands and above all of Greece, the country that he most loved to paint. No one else has managed to reproduce so simply the extraordinary light of the Greek countryside. Lear himself would have been surprised and rather shocked to find that within forty years of his death these sketches were eagerly sought after by collectors, while his oils remained unappreciated till these recent days when all Victorian art is now rehabilitated and fetches large sums in salerooms. There is a sad irony in the story.

Indeed, Edward Lear's life was full of disappointment. He gave happiness to others, but he was not a happy man. His health was never good. His eyesight was poor and always worsening. He suffered from epileptic fits which he tried desperately to conceal from his friends. The one woman whom he wanted to marry rejected him. His emotional demands on his male friends were more than they could bear. He mismanaged his financial affairs; and his publishers let him down. He was fussy and full of complaints. As he wrote of himself, 'Some think him ill-tempered and queer.' But, as he also wrote, 'How pleasant to know Mr Lear.' With his indomitable courage, his unquenchable humour and his intense personal loyalties, he must have been an enchanting companion, and he inspired deep devotion. He may himself have thought his life a failure; but he was wrong. He gave great delight while he lived and he still gives delight in this present time, through his books of travel, through his incomparable Nonsense and through the pictures such as we see in this exhibition at the Royal Academy.

Condessi, 1848 (Cat. 24*g*)

FROM THE SUBLIME TO THE RIDICULOUS
Edward Lear in his Artistic Context
Jeremy Maas

It seems scarcely credible that the daunting, once derided Victorian age was so super-abundant in formidable genius and eccentric talent that it has taken over eight years since the death of Queen Victoria, nearly a hundred years since his own, for us to re-discover through a major exhibition yet another colossus, another monumentally eccentric figure whose talent was spread liberally, almost casually, over a range of creative activity, so diverse, so peculiar even, as to astonish.

Lear's genius expressed itself through an improbable fusion of seeming incompatibles into a glorious alchemy: he could paint sublimely romantic landscapes where Western man had scarcely set foot, write travel books, compose Nonsense verse and make Nonsense drawings—all in unstinting, unflagging profusion. The irony is that this very diversity has tended to blind us to Lear's true merit as a creative artist. Lovers of his Nonsense verse are probably often as wholly unaware of his achievements as a painter as much as the other way round. Indeed the tone of self-mockery which permeates his poetry and letters, this attitude of self-deprecation which was adopted, perhaps too consciously, by some of his Pre-Raphaelite friends, has been taken at rather more face value than has been good for Lear's reputation. This is in complete contrast to the fate of his friend Holman Hunt whose high earnestness tended to compel admiration, if not understanding, for a far wider public through his life-time and, to some extent, since his death. Self-denigration, long absences abroad, the publication of funny limericks, travel books, a narrow if loyal, and mainly aristocratic, body of patronage, weakened the essential life blood of public approbation—and Lear thus paid the penalty in terms of worldly success. And in an age which demanded of its most celebrated painters that they should regularly deliver large and important subject pictures, preferably of a highly engravable nature, Lear, as a landscapist, fell lamentably short. No Scapegoats, no Derby Days, no Ophelias from *his* brush, only strange scenes in strange God-forsaken places, which tolled the death knell of public celebrity. His wayward talent was not to be nurtured by public esteem—it took root and flourished in exotic locations, always real and such as would only exist in the imagination of the greater part of his public.

Epileptic, bronchial, bulbous-nosed and ungainly, Lear, the twentieth of twenty-one children, was born to be an outsider. Like his friend Holman Hunt he regarded the Royal Academy as a highly suspect institution, wilfully rewarding mediocrity and ignoring merit alike. And yet for his waywardness and his obtuseness, even, his lack of self-confidence as a painter in oil made him only too aware of the work of his contemporaries. Minor landscape painters like Creswick he admired, even Vicat Cole, if only because he considered that Cole could paint trees better than he. In the treatment of middle-eastern landscape his closest affinity was with Hunt, whose palette most closely resembles his own. Inevitably, perhaps, he was drawn to J.F. Lewis, that fellow enthusiast for oriental places, who, unlike Lear, mastered the art of painting the human figure; with Clarkson Stanfield, another traveller, he is scarcely to be compared, although he may well have admired Stanfield's technique and feeling for composition. Stanfield's friend David Roberts is another artist often rather loosely bracketed with Lear, but nothing could be further removed from Lear's methods than the architectural technique of the latter, with his frequent use of the ruler and his muted tonal colouring. As an eccentric painter of the East perhaps George Chinnery reveals some affinity with Lear, although the teeming world of Chinese figures, cattle and junks is far removed from the quiet, serene, near surrealistic landscapes of Lear. (Their only true similarity is in liberal use of shorthand notes and hieroglyphs in their drawings; in Lear's case this departure from convention suggests a move towards modernity.)

Earlier debts to the classical landscape tradition of Salvator Rosa, Claude Lorraine and later, to the topographical work of Samuel Prout, although sometimes evident in his mature work, was to be largely dispelled by the growing affinity of his work with that of John Martin and Turner. Although Lear's taste for nature at its most awe-inspiring may well have been influenced by the cataclysmic fantasies of Martin, he is not known to have acknowledged the debt, deterred from doing so possibly as much by Ruskin's disdain for Martin's work as by its blatant popular appeal. For all Lear's contact with the Pre-Raphaelites, he remained essentially a Romantic painter. So perhaps it is only natural that he would be generous in his admiration for Turner, whom, as a young man, he had once met. Only too mindful of his own shortcomings he once confessed in his diary, 'Depressed enough already—the glory and beauty of the Turners [at the Taylorian Institution, now the Ashmolean Museum] depressed me still more' (Diary, 1.viii.77). From Turner he would have learnt not to draw back from conveying an impression of sublimity, a lesson he learnt also from another, perhaps less likely source, the work of the American landscapist Frederic Church. To Lear, he was 'the greatest Landscape Painter after Turner. . . . One of his works, "The Heart of the Andes" [Metropolitan Museum, New York] hangs always before me', he wrote in a letter to his American publisher James Fields in 1880. (Lear probably referred to a reproductive engraving). In this same letter Lear touched eloquently on the mainspring of his own art. 'The painter who all his life paints Surrey woodlands or English coast scenes arrives at a perfection in what he aims at, and

Mount Tomohrit, Albania,
c. 1849–*c.* 1852, 1872–77 (Cat. 48)

is a delight and a benefactor:—but he who can portray Arctic scenes, South American magnificences and endless other distinctly various phases of nature, is far more a delight and a far greater benefactor to his art and his country.'

As a Victorian landscape painter, Lear could not have failed to respond to the teachings of Ruskin, whom he admired. He dutifully digested *Modern Painters*: thereafter his foregrounds came to acquire a concern for more carefully rendered detail, while the middle distances and backgrounds reflected the enthusiasm of both for the revelation of the great truths in nature implicit in the grander works of Turner. Lear had, however, already shown a gift for scientific accuracy in his early ornithological illustration: Ruskin's advocacy could be said, therefore, to have been anticipated by him at an early age.

Although Lear came rather late to the old landscape tradition, his work nevertheless reveals a further element of modernity, in one respect particularly so to his contemporaries: it was an age of scientific enquiry, of which Lear's travelling reports of weird and wonderful faraway places were one expression. It was the same attitude which motivated the painstaking reconstructions of distant historical periods in the work of Alma-Tadema and Poynter.

Like Lewis Carroll, Lear was an acutely intelligent man, to whom reality became a playground of the mind; weird, majestic, wonderful scenery, strange mishaps on his wanderings were sublimated in his art—all the rest was nonsense.

LEAR ON ART

Albrecht Dürer

'All the 26th I spent very quietly in the Austrian capital—I being, as you know, no great sight seer—I went with Morier to the Archduke Charles's gallery[1]—& there I had folio after folio of Albert Dürer's drawing all to my blessed self. I never looked at anything else, but passed the whole morning on the old Nurenberger's works, getting a good lesson as to what perseverance & delicate attention to drawing may do. You would have liked to see some of the wonderfully beautiful sketches of weeds—flowers, & birds, which were there—much reminding me of certain hedgehogs, shells, flies, & pole cats etc. etc.—of other days.'

(Ann, 28.xi.57, TS.)

1. Now the Albertina, Vienna (founded by Duke Albert of Sachsen-Teschen, d. 1822, and enlarged by Archduke Charles, d. 1847, and Archduke Albrecht, d. 1895), which became a state museum in 1919.

Titian and Holbein considered superior to Gaspard Poussin and Salvator Rosa

'. . . *how* could I *ever* have looked with delight on Gaspar Poussin, or S. Rosa?—I can understand & admire Titian, Holbein, & heaps of old portraits—but those things are odious.'

(Diary, 14.vi.61)

J.M.W. Turner

'Depressed enough already—the glory & beauty of the Turners depressed me still more.'

(Diary, 1.viii.77)

'Natl. Gallery—O!!! Turner!!!'

(Diary, 14.viii.80)

'The last time I was in England (1880) I saw at Oxford (by means of a friend at one of the Colleges—R.W. Roper,) the wonderful Turners, in the Taylor (?) [*sic*] Institution.[1] A treat for which I may also take this opportunity of thanking you, as I often do mentally for having by your books caused me to use my own eyes in looking at Landscape, from a period dating many years back.'

(Ruskin, 16.ii.83, MS., Beinecke)

1. Taylorian Institution, now the Ashmolean Museum; Ruskin had given a collection of watercolours by Turner to the Institution, intending them both to be seen and to be used for copying by artists and students.

J.M.W. Turner and Frederic Church favourably compared

'Church[1] the Landscape painter . . . I consider the greatest Landscape Painter after Turner;—& one of his works, "The Heart of the Andes"[2] hangs always before me. I have heard Church's works decried as wanting in certain technical qualities, & conditions of art:—yet he is not the greatest Orator—it seems to me,—who can speak with perfect fluency & charm of rhetoric on one or two subjects,—but rather he who with less power of eloquence or popular persuasiveness can bring home to the hearts & minds of his audience convictions on a multitude of different subjects with unfailing force. The painter who all his life paints Surrey woodlands or English coast scenes arrives at a perfection in what he aims at, & is a delight & a benefactor;—but he who can portray Arctic scenes, South American magnificences & endless other distinctly various phases of nature, is far more a delight & a far greater benefactor to his art & his country.'

(Fields, 18.i.80, MS., Huntington Library, San Marino)

1. Frederic Edwin Church (1826–1900), American painter of sublime landscapes.
2. Oil on canvas, 167.9 × 302.9 cm/66⅛ × 119¼ in, 1859; Metropolitan Museum of Art, New York. Lear presumably knew this sublime mountain landscape, the product of Church's second visit to South America in 1857, through a reproductive engraving.

George Frederick Watts RA

'Watt's drawings are of the most beautiful I ever saw. But you should not compare me to him, even in a joke. We landskippers are little animals.'

(Henry Bruce, 24.ii.[55], MS., Glamorgan Record Office)

William Holman Hunt

'I wonder what you will do in the East.[1] Some one said, Dannel in the Lion's den. Of course those legends are very sure of success in multitudinous ways—but I would fain see somewhat of a truer & broader caste of poetry. (So far as popular delight would make success sure—Daniel &c—with Balaam's ass seen thro' a window—Jonah's whale on a distant shore—Elijahs ravens—& the Gadarene piggy-wiggies—would be a lovely subject.) Have you thought of Jacob & Rebekah—or rather the man sent from Jacob's wife. But you are a far better judge of these things than I.'

(Holman Hunt, n.d. [January 1865], MS., Huntington Library, San Marino)

1. Hunt visited the Near East in 1854–56, 1869–72, 1875–78.

'In what you paint I am nursing the hope that you may not have selected any subject connected with miraculous or mythical, or even traditional interest. There seems to me such a host of moral-historic truth to illustrate, that fables may nowadays be well left aside. Some parts of Jewish *History* (I don't mean traditions, speaking eagles & Lions dens,) are most touching & grand; & so also are some of the undoubtedly historic parts of the New Test. All that tends to strengthen the hands of priests—of whatever creed—the race who have preyed for ages on the foolish & helpless—should, to my fancy—be avoided.'

(Holman Hunt, n.d. [autumn 1869], MS., Huntington Library, San Marino)

'Holman Hunt writes from Jerusalem; he is getting more and more religious: you & I would say—superstitious: but don't repeat this . . .'

(Fortescue, 31.vii.70, LLEL 1911, p. 125)

John Everett Millais PRA

'O dear me I wish I had gone to the Academy when you did, & had been working with you ever since! . . . When I say, "I wish I had gone to the Academy when you did"—you may suppose I don't say that out of love for the Academy for itself. Tout au contraire, I believe that had J. Millais foregone the ambition of place & position, & had he steadily worked with all those who, as he once did, set their faces against conventionalities & still do so,—art in England & who knows where not beside—would have gained life & respectability.'

(Holman Hunt, 7.ii.57, MS., Houghton Library, Harvard University)

'Then to Millais—24. Down St Mrs M. was there,—but in the dark, & a shade over her eyes—being ill of neuralgia. The dinner was very good:—but the 2 hours I passed there, a bore. Mrs R's—I mean Mrs M's—cold Scotch accent, her vulgar queries & half suppressed jealousy about Hunt—(who is as the Sun to a Candle compared with J.E. Millais)—her catching at any Aristocratic names,—her pity of Bachelors—"it's just so melancholy!"—(as if one half of her 2 matrimonial ventures in life had turned out so happily!)—& her drawling stoniness disgusted me—wrongly or rightly I don't yet quite know—so that I don't care ever to see her again. J.E.M. has far better qualities than she—such is my impression. He walked, at 9. with me to Oxford St.: but I must say I do not care ever to see him much more. As I consider Daddy H. far his superior, this cannot be envy—nor is the feeling, I believe, anything but one arising from the utter difference of his nature & my own: he, at 30 is like a crafty aged French dancing = master,—& has neither depth nor softness in his character.'

(Diary, 22.iv.61)

'I am thankful I have never known what it is to envy anyone, but it cannot be otherwise than strange to me that with all my labour I find a difficulty in getting rid of such works, while Johnny Millais gets 1,000, 2,000, or 3,000£ for what costs him hardly any labour at all. Yet I should not use the word "strange"—for Fashion explains all things odd, & besides Johnny M's works have great talent.

For all that (though the technical workmanship is very inferior & pottering) the real likenesses of such places as Ravenna Gwalior & Argos seem to claim 300 Guineas each, not unrighteously if compared with a portrait head for a thousand pound.'

(Aberdare, 25.ix.84, MS., Robert Manning Strozier Library, Florida State University)

John Everett Millais PRA and William Holman Hunt compared

'At 7.30.—came Daddy Hunt—& our dinner & evening were, as always,—delightful. He is a very solid good fellow, & wonderful in contrast to J.E. Millais—all outside & froth. We talked much:—of many things.'

(Diary, 23.iv.61)

John Frederick Lewis RA

'I bought a Catalogue of the RA. & was disappointed in not finding any of his works named there, & now I can understand the reason of their absence. There never have been, & there never will be, any works depicting Oriental life—more truly beautiful & excellent—perhaps I might say—*so* beautiful & excellent. For, besides the exquisite & conscientous workmanship, the subjects painted by J.F. Lewis were perfect as representations of real scenes & people. In my later visits to England, (& it is 3 years since I was here,) I cared to go to the RA. chiefly on account of his pictures.'

(Mrs Lewis, 22.vi.75, MS., Private Collection)

Frederick Goodall RA

'Goodall[1] must be a man of greatest talent *because* he is elected ARA[2]—QED.'

(Holman Hunt, n.d. [November 1852], MS., Huntington Library, San Marino)

1. 1822–1904.
2. Goodall was elected ARA in 1852, RA in 1864.

The Royal Academy of Arts

'The Academy exhibition is unusually bad.[1] Sir Charles[2] had a "Giorgione & water" female head,—more like a piece of boiled veal than a woman.—McLise's[3] immense picture wants interest & variety to me. Frith's[4] "Ramsgate Sands" is his best:—he sold it to Lloyd to Engravism for £1000, & the Queen has bought it since. Creswick[5] is like himself in choice of subject, but has the best landscapes in the rooms.—Linnell[6] has an *enormous* bit of Reigate Common, with Scotch firs—in which a donkey & old man appear to account for its being called "The Syrian false prophet.—" Ward's[7] Argyle has great power in the sleeping figures. Boxall[8] has a Lady Eastlake dipped in treacle. Landseer[9] a huge canvass full of slosh—melancholy to see when one thinks of what he could do if he liked. Buckner[10] has a pyramid of babies & a mother which I would recommend you to study as an original composition were you here. Hannah[11] has a very clever picture. Jones[12]—you will hardly believe me—has a ——— battlepiece!—And Webster[13] a school, & Hart[14] an old man, & Uwins[15] a vintage, & Witherington[16] a Windermere, & Leck[17] Cooper 114 avenues,[18] & Redgrave a fiddled foreground,[19] and Roberts a Venice,[20] ditto Harding[21]—only one is painted with asphaltism & white, & the other imitates Turner with chrome & white. Stanfield[22] has a good Mountain pass. E Cooke[23] sloops & luggers. Altogether the impression of standstillness as to the general run of painters is sad enough. The watercolor, barring John Lewis,[24] who has some exquisite camels, is monotony itself.'

(Holman Hunt, 7.vii.[54], MS., Huntington Library, San Marino)

1. Lear exhibited *Marathon* (no. 105), *Sparta* (no. 561).
2. Sir Charles Eastlake PRA (1793–1865); exh. *Irene* (no. 129).
3. Daniel Maclise RA (1806–70; exh. *Richard de Clear, Earl of Pembroke. . . .* (no. 379).
4. William Powell Frith RA (1819–1909); exh. *Life at the Sea Side* (no. 157), *Anne Page (Merry Wives of Windsor)* (no.270), *The Love-token—a scene from the Bride of Lammermuir* (no. 468), *The poison cup—a scene from Kenilworth* (no. 485), *Mrs. E. M. Ward* (no.511).
5. Thomas Creswick RA (1811–69); exh. *The Woodland tees* [sic] (no. 122), *The passing cloud* (no. 302), *The blithe book* (no. 480).
6. William Linnell (1826–1906); exh. *The disobedient prophet* (no. 234).
7. Edward James Ward (1769–1859); exh. *The last sleep of Argyle before his execution, A.D. 1685* (no. 403).
8. Sir William Boxall RA (1800–79); exh. *A Portrait* (no. 205), *Viscount Downe* (no. 211), *Lewis Cubitt Esq.* (no. 296), *A Portrait* (no. 338).
9. ? Edwin Landseer RA (1802–73); exh. *Royal sports on hill and loch . . .* (no. 63), *Dandie Dinmont, the favourite old Skye terrier of Her Majesty the Queen* (no. 360).
10. Richard Buckner (*fl.* 1830–97); exh. *Mrs. F. Wickham and children* (no. 156), *Mrs. Richard Payne* (no. 533), *Portrait of Mrs. Stopford Blair* (no. 1281).

11. Robert Hannah (1812–1909); exh. *The Countess of Nithsdale petitioning George I . . .* (no. 426).
12. George Jones (1786–1869); exh. *Battle of Hyderabad, 24th March, 1843* (no. 13), *L'Embrasement du monde* (no. 915), *Ezekiel in the valley full of bones* (no. 933).
13. Thomas Webster RA (1800–86); exh. *A villager's offering* (no. 85), *A breakfast party* (no. 104), *Peasant children* (no. 159).
14. Solomon Alexander Hart RA (1806–81); exh. *Columbus, when a boy, being instructed in geography, conceives the idea of the New World* (no. 180).
15. Thomas Uwins RA (1782–1857), with whom Lear travelled to Corpo di Cava in 1838 (see Cat. 45); exh. *The cottage toilette* (no. 25), *A cabin in a vineyard* (no. 79), *The votary of San Antonio, Naples* (no. 421), *The faithful shepherdess* (no. 483).
16. William Frederick Witherington RA (1785–1865); exh. *The park* (no. 132), *Harvesting, near Derwentwater, Cumberland* (no. 286), *A Watermill* (no. 411).
17. ?
18. Thomas Sidney Cooper RA (1803–1902); exh. *Groups in the marshes* (no. 54), *Morning effect—Harbledown Park, East Kent* (no. 254), *Common fare* (no. 556), *Evening in the meadows* (with F. R. Lee) (no. 590).
19. Richard Redgrave RA (1804–88); exh. *An old English Homestead* (no. 212), *'The mid-wood shade'* (no. 326), *Foreshadows of the future* (no. 578).
20. David Roberts RA (1796–1864); exh. *A view of the canal of the Giudecca, at Venice* (no. 115), *The Church of Santa Maria della Salute, at Venice* (no. 200), *View showing the entrance to the Firth of Forth, . . .* (no. 581).
21. James Duffield Harding (1798–1863); exh. *View of Venice, taken from near the Church of the St. Giorgio Maggiore* (no. 580), *Crystal Palace, Sydenham . . .* (no. 1121).
22. William Clarkson Stanfield RA (1793–1867); exh. *The Last of the Crew* (no. 57), *La Rochelle* (no. 139), *Hulks on the Medway* (no. 187), *View of the 'Pic du Midi d'Ossau' in the Pyranees* (no. 315).
23. Edward William Cooke RA (1811–80); exh. *Zuyder Zee Botter—returning to port* (no. 264), *French lugger returning into Calais* (no. 394), *Porto del Lido—the entrance to the Lagune of Venice, from the Adriatic* (no. 469), *Dutch fishing Pincks, of Egmonde-up-Zee, hauling offshore* (no. 526).
24. John Frederick Lewis RA (1805–76); exh. *A lady—sketched at Constantinople* (no. 980), *Albanian Soldiers—sketched in Asia Minor* (no. 1004). Also exhibited at Old Water Colour Society, *Halt in the Desert, Egypt* (no. 248), *Camels and Bedouins—Desert of the Red Sea* (no. 305).

'. . . the Academy cannot change any more than the Papacy.'

(Holman Hunt, 1.iii.60, MS., Huntington Library, San Marino)

'A society like the W. Color[1] has the right to place who it pleases as 1st rate members & to exclude whom it pleases:—but on what ground do R.A.s of any small or of no power monopolize the eclat & substance accruing to them from Royal Patronage & recognised position? If 25 painters were the elite of the nation in 1780—why is the list in 1862 to exclude good & include bad & yet ever remain 25? (I do not speak of Architects or Sculptors—40 being the whole number.) Talented as many of the body are—I fear that dishonesty is a thriving deity of their pantheon: for those very talented men who can fully appreciate the merits of such as are shut out—are the most to blame for not moving the extension of the number of members, or, if they cannot do that, for not leaving the Academy . . . if the R. Academy is a National Institution, then it ought to be forced to reform:—or it might cease to be a Royal & National affair,—& then nobody can complain that it is rotten & narrow if it pleases itself so to be.'

(Fortescue, 7.v.62, MS., Somerset Record Office, Taunton)

1. A reference to one of the two watercolour societies: the Old Water Colour Society (founded 1804; became 'Royal' in 1881), and the New Water Colour Society (founded 1832; became Institute of Painters in Watercolours in 1863).

'I see you are going to have a R. Academy Commission: It will do nothing at all I fear. I wish the whole thing were abolished—for as it now is it is disgraceful. 30 men self-declared as the 30 greatest painters of England—yet having in their body—Witheringtons[1]—Frosts[2]—Coopers[3] C. Landseers[4]—& other unheard of nonentities, while Watts[5]—Linnell[6]—Hunt[7]—Maddox Brown[8]—Antony[9]—& many more are condemned to official extinction—'

(Fortescue, 8.iii.62, MS., Somerset Record Office, Taunton)

1. William Frederick RA (1785–1865).
2. William Edward Frost RA (1810–77).
3. Thomas Sidney Cooper RA (1803–1902).
4. Sir Edwin Landseer RA (1802–73).
5. George Frederick Watts RA (1817–1904).
6. ? John Linnell (1792–1882) or ? William Linnell (1826–1906).
7. William Holman Hunt (1827–1910).
8. Ford Maddox Brown (1821–93).
9. Henry Mark Anthony (1817–86).

'. . . there is one of your sentences that made my hair stand on end for four hours, & it was not without the most violent brushing from 2 new brushes that I could calm it to its former position—I mean where you put the words "Royal Academy" and "dirty work" into one paragraph!!!!!—This is truly dreadful & I trust you wrote in inadvertiently.) But seriously, when I think how many painters with infinitely greater talents than mine have had to struggle on painfully—(such for instance as Maddox Brown,[1] & for many years, Linnell,[2])—I think myself well off.'

(Prescott, 17.xi.63, MS., Private Collection)

1. Ford Maddox Brown (1821–93).
2. John Linnell (1792–1882).

'The R.A. hung 2 of my pictures[1] very well this year—the small one extremely so—& it was sold the first week. And now I am going to make 3 Watercolor drawings to try (as you did—tho' I have not the same chance of success,) to get into the Old W. Color.[2] I'm sure 8 or 10 of my various subjects would attract more than everlasting Hampstead Heaths—but perhaps they won't think so.'

(Holman Hunt, 7.vii.70, MS., Huntington Library, San Marino)

1. *Kasr es Saad* (no. 271; see Cat. 62); *Valdoniello* (no. 508; LEL 1907, p. 317, no. 229).
2. The Old Water Colour Society (founded 1804; see above).

'. . . to R. Academy, when I staid—tired out—till nearly 3 . . . Very little of the work on all those walls delighteth or gaineth respect. Hook's[1] pictures the main exception. Yet I would I could do trees as V. Cole[2] and some others, & if one could, surely one would produce far more interesting work.'

(Diary, 26.vi.75)

1. ? James Clarke Hook RA (1819–1907); exh. four pictures (nos. 47, 256, 308, 439).
2. George Vicat Cole RA (1833–93); exh. three landscapes (nos. 237, 513, 1213).

THE OLD WATER COLOUR SOCIETY

'. . . to the Water Color Exhibition'—about 11.30—to 12.45—it interests me much—but principally as to the various modes of execution—so much more liquid than my own.'

(Diary, 19.vi.75)

1. The Old Water Colour Society (founded 1804; see above).

TRUTH TO NATURE

'Yesterday however I got out for the first time, & was much pleased to find that the picture[1] has literally *the* best place in the whole exhibition,[2]—over the line in the centre of the middle room,—so that all can see it. And the opinions I have from artists whose opinions are valuable to me, are most satisfactory & encouraging, though of course there are many who think that trees should never be painted green, (because they *are* so), & that all Landscapes should be filled up with trees like Claudes,—(because they *ain't* so). To such, strict copies of nature are odious.'

(Lord Derby, 3.iii.[55], MS., Private Collection)

1. *Windsor Castle from St Leonard's Hill*, 1853; commissioned by Lord Derby (exhibited 1855, London, The British Institution, no. 317; 1964, with Appleby and Son Ltd, London).

'O Pa! I ain't a sloshing, but contrary:—so as that one of my friends here[1] says—Do you call *that* a picture!—with the utmost contempt, for he says there is *nothing but careful painting* & reality—(nothing but!) & no composition. He would like a large group of Oaks by the side of the Dead Sea, & innumerable Palms on the hills from which you look down on Damascus.'

(Holman Hunt, 1.iii.60, MS., Huntington Library, San Marino)

1. Rome.

'I go daily to a villa near here,[1] from which is that wonderful view wh. Turner painted.[2] And I am drawing this, partly because I have no topographic illustrations of this beautiful place,—partly because I believe I can do the subject pretty well out of my own brains—placing vines & olives as they really are,—& not calling in to my aid, broken pillars, upset capitals, immense gourds, & 15 Ladies in pink & yellow satin playing on Guitars.

(Holman Hunt, n.d. [summer 1861], MS., Huntington Library, San Marino)

1. Florence.
2. ?*Florence from San Miniato* (three versions, see A. Wilton, *The Life and Work of J. M. W. Turner*, 1979, nos 727–29).

'I suppose I must so far sacrifice to propriety as to go & see some "pictures." Very few I intend to see.[1] All the best I know by copies: & looking into the Guide book I see "This is one of the best speciments of Tintoretto's corrupter style,—or his blue style—or Basano's green style—or somebody else's hoshy boshy lovely beautiful style—all looked on & treated as so many artificialities—&, as not the least as more or less representing nature. The presentation of Christ in the Temple—with Venetian Doges & Senator's dresses—& Italian palaces in the background!—fibs in fibs—wrapped up in pretty colour or not. And besides—looking at pictures wearies me always. It is quite hard work enough to try to make them.'

(Ann, 23.v.57, TS.)

1. Written on Lear's first visit to Venice in 1857 (see Cat. 59).

THE PLEASURES AND PAINS OF PAINTING

'If I am able to leave behind me correct representations of many scenes little cared for or studied by most painters, perhaps I shall have done somewhat; at least as you have before observed, I certainly give great pleasure to numbers at present.'

(Emily Tennyson, 9.x.56, MS., Tennyson Research Centre, Lincoln)

'It seems to me that in converting memories into tangible facts,—recollections & past time as it were into pictures,—lies the chief use & charm of a painter's life. (I'm sure if it isn't, I don't know where it is, for technical study & manipulation will always be a bore to me.)'

(Lady Waldegrave, 5.i.62, LEL 1907, p. 216)

'No life is more *shocking* to me than sitting motionless like a petrified gorilla as to my body & limbs hour after hour—my hand meanwhile, peck peck pecking at billions of damnable little dots & lines, while my mind is fretting & fuming through every moment of the weary day's work.'

(Fortescue, 29.viii.61, LEL 1907, p. 189)

'Yes—: I certainly *do* hate the act of painting: & although day after day I go steadily on, it is like grinding my nose off.'

(Fortescue, 5.ix.61, LEL 1907, p. 193)

'I agree with you Daddy. Art is the Devil. I believe that originally in the Hebrew version of Job, the Devil was made to set Job about a painting, & that that excellent & unfortunate individual took it in hand until he was worn out, & bust into cusses no end. But the later transcribers of the Bible could not see the wit of this, so they cut it out. More fools they.'

(Holman Hunt, 22.x.62, MS., Huntington Library, San Marino)

'How few can realise the labour—simply the manual labour, of an Artist's life—let or be the work of brain, & the vexatious failures of infinitely repeated experiments.'

(Diary, 6.ix.73)

'O! the difficulty of dovetailing the charm of early artist life, with the formality of later days! The calm & brightness of the view, & the lovely sweetness of the air, bring back infinite days & years of outdoor delight;—& I am thankful for this blessing,—though it can only last a few minutes.'

(Diary, 8.viii.81)

'When you & I go to heaven we won't paint any more, but will sit in Chesnut trees & smoke & drink champagne continual.'

(Holman Hunt, n.d. [November 1864], MS., Huntington Library, San Marino)

COMMERCIAL CONSIDERATIONS AND THE QUALITY OF HIS OWN ART

'Regarding my copying my own drawings, it is a thing the effects of doing which would overbalance any good I should gain by making money—because I know my own irritation if I work at anything mechanical, & that my only chance of tolerable ease is constant attempt at *progress* & improvement. If I constantly copied my own works, I should grow crosser & stupider every day, & finally might turn into something between a spider & a polar bear.'

(Ann, 15.iii.57, TS.)

'. . . tho' I have 400£ of commissions, yet people don't pay their money till the pictures are done usually—not always then. So I have been obliged to write for an advance on two paintings. / I much wish I could get so far beforehand as to be out of that constant worry of "daily bread" wh. is a bore—but there is no remedy:—& one ought to think how many unknown artists have no bread at all.'

(Fortescue, 6.iv.62, MS., Somerset Record Office, Taunton)

'Bother the necessity of getting money always!'

(Fortescue, 8.ii.63, MS., Somerset Record Office, Taunton)

'. . . it is hopeless to think of saving enough to allow of my working quietly at progressive art.'

(Fortescue, 24.xi.67, MS., Somerset Record Office, Taunton)

'. . . private patronage must end in the natural course of things, but eating & drinking & clothing go on disagreeably continually.'

(Fortescue, 6.vii.70, LLEL 1911, p. 117)

'I have to work for vulgar food &c &c—& cannot go in for improvement always'

(Gibbs, 23.i.84, MS., Private Collection)

'I am now working on the last commission but one wh. I have . . . when these are done I shall have like Sir Simon Skylights to live "on my Capital".'

(Fortescue, 22.iii.85, MS., Somerset Record Office, Taunton)

'A keen sense of every kind of beauty, is, I take it, if given in the extreme—always more or less a sorrow to its owner,—tho' productive of good to others.'

(Diary, 29.i.62)

5c *Javanese Peacock*, 1831

11d *Wattled Crown Crane*, 1835

109 *Spectacled Owl*, 1836

94 *Coloured Birds* (2), 1880

7d Lesser Sulphur-Crested Cockatoo, 1830

7c Leadbeater's Cockatoo

8*b* *The Red and Yellow Macaw* (preliminary study)

8*c* *The Red and Yellow Macaw* (study)

8d *The Red and Yellow Macaw* (lithograph), 1832

45 *Tree Roots*, 1838

55 *Mount Sinai with the Monastery of St. Catherine in the Distance*, 1858

58 *Mont Blanc from Pont Pellisier*, 1862

48 *Mount Tomohrit, Albania*, *c.* 1849–*c.* 1852, 1872–77

51 *The Temple of Bassae or Phigaleia, in Arcadia from the Oakwoods of Mt. Cotylium. The Hill of Sparta, Ithome and Navarino in the Distance*, 1854

50 *The Mountains of Thermopylae*, 1852

52 *Philae* [1855]

61 *The Pyramids Road, Gizah*, 1873

60 *Mount Lebanon*, *c.* 1866

62 *Kasr-es-Saad*, 1877

56 *Jerusalem from the Mount of Olives, Sunrise*, 1859

13*h* *Wastwater*, 1837

19*b* *Girgenti*, 1847

15g *Narni*, 1839

15*d* *Village with hilltop ruin*, 1838

15*a* *Temple of the Sybil, Tivoli*, 1838

15c *Amalfi*, 1838

37*b* *Athens*, 1850

20*b* *Temple of Olympian Zeus, Athens*, 1848

19c *Quarries of Syracuse*, 1847

208 *Meteora*, 1849

20c *Leondari*, 1849

24a *Ohrid*, 1848

24e *Berat*, 1848

24*c* *Elbassan*, 1848

24*f* *Berat*, 1848

21a *View of the Islands from Kanoni Point, Corfu*, 1855

27*e* *Aswan*, 1854

25*c* *Masada*, 1858

37e *View from Luxor* [1865]

39a *Jerusalem*

39b *Corfu*

37c *Mount Athos*, 1857

29 *Near Sestri Levante*, 1860

32b Finale, 1864

33*b* *Forest of Bavella*, 1868

33a Sartene, 1868

34*f* *Gwalior*, 1874

34*k* *Hyderabad*, 1874

34e *Agra. The Taj*, 1874

34d *Benares*, 1873

34*b* *Landoor-Massoorie*, 1874

34*c* *Lucknow*, 1873

34j Poonah, 1874

35e *Teog*, 1874

35c *Simla*, 1874

35*a* *Barrackpore*, 1873

35*b* *Kersiong*, 1874

26 *The Cedars of Lebanon*, 1858

38 *San Remo from Villa Congreve*, 1870

27d Richard Burton, 1853

EARLY YEARS

4*b*

Writing in 1884, Lear said: 'I think a great deal in these latter days of all my life, *every particle* of which from the time I was 4 years old, I—strange to say,—can perfectly remember. (Even earlier, for I well remember being wrapped in a blanket & taken out of bed to see the illuminations in the house at Highgate, on the Battle of Waterloo occasion—& I was then, 1815, just 3 years old & odd weeks' (Fortescue, 27.vi.84, LLEL 1911, p. 311).

He had a strange, sad childhood. He was the twentieth of twenty-one children of whom eleven survived into adult life. In 1816 his father was a defaulter on the Stock Exchange. Family tradition says that he was imprisoned for debt, but there is evidence that this was not so. However, the family split up and Lear was given into the charge of his oldest sister, Ann. Although once the crisis had passed the family was reunited, Lear had little more to do with his mother.

When he was five or six he had his first attack of what he called 'the Demon', the epilepsy that was to pursue him for the rest of his life. He suffered also from bronchitis and asthma, and from short-sight, and from the age of about seven he was subject to bouts of acute depression which he called 'the Morbids'.

Fortunately Ann seems to have been a warm and loving woman who guided him through the distresses of his childhood. He did not go to school, but had lessons at home from her and another of his sisters, Sarah. 'I am almost thanking God that I was never educated,' he wrote in his middle years, 'for it seems to me that 999 of those who are so, expensively and laboriously, have lost all before they arrive at my age—& remain like Swift's Stulbruggs—cut & dry for life, making no use of their earlier=gained treasures:—whereas, I seem to be on the threshold of knowledge' (Fortescue, 2.ix.59, LEL 1907, p. 148). One of the most important parts of his sisters' tuition, however, were lessons in drawing and painting.

In 1822 Sarah married and went to live near Arundel, Sussex. Lear spent long periods of his later childhood staying with her, and one of his earliest pieces of poetry was written on Bury Hill (MS., National Library of Scotland, Edinburgh, Cat. 5*a*). From there the wide view across the valley of the River Arun reaches the North Downs in a landscape which called to mind the Great Gromboolian Plain and the Hills of the Chankly Bore of Lear's later Nonsense world (see Cat. 86). As with so much of his Nonsense, the theme of the poem is the transitory nature of happiness.

The earliest hints of Lear's Nonsense appear in other ways during this time, with poetic letters to Ann and absurd poems and parodies. 'My Sussex friends always say that I can do nothing like other people,' he wrote (Empson, 1.x.31, MS., Pierpont Morgan Library, New York); from what little has survived from this stage of his life we can see that he had cast himself in the role of joyful clown. Such merriment helped to balance the other aspects of his life. 'Considering all I remember to have passed through from 6 years old to 15—is it not wonderful I am alive?—far more to be able to feel & write,' he wrote, many years later (Diary, 29.iii.68). V.N.

1 Lear's Birth

a) Birth certificate
Pen on paper: 6.7 × 17.5 cm/$2\frac{5}{8} \times 6\frac{7}{8}$ in
Trustees of the Victoria and Albert Museum

b) *Bowman's Lodge, Upper Holloway, c.* 1850
Engraving: 8.8 × 10.8 cm/$3\frac{1}{2} \times 4\frac{1}{2}$ in
Islington Libraries

Edward Lear was born at Bowman's Lodge, Upper Holloway (Cat. 1*b*) in May 1812. There is some doubt about the exact date. His birth certificate (Cat. 1*a*) gives it as 13 May 1812, and until 1858 Lear celebrated his birthday on that date. However, in 1859 he noted it in his diary as 12 May, a date which he kept for the rest of his life. Writing to Hubert Congreve on 12 May 1882 he said, 'I ain't 70 till 11.30 tonight' (MS., Houghton Library, Harvard University). The following year he told Rev. E. Carus Selwyn, 'As for memory, I remember lots of things before I was born, & quite distinctly being born at Highgate 12 May 1812' (MS., 28.xii.83, Private Collection), which seems to settle the matter. His birth was not registered until 1 November 1822, when it was placed as no. 2822 on the General Register of Births of the children of Protestant dissenters kept at Doctor William's Library. On the same day his parents registered the births of the twelve children surviving of the twenty-one born to them—Ann, Sarah, Mary,

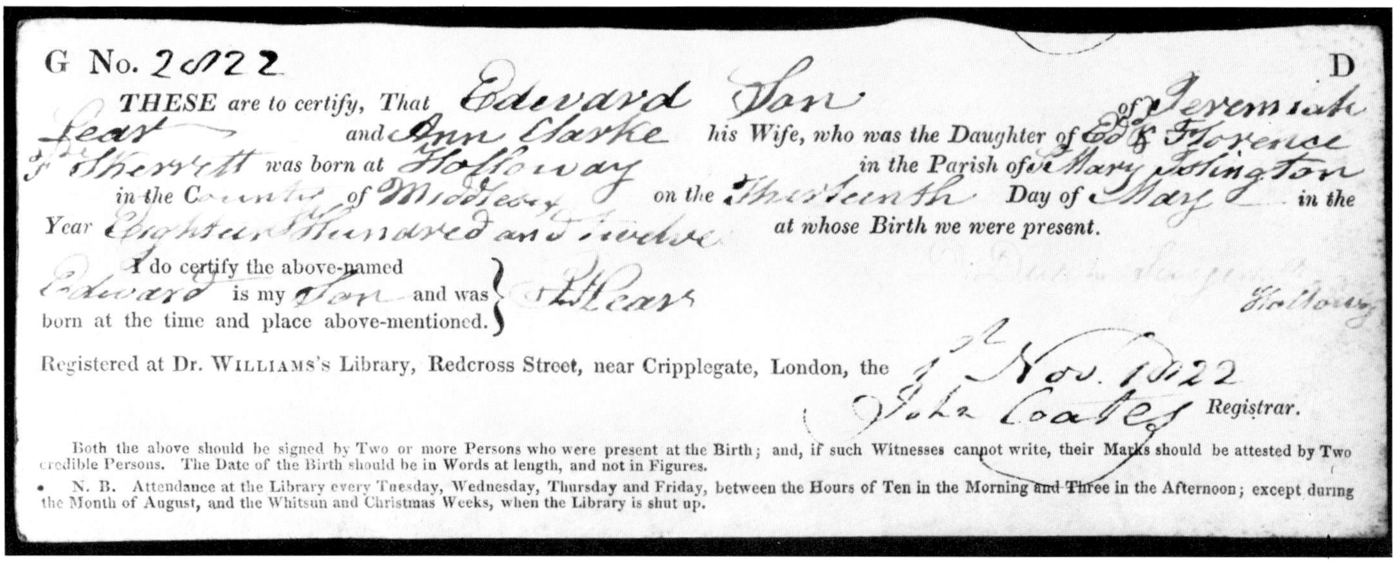
G No. 2822 D

THESE are to certify, That Edward Son of Jeremiah Lear and Ann Clarke his Wife, who was the Daughter of Edw & Florence Skerrett was born at Holloway in the Parish of St Mary Islington in the County of Middlesex on the Thirteenth Day of May in the Year Eighteen Hundred and Twelve at whose Birth we were present.

I do certify the above-named Edward is my Son and was born at the time and place above-mentioned. } J Lear

Registered at Dr. WILLIAMS's Library, Redcross Street, near Cripplegate, London, the 1 Nov. 1822
John Coates Registrar.

Both the above should be signed by Two or more Persons who were present at the Birth; and, if such Witnesses cannot write, their Marks should be attested by Two credible Persons. The Date of the Birth should be in Words at length, and not in Figures.

• N. B. Attendance at the Library every Tuesday, Wednesday, Thursday and Friday, between the Hours of Ten in the Morning and Three in the Afternoon; except during the Month of August, and the Whitsun and Christmas Weeks, when the Library is shut up.

1*a*

1*b*

Eleanor, Henry, Harriet, Cordelia, Frederick, Florence, Charles, Edward and Catherine.

Bowman's Lodge stood on the corner of Holloway Road and Seven Sisters' Road, and took its name from the archery range which had occupied the site in the sixteenth century. In the early nineteenth century Upper Holloway was still a rural village.

The Lears lived in Bowman's Lodge from 1806 until 1828, although they had to leave the house for a while during a period of acute financial hardship. It later became an Establishment for Young Ladies, and it was during this time that the engraving exhibited here was made. Lear did not return there again until 10 September 1863, when he was walking past and saw that it was being demolished. He went inside and wandered through the empty rooms: there are plans for the two storeys in his diary for that day.

PROVENANCE *(a)* Eleanor Newsom (née Lear), by family descent; 1984, given by Mrs Z.E. Clark to the Victoria and Albert Museum. *(b)* not known.

EXHIBITIONS *(b)* 1958, London, Arts Council of Great Britain, *Edward Lear* (no. 121); 1968, London, Gooden and Fox Ltd, *Edward Lear* (no. 128).

REFERENCES *(a)* Noakes 1979 edn, p. 324. *(b)* Murphy 1953, pp. 12–14; Noakes 1968 edn, pp. 12, 17–18, 198, repr. p. 16; Lehmann 1977, repr. p. 10.

2a

2 Jeremiah and Ann Lear, Edward's Parents

a) Frederick Harding, *Jeremiah Lear*
Photograph of miniature: 10.5 × 6.5 cm/4⅛ × 2½ in
D.R. Michell Esq.

b) ?Margaret Carpenter, *Ann Lear*
Pencil and grey wash on buff paper, heightened with white chalk: 23 × 19 cm/9 × 7½ in
D.R. Michell Esq.

2b

Jeremiah and Ann Lear were married on 24 August 1788; he was 31, she was 19.

Lear himself claimed Danish descent, and until 1968 this remained unchallenged (Noakes 1968 edn, p. 14). 'My own [name] as I think you know is really LØR, but my Danish grandfather picked off the two dots and pulled out the diagonal line and made the word Lear (the two dots and the line and the O representing the sound —ea). If he threw away the line and the dots only he would be called *Mr Lor* which he didn't like' (Congreve, 31.xii.82, LLEL 1911, pp. 18–19). This would seem to be Lear indulging in phonetic play were it not that even his closest friend, Franklin Lushington, believed it to be true (see introduction to *Poems of Alfred, Lord Tennyson, illustrated by Edward Lear*, 1889; see Cat. 44*b*).

In fact, his father's forebears came from Dorset. His great-grandfather, George Leare, came up to London and established a successful sugar refining business. In 1799, Jeremiah Lear, Edward's father, was elected Master of the Fruiterer's Company. However, in the same year he left the family business and became a stockbroker. The exact nature of Jeremiah Lear's subsequent financial misfortunes is not fully known. In 1816, his name appears as a defaulter on the Stock

Exchange, and it is possible that he served a short prison sentence for debt.

Edward's mother, Ann Lear (née Clarke Skerrett), was descended from a landed Durham family whose wealth had passed down through another branch. From a boyhood poem written by Lear on 24 July 1828, now surviving only in a copy, it appears that his mother brooded on the loss of her family's fortune. There was a time when 'all Durham had been ours', but those days were past. Ann Lear probably felt that she had married beneath her, and the nagging of Mrs Discobbolos in the second part of 'Mr and Mrs Discobbolos' (see Cat. 87*b*) may have echoed complaints which Edward had been accustomed to hear in his youth.

Referring to the miniature of Jeremiah Lear (Cat. 2*a*), Lear said that 'the portrait of my father is good but less agreeable in face that he was' (Diary, 10.x.77). The drawing of Ann Lear (Cat. 2*b*) is unsigned but may be by Margaret Carpenter: her studio book for 1812 (National Portrait Gallery, London) records two entries for 'Mr Lear'. The first, in 1812, is for '£6.6.0', and the second, in 1816, is for £5. These may refer to Jeremiah Lear.

PROVENANCE *(a) (b)* Sarah Street (née Lear), by family descent.

REFERENCE *(a) (b)* Noakes 1968 edn, repr. p. 19. *(b)* Lehmann 1977, repr. p. 10.

[The compiler is indebted to John Anderson Esq. for his information about Margaret Carpenter.]

3

3 Ann Lear, Edward's Sister

Artist unknown, *Ann Lear*
Miniature on ivory: 9.8 × 7.6 cm/$3\frac{7}{8}$ × 3 in
National Portrait Gallery, London

Ann Lear was Edward's oldest sister. She was born on 17 January 1791, and it was she, rather than Edward's mother, who was responsible for his upbringing. 'Ever all she was to me was good,' he wrote in 1865, '& what I should have been unless she had been my mother I dare not think' (Diary, 17.i.65). She seems to have been a gentle, loving and infinitely unselfish woman with a sense of fun, and the value of her influence on Edward cannot be underestimated. Despite her affection for a Major Wilby, and a proposal from Sir Claudius Hunter, Ann remained unmarried. She and Edward shared a home until his departure for Rome in 1837 (see Cat. 14). She then lived alone, or shared lodgings with friends. When they were apart Edward wrote her long, affectionate letters. Although those written from Knowsley were subsequently destroyed, his letters from the summer of 1837 until Ann's death in 1861 cover a period for which no diaries survive and are an invaluable source of information. The letters themselves—apart from two now in a private collection (see Cat. 26, 27)—have disappeared. However, they are known to have existed until the end of the 1930s, and at some time typed copies were made from them.

Ann died on 11 March 1861. She 'speaks of dying as a change about to bring such delight that she only checks herself from thinking of it too much. She has always been indeed as near Heaven as it was possible to be,' wrote Lear (Fortescue, 7.iii.61, LEL 1907, p. 183). She was buried in Highgate cemetery, but, although the location of her grave is known (no. 10948, square 51), it has not been possible to find it.

On receipt of a miniature portrait of Ann, possibly the one exhibited here, Lear wrote to his sister: 'I am so delighted with your likeness; I hope when you see Mrs. Arundale you will thank her for having taken so much pains with it; it is a *most beautiful* miniature, quite apart fom the resemblance, which, now I have looked at it a great deal, I really think cannot be improved in any one particular' (28.x.47, TS.).

PROVENANCE Mary Boswell (née Lear); by family descent to Francis Adeney Allen; 1915, given by him to the National Portrait Gallery, London.

REFERENCES Strachey 1911, pp. 7–10, repr. opp. p. 48; Lehmann 1977, repr. p. 11; Kai Kin Yung, *National Portrait Gallery, Concise Illustrated Catalogue*, London 1981.

4 Portraits

a) Edward Lear's sister, 1832
Pencil on grey paper, heightened with white chalk: 31.5 × 21.5 cm/$12\frac{1}{2}$ × $8\frac{1}{2}$ in
Signed and dated br.: *E. Lear del. 1832*
D.R. Michell Esq.

b) Artist unknown, *Boyhood Silhouette of Edward Lear*
Ink on black paper: 6.4 × 2.8 cm/$2\frac{1}{2}$ × $1\frac{1}{8}$ in [Repr. p. 73
National Portrait Gallery, London

Lear produced few portraits (see Cat. 27*c*, *d*). The early drawing exhibited here (Cat. 4*a*) is thought to be one of his sisters, and certainly the family resemblance is strong, particularly in the shape of the nose. Lear recognised that the weakest area of his work was figure drawing. Though he attempted to rectify this (see Cat. 103), he never fully understood the human form.

The silhouette of Lear by an unknown artist (Cat. 4*b*) is undated, but was probably drawn in the early 1830s. It is one of a pair; the other is of his youngest sister, Catherine (National Portrait Gallery, London).

PROVENANCE *(a)* Sarah Street (née Lear), by family descent. *(b)* Mary Boswell (née Lear), by family descent to Francis Adeney Allen; 1915, given by him to the National Portrait Gallery, London.

EXHIBITION *(b)* 1968, London, Gooden and Fox Ltd, *Edward Lear* (no. 129).

REFERENCES *(a)* Noakes 1968 edn, repr. p. 27. *(b)* Strachey 1911, pp. 9–10, repr. opp. p. 188; Lehmann 1977, repr. p. 7; Hyman 1980, repr. p. 10.

4*a*

5 Work from Early Scrapbooks

a) Lear's notebook, 1829
Containing drawings, watercolours and poems
Volume 18.4 × 11.1 cm/7¼ × 4⅜ in
Open at poem signed and dated: *E. Lear.— / December. 3d 1829.*
Inscribed:

From the pale and the deep—
From the dark and bright—
From violets that sleep—
Away from light:—
From the lily that flashes
At morn's glad call—
The bee gathers honey
And sweets from all.

There are hearts like bees
In a world such as this,
That are given to please
Through sorrow and bliss:—
Be the heaven of life
As dark as it will—
Amid pleasure and strife
They are smiling still.

They've a tear for the sad—
But there's balm in their sigh,—
And they laugh with the glad
In sunshine and joy:—
They give hope to the gloom
Of the mourner's thrall—
Like the bee they find honey
And sweets in all.—

The Trustees of the National Library of Scotland

b) *Eleanor's geranium*, 1828
Watercolour on paper: 35 × 25 cm/13$\frac{13}{16}$ × 9⅞ in
Signed, inscribed and dated bc.: *E. Lear Eleanor's Geranium, Twickenham June 18. 1828*
Private Collection

c) *Javanese peacock*, 1831 [Col. pl. p. 25
Watercolour on card: 22.8 × 17.7 cm/9 × 7 in
Signed br.: *E. Lear*
Dated bl.: *1831*
The Department of Printing and Graphic Arts, The Houghton Library, Harvard University

In 1858 Lear told Fortescue, 'Brought up by women—& badly besides—& ill always, I never had any chance of manly improvement & exercise' (9.iii.58, LEL 1907, p. 92). Tutored at home by his sisters, particularly Ann and Sarah, he learned such feminine accomplishments as drawing and painting. Indeed, a room at Bowman's Lodge was set aside as the painting room.

The earliest of his work to have survived, dated *c.* 1828, is in an album of birds, butterflies and flowers (Houghton Library, Harvard University). The drawings follow the amateur conventions of their day. The volume exhibited here (Cat. 5*a*) contains youthful poems as well as drawings dated variously in 1829. Though both the writing and the drawing show talent, there is no hint of the bold zest of his later work.

Eleanor's geranium (Cat. 5*b*), drawn when Lear was sixteen, is an early indication of his lifelong interest in flora (Cat. 35). Eleanor was his fourth sister, married to William Newsom of Leatherhead.

The *Javanese peacock* (Cat. 5*c*), though dated 1831, is closer to Lear's childhood drawings than the professional work in which he was already involved (Cat. 6–9). It shows clearly Lear's early interest in landscape backgrounds; his free handling of large shapes is typical of much of his early Italian landscape (Cat. 15).

As with his early Nonsense drawings (Cat. 71), Lear's progression from small, derivative bird drawing to bold, powerfully characteristic work was rapid. In fact, the two seem to go side by side, and his youthful, imitative style was not fully abandoned until after he had established himself as a considerable ornithological draughtsman.

PROVENANCE *(a)* Gertrude Lushington; Hugh Sharp; 1938, given to the National Library of Scotland. *(b)* Eleanor Newsom (née Lear), by family descent; 10 February 1970, Christie's (lot. 44); bt by present owner. *(c)* W.B. Osgood Field; The Houghton Library, Harvard University.

EXHIBITIONS *(a)* 1958, London, Arts Council of Great Britain, *Edward Lear* (no. 103). *(b)* 1958, London, Arts Council of Great Britain, *Edward Lear* (no. 8).

REFERENCES *(a)* W.M. Parker, Edward Lear, 'Three New Poems', *Poetry Review* vol. XLI (April 1950), pp. 81–83. *(b)* Lehmann 1977, repr. p. 6. *(c)* Osgood Field 1933, p. 239; Hofer 1967, pl. 1b; Hyman 1980, repr. p. 14.

5*b*

NATURAL HISTORY

Writing in 1831, Lear explained that he 'at the age of 14 & a half, was turned out into the world, *literally without a farthing*—& with nought to look for a living but his own exertions' (Empson, 1.x.31, MS., Pierpont Morgan Library). He was not destitute, however, for he shared a home with his sister Ann, who had a small inheritance.

The precise date when he became a professional ornithological draughtsman cannot now be established (see Cat. 6), but by the time he was nineteen he was working on *Illustrations of the Family of Psittacidae, or Parrots*, which he published himself for subscribers (see Cat. 9). However, without financial backing and with 'the tardy paying of many of my subscribers' (Empson, 1.x.31, MS., Pierpont Morgan Library), Lear was unable to complete the work, and from April 1832 until July 1837 he worked as an ornithological and natural history draughtsman for other people (see Bibliography), in particular John Gould and the 13th Earl of Derby.

The relationship between Lear and Gould was not an easy one. When Gould died in 1881 Lear wrote, 'he was one I never liked really, for in spite of a certain jollity and bonhommie, he was a harsh and violent man. At the Zoological S. at 33 Bruton St.—at Hullmandels—at Broad St. ever the same persevering hardworking toiler in his own (ornithological) line,—but ever as unfeeling for those about him. In the earliest phase of his bird=drawing, he owed everything to his excellent wife, & to myself,—without whose help in drawing he had done nothing' (Diary, 2.ii.81).

Lear's relationship with Lord Derby—who was Lord Stanley when Lear first worked for him—was quite different. He lived and worked at Knowsley, at intervals, between 1831 and 1837, making drawings of the birds and animals in the menagerie there.

Because Lear abandoned this career so early—he was only twenty-five when he became a landscape painter—it is easy to pass too swiftly over this stage in his life and to underestimate his contribution to the ornithological illustration of his time. This came particularly from his Book of Parrots, which was the first book to be devoted to a single species. Perhaps the most important part of his contribution was his insistence on drawing from living birds rather than from stuffed skins. This made his task difficult but resulted in more truthful representations, both anatomically and in the characteristics of the birds he portrayed. His pursuit of truth to nature, begun before his contemporaries formalized the idea, was one that he carried into his landscape work.

His choice of lithography, and his decision to reproduce the drawings life-size, meant that the vitality and scale of his work could be sustained. His lithographs were printed by Charles Hullmandel, whose *Art of Drawing on Stone* had been published in 1824, and who set a high standard of reproduction. Lear's Book of Parrots, published when he was nineteen, contributed significantly to the quality of ornithological publication which reached such heights during the nineteenth century.

10*d*

As an indication of Lear's contribution to ornithological draughtsmanship it is worth noting that three species of birds are named after him—*Anodorhynchus leari*, *Lopochroa leari* and *Pyrrhulopsis leari* (see Bibliography).

V.N.

6 Early Bird Drawings

a) *Bird*, *c.* 1830
Watercolour on paper: 16.5 × 14 cm/6½ × 5½ in
Nigell D'Oyly Esq.

b) *Great Auk*, 1831
Drawing for Prideaux Selby's *Illustrations of British Ornithology*, vol. 2 ('Sea Birds'), pl. 82
Pencil on paper (two pieces glued together): 52.4 × 37.1 cm/20½ × 14½ in
The Blacker-Wood Library, McGill University, Canada

Lear tells us that he 'began to draw, for bread and cheese, about 1827, but only did uncommon queer shop-sketches—selling them for prices varying from ninepence to four shillings: colouring prints, screens, fans; awhile making morbid disease drawings, for hospitals and certain doctors of physic. In 1831 through Mrs. Wentworth, I became employed at the Zoological Society, and, in 1832, published "The Family of Psittacidae"' (*Nonsense Songs and Stories*, 6th edn, 1888, 'By Way of Preface').

The watercolour study of a bird (Cat 6*a*) comes from a group of bird drawings, now largely dispersed, which Lear gave to Mrs Godfrey Wentworth as a token of gratitude. The group was accompanied by a sheet inscribed: 'To Mr. and Mrs. Wentworth, / and their family, / In acknowledgement of their kindness towards him / These drawings are respectfully and gratefully presented / by / E. Lear / 24th April 1830 / 35 Upper North Place, / Grays Inn Road' (MS., Nigell D'Oyly).

Lear spoke of Mrs Wentworth as the person responsible for launching him into his artist's life (see LEL 1907, pp. xvii-xviii), and it was probably she who introduced Lear to the naturalist Prideaux Selby (1788–1867). In a letter to Fortescue dated 21 January 1862, Lear speaks of having met 'One Luard—which I made drawings when I was 16 for his grandfather who was very kind to me' (LEL 1907, p. 222). Luard's grandfather was Prideaux Selby. Lear's dating is unreliable but this reference would seem to place the introduction as 1828 or early 1829.

6*a*

It is likely that Lear served an informal apprenticeship with Selby. If so, it was a fortunate training, for Selby demonstrated a bold and lively approach to his ornithological work which was ahead of his time, and which Lear was to develop with such skill in his later bird drawings.

The drawing of the *Great Auk* (Cat. 6*b*) is a preliminary study for an engraving which Lear contributed to Prideaux Selby's *Illustrations of British Ornithology*. The work was published in nineteen parts between 1821 and 1834.

The engraving is signed with Selby's name alone, but a pencil and watercolour wash drawing (Martin Bradley Collection), based on his sketch which comes from a collection of ornithological drawings known to be by Lear, is signed by both Lear and Selby and dated 1831.

PROVENANCE *(a)* Mrs Godfrey Wentworth, by family descent. *(b)* 1927, 29 May, bt from Fogg (Bookseller), Crystal Palace, London; The Blacker-Wood Library of Zoology and Ornithology, Montreal, Canada.

[The compiler is indebted to Miss Gillian Kyles for her information about the watercolour of the *Great Auk*]

7 Preliminary Studies for Illustrations of The Family of Psittacidae, Or Parrots, 1830–32

a) *Platycercus tabuensis* (Tabuan Parakeet)
Study for pl. 16 on verso of lithographic proof of *Psittacula torquata*, pl. 40
Pencil, ink and grey wash on paper: 56.1 × 38.1 cm/22⅛ × 15 in
Department of Printing and Graphic Arts, The Houghton Library, Harvard University

b) Unidentified parrot (Rose-ringed Parakeet?)
Pencil on paper: 27.9 × max. 22.2 cm/11 × 8¾ in
Department of Printing and Graphic Arts, The Houghton Library, Harvard University

c) *Plyctolophus Leadbeateri* (Leadbeater's Cockatoo)
Study for pl. 5 [Col. pl. p. 29
Pencil, ink, watercolour, with notes on paper: max. 52 × 35.8 cm/20½ × 14⅞ in
On verso: pencil and wash drawings of parrots and two drawings of trains
Department of Printing and Graphic Arts, The Houghton Library, Harvard University

d) *Plyctolophus sulphureus* (Lesser Sulphur-crested Cockatoo), 1830 [Col. pl. p. 29
Study for pl. 4
Pencil, ink, watercolour on paper (the larger bird is cut out and mounted on the leaf): 50.8 × max. 31.4 cm/20 × 12⅜ in
Inscribed and dated tl.: *September 1830 Plyctolophus Sulphureus. from a living specimen at Bruton Street*
Department of Printing and Graphic Arts, The Houghton Library, Harvard University

In June 1830 Lear applied for permission to make drawings of the parrots belonging to the Zoological Society of London.

7a

ship, with added colour wash and often extensive notes—'rather too pink', 'rather too deep', 'soft undulating feathers'—which would act as guides to both form and colour when he worked on more finished paintings based on these studies.

7b

This was granted on 16 June at a meeting chaired by Lord Stanley, President of the Zoological Society, later the 13th Earl of Derby and one of Lear's most important patrons (see Cat. 11).

During the next two years Lear prepared drawings for *Illustrations of the Family of Psittacidae, or Parrots*. This he published privately by subscription in twelve folio parts between 1830 and 1832 (Cat. 9). He found his subjects in the recently opened Zoological Society Gardens in Regent's Park, in the Society's museum in Bruton Street and in private collections.

He later considered the project to have been innovatory in three ways: it was the first work devoted to a single species; it was 'the first book of the kind drawn on stone in England of so large a size' (Northbrook, 11.x.67, MS., The Houghton Library, Harvard University); and he worked from living birds rather than from stuffed skins.

Two features of Lear's later landscape watercolours can be seen in his studies for the parrots: the importance of accuracy achieved by working directly from nature, which is endorsed in Lear's claim that his landscape drawings were 'really topographically correct' (Fortescue, 8.iv.83, MS., Somerset Record Office, Taunton); and the emphasis on draughtsmanship, with added colour wash and often extensive notes—'rather too pink', 'rather too deep', 'soft undulating feathers'—which would act as guides to both form and colour when he worked on more finished paintings based on these studies.

Though working from the parrots demanded considerable concentration, his attention sometimes turned from his subject to the people who watched him at work. Visitors to the aviary probably found the young artist as interesting as the birds, and he reciprocated by drawing them. Among the fine collection of preliminary parrot studies at Harvard are a number of examples of Lear's temporary boredom or distraction—parrot drawings are adorned with figures, puns and even messages in code. The interpolation of the absurd into otherwise serious matters is characteristic of Lear, and can be seen in his landscape drawings (Cat. 17*d*), his Nonsense, his letters (Cat. 95) and his conversation with friends (see Cat. 89).

PROVENANCE *(a)–(d)* W.B. Osgood Field; The Houghton Library, Harvard University.

EXHIBITION *(d)* 1962, San Marino, Calif., Henry E. Huntington Library and Art Gallery, *Drawings by Edward Lear* (no. 4).

REFERENCES *(a)* Osgood Field 1933, p. 246, repr. (detail) p. 122. *(b)* Osgood Field 1933, p. 245, repr. (detail) p. 141; Hyman 1980, repr. p. 20. *(c)* Osgood Field 1933, p. 245; Reade 1949, p. 16. *(d)* Osgood Field 1933, p. 244; Hyman 1980, repr. p. 20.

8 The Red and Yellow Macaw

Red and Yellow Maccaw, Macrocercus aracanga, pl. 7 in *Illustrations of The Family of Psitaccidae, Or Parrots*

a) Preliminary drawing for pl. 7
Pencil on paper: 33 × max. 37.1 cm/13 × $14\frac{5}{8}$ in
Verso has been rubbed over with soft pencil and the drawing traced through
Department of Printing and Graphic Arts, The Houghton Library, Harvard University

b) Preliminary study for pl. 7 [Col. pl. p. 30
Pencil, watercolour with colour notes and trial colour washes on paper: 31 × 37.1 cm/13 × $14\frac{5}{8}$ in
Department of Printing and Graphic Arts, The Houghton Library, Harvard University

c) Study for pl. 7 [Col. pl. p. 30
Pencil, ink, watercolour on paper with colour notes: 36.8 × 37.7 cm/$14\frac{1}{2}$ × $14\frac{7}{8}$ in
Department of Printing and Graphic Arts, The Houghton Library, Harvard University

d) *Illustrations of The Family of Psittacidae, Or Parrots The Greater Part of Them Species Hitherto Unfigured, Containing Forty-two Lithographic Plates, Drawn from Life, And On Stone by Edward Lear, A.L.S.*, 1832 [Col. pl. p. 31
Printed by Charles Hullmandel
Volume: 54 × 36.2 cm/$21\frac{1}{4}$ × $14\frac{1}{4}$ in
Open at pl. 7
Hand-coloured lithograph: 53.3 × 35.6 cm/21 × 14 in
Private Collection

8*a*

Lear's parrot drawings, apart from the few cases clearly indicated in both his studies and the published lithographs, were life-size. Having decided upon a characteristic pose, he made a careful drawing (Cat. 8*a*). This was then traced through onto a fresh sheet of paper, and he began to block in colour (Cat. 8*b*). Probably deriving the outlines from the first drawing, he produced a series of increasingly detailed studies (Cat. 8*c*). When he was satisfied that both the drawing and the colour were accurate, the work was ready for transferring to the lithographic stone.

It is believed that Lear transferred the drawings onto the lithographic stones himself. In doing so, he traced them directly onto the stone so that the lithographic print is the reverse of the final drawing. This is the only occasion in Lear's work where this is the case: in the *Gleanings from the Menagerie and Aviary at Knowsley Hall* (1846; see Cat. 11*i*) and Lear's travel journals where he employed lithography (see Cat. 64, 65, 67, 68, 69) the reproductions are not mirror images. At the time he was working on the parrots, Lear was unfamiliar with *papier rapport* or transfer paper, and in a letter dated 13 March 1833, he wrote: 'I have recd. from the Society a sheet of transferring lithographic paper—desiring my opinion of its suitableness for that purpose—and had I been at all accustomed to practice transferring, I should have felt very glad to have given it. As however I understand nothing of that part of the art of Lithography—I have taken it to Mr. Hullmandel' (Arthur Aiken, MS., Royal Society of Arts).

He checked the quality of the lithographic proofs, rejecting those that were too dark or indistinct. The final process of handcolouring, based on his finished watercolour, was done by an assistant working under his guidance.

The *Red and Yellow Maccaw* is one of the finest of Lear's bird illustrations. Writing on 26 November 1831, William Swainson, who had studied with the American illustrator of natural history, Audubon, wrote: 'Sir, I received yesterday with great pleasure the numbers of your beautiful work. To repeat my recorded opinion of it, as a whole, is unnecessary but there are two plates which more especially deserve the highest praise: they are the New Holland Palaeornis, and the red and yellow maccaw. The latter is in my estimation equal to any figure ever painted by Barraband or Audubon, for grace of design, perspective, or anatomical accuracy. I am so particularly pleased with these, that I should feel much gratified by possessing a duplicate copy of each. They will then be framed, as fit companions in my drawing room to hang by the side of a pair by my friend Audubon' (MS., Houghton Library, Harvard University).

PROVENANCE *(a)–(c)* W.B. Osgood Field; The Houghton Library, Harvard University. *(d)* by family descent to present owner.

EXHIBITION *(c)* 1962, San Marino, Calif., Henry E. Huntington Library and Art Gallery, *Drawings by Edward Lear* (no. 5).

REFERENCES *(a)* Osgood Field 1933, p. 246, repr. p. 21. *(b)* Hyman 1980, repr. p. 25. *(c)* Osgood Field 1933, p. 246; Hyman 1980, repr. p. 24.

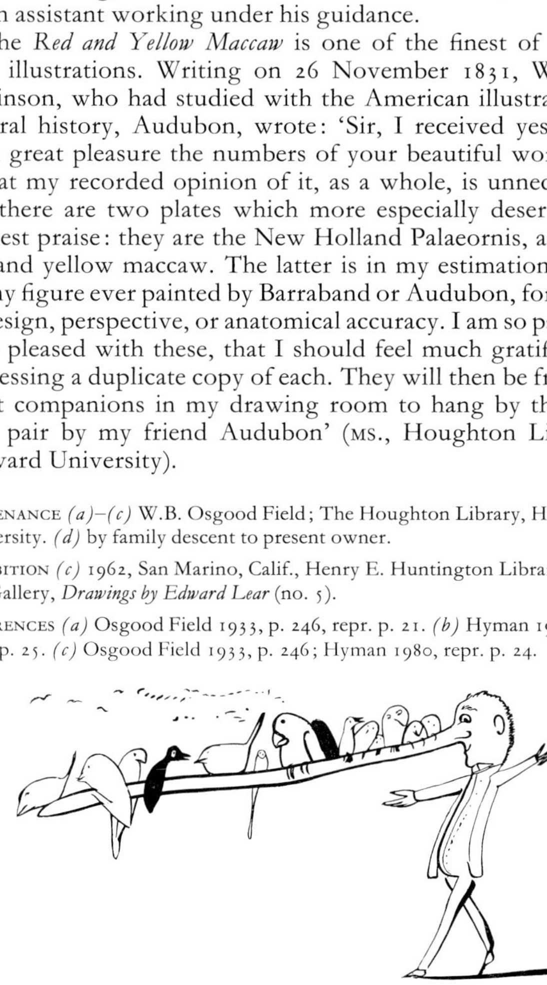

76

9 Illustrations of The Family of Psittacidae, Or Parrots, 1830–32

a) Folio wrapper for part 1
Lithograph on paper: 56.5 × 38.1 cm/$22\frac{1}{4}$ × 15 in
Private Collection

b) Folio wrapper for part 12
Lithograph on paper: 55.8 × max. 38.1 cm/22 × $14\frac{1}{4}$ in
Department of Printing and Graphic Arts, The Houghton Library, Harvard University

c) *Illustrations of The Family of Psittacidae, Or Parrots: The Greater Part of Them Species Hitherto Unfigured, Containing Forty-two Lithographic Plates, Drawn from Life, And On Stone by Edward Lear, A.L.S.*, 1832
Inscribed in Lear's hand facing title page: *Ann Lear / with the sincere regards of her brother / E. Lear / April. 15. 1832. / 61. Albany St. Regent's Park.*
Department of Printing and Graphic Arts, The Houghton Library, Harvard University

d) Proposal for Associate Membership of the Linnean Society
Sepia ink on paper: 24.9 × 20 cm/$9\frac{13}{16}$ × $7\frac{7}{8}$ in
Dated *18 January 1831*
The Council of the Linnean Society, London

In order to finance his *Illustrations of the Family of Psittacidae, or Parrots*, Lear invited subscribers; the list is headed by Mrs Godfrey Wentworth (see Cat. 6) and members of her family. Only 175 impressions were made from each drawing, and the stones were then destroyed. As Lear explained, 'My reasons for so soon destroying my drawings were these . . . I was obliged to limit the work—in order to get more subscribers—and to erase the drawings—because the expense is considerable for keeping them on and I have pretty great difficulty in paying my monthly charge,—for to pay colourer and printer monthly I am obstinately prepossessed—since I had rather be at the bottom of the River Thames than be one week in debt,—be it never so small' (Empson, 1.x.31, MS., Pierpont Morgan Library, New York).

Lear had originally intended to publish fourteen parts, but the work was never completed. The reason was almost certainly financial, for in October 1831 he wrote, 'the tardy paying of many of my subscribers—renders it but too difficult to procure food and pay for publishing at once.—With Mr. Gould all this is very different—he has sufficient to live on, whether his subscribers pay or not and can well afford the innumerable little expenses of printing—but for poor I—I have just nine and twenty times resolved to give up parrots and all—and should certainly have done so had not my good genius with vast reluctance just 9 and 20 times set me going again' (Empson, 1.x.31, ibid.).

Writing to Sir William Jardine in 1834, Lear explained: 'I had originally intended to have figured all the Psittacidae, but I stopped in time, neither will there be (from me) any letter-press. Their one publication was a speculation which so far as it made me known procured me employment, but in the matter of money occasionally caused loss' (23.i.34, quoted Reade, 1949, p. 16). A few days earlier, John Gould (see Cat. 12) had told Jardine, 'Mr Lear's Parrots stopped at the 12th number. I have purchased from him the whole of his stock so that if you are not complete as far as published I can make them so—I have some idea of finishing them myself' (16.i.34, quoted Reade, 1949, p. 16).

9*a*

9*b*

The first two folio parts were issued on 1 November 1830 (Cat. 9*a*), and others throughout 1831 and the early months of 1832 (see Cat. 9*b*, Bibliography). The final volume (Cat. 9*c*), published by April 1832, contained 42 hand-coloured lithographs, a list of subscribers and another of plates, a dedication to Queen Adelaide and a title page. Ann's copy (Cat. 9*c*) is inscribed by Lear and dated 15 April 1932.

The day after the publication of the first two folios, Lear was recommended for Associate Membership of the Linnean

Society (Cat. 9*d*). His sponsors were N.A. Vigors (1785–1840), the zoologist who owned some of the parrots that Lear drew; Thomas Bell (1792–1880), to whose zoological works Lear later contributed drawings (see Bibliography); and E.T. Bennett (1797–1836), who had played an important part in establishing the Zoological Society of London, and to whose 1831 publication, *The Gardens of the Zoological Society Delineated*, Lear contributed a drawing of Blue and Yellow Macaws (see Bibliography). Lear remained an Associate of the Linnean Society until 1862, when the Society requested that he should drop the A.L.S., 'if I did not communicate science' (Diary, 26.iv.62).

PROVENANCE *(a) c.* 1945, purchased by present owner. *(b) (c)* W.B. Osgood Field; The Houghton Library, Harvard University. *(d)* The Linnean Society.

EXHIBITION *(c)* 1968, Worcester Mass., Worcester Art Museum, *Edward Lear, Painter, Poet and Draughtsman* (no. 85).

REFERENCES *(b)* Osgood Field 1933, p. 246; Hofer 1967, repr. pl. 2; Hyman 1980, repr. p. 18. *(c)* Osgood Field 1933, p. 116–17, 242–46; Reade 1949, pp. 12–24.

10 Watercolours for Lord Derby

a) Unidentified marsupial, 1835
Watercolour, watercolour mixed with gum, with touches of bodycolour on paper: 53.4 × 36.5 cm/$21\frac{1}{16} \times 14\frac{3}{8}$ in
Signed and dated bl.: *Edward Lear del. Sept. 1835*
Inscribed in pencil b.: *Macropus . . . ?*
Private Collection

b) *Circaëtus gallicus* (Short-toed Eagle), 1835
Watercolour, watercolour mixed with gum on paper: 53.4 × 36.8 cm/$21\frac{1}{16} \times 14\frac{1}{2}$ in
Signed and dated br.: *Edward Lear. del. Sept. 1835.*
Inscribed b.: *Circaëtus gallicus (Gmel.) Mogador*
Private Collection

c) *Viverra binotata* (Civet), 1836
Watercolour, watercolour mixed with gum on paper: 36.6 × 53.4 cm/$14\frac{7}{16} \times 21\frac{1}{16}$ in
Signed and dated br.: *Edward Lear. del. Decbr 1836*
Inscribed b.: *Viverra Binotata, Temm. Western Africa.*
Private Collection

10*a*

10*b*

d) *Palaeornis melanorhynchus* (? Parakeet), 1835
[Repr. p. 79
Watercolour, watercolour mixed with gum on paper: 53.4 × 36.8 cm/$21\frac{1}{16}$ × $14\frac{1}{2}$ in
Signed and dated bc.: *Edward Lear. del Sept. 1835*
Inscribed b.: *Palaeornis melanorhynchus, Sykes Ghauts, India.*
Private Collection

e) *Scolopax rusticola* (European Woodcock), 1835 (left); *Scolopax gallinago* (Common Snipe), 1835 (right)
Watercolour, watercolour mixed with gum, and chinese white on paper: 36.1 × 53.4 cm/$14\frac{1}{4}$ × $21\frac{1}{16}$ in
Signed and dated bc.: *Mr. Lear. / 28 Southampton / Decr. 1835.*
Inscribed b.: *Scolopax rusticola, Linn. British*; *Scolopax gallinago, Penn.*
Private Collection

10*c*

10*e*

10*f*

f) *Heliornis senegalensis* (Sun-grebe), 1836
Watercolour, watercolour mixed with gum, and chinese white on paper: 36.9 × 53.4 cm/$14\frac{9}{16} \times 21\frac{1}{16}$ in
Signed and dated bl.: *Edward Lear. del. July. 1836.*
Inscribed b.: *Heliornis senegalensis*
Private Collection

g) *Strix perspicillata* (Spectacled Owl), 1836 [Col. pl. p. 27
Watercolour, watercolour mixed with gum, and chinese white on paper: 53.4 × 36.6 cm/$21\frac{1}{16} \times 14\frac{7}{16}$ in
Signed and dated bl.: *Edward Lear. del. August. 1836*
Inscribed in pencil b.: *Spectacled Owl Strix perspicillata*
Private Collection

h) Unidentified tree rat, 1834
Watercolour, watercolour mixed with gum, and bodycolour on paper: 53.4 × 36.5 cm/$21\frac{1}{16} \times 14\frac{3}{8}$ in
Signed and dated br.: *E. Lear. del. March 18. 1834*
Private Collection

Although the opening of the Zoological Society Gardens in Regent's Park in 1829 gave a new opportunity for the public to see the strange and extraordinary birds and animals that were brought back to England by explorers and zoologists on scientific voyages, there remained a tradition of private menageries. One of the most important of these was built up by Lord Stanley on an existing collection of animals at his family home, Knowsley Hall, just outside Liverpool.

The most important immediate consequence of Lear's *Illustrations of the Family of Psittacidae, or Parrots* (see Cat. 9*c*) was that it brought his work to the attention of Lord Stanley (who in 1834 became Lord Derby), who invited him to make drawings of some of the creatures in his collection at Knowsley and in that part of it housed at the Zoological Society. Lord Stanley wished both to catalogue his collection and to build a record for classification. It was essential that he should employ a draughtsman capable of making accurate drawings; Lear's publication on parrots provided evidence of these skills.

Although Lear's early work had been with birds he now had the opportunity of drawing animals as well, and in the library at Knowsley there are more than a hundred Lear watercolours of the creatures in the menagerie. The earliest dated

10*h*

drawing in the collection is 1831, and in October of that year he was writing, 'I am delighted with the flowers—if you have any more sketches of S. American *trees* (correct) they would be invaluable to me for I often want to put birds on when I draw for Lord Stanley—which is very frequently' (Empson, 1.x.31, MS., Pierpont Morgan Library, New York).

But Lear did not spend all his Knowsley days in the menagerie. He found time to mix with 'half the fine people of the day' (LEL 1907, p. xix), and to entertain their children with his Nonsense (Cat. 72*c*). When not at Knowsley he lived with Ann in rooms at 28 Southampton Row, and it was to this address that Lord Derby sent Lear the brace of snipe shot on the estate at Knowsley (Cat. 10*e*).

PROVENANCE by family descent to present owner.

EXHIBITIONS *(b)* 1975, Liverpool, Walker Art Gallery, *Edward Lear and Knowsley* (no. 18). *(d)* 1968, London, Gooden and Fox Ltd, *Edward Lear* (no. 1). *(e)* possibly 1836, London, Royal Society of British Artists, (as *Dead Birds*); 1975, Liverpool, Walker Art Gallery, *Edward Lear and Knowsley* (no. 22). *(g)* 1975, Liverpool, Walker Art Gallery, *Edward Lear and Knowsley* (no. 31).

REFERENCE *(g)* Hyman 1980, repr. p. 83.

11 Gleanings From The Menagerie And Aviary At Knowsley Hall, 1846

a) *Leopardus Yagouarondi* (Yagouarondi), 1836
Published as pl. IV
Watercolour, watercolour mixed with gum, heightened with white on paper: 53.4 × 35.9 cm/21$\frac{1}{16}$ × 14$\frac{3}{8}$ in
Signed and dated br.: *Edward Lear del. May. 1836*
Inscribed b.: *Leopardus Yagouarondi (Lacep.) Tropical America The Original of the Plate in the 'Gleanings'*
Private Collection

b) *Chenalopex jubata* (Maned Goose), 1836
Published as pl. XV
Watercolour, watercolour mixed with gum on paper: 36.8 × 53.4 cm/14$\frac{1}{2}$ × 21$\frac{1}{16}$ in
Signed and dated bl.: *Edward Lear. del. July. 1836.*
Inscribed b.: *Chenalopex jubata (Spix) Tropical America The Original of the Plate in the 'Gleanings'.*
Private Collection

c) *Balearica regulorum* (Wattled Crown Crane)
Sheet of preliminary studies for pl. XIII
Pencil, ink, watercolour and notes on paper: 52.8 × 36 cm/20$\frac{13}{16}$ × 14$\frac{3}{16}$ in
Inscribed and numbered in modern hand
Blacker-Wood Library, McGill University, Canada

d) *Balearica regulorum* (Wattled Crown Crane), 1835
Published as pl. XIII [Col. pl. p. 26
Watercolour, watercolour mixed with gum, heightened with chinese white on paper: 53.4 × 37.3 cm/21$\frac{1}{16}$ × 14$\frac{11}{16}$ in
Signed bl.: *Edward Lear. del.*
Dated br.: *Sept. 1835.*
Inscribed: *Balearica regulorum. South Africa. The Original of the Plate in the 'Gleanings'.*
Private Collection

e) *Scops Paradisea* (Stanley Crane), 1835
Published as pl. XIV
Pencil, watercolour, watercolour mixed with gum on paper: 53.4 × 36.9 cm/21$\frac{1}{16}$ × 14$\frac{9}{16}$ in
Signed bl.: *Edward Lear. del.*
Dated br.: *Sept. 1835.*
Inscribed b.: *Stanley Crane Scops Paradisea (Licht.) South Africa. The Original of the Plate in the 'Gleanings'.*
Private Collection

f) *Sciurus Javensis* (Tree Squirrel), 1836
Published as pl. VI
Watercolour, watercolour mixed with gum and bodycolour on paper: 32.6 × 53.4 cm/14$\frac{7}{16}$ × 21$\frac{1}{16}$ in
Signed and dated br.: *Edward Lear. del. July. 1836*
Inscribed b.: *Sciurus Javensis, Schreb. India. The Original of the figure in the 'Gleanings'.*
Private Collection

11*a*

Chenalopex jubata (Spix) Tropical America.
The Original of the Plate in the 'Gleanings'.

11*b*

11*c*

11*e*

11*f*

11*g*

g) *Tyrse Argus* (Eyed Tyrse), 1836
Published as pl. XVII
Watercolour, watercolour mixed with gum on paper: 53.4×36.5 cm/$21\frac{1}{16} \times 14\frac{3}{8}$ in
Signed and dated br.: *Edwd. Lear. del. May. 1836*
Inscribed b.: *upper side Tyrse Argus. Gray Western Africa Brought home, alive, by Mr. Whitfield. The Original of the figure in the 'Gleanings'*
Private Collection

h) *Account sent by Lear to Lord Derby*
Ink on paper: 38.8×11.7 cm/$7\frac{7}{16} \times 4\frac{5}{8}$ in
Dated b.: *2 June 1836*
On deposit with the Public Records Office, Liverpool

i) *Gleanings From The Menagerie And Aviary At Knowsley Hall* (Knowsley, 1846), printed for private distribution
J. W. Moore, printed by Hullmandel & Walton and coloured by Mr Bayfield
10 pages of titles and notes, and 17 lithographic plates
Volume 56.8×39 cm/$22\frac{3}{8} \times 15\frac{3}{8}$ in
Preface dated and signed: *British Museum, August 1, 1846. J.E. Gray.*
Private Collection

It was not until 1846, nine years after Lear left England, that Lord Derby published a selection of Lear's watercolours in *Gleanings From The Menagerie And Aviary At Knowsley Hall.* This was a privately printed book, and contained seventeen of Lear's drawings. The lithography was by J. W. Moore, and the printers were Hullmandel & Walton (see Cat. 9, 65, 67, 68). The plates were-hand-coloured by Mr Bayfield.

The Preface, written by J.E. Gray of the British Museum and dated 1 August 1846, paid tribute to Lear's accuracy in representing living specimens, but Lear had not always found such accuracy easy to achieve. He wrote to Lord Derby on

2 June 1836: 'My Lord, I do not know what to say for myself for having so long delayed sending the drawings which will reach Knowsley about the same time this letter does. I took the sketches very carefully from the living animals, but owing to their not being in a good light, I have had very great trouble in getting the drawings to look satisfactory: even now, only the under side of the Trionyx is what I really like. The cat was very difficult to represent, & the Trionyx, although James Hunt held it for me for two whole mornings—not much less so:—I shall be very glad to hear if your Lordship is pleased with them—as I have been very much of out of temper with all three at times' (MS., Public Record Office, Liverpool; Cat. 11*a*, *g*).

In the same letter he tells Lord Derby of the newly arrived giraffes which were creating a sensation at the Zoological Gardens: 'I never imagined any thing living of such extreme elegance,' he says, '& I much wish your Lordship could see them.' He also encloses an account for the drawings of the cat and the tortoise (Cat. 11*h*).

PROVENANCE *(a)–(g)(i)* by family descent to present owner. *(h)* by family descent to present owner; on deposit with Public Records Office, Liverpool.

EXHIBITIONS *(e)* 1958, London, Arts Council of Great Britain, *Edward Lear* (no. 12); 1975, Liverpool, Walker Art Gallery, *Edward Lear and Knowsley* (no. 20). *(f)* 1975, Liverpool, Walker Art Gallery, *Edward Lear and Knowsley* (no. 40, as *Ratufa bicolor* [*Sparrman*]). *(g)* 1975, Liverpool, Walker Art Gallery, *Edward Lear and Knowsley* (no. 38, as Trionyx triunguis [Forskål]).

REFERENCE *Catalogue of the Library at Knowsley Hall*, London, 1893, vol. III, p. 515.

12*a*

12 Work for John Gould

a) *Haliaectus albicilla* (Sea Eagle)
Preliminary study for J. Gould, *Birds of Europe*, vol. I, pl. 9
Pencil, ink and watercolour with notes on paper:
47.4 × 31.9 cm/18⅞ × 12 11/16 in
Blacker-Wood Library, McGill University, Canada

b) *Grus cinerea* (Common Crane)
Study for J. Gould, *Birds of Europe*, vol. IV, pl. 270
Pencil, ink, watercolour with notes on paper:
47.1 × 36.6 cm/18⅞ × 13 in
Blacker-Wood Library, McGill University, Canada

c) *Ramphastos Erythrorhynchus* (Red-billed Toucan)
Study for J. Gould, Monograph of the *Ramphastidae, or Family of Toucans*, pl. 3
Pencil, ink, watercolour and tempera on paper:
51.3 × 37 cm/20 3/16 × 14⅝ in
Blacker-Wood Library, McGill University, Canada

12*a–c* are inscribed and numbered in a modern hand

From the earliest days of his natural history work, Lear was employed in making drawings for various zoological publications (see Bibliography). The man for whom he did most work was John Gould (1804–81). Writing to Northbrook in 1867,

94

94

12*b*

12*c*

Lear said of his book of parrots (Cat. 9*c*) that it 'led to all Mr. Gould's improvements—vide that gentleman's Birds of Europe—Toucans &c—many of which the said foolish artist drew' (11.x.67, MS., Houghton Library, Harvard University).

The plates he contributed to Gould's *Birds of Europe* are some of the finest of his ornithological works; the larger, less pretty birds are drawn with an understanding which he never exceeded. Plans for Lear's part in this work probably date back to a visit he made with Gould to Rotterdam, Berne, Berlin and Amsterdam. Lear dates this tour as 1828 or 1830—the later date is more likely. '. . . at Amsterdam we laid the foundation of many subsequent years of misery to me,' Lear wrote (quoted Reade 1949, p. 26). Two preliminary drawings for this work (Cat. 12*a*,*b*) and a drawing for the volume of Toucans (Cat. 12*c*) are exhibited here.

Lear's relationship with Gould was not always easy (see p. 79). One probable reason for Lear's mistrust was that Gould frequently used his work without acknowledgement. There are plates where the drawing is clearly signed with Lear's name, whilst the attribution reads: 'Drawn from nature and on stone by J.&E. Gould' (see Bibliography). Unless more preliminary studies are discovered it will be impossible now to know which plates in Gould's early works were drawn by Lear, for many that are almost certainly his contain no signature and no attribution.

PROVENANCE *(a)–(c)* 1927, 29 May, bt from Fogg (Bookseller), Crystal Palace, London by Blacker-Wood Library of Zoology and Ornithology, McGill University, Montreal, Canada.

76

15*i*

EARLY LANDSCAPE 1834–1848

Although Lear continued to work as an ornithological draughtsman until the summer of 1837, his interest in landscape dates from the early 1830s. It is first seen in the freely handled watercolour backgrounds to his bird drawings which, whilst within the convention of ornithological illustration of his day, he uses with imagination and skill.

Apart from these, and a few slight works in youthful sketchbooks, Lear's earliest surviving landscape drawings date from 1834. The vigorous use of soft, dark line and white chalk highlights is characteristic of much of his work until the early 1840s, and shows an awareness of the work of J.D. Harding. From the time of his arrival in Rome in 1837, Lear experimented with different ways of drawing and painting in watercolour, and his work during these years demonstrates a wide range and a rapid mastery of both media. These early drawings and watercolours call to mind the work of Samuel Prout, the Varleys, Cox and de Wint, but during the later 1840s his mature style developed and his work acquired its own distinctive character.

His earliest landscape drawings were made near his sister's home in Sussex, but in 1835 he went to Ireland and the following year to the Lake District, returning with portfolios of drawings made on his travels. For Lear, such travel became synonymous with freedom, and the completeness with which he abandoned his ornithological career and his total lack of regret at having done so, derive partly from his finding in landscape work something which satisfied other needs. In 1880 he wrote of 'the charm of early artist life' with its 'days & years of outdoor delight' (Diary, 8.viii.81). 'The Elements—trees, clouds, &c—silence . . . seem to have far more part with me or I with them, than mankind,' he wrote (Diary, 12.v.62).

The immediate reason he gave for his change to landscape painting was ill-health. During the years he spent in the damp northern climate of Knowsley, his childhood illnesses of bronchitis and asthma returned. As well as this, the close work demanded by his study of birds and animals strained his already weak sight, so that in 1836 he wrote to John Gould: 'my eyes are so sadly worse, that no bird under an ostrich shall I soon be able to see to do' (31.x.36, MS., Houghton Library, Harvard University). It seems likely, however, that these factors provided him with the excuse he needed to move on to the work he really wanted to do, and when Lord Derby and his cousin Robert Hornby offered to send him to Rome where he could improve his health and learn to paint, Lear accepted eagerly. V.N.

13 Early Watercolours

a) *Parham*, 1834
Pencil, heightened with chinese white, on buff paper: 26.7 × 36.8 cm/$10\frac{1}{2} \times 14\frac{1}{2}$ in
Inscribed bl.: *E. Lear. del: Parham. 1834*
Lord Aldington

b) *Peppering*, 1834
From a sketchbook originally containing 34 sheets
Pencil on paper: 11.4 × 14.4 cm/$4\frac{1}{2} \times 5\frac{5}{8}$ in
Inscribed bl.: *Peppering. Oct. 3. 1834*
Private Collection

c) *Peppering*, 1834
From a sketchbook originally containing 34 sheets
Pencil on paper: 11.4 × 14.4 cm/$4\frac{1}{2} \times 5\frac{5}{8}$ in
Inscribed and dated bl.: *Peppering Oct. 3. 1834*
Private Collection

d) *Wicklow Head from the Glen of the Downs*, 1835
Pencil heightened with white chalk on feint grey paper: 10.8 × 16.5 cm/$4\frac{1}{4} \times 6\frac{1}{2}$ in
Private Collection

e) *Levens Hall (interior)*, 1836
Pencil on buff paper: 23.3 × 36 cm/$9\frac{3}{16} \times 14\frac{3}{16}$ in
Inscribed br.: *Augt 18 1836 (7) Levens Hall, Westmorland*
Trustees of the British Museum

f) *Umbrellifera, Kendal, August 1836*
Pencil on blue paper: 11.4 × 17.1 cm/$4\frac{1}{2} \times 6\frac{3}{4}$ in
Inscribed bl.: *Umbrellifera. / Kendal, / Aug. 20th. 1836*
Numbered br.: *188*
Department of Printing and Graphic Arts, The Houghton Library, Harvard University

g) *Crummock*, 1836
Pencil, heightened with chinese white on grey paper: 38 × 45 cm/$15 \times 17\frac{5}{8}$ in
Inscribed br.: *Crummock 27. Sept. 1836.*
Numbered bl.: *54*
Collection of Mr and Mrs David Mawson

h) *Wastwater*, 1837 [Col. pl. p. 42
Ink, watercolour, gum arabic and some scratching out on paper: 35 × 58 cm/$13\frac{3}{4} \times 22\frac{7}{8}$ in
Signed and dated br.: *Edward Lear del. 1837*
Inscribed on label attached to backboard: *Wastwater / For the Rev. J.J. Hornby / 1837 /* E. Lear
Mr Roger Ebert

The drawings in the group exhibited here demonstrate a freedom of handling quite different from the precision and attention to small detail which was necessary in Lear's ornithological work. At this time he worked mostly in soft pencil, a medium he continued to use throughout his time in Rome (see Cat. 15, 17). The rhythmic patterns of drawing characteristic of his birds continue into his landscape; so, too, does his humorous observation (Cat. 13*f*).

Parham (Cat. 13*a*), an Elizabethan house a few miles south-east of Pulborough, Sussex, was the home of Lady de la Zouche whom Lear had first met in 1828. From tree studies made there (Private Collection), we know that Lear was at Parham in October 1834.

13*a*

13*b*

13*c*

13*d*

13*e*

13*f*

Peppering House (Cat. 13*b*, *c*), in the downland village of Burpham, just outside Arundel, was the home of the Drewitt family (see Cat. 90) whom Lear first met when he was ten years old. There is another drawing made at Burpham on the same day in the Houghton Library. One of Lear's earliest humorous poems (TS., Private Collection) relates to the Peppering turkeys.

In 1835 Lear went to Ireland (Cat. 13*d*). He travelled with Edward Stanley, Bishop of Norwich, whom Lear had met at Knowsley, and his son Arthur Penrhyn Stanley, later Dean of Westminster (see Cat. 42). (The visit is recalled in *The Life and Correspondence of Arthur Penrhyn Stanley, D.D.* by Rowland E. Prothero, 1894, vol. 1, pp. 146–47). Some of Lear's early parody of Thomas Moore (see Cat. 71) was prompted by this tour.

In 1836 Lear visited the Lake district (Cat. 13*e*–*h*), and on 31 October he wrote to John Gould (see Cat. 12) 'I left Knowsley . . . on the 12th August for a sketching tour, & really it is impossible to tell you *how*, and *how enormously* I have enjoyed the whole Autumn. The counties of Cumberland & Wesmorland are superb indeed, & tho the weather has been miserable, yet I have contrived to walk pretty well over the whole ground, & to sketch a good deal besides' (31.x.36, MS., Houghton Library, Harvard University).

Levens Hall (Cat. 13*e*) is an Elizabethan house in Westmorland. The chimneypiece dates from 1595, and is one of the very few interiors that Lear drew. He also made a drawing of the topiary (British Museum), which is the most famous feature of the house and dates from 1700.

Lear painted his finished watercolour of Wastwater in 1837 from drawings made there the previous year. This is the earliest known example of his landscape work executed in the studio (see Cat. 37), and was painted for Rev. J.J. Hornby whose nephew, also J. J. Hornby, was later Headmaster and Provost of Eton. In 1884 Lear recalled how 'He & I—(the Provost), used to run races all over that part of the country—& perhaps you don't know that I know every corner of Westmorland; Scawfell Pikes is my cousin, and Skiddaw is my mother in law' (Selwyn, 29.xii.84, MS., Private Collection).

PROVENANCE *(a)* given as a wedding gift to present owner. *(b) (c)* Franklin Lushington, by family descent; bt by Craddock and Barnard, Tunbridge Wells; 12 December 1945, bt by present owner. *(d)* 1983, bt by present owner. *(e)* 1942, acquired by the British Museum, London. *(f)* W.B. Osgood Field; The Houghton Library, Harvard University. *(g)* Edward Seago; Spink and Son Ltd; bt by present owner. *(h)* Rev. J.J. Hornby, by family descent; 1982, March, Sotheby's London (lot 117); bt by Spink and Son Ltd; 1985, bt by present owner.

EXHIBITIONS *(f)* 1968, London, Gooden and Fox Ltd, *Edward Lear* (no. 37). *(h)* 1984, London, Spink and Son Ltd, Autumn Exhibition (no. 57).

REFERENCES *(f)* Hofer 1967, p. 17 repr. pl. 5; Lehmann 1977, repr. p. 17.

14 The Journey out to Rome

a) *Frankfurt. The Jews' Quarter*, 1838
Black chalk, heightened with white, on blue paper: 27.9 × 19.3 cm/11 × $7\frac{5}{8}$ in
Signed, inscribed and dated in chalk br.: *Frankfurt. The Jews' Quarter E. Lear del. 1838*
Trustees of the Victoria and Albert Museum

b) *Castle of Elz, Germany*, 1837
Pencil and chinese white on buff paper: 27.7 × 20 cm/ $10\frac{15}{16}$ × $7\frac{7}{8}$ in (corners cut)
Inscribed bl.: [ ] *Elz. Mosel* [part of inscription removed]
Inscribed br.: *8. August 1837*
Department of Printing and Graphic Arts, The Houghton Library, Harvard University

Lear left England with his sister, Ann, at the end of July 1837; she travelled with him as far as Brussels, where she stayed until the following May. From there, Lear set out on his own for Rome. He travelled slowly, stopping to draw on the way. His route took him through Luxembourg and Germany (Cat. 14*a*,*b*), and he crossed into Italy in September, reaching Florence at the beginning of November. There he found many English friends, and stayed until the end of the month, exploring the city and supporting himself by giving drawing lessons to some of the English residents. He reached Rome on 3 December, 1837.

Lear had visited the Continent with Gould a few years earlier (see Cat. 12), but this was his first journey there alone. His response was one of enthusiasm and excitement—it was all 'a hurly-burly of beauty and wonder' (Ann, 3.xi.37, TS.). The earliest consistent records of Lear's life—his letters to Ann—date from this time; they are filled with descriptions of the scenery (which frequently reminded him of the paintings of Claude Lorraine [see Cat. 15]), the cities, the people, the animals and the food. The man who had once been a delicate child had now begun on the travels which would take him to wild, remote places where no Englishman had been before (Cat. 24) and open up to him scenes of great beauty. For the first time he experienced real freedom, and the joys of discovery; his early Nonsense songs (see Cat. 78) were to echo these themes over and over again.

The drawing of Frankfurt (Cat. 14*a*) was produced in the studio from a study made in Frankfurt on 25 August 1837 (Houghton Library, Harvard University).

PROVENANCE *(a)* 1887, acquired by the Victoria and Albert Museum, London. *(b)* W. B. Osgood Field; The Houghton Library, Harvard University.

EXHIBITION *(a)* 1958, London, Arts Council of Great Britain, *Edward Lear* (no. 14).

REFERENCES *(b)* Osgood Field 1933, p. 281, repr. p. 247.

14*a*

14*b*

15 The Early Roman Years

a) *Temple of the Sybil, Tivoli*, 1838 [Col. pl. p. 46
Pencil and chinese white on buff paper: 42.5 × 25.7 cm/ $16\frac{3}{4} \times 10\frac{1}{8}$ in
Signed, inscribed and dated br.: *TIVOLI. E. LEAR. del. 1838*
Private Collection

b) *St. Peter's from Monte Pincio, Rome*
Pencil and chinese white, with notes on buff paper: 28.6 × 44 cm/$11\frac{1}{4} \times 17\frac{3}{8}$ in
Department of Printing and Graphic Arts, The Houghton Library, Harvard University

c) *Amalfi*, 1838 [Col. pl. p. 47
Black chalk, heightened with white on blue paper: 34.2 × 25 cm/$13\frac{1}{2} \times 9\frac{7}{8}$ in
Signed, inscribed and dated br.: *Amalfi. E. Lear. Del. 1838*
Trustees of the Victoria and Albert Museum

d) *Village with hilltop ruin*, 1838 [Col. pl. p. 45
Ink, watercolour with chinese white on blue paper: 16.5 × 24.9 cm/$6\frac{1}{2} \times 9\frac{13}{16}$ in (corners cut off)
Dated bl: *1838*
Department of Printing and Graphic Arts, The Houghton Library, Harvard University

e) *Val Montone*, 1839
Pencil on blue paper: 30.7 × 45.4 cm/$12\frac{1}{8} \times 17\frac{7}{8}$ in
Signed and dated br.: *Edward Lear del. Val Montone 1839*
Trustees of the British Museum

f) *Isola S. Giulio, Orta*, 1839
Pencil on blue paper: 25.2 × 34.2 cm/$9\frac{15}{16} \times 13\frac{1}{2}$ in
Signed, inscribed and dated br.: *Edward Lear del. 1839 Isola S. Giulio Orta*
Trustees of the British Museum

g) *Narni*, 1839 [Col. pl. p. 44
Pencil, watercolour on buff paper: 26.3 × 42.7 cm/ $10\frac{3}{8} \times 16\frac{13}{16}$ in
Inscribed and dated bl.: *Narni 16. May. 1839*
Department of Printing and Graphic Arts, The Houghton Library, Harvard University

h) *Bridge over a river on the Roman Campagna*
Pencil, watercolour with notes on buff paper: 20.7 × 29.3 cm/$8\frac{3}{16} \times 11\frac{9}{16}$ in (corners cut off)
Department of Printing and Graphic Arts, The Houghton Library, Harvard University

i) *Val Montone*, 1840 [Repr. p. 92
Pencil on paper: 26 × 39.6 cm/$10\frac{1}{4} \times 15\frac{5}{8}$ in
Inscribed and dated bl.: *Val Montone 17. Octr. 1840*
Private Collection

Apart from two visits to England in 1841 (see Cat. 64) and 1845–46 (see Cat. 65), Lear stayed in Italy for the next ten years. For the only time in his life he was part of an international community of artists (see Cat. 16), and free from financial hardship. Part of his income, particularly in the early years, came from teaching drawing to English residents; the rest was from the sale of his drawings, watercolours and oil paintings.

15*b*

15*e*

15*f*

15*h*

Two illustrated books about Italy (see Cat. 64 and 65) brought additional funds, but because of his anxiety about his deteriorating eyesight he put this money aside for the time when he feared he may no longer be able to work.

Each year Lear spent the winter months in and around Rome. One of his favourite views of the city was from the Pincian Mount (Cat. 15*b*) 'a beautiful garden overlooking all Rome, and from which such sunsets are seen!' (Ann, 14.xii.37, TS.). There is a slightly different view from the Pincian Mount as plate 15 of *Views in Rome and its Environs* (see Cat. 64).

In May 1838 he was in Tivoli (15*a*), to which he responded with typical eighteenth-century enthusiasm, seeing it to be 'the height of landscape perfection' (Ann, 11.v.38, TS.); he returned there many times. He described to Ann the 'beautiful ruin of the Sybil's temple—very old, & standing on a great precipeice; for Tivoli . . . stands on a ledge of rock which projects like a tongue into a long valley,—& as the river comes to Tivoli, it is obliged to tumble, (with such a noise,) *down* the rocks before it gets to the valley below,—& it is over this chasm that the temple stands' (3.v.38, TS.). In 1839 Lear made a drawing similar to that exhibited here as a present for Lord Derby. There are two different views of Tivoli in *Views in Rome and its Environs* (plates 23 and 24). He also made frequent visits into the Campagna (Cat. 15*g*, *h*), a landscape favoured by artists for more than two centuries, and subsequently made at least fourteen oil paintings of Campagna scenes. He thought Val Montone (Cat. 15*e*,*i*) 'one of the most elegant campagna towns and very curious: it is in a deep dell in the Latin valley—but rises on a mound—crowned with a superb church and castle—though the town itself is wretchedly poor. . .Fine trees are all around Val Montone—and it is altogether a delightfully quiet place' (Ann, 11.x.38, TS.). A different view of Val Montone is plate 25 of *Views in Rome and its Environs*.

In the summer months Lear travelled to other parts of Italy. In 1838 he went with Thomas Uwins RA (1782–1857) to Naples, where he stayed at the same hotel as Samuel Palmer (1805–81). Lear and Uwins went on south to Amalfi (Cat. 15*c*) and Corpo di Cava (see Cat. 45). The following May he set out on a walking tour towards Florence (Cat. 15*f*), 'after which, I went to a little town at the top of a high hill, where I have remained in company with sundry other artists until yesterday evening, when I returned here for the winter campaign' (Gould, 17.x.39, MS., Houghton Library, Harvard University).

The watercolours from Lear's early Italian period (1838–42) display both a close connection with the watercolour landscapes introduced into his early bird drawings (see Cat. 10, 11) and an awareness of contemporary handling of watercolour, especially that of J. Varley and de Wint.

PROVENANCE *(a)* Edward Cheney, by family descent. *(b)(d)(g)(h)* W.B. Osgood Field; The Houghton Library, Harvard University. *(c)* 1887, acquired by the Victoria and Albert Museum. *(e)(f)* 1892, acquired by the British Museum. *(i)* Sir Robin Darwin RA; Spink and Son Ltd; 1984, bt by present owner.

EXHIBITION *(c)* 1958, London, Arts Council of Great Britain, *Edward Lear* (no. 17).

REFERENCE *(b)* Hofer 1967, repr. pl. 15.

16 Wilhelm Marstrand

Wilhelm Marstrand, *Portrait of Edward Lear*, 1840
Pencil on paper: 17.8 × 10.8 cm/7 × 4¼ in
Inscribed bl.: *Edward Lear 14 nel Luglio 1840*
National Portrait Gallery, London

Particularly during his early years in Rome, Lear enjoyed being part of a community of artists. A few days after his arrival he was telling Ann: 'At 8 I go to the Cafe, where all the artists breakfast . . . then—I either see sights—make calls—draw out of doors—or, if wet—make models indoors till 4. Then most of the artists walk on the Pincian Mount . . . and at 5 we dine very capitally at a Trattoria or eating house' (14.xii.37, TS.). Two years later he wrote to Gould: 'I know all the English artists who are universally kind to me . . . & our little supper parties in the winter & our excursions in spring & autumn are very lively & agreeable' (17.x.39, MS., Houghton Library, Harvard University).

But it was not only English artists whom Lear knew. There was also a group of Danish painters, amongst them Wilhelm Marstrand who made this drawing of Lear in July 1840. Later Lear recalled the days 'when W. Marstrand & I used to be always together!' (Diary, 7.iv.60). Hearing of Marstrand's death in 1873, he wrote: 'So: I can never see dear gentle good clean Marstrand more! . . . He was the F[ranklin] L[ushington] of those days: & I dare not think of them!' (Diary, 18.x.73).

Among other artists whose names recur in Lear's letters from Rome are John Gibson (1790–1866), who revived polychrome sculpture; William Theed (1804–91), who sculpted the figure of Africa on the Albert Memorial; Penry Williams (1798–1885) the painter (see Cat. 47); Thomas Uwins RA (1782–1857; see Cat. 45); Thomas Wyatt (1807–80) the architect; and Samuel Palmer (1805–81; see Cat. 45).

PROVENANCE Aage Marcus; 1939, bt by the National Portrait Gallery.

EXHIBITION 1968, London, Gooden and Fox Ltd, *Edward Lear* (no. 130).

REFERENCES National Portrait Gallery, *British Historical Portraits*, 1957, p. 239, repr. pl. 325; National Portrait Gallery, *Complete and Illustrated Catalogue*, 1981; Davidson 1968 edn, repr. p. 17; Noakes 1968 edn, p. 57; Hyman 1980, p. 40.

16

17 The Middle Roman Years

a) *Villa Adriana*, 1842
Pencil heightened with white on blue paper: 40 × 22.2 cm/15¾ × 10⅞ in
Signed, inscribed and dated b.: *Villa Adriana Edward Lear del. 1842*
Trustees of the British Museum

b) *St. Pietro in Vincoli, Rome*, 1842
Pencil heightened with white on buff paper: 31.4 × 23.1 cm/12⅜ × 9⅛ in
Signed, inscribed and dated b.: *near St Pietro in Vincolis, Roma Edward Lear del. 1842*
Trustees of the British Museum

c) *Ponciglioni, near Pontone*, 1844
Pencil and sepia ink, with notes on blue paper: 33.6 × 52 cm/13¼ × 20½ in
Inscribed, dated and numbered b.: *near Pontone. 9. June. 1844. (27)*
Inscribed bl.: *Ponciglioni old church. Chinese boy. Francis & Pansa. Storia of Amalfi.*
Department of Printing and Graphic Arts, The Houghton Library, Harvard University

d) *The Siren Isles*, 1844
Pencil, sepia ink on paper: 40.3 × 55.2 cm/15⅞ × 21¾ in
Inscribed and numbered br.: *S. Pietro [?] In Crapollo 52*
Inscribed and dated br.: *I Galli. The Sirens isles. 12. June. 1844*
1. *A blind Doge—a bathing.*
2. *A Siren—a singing to the 'Arp.*
Trustees of the Tate Gallery

e) *Morle Sant' Angelo*, 1844
Pencil, sepia ink, sepia and blue wash on blue paper: 51.5 × 35.8 cm/20 5/16 × 14⅛ in
Inscribed, dated and numbered br.: *Morle Sant' Angelo 19. June. 1844. 103*
Department of Printing and Graphic Arts, The Houghton Library, Harvard University

f) *Civitella*, 1844
Mounted with Cat. 17*g* by Lear
Pencil, sepia ink and watercolour with notes on buff paper: 33.1 × 31.7 cm/13 1/16 × 12½ in
Inscribed and dated bl.: *Civitella 20 August. 1844*
Private Collection

g) *Civitella*, 1844
Pencil, sepia ink and watercolour with notes on paper: 14.7 × 29.5 cm/5 13/16 × 11⅝ in
Inscribed and dated bl.: *Civitella. 21. August. 1844*
Private Collection

Lear returned to Rome in December 1841, and from then until he left in 1848 his mature watercolour style gradually developed. In 1842 he was still using the conventions of drawing and composition which had been typical of his earlier Roman work (Cat. 15), but now the purpose of his watercolours was beginning to change. In 1840 he made his first oil paintings (see Cat. 46), and whereas most of his earlier works prepared out of doors in front of the subject were used as a basis for further pencil drawings or for lithographic reproduction (see Cat. 64, 65), from the early 1840s onwards such watercolours were prepared increasingly as works of

17*a*

17*b*

17*c*

17*e*

reference on which he would base oil paintings and more highly finished watercolours (see Cat. 37). They had to give him the topographically accurate information he would need when laying in his work in his studio, while the notes—which are reminiscent of the notes he made on his bird studies (see Cat. 8)—guided him in colour and details of content. His line became finer and more sculptural, and he began to go over his pencil drawing with ink (Cat. 17*c*–*g*).

Cat. 17*d* is an example of Lear introducing absurdity into landscape (see Cat. 18*a*) as he had done into his bird drawings (see Cat. 7*a*, *b*).

In August 1844 he was in Civitella Cat. 17*f*, *g*; see Cat. 47). He spent the winter in Rome, and the following May left for a second extended visit to England.

PROVENANCE *(a)* ?Franklin Lushington; British Museum. *(b)* November 1892, presented by Alexander Malcolm to the British Museum. *(c) (e)* W.B. Osgood Field; The Houghton Library, Harvard University. *(d)* Lord Northbrook; 1910, presented to the Tate Gallery. *(f) (g)* by family descent to present owner.

17*d*

96*a*

18 Charles Knight

a) *Scene in the Roman Campagna*, 1842
In volume: 40.6 × 23.6 cm/16 × $9\frac{5}{16}$ in
i Sepia ink on cream paper: 25.4 × 20.3 cm/10 × 8 in
Signed and dated b.: *Edward Lear. del. 1842*
ii Sepia ink on light green paper: 25.4 × 20.3 cm/10 × 8 in
Inscribed b.: *Scene in the Campagna of Rome 1842*
Trustees of the British Museum

18*a*

18*b*

18*b*

18*b*

b) 18 drawings from a group illustrating an Italian tour made by Charles Knight and Edward Lear, 1842
Pencil and sepia ink: av. size 13.5 × 19 cm/$5\frac{3}{8}$ × $7\frac{1}{2}$ in

1 Inscribed and dated tl.: *L. & K. leave Frascati—July 28th. 1842.—Villa Taverna.*; b.: *L. contemplates a ferocious horse with feelings of distrust.*
2 Inscribed tl.: *Frascati. V. Taverna*; b.: *L. declares that he considers his horse far from tame.*
3 Inscribed tl.: *Frascati. V. Taverna.*; b.: *L. casually seats himself on the wrong side of his saddle.*
4 Inscribed tl.: *—V. Taverna. Frascati*; b.: *L. changes his position for the sake of variety.*
5 Inscribed tl.: *—V.. Mondragone. Frascati.*; b.: *L. perceives he has not seated himself properly.*
6 Inscribed tl.: *—K.L. Commence their journey.*; b.: *L. is advised by K. to hold his reins short.*
7 Inscribed tl.: */ Frascati. Villa Mondragone.*; b.: *L. is politely requested by K. to stop his horse.*
8 Inscribed tl.: */ M. Porzio.*; b.: *K. enquires amiably of L. if his stirrups are sufficiently short.—*

18*b*

9 Inscribed tl.: / —*M. Porzio.*; bl.: *K & L. are pursued by an irascible ox.*—
10 Inscribed tr.: *K. & L. pass M. Porzio & M. Compatri.*; bl.: *L. is requested by K. not to rise so exceedingly high from his saddle.*
11 Inscribed tl.: / *Monte Compatri.*; b.: *L. descends an unsatisfactory hill in a pensive manner.*
12 Inscribed tl.: / *K. & L. pass Colonna.*; b.: *L. is besought by K. to sit back on his saddle.*
21 Inscribed tl.: *K. & L. proceed to Tivoli.*; b.: *L. becomes suddenly and imperceptibly entangled in an obtrusive Olive=tree.*
23 Inscribed tc.: *K. & L. visit the temple by Moonlight.*; br. *K. & L. discern a predominant Ghost.*—
25 Inscribed t.: *Tivoli—K. & L. commence their journey back to Frascati.*; b.: *L. is confidentially assured by the groom that he has mounted his horse incorrectly.*
26 Inscribed t.: *K. & L. pass through San Gregorio.*; b.: *K. affectionately induces L. to perceive that a thornbush has attached itself to his repugnant horse.*
27 Inscribed tl.: / *K. & L. pass Casape & Poli: returning to Gallicano to Zagarolo.*; b.: *L. is much disturbed by several large flies.*—
33 Inscribed t.: *K. & L. proceed from Zagarolo to Frascati.*; b.: *K. & L. are attacked by several very venomous Dogs in the vicinity of Colonna*—

Trustees of the British Museum

Shortly after his arrival in Rome in 1837 Lear met Charles Knight and his family. One of Knight's sisters, Margaret, married the Duke of Sermoneta; the other, Isabella, was an invalid.

The commonplace book exhibited here (Cat. 18*a*) was kept by Isabella Knight, and contains a number of drawings and a poem about the return of the dove to the ark contributed by Lear. His 'Scene in the Campagna of Rome—1842' is both a play on words and one of a number of examples of Lear bringing absurdity into his landscapes (see Cat. 17*d*), just as he had done in his parrot drawings (see Cat. 7*a*, *b*).

The eighteen drawings exhibited here (Cat. 18*b*) are part of a series describing Lear's adventures on horseback during his first tour of the Abruzzi in the company of Knight (see Cat. 65). Knight had already given Lear riding lessons 'round the walls of Rome' (see Diary, 25.vii.71), and he now lent him his arab, Gridiron. Despite disasters, Lear and Gridiron survived their adventures, travelling together until 10 August, when Knight left with the arab, and Lear returned to his more placid old grey.

Lear frequently illustrated his travel adventures in Nonsense form (see Cat. 92). The earliest dated examples to have survived were made in the autumn of 1841, when he travelled with Phipps Hornby to Scotland (Private Collection).

PROVENANCE *(a)* Isabella Jane Knight, by family descent; presented by Lt.-Col. C.L.W. Morley Knight to the British Museum. *(b)* 1969, 11 December, Christie's London (lot 163); bt by the British Museum.

REFERENCES *(a)* Noakes 1968 edn, p. 66; Noakes 1979 edn, p. 52. *(b)* Noakes 1979 edn, p. 11; Liebert, 1975, pp. 27–28.

19*a*

19 The Last Roman Years

a) *Tellena*, 1847
Pencil, sepia ink and watercolour on blue paper:
21.1 × 48.2 cm/$8\frac{5}{16}$ × 19 in
Inscribed and dated bl.: *Tellena March. 20. 1847*
Department of Printing and Graphic Arts, The Houghton Library, Harvard University

b) *Girgenti*, 1847 [Col. pl. p. 43
Pencil, sepia ink and watercolour on blue/grey paper:
21.1 × 31.1 cm/$8\frac{5}{16}$ × $12\frac{1}{4}$ in
Inscribed and dated br.: *Girgenti 29. May. 1847*
Department of Printing and Graphic Arts, The Houghton Library, Harvard University

c) *Quarries of Syracuse*, 1847 [Col. pl. p. 50
Pencil, sepia ink and watercolour with notes on paper:
35.2 × 50.5 cm/$13\frac{7}{8}$ × $19\frac{7}{8}$ in
Inscribed, dated and numbered br.: *Siracusa. Jackdaw gardens. 12. June. 1847. (138)*
Lent by Merseyside County Council, Walker Art Gallery, Liverpool

By the time Lear returned to Rome in December 1846, increasing political unrest in Italy made life there less settled. He spent the winter of 1846–47 in Rome, and as the spring came he made excursions into the Campagna to draw (Cat. 19*a*). On 27 March 1847 he wrote to Ann: 'There is a charm about this Campagna when it becomes all purple & gold, which it is difficult to tear one'sself from. Thus—climate & beauty of atmosphere regain their hold on the mind—pen—& pencil' (TS.).

In April he travelled south, and from 3 May to 19 July was in Sicily. His companion for the journey was John Proby, heir to the Earl of Carysfort; a volume containing twenty Nonsense drawings of their adventures on the island was published in 1938 as *Lear in Sicily*. At the end of May they were in Girgenti (Cat. 19*b*), the city founded by Greek colonists in about 580 BC, and from there Lear wrote: 'Nothing of earth can be so beautiful as Girgenti with its 6 Temples—I speak of the old town—& the flowers & birds are beyond imagination lovely. I must however, need say that the gnats, fleas, flies, wasps, etc. etc.—require much philosophy to bear' (Ann, 23.v.47, TS.). They reached Syracuse on 8 June, and Lear told Ann that 'the vast quarries whence this enormous city was dug are now used as gardens, & being sheltered are really quite like Paradise. Every kind of tree & flower grows luxuriantly in them, & they are as full as possible of nightingales' (17.vi.47, TS.). This drawing, made on 12 June, is an early example of the fully developed style of travel watercolours Lear was to use from now on (see Cat. 20). It formed the basis of his oil painting, *The Quarries of Syracuse* (see Cat. 49).

PROVENANCE *(a) (b)* W.B. Osgood Field; The Houghton Library, Harvard University. *(c)* 1948, bt from The Art Exhibition Bureau by The Walker Art Gallery.

EXHIBITIONS *(c)* 1952, London, Empire Art Loans Society, *British Watercolour Exhibition 1850–1914* (no. 5*c*), subsequently went to Australia; 1968, Detroit, Institute of Art and Philadelphia Museum of Art, *Romantic Art in Britain 1760–1860* (no. 197).

REFERENCES *(c)* W. Holman Hunt, *Pre-Raphaelitism and The Pre-Raphaelite Brotherhood*, 1905, p. 328; A. Staley, *The Pre-Raphaelite Landscape*, 1973, pp. 152–53, repr. pl. 84*a*.

LEAR'S TRAVELS

1848–1888

20f

When Lear left Rome in 1848, his plan was to spend some months travelling round the Mediterranean before returning to settle permanently in England. He visited Malta, Greece, Turkey, Albania, Egypt and Sinai, collecting drawings as he went, and by July 1849 he was back in London.

He remained in England only until the end of 1853, when the combination of ill-health and the constraints of city life forced him to abandon his plan, and he set off once more on his travels. The last of his extended journeys—to India between 1873 and 1875—was made when he was in his sixties, though he continued to go into the mountains above San Remo until the last year of his life.

The immediate purpose of these travels was to build up a collection of drawings of interesting and beautiful places on which he could base both oils and finished watercolours. He went to places popular with artists, such as Athens and Jerusalem, and also remote areas which no other artist had attempted to paint. 'I suppose no "dirty Landscape-painter" ever got together so curiously diversified a collection of Topographical illustrations', he wrote in 1880 (Hallam Tennyson, 16.x.80, MS., Tennyson Research Centre, Lincoln).

He liked to wander slowly in a 'stopping, prying, lingering mode of travel' (Ann, 14.v.58, TS.), but when he settled down to work he drew with concentration and speed. These drawings were done in pencil, with often extensive notes about colour and content which would provide the necessary reference for later work back in his studio. He wrote in the location, date and occasionally the time of the drawing, numbering the works in a sequence which would begin again when he moved from one country to the next. After his return, he laid in colour washes based on the notes he had made, and 'penned out' the pencil drawing and writing in ink, a task which filled winter evenings when the light had gone.

In these unselfconscious, freely handled works done for his own reference, Lear demonstrated a mastery and confidence which is sometimes lacking in the more anxious works he prepared for public exhibition and sale. V.N.

20 Greece

a) *Athens*, 1848
Pencil, sepia ink, watercolour, with touches of bodycolour: 28.8 × 45 cm/$11\frac{3}{8}$ × $17\frac{3}{4}$ in
Inscribed, dated and numbered br.: *Athens June 5th–9th & 10 June 1848 10*
Department of Printing and Graphic Arts, The Houghton Library, Harvard University

b) *Temple of Olympian Zeus, Athens*, 1848, [Col. pl. p. 49
Pencil, sepia ink, touches of bodycolour, with notes on paper: 27.9 × 49.8 cm/11 × $19\frac{5}{8}$ in
Inscribed, dated and numbered br.: *Athens. 14. June. 1848 30*
H.M.N. Hollis Esq.

c) *Leondari*, 1849 [Col. pl. p. 52
Pencil, sepia ink, watercolour, with notes on buff paper: 32.2 × 52.5 cm/$12\frac{5}{8}$ × $20\frac{11}{16}$ in
Inscribed, dated and numbered br.: *Leondari. 22^d March. 1849. (10–11½. A.M.) (60)*
Department of Printing and Graphic Arts, The Houghton Library, Harvard University

d) *Parga*, 1849
Mounted with Cat. 20*e* by Lear
Pencil, sepia ink, sepia and blue wash, with notes on buff paper: 12 × 22.5 cm/$4\frac{3}{4}$ × $8\frac{7}{8}$ in
Inscribed and dated bl.: *Parga. 30. April. 1849*
Numbered br.: *(1)*
Department of Printing and Graphic Arts, The Houghton Library, Harvard University

e) *Nicopolis*, 1849
Pencil, sepia ink, watercolour, with notes on buff paper: 25 × 43.1 cm/$9\frac{7}{8}$ × 17 in
Inscribed and dated bl.: *Nicopolis, May.1. 1849*
Numbered br.: *(3)*
Department of Printing and Graphic Arts, The Houghton Library, Harvard University

f) *Suli*, 1849 [Repr. p. 105
Pencil, sepia ink, watercolour, with notes on paper: 31.1 × 56.2 cm/$12\frac{1}{4}$ × $22\frac{1}{8}$ in
Inscribed and dated bl.: *Suli. 6. May. 1849*
The Hon. Sir Steven Runciman, CH

g) *Meteora*, 1849 [Col. pl. p. 51
Pencil, sepia ink, watercolour with touches of bodycolour, with notes on mauvish paper: 34.6 × 52.5 cm/$13\frac{5}{8}$ × $20\frac{11}{16}$ in
Inscribed and dated bl.: *Meteora 16 May. 1849*
Numbered br.: *(56)*
Department of Printing and Graphic Arts, The Houghton Library, Harvard University

20*a*

20*d*

20*e*

The idea of visiting Greece had long excited Lear. As a child he had been introduced to the Greek myths, and during the 1820s had watched the Greek struggle for freedom from Turkish domination. Byron was his boyhood hero.

He arrived in Athens (Cat. 20*a*, *b*) from the Ionian Islands on 2 June 1848 (see Cat. 21), and the next day wrote excitedly to Ann, '. . . surely never was anything so magnificent as Athens!—far more than I could have had any idea of. The beauty of the temples I well knew from endless drawings—but the immense sweep of plain with exquisitely formed mountains down to the sea—& the manner in which that huge mass of rock—the Acropolis—stands above the modern town with its glittering white marble ruins against the deep blue sky is quite beyond my expectations . . . You walk about in a wilderness of broken columns, friezes etc. etc. Owls, the bird of Minerva, are extremely common, & come & sit very near me when I draw' (3.vi.48, TS.).

He left Greece at the end of July and moved on to Turkey, Albania, Egypt and Sinai, but the following March and April he was back, travelling through the Peloponnese with Lushington (Cat. 112). 'No one can form any idea of what the spring is in Greece,' he told Ann, delightedly, 'it is all very well to say that there is a mile of bright scarlet ground, then half a mile of blue or pale pink—but it is difficult for you to realise that the whole earth is like a rich Turkey carpet. As for Lushington & I, equally fond of flowers, we gather them all day like children, & when we have stuck our hats & coats & horses all over with them—it is time to throw them away, & get a new set' (21.iv.49, TS.). They went to Bassae (see Cat. 51) and on 22 March were in Leondari (Cat. 20*c*). This medieval village, with its hilltop Frankish castle, had been overrun by the Turks in 1460; they massacred the people and converted the two-domed church into a mosque.

After six joyful weeks the two men parted, and Lear travelled north on his own. By the end of April he was in Parga (Cat. 20*d*), and the next day reached Nicopolis, the town from where St Paul wrote his Epistle to Titus (Cat. 20*e*). A few days later he reached Suli with its magnificent but forbidding mountain scenery (Cat. 20*f*). The Christians of Suli had fiercely resisted the Turks, but in 1803 they were defeated and crossed to the Ionian Islands. They returned to the mainland at the outbreak of the Greek War of Independence. It was from the Suliots that Lear's man-servant, Giorgio Kokali came (see Cat. 116).

By 16 May he was in the Meteora, the dramatic valley from which huge, precipitous rocks rise, each topped with a monastery (Cat. 20*g*). By the date of Lear's visit these hermit retreats had declined and become little more than curiosities.

Writing to Fortescue at the beginning of his Greek travels, Lear had said, 'I cannot but think that Greece has been most imperfectly illustrated . . . the vast yet beautifully simple sweeping lines of the hills have hardly been represented I fancy —nor the primitive dry foregrounds of Elgin marble peasants &c. What do you think of a huge work (if I can *do* all Greece)?' (26.viii.48, MS., Somerset Record Office, Taunton). Several years later, he told Ann, 'it appears to me more & more that my painter's reputation will be that of a painter of Greek scenery principally' (15.iii.57, TS.), but though he was constantly drawn back to Greece, the *magnum opus* never materialised.

PROVENANCE *(a)* Philip Hofer; The Houghton Library, Harvard University. *(b)* Prof. Charles M. Church, by family descent; H.M.N. Hollis Esq. *(c)–(d) (e), (g)* W.B. Osgood Field; The Houghton Library, Harvard University. *(f)* 14 June 1950, Sotheby's London (lot 10); bt by the Fine Art Society, London; The Hon. Sir Steven Runciman.

EXHIBITIONS *(a)* 1968, Worcester, Mass. Worcester Art Museum, *Edward Lear, Painter, Poet and Draughtsman* (no. 17). *(f)* 1979, London, Fine Art Society, *The Rediscovery of Greece* (no. 130).

REFERENCES *(a)* Hofer 1967, p. 23, repr. pl. 27, *(c)* Osgood Field 1933, p. 310, no. 186, repr. pp. 290–91. *(f)* Lehmann 1977, repr. p. 91.

21 The Ionian Islands

a) *View of the Islands from Kanoni Point, Corfu*, 1855
Pencil, ink and watercolour on paper: [Col. pl. p. 55
24.7 × 22.8 cm/$9\frac{3}{4}$ × 9 in
Numbered and dated br.: *15/28 Dec. 1855*
Inscribed on verso in pencil (in Mr Adkin's hand): *Corfu/ Edward Lear/E. Lear*
The Syndics of the Fitzwilliam Museum, Cambridge

b) *Plain of Zante from Galaro*, 1863
Pencil, sepia ink, watercolour, with notes on paper:
34.2 × 52.7 cm/$13\frac{1}{2}$ × $20\frac{3}{4}$ in
Inscribed and dated bl.: *Plain of Zante from Galaro May 30 11–11.15 AM. 1863*
Numbered br.: *(213)*
Private Collection

The Ionian Islands had been ceded to the British under the terms of the Congress of Vienna in 1815 and remained under their rule until 1863. During that time there was a substantial British colony in Corfu, and for several years Lear made the island his home. It offered what he needed—a good climate, beautiful scenery, and a community which was prepared to buy and commission pictures.

His first visit had been in 1848, and he returned with Franklin Lushington (see Cat. 112) in December 1855, when Lushington had been appointed Judge to the Supreme Court of Justice in the Ionian Islands. It was shortly after his arrival in 1855 that Lear made the watercolour drawing of the view from Kanoni Point (Cat. 21*a*). He remained in Corfu until summer 1857, returning again for the winters of 1858–59, 1861–62 and 1862–63. After a brief visit early in 1864 he left in March after the transfer of the Ionian Islands to Greece.

Though he found the beauty of the island astonishing, he disliked the lifestyle of the English: 'what a place this might be if there were any good people to give it a twist,' he wrote to Ann. 'As it is—a more disorganised fiddlefaddle Poodlypumpkin place never was . . . at the Palace that are active—dancing & rushing about pauselessly & continually. I suspect Lady Young would not be happy in Heaven if she did not get up an immense ball & land & water picnics, among the angels' (22.iii.57, TS.); '. . . this rustymustyfustydustybustycrusty Corfu,' he concluded (ibid.).

21*b*

He twice toured the other Ionian islands, first in 1848 and again between March and June 1863. In his diary for 30 May 1863 he noted: 'From 10 to 11 went in a violent=odious descent between 2 sides of a ravine—& the pale green plain of Zante came out by degrees in a vivid triangle at the end.' He spent fifteen minutes making the drawing (Cat. 21*b*). According to Hubert Congreve, when he 'came to a good subject, Lear would sit down, and taking his block from George, would lift his spectacles, and gaze for several minutes at the scene through a monocular glass he always carried; then, laying down the glass, and adjusting his spectacles, he would put on paper the view before us, mountain range, villages and foreground, with a rapidity and accuracy that inspired me with awestruck admiration' (LLEL 1911, Preface, p. 23).

In 1863 the Greeks invited the youthful Prince William of Denmark to accept their throne. 'You may not have heard (it is not generally known,) that I refused the throne of Greece,' Lear wrote to Drummond, 'King Lear the first—on account of the conduct of Goneril & Regan my daughters, wh. has disturbed me too much to allow of my attention to governing' (23.iii.63, MS., Private Collection). Deprived of his crown, he left Corfu with the rest of the British residents, and on 4 March 1864 he saw 'the loveliest place in the world' disappear beneath the horizon (Diary, 4.iii.64).

PROVENANCE *(a)* M.B.C. Adkin; 1964, given to Fitzwilliam Museum, Cambridge. *(b)* Lady Darwin; Spink and Son Ltd, London; April 1981, bt by present owner.

EXHIBITION *(b)* 1981, London, Spink and Son Ltd, *Spring Exhibition* (no. 63).

REFERENCE *(a) Annual Report*, Fitzwilliam Museum, 1964, repr. pl. XIII.

22 Mount Athos

Athos from near Neochorio, 1856
Pencil, sepia ink and watercolour with notes on paper: 23.3 × 30.6 cm/9 3/16 × 12 1/16 in
Inscribed numbered and dated br.: *Athos—from near ΝΕΟΧΥΡΙΟ 21 Sept 1856 (106)*
The Hon. Sir Steven Runciman, CH

Despite his feelings about the monks of Athos (Cat. 53) Lear found it a place of fascination and beauty. Approaching it, 'one crosses a ridge of hills, whence Mount Athos is first discovered —a blue peak on a bluer sea—seen above the most wondrous forests of beech I ever beheld. Nothing did I ever behold more lovely that those views' (Ann, 8.x.56, TS.). As he crossed onto the isthmus itself, the path became 'most toilsome through the wildest & grandest forest scenery—from which every now & then you looked out on such screens & depths of green wood as would astonish those who talk of England as having more trees than other countries' (ibid.: this letter contains a thumbnail sketch of this view).

During his three weeks on Mount Athos, Lear visited the twenty principal monasteries, receiving in each a warm welcome. He made a collection of fifty drawings which he hoped would be valuable, 'for I believe no such collection of illustrations has yet been known in England' (ibid.).

PROVENANCE 21 May 1952, Walkers Art Gallery, London; 1953, the Fine Art Society; bt by the Hon. Sir Steven Runciman.

REFERENCE Lehmann 1977, repr. p. 35.

22

23 Crete

Kanea from Akrotiri, 1864
Pencil, ink, watercolour and bodycolour with notes on paper: 33.3 × 54 cm/13 1/8 × 21 1/4 in
Inscribed and dated bl.: *Kanea Crete from Αυροτυρι 22 April. noon—12.30 1864*
Numbered br.: *31*
Museum of Art, Rhode Island School of Design

23

Having left Corfu in March 1864, Lear travelled via Athens to Crete, where he spent the months of April and May. By mid-April he was in Hania, and on the 22nd wrote in his journal: 'scantily little in this land is there to draw; its stunted harsh small olives, & its ever stony surface. I begin to think Crete is a "sell".' At 10.30 he 'reached the spot looking over the bay and Hanía; &, as the weather is lovely, so there is a certain charm in the view. . . Drew till 1 p.m. Alas! for Crete, it seems a sell—& when I think of Sicily & its every step & every moment of interest, while here is so little, except that of floral nature & the delight of the sweet morning air & thorough calm.' It is perhaps characteristic of Lear, however, to grumble at the time and look back with affection later.

Mount Ida, which he drew a month later (24.v.64, British Museum), he found more beautiful. It was here that he encountered the mountain goats of Crete (see Cat. 92).

PROVENANCE P. and D. Colnaghi, London; anonymous gift to the Museum of Art, Rhode Island School of Design.

EXHIBITIONS 1965, Newport, R.I., Art Association of Newport, *Watercolours by Edward Lear*; 1982, Providence, R.I., Museum of Art, Rhode Island School of Design, *How Pleasant to know Mr Lear* (no. 27); 1983, London, the Fine Art Society, *The Travels of Edward Lear* (no. 59).

24 Albania

a) *Ohrid*, 1848 [Col. pl. p. 52
Pencil, sepia ink, watercolour, with notes on paper: 34.4 × 53 cm/$13\frac{9}{16} \times 20\frac{7}{8}$ in
Inscribed, dated and numbered br.: *Akhrida. 23. Sept. 1848 (56)*
Inscribed in pencil br.: *Ochrida 23. Septer 1848. (56)*
Department of Printing and Graphic Arts, The Houghton Library, Harvard University

b) *Between Ohrid and Elbassan*, 1848
Pencil, sepia and blue ink, watercolour on buff paper: 33.6 × 52.5 cm/$13\frac{1}{4} \times 20\frac{11}{16}$ in
Inscribed and dated bl.: *between Akhrida & Elbassan. Sept. 24. 1848*
Numbered br.: *(64)*
Department of Printing and Graphic Arts, The Houghton Library, Harvard University

c) *Elbassan*, 1848 [Col. pl. p. 54
Pencil, sepia ink and watercolour on paper: 20.8 × 29 cm/$8\frac{3}{16} \times 11\frac{7}{16}$ in
Inscribed, dated and numbered br.: *26. September. 1848 (80)*
Department of Printing and Graphic Arts, The Houghton Library, Harvard University

24*b*

d) *Scutari* [1848]
Pencil, sepia ink, watercolour, with notes on paper: 18 × 53.1 cm/$7\frac{1}{8} \times 20\frac{15}{16}$ in
Inscribed, dated and numbered br.: *Scutari 4 October. 1849 107*
Department of Printing and Graphic Arts, The Houghton Library, Harvard University

e) *Berat*, 1848 [Col. pl. p. 53
Pencil, ink watecolour, Chinese white, with notes on grey paper: 20.5 × 29.3 cm/$8\frac{1}{4} \times 11\frac{1}{2}$ in
Inscribed and dated in ink bl.: *Berat Octbr 15. 1848*
Inscribed and dated in pencil br.: as above
Numbered br.: *134*
Department of Printing and Graphic Arts, The Houghton Library, Harvard University

f) *Berat*, 1848 [Col. pl. p. 54
Pencil, sepia ink, watercolour, touches of bodycolour with notes on paper: 53 × 96.1cm/$20\frac{7}{8} \times 14\frac{1}{4}$ in
Inscribed and dated bl.: *Berat. October. 1848*
Numbered br.: *132*
Department of Printing and Graphic Arts, The Houghton Library, Harvard University

g) *Condessi*, 1848 [Repr. p. 17
Pencil, sepia ink, watercolour, with notes on paper: 24.9 × 51.3 cm/$9\frac{13}{16} \times 20\frac{3}{16}$ in
Inscribed and dated br.: *Condessi 31 October. 1848*
Numbered in pencil br.: *202*
Department of Printing and Graphic Arts, The Houghton Library, Harvard University

h) *Tree at Tepelene*, 1857
Pencil, sepia ink, watercolour, with notes on paper: 23.4 × 32.3 cm/$9\frac{1}{4} \times 12\frac{3}{4}$ in
Inscribed and dated bl.: *2 hours from Tepelene 19 April 1857*; br.: *on the road, 2 hours from τεπεδελένη*
Private Collection

Lear's first and longest visit to Albania took place between September and November 1848. It took him through some of the wildest and most dramatic countryside he ever visited. Few foreigners had been to the remote area beyond Yannina. The conditions of travel were taxing, and on occasion Lear was prevented from making drawings in this Islamic country

24*d*

where pictorial representations were regarded with fear and suspicion.

In Ohrid (Cat. 24*a*) he began to make drawings of the town and castle, when 'a shepherd ventured to approach and look at my doings; but no sooner did he discover the form of the castle, on the paper than shrieking out "Shaitán!" [Devil!] he fled rapidly from me, as from a profane magician' (J. Alb., pp. 68–69). Word soon spread, and as he walked around the town 'several of these wild and shy people espied me afar off, and rushed screaming into their houses, drawing bolts, and banging doors with the most emphatic resolve against the wandering apparition' (J. Alb., p. 69). Others threw stones, and it was only after the local Bey had arranged a guard to accompany him that he was able to settle to his work.

At the beginning of October, he was in Scutari (Cat. 24*d*), on the frontier between Montenegro and Albania. He stayed there for three days, and on 4 October 'drew throughout the whole day unremittingly, from various points below the south side of the castle, where the view is very imposing, and near a wondrous old bridge across to Bryana, constructed of pointed arches of irregular width, and having somewhat the effect of the columns in a Gothic cathedreal . . .' (J. Alb., pp. 141–42). The date of 1849 inscribed by Lear on his watercolour of Scutari (Cat. 24*d*) was added later. It was his habit to work over his drawings in pen in the winter evenings, sometimes many years after he had made the initial study. In this case he has mistaken the date of his Albanian journey.

From Scutari he then turned back, reaching Berat ten days later (Cat. 24*e*, *f*). Here, as throughout his Albanian journey, he was fascinated by the local costume, and welcomed the chance to make drawings of the local people undisturbed: 'Beyond the bazaars, which are extensive and well filled, is a wide open space by the river, whence the view of the dark gorge of the Beratíno, and town and castle are truly wonderous. On one side of this piazza or market place is a large new khan, and here I took possession of a corner room looking out on to the busy scene that extends to the foot of the hill—a space in which hundreds of figures sat continually before me for their pictures without suspicion or restraint' (J. Alb., pp. 188–89).

24*b*

He was in Condessi (Cat. 24*g*) by the end of the month, and as he approached the village he saw that: 'Numerous small hamlets cluster round the sides of Kúdhesi, and are all called by the mountain's name. To one of these, on the banks of the Viósa, we descended . . . In the stable below, the Zaftí and his two friends sung half "the live-long night."' (J. Alb. pp. 301–02)

Lear visited Tepelene, but it was on a return visit in 1857 that he drew the tree (Cat. 24*b*), two hours' journey from the ruined stronghold of Ali Pasha, the Turkish ruler and Byronic hero, whose palace recalled to Lear lines from *Childe Harold*.

PROVENANCE *(a)–(g)* W.B. Osgood Field; The Houghton Library, Harvard University. *(b)* 1944, acquired from Redfern Gallery, London, by present owner.

EXHIBITIONS *(a)* 1968, Worcester, Mass., Worcester Art Museum, *Edward Lear, Painter, Poet and Draughtsman* (no. 22). *(d)* 1968, Worcester, Mass., Worcester Art Museum, *Edward Lear, Painter, Poet and Draughtsman* (no. 27). *(f)* 1968, Worcester, Mass., Worcester Art Museum, *Edward Lear, Painter, Poet and Draughtsman* (no. 23). *(b)* 1951, New Haven, Conn., Jonathan Edwards College, Yale University, *Edward Lear* (no no.).

REFERENCES *(a)* Hofer 1967, repr. pl. 34. *(d)* Hofer 1967 repr. pl. 4. *(f)* Hofer 1967, p. 25, repr. pl. 36.

25 Palestine

a) *Petra*, 1858
Pencil, sepia ink watercolour and bodycolour on paper: 25.4 × 51.8 cm/10 × $20\frac{1}{2}$ in
Numbered br.: *(172)*
Private Collection

b) *The Dead Sea*, 1858
Pencil, sepia ink, watercolour, with notes on paper: 36.9 × 55.3 cm/$14\frac{1}{2}$ × $21\frac{3}{4}$ in
Inscribed, dated and numbered br.: *Wady Mabookoo? 16 & 17 April 1858 (60)*
Yale Center for British Art, Paul Mellon Collection

c) *Masada*, 1858 [Col. pl. p. 56
Pencil, sepia ink, watercolour with notes: 34.3 × 49.5 cm/$13\frac{1}{2}$ × $19\frac{1}{2}$ in
Inscribed, dated and numbered br.: *Masade. (73) 19. April 1858 5. AM*
Private Collection

d) *Jerusalem*, 1858
Pencil, sepia ink, watercolour with notes on blue paper: 33.8 × 21.2 cm/$13\frac{5}{16}$ × $21\frac{3}{16}$ in
Inscribed and dated bl.: *Jerusalem 4. May. 1858*
Numbered br.: *(142)*
Department of Printing and Graphic Arts, The Houghton Library, Harvard University

e) *Jericho*, 1858
Pencil, sepia ink, watercolour, with notes on paper: 18.2 × 50.5 cm/$7\frac{1}{8}$ × $19\frac{7}{8}$ in
Inscribed, dated and numbered br.: *Jericho—/May 7. 1858./ (157)*
Yale Center for British Art, Paul Mellon Collection

Having considered visiting Palestine in 1849 and again at the beginning of 1854, Lear arrived in Jerusalem on 28 March

25*a*

25*e*

25*b*

25*d*

82

1858. He found the city so crowded with Easter pilgrims that he moved on into the desert, reaching Petra on 13 April (Cat. 25*a*). 'It is absurd to attempt to describe this place which is one of the great marvels of the world,' he wrote to Ann. 'I had expected a great deal, but was overwhelmed with extra surprise & admiration at the truly beautiful & astonishing scenes. The whole valley is a great ruin—temples—foundations—arches—palaces—in inconceivable quantity & confusion; & on 2 sides of the valley are great cliffs, all cut into millions of tombs—magnificent temples with pillars,—theatres etc. so that the whole place is like magic; & when I add that every crevice is full of Oleander & white Broom, & alive with doves, gazelles & partridges—you may suppose my delight was great. All the cliffs are of a wonderful colour—like *ham* in stripes; & parts are salmon colour' (23.iv.58, TS.). But Lear and his guides were soon surrounded by threatening Arabs demanding payment, and when the situation became really dangerous they were forced to leave. 'I was greatly vexed at getting so few drawings of this wonderful place,—but to have seen it is something, & to have got away safely is no little matter' (ibid.).

From Petra they went on to the Dead Sea (Cat. 25*b*), and then to Masada (Cat. 25*c*), 'that great fortress in which Eleazar & a thousand Jews held out, after the destruction of Jerusalem, for 3 years—at the end of which the Romans took it, but the beseiged had all put themselves to a voluntary death. This fort is one of the finest scenes I ever beheld—& as the weather was lovely, I am obliged to say that the Dead Sea is more like a calm Italian lake than as I have heard it described. Only there is no fish, or shell, or insect on the waters, which their taste you may imitate if you like by putting a little bark mustard, & cayenne, with Epsom salts' (ibid.). There is a thumbnail sketch of the drawing of Masada (Cat. 25*c*) in a letter to Lady Waldegrave (27.v.58, LEL 1907, p. 100). Lear appears to have selected certain sites before his arrival in the Near East, as suitable subjects for major landscape paintings which combined topographical interest with historical associations. In the case of Masada, for example, he wrote to Fortescue from Corfu on 27 December 1857: 'The uppermost subject in my feeble mind just now is my Palestine visit . . . Now my particular idea at the present hour is to paint Lady Waldegraves 2nd picture from *Masada* whither I intend to go on purpose to make correct drawings . . . My reason for this choice is, that not only I know the fortress of Masada to be a wonder of picturesqueness, but that I consider it as embodying one of the extremist developments of the Hebrew character, i.e. consistency of purpose & immense patriotism. This subject I believe will as it were "match" Jerusalem well.' (LEL

1907, pp. 69–70) The painting of Jerusalem referred to by Lear had been one of two commissioned by Lady Waldegrave before the artist's departure for Palestine (see Cat. 56).

When he reached Jerusalem again (Cat. 25*d*), the crowds had gone and he could move freely round the city. '. . . there is enough in Jerusalem to set a man thinking for life,' he told Lady Waldegrave, '& I am deeply glad I have been there' (27.v.58, LEL 1907, p. 106).

Moving on to Jericho (Cat. 25*e*), he found the heat of the lowest spot on earth overwhelming. He abandoned his plans to go on to Nazareth and Gallilee and returned to Jerusalem, before going onto Lebanon (see Cat. 26).

'I went to Holman Hunt's the other evening,' the Pre-Raphaelite sculptor Thomas Woolner (1825–92) told Emily Tennyson some time later, 'and met Lear who shewed me all his sketches done in the Holy Land: I think that they are the most beautiful things he has ever done: if you have not seen them I hope you will, for they would give much delight and interest you extremely, not only for the mystery and history attached to the places themselves but also for the excessive fineness, tenderness and beauty of the art displayed in them' (Woolner-Emily Tennyson 22.x.58, quoted in A. Woolner, *Thomas Woolner, R.A., Sculptor and Poet: His Life in Letters*, London 1917, p. 154).

PROVENANCE *(a)* Spink and Son Ltd; bt by present owner. *(b)* Thomas Agnew and Sons, London; March 1971, bt by Mr Paul Mellon; 1975, Paul Mellon gift to The Yale Center for British Art. *(c) c.* 1905, bt by present owner's grandfather, by family descent. *(d)* W.B. Osgood Field; The Houghton Library, Harvard University. *(e)* Mrs A. Meldrum; March 1967, bt by Mr Paul Mellon; 1975, Paul Mellon gift to The Yale Center for British Art.

EXHIBITIONS *(b)* 1971, London, Thomas Agnew & Sons Ltd, *Watercolours and Drawings Exhibition* (no. 55). *(d)* 1968, Worcester, Mass., Worcester Art Museum, *Edward Lear, Painter, Poet and Draughtsman* (no. 37).

26 Lebanon

The Cedars of Lebanon, 1858 [Col. pl. p. 70
Pencil, sepia ink and watercolour on paper:
36.5 × 55.5 cm/$14\frac{2}{5} \times 21\frac{4}{5}$ in
Inscribed, dated and numbered br.: *The Cedars. Lebanon 20.21 May 1858. (193)*
Private Collection

Lear decided against travelling to Nazareth and Galillee because of heat, weariness and the demands of local arabs, and he went instead to Lebanon. He arrived in Beirut on 11 May 1858. Writing to Ann he described his approach to the cedars: 'So fine a view I suppose can hardly be imagined—more perhaps like one of Martin's ideal pictures:—the whole upper part of the mountain is bare & snowy, & forms an amphitheatre of heights, round a multitude of ravines & vallies—full of foliage & villages most glorious to see:—and all that descends step by step to the sea beyond!—Far below your feet, quite alone on one side of this amphitheatre is a single dark spot—a cluster of trees: these are the famous Cedars of Lebanon. = Lebanon doubtless was once thickly covered with such, but now there are these only left.—I cannot tell you how delighted I was with those cedars!—those enormous old trees—a great dark grove—utterly silent, except the singing of birds in numbers. Here I staid all that day—the 20th & all the 21st working very hard. . . . only there was a leettle drawback to my pet cedars—& that was, that being 6000 feet above the sea, & surrounded by high snow peaks, the cold was so great I could not hold my pencil well . . .' (Ann, 26.v.58, MS., Private Collection).

He made several drawings of the cedars (e.g. dated 21 May 1858, Victoria and Albert Museum, London). The one exhibited here was later used as the basis for what he considered to be his most important oil painting (executed winter 1860–61; see Noakes 1979 edn, pp. 177–234). This nine-foot canvas is now lost, but its failure to sell at the initially high price of £735 or to receive sustained critical acclaim was the turning point in Lear's hopes to find a place amongst the leading landscape painters of his day.

It is interesting to speculate on why Lear should have chosen this particular subject for so important a work; he himself gave no explanation for this choice. By the 1850s, Orientalist subject matter was popular both in England and abroad, so it was a subject likely to sell. Whilst it biblical associations gave it the overtones considered necessary for a major work, the cedars in which the birds of the air made their nests may have offered a particular charm to the Nonsense writer who found birds nesting in his beard. Possibly he saw the subject as a counterbalance to the work that Hunt was now doing. By 1860, Hunt's direct influence on Lear's work had declined; whilst admiring his talent, Lear was increasingly unhappy about Hunt's choice of subject matter which he felt was becoming removed from reality and tending to superstition (see p. 20). In choosing the cedars, Lear could combine the biblical association with a subject drawn direct from nature. It is also possible that Lear felt that his particular strength lay in his depictions of natural history, an area in which he might excel over his contemporaries. He spoke often of his 'poetical, & accurate typographical delineation' (Diary, 3.iv.72); the lifelike quality of his work was important to him. Certainly he seems to have succeeded with the cedars, for he wrote to Marianne North, 'The cedars are so advanced that millions of sparrows are said to sit—(I never saw them myself,) on the window ledges, pining with hopeless despair at not being able to get inside' (30.iv.61, MS., Perkins Library, Duke University).

PROVENANCE F. Lushington; bt by present owner's father.

EXHIBITIONS 1958, London, Arts Council of Great Britain, *Edward Lear* (no. 34); 1968, London, Gooden and Fox Ltd, *Edward Lear* (no. 66); 1983, London, the Fine Art Society, *The Travels of Edward Lear* (no. 86).

REFERENCE Noakes 1979 edn, repr. opp. p. 240.

76

27 Egypt and the Nile

a) *Outside the walls of Suez*, 1849
Pencil, sepia ink, watercolour with notes on paper: 20 × 13 cm/$7\frac{7}{8} \times 5\frac{1}{8}$ in
Inscribed in pencil bl.: *Outside walls of Suez*
Dated bl.: *$8\frac{1}{2}$ A.M. Jany 17 1849*
Inscribed cr.: *Outside the walls of Suez*
Numbered br.: *54*
Private Collection

b) *Near Suez*, 1849
Pencil, sepia ink, watercolour with notes on paper: 13.4 × 23.3 cm/$5\frac{5}{16} \times 9\frac{3}{16}$ in
Inscribed and dated bl.: *near Suez. Evening. Jany 15. 1849*
Numbered br.: *43*
Private Collection

d) *Richard Burton*, 1853
Mounted with Cat. 27*d* by Lear
Pencil, sepia ink, watercolour: 16.9 × 14.3 cm/$6\frac{11}{16} \times 5\frac{5}{8}$ in
Inscribed and dated bl.: R. *Burton. Cairo. Decbr. 23. 1853*
Department of Printing and Graphic Arts, The Houghton Library, Harvard University

d) *Richard Burton*, 1853 [Col. pl. p. 72
Pencil, sepia ink, watercolour: 22.9 × 15.5 cm/$9 \times 6\frac{1}{8}$ in
Inscribed and dated bl.: *Cairo. Decr. 23. 1853*
Numbered br.: *(2)*
Department of Printing and Graphic Arts, The Houghton Library, Harvard University

e) *Aswan*, 1854 [Col. pl. 56
Pencil, sepia ink, watercolour, with extensive colour notes on paper: 33.6 × 50.4 cm/$13\frac{1}{4} \times 19\frac{7}{8}$ in
Inscribed and dated bl.: *Asswan 8. Feby. 1854. 6.P.M.*
Numbered br.: *186*
Merseyside County Council, Walker Art Gallery, Liverpool

f) *Aswan*, 1867
Mounted with Cat. 27*g* by Lear
Pencil, sepia ink, watercolour, touches of chinese white, with notes on grey paper: 7.1 × 26.9cm/$2\frac{13}{16} \times 10\frac{5}{8}$in
Inscribed and dated bl.: *Aswan. 8.30. AM. 28 Jany 1867*
Numbered br.: *(246)*
Private Collection

g) *Shelaal*, 1867
Pencil, black ink, bodycolour and chinese white on grey paper: 7.62 × 27.6 cm/$3 \times 10\frac{7}{8}$ in
Inscribed and dated bl.: *Shelaal. 2.30. PM. Jany 29. 1867*
Numbered br.: *(260)*
Private Collection

h) *Philae*, 1867
Pencil, sepia ink, watercolour, with notes on paper: 9.5 × 18.4 cm/$3\frac{3}{4} \times 7\frac{1}{4}$ in
Inscribed and dated bl.: *Philae 30 Jany 1867 5.20 PM*
Numbered br.: *275*
Private Collection

27*a*

27*b*

Before his first visit to Egypt in January 1849, Lear had written to Fortescue: 'I strongly long to go to Egypt for the next winter as ever is, if so be as I can find a sufficiency of tin to allow of my passing 4 or 5 months there. I am quite crazy about Memphis & On & Isis & crocodiles and ophthalmia & nubians, and simooms & sorcerers, & sphingidoe. Seriously the contemplation of Egypt must fill the mind, the artistic mind I mean, with great food for the rumination of long years' (12.ii.48, LEL 1907, pp. 8–9). The visit was, however, brief. He spent a week in Cairo and visited the Pyramids (see Cat. 61), finding everything 'so very very bright—all the sky blue—& all the earth light yellow or white' (Ann, 11.i.49, TS.). Indeed on each of his visits to Egypt, Lear found the colours extraordinary; his diary is filled with descriptions of their brilliance, or their delicacy, or their mournful greyness: 'Egypt is at least a land to learn color in' (Diary, 9.i.67). Easier to draw were the camels as they settled round the campfire at night (Cat. 27*a*, *b*). 'At night, when our tent is pitched, all the camels stride away—just where they please—looking for little thorny shrubs they feed on—till quite out of sight: but after sunset—when the Arabs call them, they all appear in 2s of threes—& are soon round the tent fires . . .' (Ann, 16.i.49, MS., Private Collection).

27*f*

27*g*

27*h*

He visited Egypt for the second time at the end of 1853, a trip which he and Holman Hunt had discussed while living at Clive Vale Farm in summer 1852 (see Cat. 49, 104). He arrived in Cairo in December to find Thomas Seddon (1821–56) already there; Holman Hunt was expected on the next boat. Strangely, Lear makes no mention of a meeting with Sir Richard Burton (1821–90), the explorer, nor of the drawings which were the first he did after his arrival in Egypt and two of the very few portrait studies Lear ever attempted (Cat. 27*c*, *d*). There is a watercolour portrait of Burton in an almost identical pose to Cat. 27*d*, painted by Seddon but dated 1854 (Andrew McIntosh Patrick, London); the relationship between the two portraits has yet to be resolved.

Lear had expected to stay in Cairo until Hunt arrived, but when he received an offer immediately after Christmas to go up the Nile he decided to accept, and the two men never travelled together as they had planned. At Aswan (Cat. 27*e*) Lear found the river 'all close & rocky' (Ann, 15.ii.54, TS.), and his colour notes, which are unusually extensive, indicate something of the difficulty he found in painting Nile scenery.

It was thirteen years before he returned to Egypt, travelling as far up the Nile as the Second Cataract. He reached Aswan once more early on the morning of 28 January 1867 (Cat. 27*f*). 'The Nile scenery here is beautiful,' he wrote, '. . . What beautiful slopes of clear sand! & rounded blotting paper colored granite boulders;' (Diary, 28.i.67). But the next day he found 'the details of this scenery, being infinite, are very difficult to get' (Diary, 29.i.67). And then, 'lo!—after 13 years—Beautiful Philae once again!!—and more beautiful than ever.—I sit & draw till 2. (N.B. I have never made enough of the *dark gray* & *black* rooted granite rox in the water—always too red & yellow in my drawings.)' (Diary, 30.i.67; Cat. 27*h*). 'In no place—it seems to me, can the variety & simplicity of colors be so well studied as in Egypt; in no place are the various beauties of shadow more observable, or more interminably numerous' (Diary, 25.ii.67), he wrote at the end of his journey.

Between 1852 and 1873, Lear made at least 45 oil paintings of the Nile, 19 of them at or near Philae (see Cat. 52, 62; see also LEL 1907, pp. 314–18).

PROVENANCE *(a) (b) (f)–(h)* 1944, bt by present owner from S. R. Meatyard, London. *(c) (d)* W.B. Osgood Field; The Houghton Library, Harvard University. *(e)* Art Exhibition Bureau; 1943, bt by the Walker Art Gallery, Liverpool.

EXHIBITIONS *(c)* 1968, Worcester, Mass., Worcester Art Museum, *Edward Lear, Painter, Poet and Draughtsman* (no. 28).

REFERENCE *(d)* Hofer 1967, pp. 27–28, repr. pl. 50a.

28 Switzerland

Interlaken, 185[4]
Pencil, blue and sepia ink, blue-grey wash, with notes on paper: 28.5 × 46.6 cm/11¼ × 18⅜ in
Inscribed and dated bl.: *Interlaken 2 Sept. 185*
Inscribed br.: *How is the father of the mother in the Faulhorn ascending on the top?*
Private Collection

Lear left London for a walking tour of Switzerland on 1 August 1854. On 6 August he wrote to Ann, 'I had no idea really of the beauty of Switzerland—for I never was in the really fine parts, except in 1841—when I came thro' by night . . . The Lake of Thun is one of the most beautiful of all the Swiss Lakes;—such a wonderful pea-blue sea-green! . . . I set out to walk to Interlacken . . . along the north side of the Lake which is like a garden or park till, towards the east end, when one walks through beautiful shady woods. The mountains grow higher & higher till you reach the end of the Lake, & the valley of Interlacken. This is a village of inns & lodging houses, & is a sort of Tunbridge Wells—or general Swiss summer retreat' (TS.).

On 2 September, towards the end of his Swiss tour, he made the drawing of a view across the Brienzer See towards the Faulhorn near Interlaken. A few days later he wrote to Holman Hunt, 'I can hardly tell why I so much wished to see the Alps—partly because (perhaps) I was tired of having talked of without having seen them. Now that I have done so, I feel I was right in coming, as there is so much of the astonishing & majestic in Swiss scenery that no Landscape painter who wishes his mind to open at the admiration and comprehension of *all kinds* of nature, should pass through life without seeing this country . . . There is a want of horizontal distance here, which is not exactly desirable, but en revanche you have what may be termed "*the perpendicular style*" of landscape in perfection' (11.ix.54, MS., Huntington Library, San Marino).

Despite the tradition for portraying the Swiss Alps which went back to the mid-eighteenth century and was epitomised in the work of J.M.W. Turner (1775–1851), Lear did not respond as a painter to this mountainous landscape (see Cat. 58). Although he enjoyed his visit, he did not return to the country until 1878 when, to escape the summer heat of San Remo, he went to the mountains above Lake Como (see Cat. 36).

PROVENANCE 1982, 11 November, Sotheby's London (lot 21); Spink and Son Ltd; from where bt by present owner.

EXHIBITION 1983, London, Spink and Son Ltd, *Annual Watercolour Exhibition* (no. 91).

29 Riviera di Levante

Near Sestri Levante, 1860 [Col. pl. p. 60
Pencil, sepia ink, watercolour with notes on paper: 34.9 × 50.1 cm/13¾ × 19¾ in
Inscribed and numbered br.: *near Sestro Levante 22 May. 1860 (40)*
Department of Printing and Graphic Arts, The Houghton Library, Harvard University

During the summer of 1858, Lear decided that he would spend the following winter in Rome, the city he had left ten years before. He returned again for the winter of 1859–60, but that was his last extended visit to the city he had loved so well in his youth (see Cat. 15–19). In the spring of 1860, before leaving for England, he spent two weeks walking around La Spezia and the Gulf of Genoa. Part of his interest in the region was its association with Shelley, whose work Lear much admired. Lear set at least one of Shelley's poems to music ('O world, O life, O time!') which was subsequently written down for him by the poet's son, Sir Percy Shelley, who visited Corfu in early 1862. In addition, as he told Ann in a letter from La Spezia, 'My plan had been to see something new, & get some drawings of parts of Italy I had not yet seen . . . I really did

28

not believe in the existence of so beautiful a place as this has turned out to be—more like Corfû than any other' (18.v.60, TS.).

He passed through La Spezia again in July 1861, on his way from Florence to England.

PROVENANCE W.B. Osgood Field; The Houghton Library, Harvard University.

30 Malta

Valletta, 1862
Pencil, sepia ink, watercolour with extensive notes on paper: 19 × 24.5 cm/7½ × 9⅝ in
Dated cl.: *28 May 1862*
Inscribed b.: *Just after sunset—all the water is grayer purple—vinous, ocrious, the lights of the wall & houses oker all, still reflected very far down, as are all the boats. The upper 2 churches remain reddest & most prominent, & the wall & the furthest Church at x; the sky behind being gray, At x ash & pink ochre clouds above delicate lilac gray. I think the whole should be without distinct light & shade, the end (at 8;) & the churches above brighter,—all else pretty monochromatic/Half an hour or more after sunset, it is more beautiful than ever,—so chose that time i.e. 7.30 P.M.—May 28th. Then the whole mass of building becomes one soft red pearly gray, on a dark ground of sea, the shades of daylight still remaining. Sky paler grayer*
Merseyside County Council, Walker Art Gallery, Liverpool

Lear left Corfu for England by boat on 20 May 1862, and stopped at Malta on the way. One is reminded of how slow travel was in those days, for he discovered that the boat was stopping in Zante, Malta, Messina and Palermo, and that the journey would take three weeks, 'Witch fax I only came at granulously as it were,' he wrote to Fortescue, 'grain by grain, as the pigeon said when he picked up the bush of corn slowly. Whereon—said I to myself—if so be as I can get my fare back again, I will even go ashore at Malta—and see that much beloved place—and wait for a Marseilles boat . . . meanwhile resting my weary lims in beds of hashphodil, and moreover escaping the chance of bad weather in the Bay of Biscuits and the Irish Channel' (29.v.62, LEL 1907, pp. 243–44).

30

Lear had first visited Malta in 1848 on his way from Italy to Greece, but on that occasion had had little time for drawing. Waiting in Malta in 1862 he took the opportunity to make drawings of the island. In his diary for 27 May there is a thumbnail sketch of the view shown in the watercolour exhibited here. On the following day he returned and noted in his diary: 'From 4.30, to 7.40 drew on the Barracca—the dreamy quiet haze of the scene after the sun is gone is a wonderful beauty' (28.v.62).

He was later to spend a sad and lonely winter in Malta in 1865–66, and the island ceased to have any charm for him.

PROVENANCE 1960, 6 October, Sotheby's London (part of lot 33), withdrawn; 1960, 30 November, Sotheby's London (part of lot 19); bt by The Fine Art Society, London; 1972, bt by C.F.J. Beausire; bequeathed to the Walker Art Gallery, Liverpool.

EXHIBITION 1970, Liverpool, Walker Art Gallery, *English Watercolours in the Collection of C.F.J. Beausire* (no. 28).

31 Venice

Venice, 1865
Pencil, sepia ink, watercolour: 32.3 × 50.1 cm/12¾ × 19¾ in
Inscribed and dated bl.: *Venice 13. & 16th Novr 1865. 8.AM.*
Numbered br.: *(15)*
Private Collection

Lear had first visited Venice in 1857. In November 1865 he returned, to make studies for an oil painting which had been commissioned by Lady Waldegrave (see Cat. 59). Despite bitterly cold weather, he was impressed by the architecture and the light of the city. On the morning of 13 November he rose early, 'Had a cup of cafe noir in the Hotel—& then got a gondola for the day. First drew S[anta] M[aria] de S[alute] by the Doge's Palace—then from the Iron Bridge . . . but it was very cold' (Diary, 13.xi.65). It was so cold that he was unable to finish the drawing, and he returned to it on the 16th, when he wrote, 'The same bright gorgeous—but cold weather. Anything so indescribably beautiful as the color of the place I never saw' (Diary, 16.xi, 65).

However, the brilliant weather did not last. A few days later the city was covered by 'Thikphoggs' and he could draw nothing. 'I am suffering from cold & asthma in consequence,' he told Drummond, 'nor must I podder any more by canal sides & in gondolas . . . Altogether this city of palaces, pigeons, poodles, & pumpkins (I am sorry to say also of innumerable pimps—to keep up the alliteration,) is a wonder & a pleasure' (21.xi.65, MS., Private Collection).

PROVENANCE *c.* 1905, bt by present owner's grandfather, by family descent.

31

32 The Corniche

a) *Eze*, 1864
Pencil, sepia ink, watercolour, touches of chinese white on blue paper: 36.6 × 53.6 cm/$14\frac{7}{16} \times 21\frac{1}{8}$ in
Inscribed, dated and numbered br.: *Eza Dec^br 6.1864 (3)*
Department of Printing and Graphic Arts, The Houghton Library, Harvard University

b) *Finale*, 1864 [Col. pl. p. 61
Pencil, sepia ink, watercolour, chinese white on buff paper: 36.8 × 54 cm/$14\frac{1}{2} \times 21\frac{1}{4}$ in
Inscribed and dated bl.: *Finále 4.15.P.M. 16. Dec^br (& 17th) 1864*
Numbered br.: *(52)*
Department of Printing and Graphic Arts, The Houghton Library, Harvard University

32*a*

Lear spent the winter of 1864–5 in Nice. Shortly after his arrival in November 1864, he settled down to draw 240 Tyrants (Cat. 39). Although necessary from a financial point of view, this mass production of watercolours was a soulless task, and after a month he decided to break away and spend a few weeks walking along the coast into Italy.

On 6 December he settled down to make drawings at Eze (Cat. 32*a*). 'A strangely wild & magnificent coast scene is this,' he wrote, 'I know no finer. It was bitterly cold & the wind very high, & I was glad to have a thick cloak' (Diary, 6.xii.64).

A few days later he reached San Remo where he found 'nothing to draw:—the town, on a hill, slopes back, so far, that you must go a mile or two out to see it, & then it is only a ridge of common buildings. S. Remo is an absolute failure' (Diary, 11.xii.64). This was the first mention of the place that would be his home for the last eighteen years of his life, and where he is buried (see Cat. 110, 118). On 16 December he was in Finale, where 'The rolling sea was magnificent' (Diary, 16.xii.64). The drawing of Finale exhibited here (Cat. 32*b*) was later used by Lear as no. 164 in his series of illustrations to Tennyson's poems (see Cat. 42).

He was back in Nice on New Year's Eve 1864 with a folio of 144 drawings, amongst which were some of the most powerful he ever did. He planned to publish a journal of this walk, but did not do so; the whereabouts of the fair copy is not known (see Cat. 109).

PROVENANCE *(a) (b)* W. B. Osgood Field; The Houghton Library, Harvard University.

EXHIBITION *(b)* 1968, Worcester, Mass., Worcester Art Museum, *Edward Lear, Painter, Poet and Draughtsman* (no. 47).

REFERENCES *(a)* Osgood Field 1933, p. 331, no. 291. *(b)* Osgood Field 1933, p. 332, no. 294; Hofer 1967, pp. 33, 46, repr. pl. 64.

33 Corsica

a) *Sartene*, 1868 [Col. pl. p. 63
Pencil, sepia ink, watercolour, with notes on paper: 15.4 × 20.5 cm/$6\frac{1}{16} \times 8\frac{1}{16}$ in
Inscribed and dated bl.: *Sarténé 5.45.PM. April 20 1868*
Numbered br.: *(58)*
Department of Printing and Graphic Arts, The Houghton Library, Harvard University

b) *Forest of Bavella*, 1868 [Col. pl. p. 62
Pencil, sepia ink, watercolour, touches of chinese white on paper: 36.5 × 53.6 cm/$14\frac{3}{8} \times 21\frac{1}{8}$ in
Inscribed and dated bl.: *Forest of Bavella 4.PM. 29. April. 1868*
Numbered br.: *(144)*
Department of Printing and Graphic Arts, The Houghton Library, Harvard University

c) *Ponte del Vecchio*, 1868
Pencil, sepia ink, watercolour, with notes on paper: 37.8 × 54.6 cm/$14\frac{7}{8} \times 21\frac{1}{2}$ in.
Inscribed and dated bl.: *2.30 PM. June 1. 1868*
Numbered br.: *333*
Department of Printing and Graphic Arts, The Houghton Library, Harvard University

33*c*

Having spent the winter of 1867–68 in Cannes, Lear left for Corsica on 8 April 1868 in the company of the writer John Addington Symonds (1840–93) and his family (see Cat. 78). From Ajaccio he set out alone to explore the island. He spent three days in Sartene (Cat. 33*a*), and in the entry for 20 April in his *Journal of a Landscape Painter in Corsica* he wrote: 'First part of the day is passed in completing drawings of the town and valley already commenced, and in making other small sketches characteristic of a place I may perhaps never revisit . . . there is hardly a path round Sarténé that does not lead to some surpassingly fine bit of landscape, and excepting Civitella and Olevano, I have known no such place for study combining so many features of grandeur and beauty' (pp. 51–52).

He reached the Forest of Bavella (Cat. 33*b*) on 28 April. It was a day of many showers. 'At times the mist is suddenly lifted like a veil, and discloses the whole forest—as it were in the pit of an immense theatre confined between towering rock-wall, and filling up with its thousands of pines all the great hollow . . . As I contemplate the glory of this astonishing amphitheatre, I decide to stay at least another day within its limits, and I confess that a journey to Corsica is worth any amount of expense and trouble, if but to look on this scene alone' (J. Cors., p. 92).

The next day he returned to draw what he had seen. The rain had gone, and, 'owing to the perfect clearness of to-day, there cannot be that wealth of effect produced yesterday by the passing and lifting of clouds across the enormous crags—sublime and continually changing—and that infinite variety of light and shadow thrown over the pines and all the foliage of the deep hollow valley.' He soon realised that the wild beauty of the forest could not be adequately 'represented in a sketch, and to attempt to do so seems like endeavouring in one day to make satisfactory notes from the contents of a whole library . . .' (J. Cors., pp. 94, 96). He did, however, make at least three oil paintings of the Forest of Bavella.

On 1 June he came to Ponte del Vecchio (Cat. 33*c*) in a thunderstorm, and, although he began work on a drawing, he had to abandon it. At 6 p.m., shortly after he had settled down to dinner at the local inn, 'the storm clouds roll away, and the mountains all at once become so perfectly clear, that I resolve to go down once more to the Ponte del Vecchio' (J. Cors., p. 241). It was a dramatic scene with 'the great snowy summit of Monte Rotondo—if that be it which appears to the left up this wild ravine—the line of crags and dark pine woods all along the centre of the gorge, the immense granite precipices hanging just above the rapid stream, its profound shadow and narrow depths here and there lighted up with gleams and flashes of brightness . . .' (ibid.).

From the handling, it is clear that the watercolour exhibited here was executed at speed before the thunderstorm forced Lear to abandon work. It was used as a preliminary study for plate XXXVIII of his *Journal of a Landscape Painter in Corsica* (London 1870; see Cat. 70).

PROVENANCE *(a)–(c)* W.B. Osgood Field; The Houghton Library, Harvard University.

34 India

a) *Lucknow*, 1873
Pencil, sepia ink, watercolour with notes on paper: 8.6 × 17.5 cm/$3\frac{3}{8} \times 6\frac{7}{8}$ in
Inscribed, dated and numbered bl.: *Lucknow Decr. 2. 1873. 4 PM (56)*
Department of Printing and Graphic Arts, The Houghton Library, Harvard University

b) *Lucknow Residency Ruins*, 1873
Pencil, sepia ink, watercolour, with notes on paper: 8.6 × 17.8 cm/$3\frac{3}{8} \times 7$ in
Inscribed and dated bl.: *Lucknow Residency ruins 2 Decr. 1873. 4.30 PM*
Department of Printing and Graphic Arts, The Houghton Library, Harvard University

34a

34b

c) *Lucknow*, 1873 [Col. pl. p. 66
Pencil, sepia ink, watercolour, with notes on paper: 35.6 × 50.8 cm/14 × 20 in
Inscribed, dated and numbered bl.: *39 Lucknow 1 PM. 8 Dec: 1873*
Department of Printing and Graphic Arts, The Houghton Library, Harvard University

d) *Benares*, 1873 [Col. pl. p. 65
Pencil, sepia ink, watercolour, bodycolour on paper: 34.1 × 50.8 cm/$13\frac{7}{16}$ × 20 in
Inscribed, dated and numbered bl.: *Benares 14 December 1873 2.15. PM (63)*
Department of Printing and Graphic Arts, The Houghton Library, Harvard University

e) *Agra. The Taj*, 1874 [Col. pl. p. 65
Pencil, sepia ink, watercolour, on paper: 34.9 × 19.6 cm/$13\frac{3}{4}$ × $19\frac{9}{16}$ in
Inscribed, dated and numbered bl.: *Agra The Taj 3 PM & 1 to 3.PM 15th: & 16 Feby. 1874 (248)*
Department of Printing and Graphic Arts, The Houghton Library, Harvard University

f) *Gwalior*, 1874 [Col. pl. p. 64
Pencil, sepia ink, watercolour, with notes on paper: 18.6 × 55.4 cm/$7\frac{5}{16}$ × $21\frac{13}{16}$ in
Inscribed, dated and numbered bl.: *Gwalior 22. Feb: 1874 2.30 PM (280)*
Numbered on mount in Lear's hand: *173*
Department of Printing and Graphic Arts, The Houghton Library, Harvard University

g) *Delhi. Tughlukubud*, 1874
Pencil, sepia ink, watercolour on paper: 33.8 × 54.6 cm/ $13\frac{15}{16}$ × $21\frac{1}{2}$ in
Inscribed, dated and numbered bl.: *Delhi. Tooklookabad. 10. AM. 12. March 1874 (335)*
Numbered on mount in Lear's hand: *213*
Department of Printing and Graphic Arts, The Houghton Library, Harvard University

h) *Landoor-Massoorie*, 1874 [Col. pl. p. 66
Pencil, sepia ink, watercolour, with notes on paper: 37.1 × 54.3 cm/$14\frac{5}{8}$ × $21\frac{3}{8}$ in
Inscribed, dated and numbered bl.: *Landoor-Massoorie 8–9.30 AM. 27 March 1874 (385)*
Numbered on mount in Lear's hand: *237*
Department of Printing and Graphic Arts, The Houghton Library, Harvard University

i) *Simla*, 1874
Pencil, sepia ink, watercolour, with notes on paper: 37.8 × 55.7 cm/$14\frac{7}{8}$ × $21\frac{15}{16}$ in
Inscribed, dated and numbered bl.: *Simla 14. April. 1874 6 P.M & 15th & 16 7. to 9. AM no. 432*
Numbered on mount in Lear's hand: *280*
Department of Printing and Graphic Arts, The Houghton Library, Harvard University

34g

j) *Poonah*, 1874 [Col. pl. p. 67
Pencil, ink, watercolour heightened with bodycolour, with notes on blue paper: 17.9 × 25.4 cm/$7\frac{1}{16}$ × 10 in
Inscribed, dated and numbered bl.: *Poonah. [June] 7.1874. 4.30 PM (563)*
Department of Printing and Graphic Arts, The Houghton Library, Harvard University

k) *Hyderabad*, 1874 [Col. pl. p. 64
Pencil, sepia ink, watercolour, with notes on paper: 35.2 × 55.4 cm/$13\frac{7}{8}$ × $21\frac{13}{16}$ in
Inscribed and dated br.: *Hyderabad 27 July 1874 7.15 to 9.AM.*
Numbered bl.: *(625)*
Numbered on mount in Lear's hand: *453*
Department of Printing and Graphic Arts, The Houghton Library, Harvard University

Lear's trip to India and Ceylon was the last, and the longest, journey of his life. He was over sixty when Lord Northbrook (see Cat. 114), who was then Viceroy, invited him to travel over the sub-continent at his expense. Lear was not certain that he wanted to go. After years of wandering he had just settled into his new home in San Remo (see Cat. 110), and he had no wish to be on the move once again.

He spent the summer of 1872 in England, and received so many commissions for Indian paintings that he knew he would be foolish not to go. That autumn he began the journey, but after a combination of misunderstandings at Suez he turned back, and 'the landscape painter does not purSuez eastern journey farther' (Fortescue, 24.xi.72, LLEL 1911, p. 151).

The following year he set out again, reaching Bombay on 22 November 1873. His immediate response was one of 'Violent and amazing delight at the wonderful variety of life and dress'. He felt 'nearly mad from sheer beauty & wonder of foliage! O new palms!!! O flowers!! O creatures!! O beasts!!—anything more overpoweringly amazing cannot be Conceived!! Colours, & costumes, & myriadism of imposs-

34*i*

ible picturesqueness!!! These hours are worth what you will' (I.J., MS., 22.xi.73).

He was launched immediately into Viceregal life, and on 2 December he found himself in a procession in Lucknow (Cat. 34*a*). They drove through the streets to the ruined Residency (Cat. 34*b*), where there were 'vast numbers of people. Immensely fine spectacle. Astonishing Elephants! Quite the finest thing of the sort I ever saw' (I.J., MS., 2.xii.73).

On 8 December he made drawings of the Elephant River (Cat. 34*c*), and after taking leave of Northbrook, he set off on his travels the next morning. He reached Benares on 12 December, and spent much of the next day searching for a possible view for a painting commissioned by Lord Aberdare (see Cat. 63) On the 14th he hired a boat, deciding that this was the only way to see Benares (Cat. 34*d*). 'Utterly so wonderful is the rainbow like edging of the water with thousands of bathers,—(all) reflected in the river. Then, the color of the Temples! & the strangeness of the huge umbrellas!! & the expressibly multitudinous detail of Architecture, Costume &c. &c. &c. &c. !!!! . . . How well I remember the views of Benares by Daniell, R.A.—pallid,—gray—sad,—solemn,—I had always supposed this place a melancholy,—or at least a "staid" and soberly coloured spot,—a gray record of bygone days!—Instead, I find it one of the most abundantly bruyant, and startlingly radiant of places of infinite bustle & movement!!! About 1.30 or 2, after having sate in the boat (doubled up,) to avoid the hot sun, and gazing at the wondrous world of bathers, huddled close together, or shewing themselve singly to the devout multitude of Benares,—I began a drawing of the Temples which I had vainly tried yesterday,—and managed to get what, should Photographs be attainable,—may one day prove more or less useful' (I.J., MS., 14.xii.73).

On 15 February 1874 he reached Agra, and went at once to see the Taj Mahal (Cat. 34*e*). 'This perfect & most lovely building infinitely surpassed all I had expected,' he wrote, 'principally on account of its size, & its colour. It is quite impossible to imagine a more beautiful or wonderful sight!' (I.J., MS., 15.ii.74). He returned the next day. '. . . descriptions of this wonderfully lovely place are simply silly, as no words can describe it at all. . .effects of colour absolutely astonishing,—the Great Centre of the Picture being ever the vast glittering Ivory=white Taj . . . *What* can I do here? Certainly not the Architecture, which I naturally shall not attempt, except perhaps in a slight sketch of one or two direct garden views. Henceforth, let the inhabitants of the world be divided into 2 classes,—them as has seen the Taj,—and them as hasn't' (I.J., MS., 16.ii.74).

When he reached Gwalior (Cat. 34*f*) in late February, he was feeling unwell, but set out and 'moved "athwart" the plain to a rising ground covered with Mussulman tombs,—some very pretty,—others mere heaps of stones,—all more or less in decay. Here I got a very good distant view of Gwalior Fortress' (I.J., MS., 22.ii.74). He subsequently made two oil paintings of this subject (see, for example, *View of Gwalior*, 1874, The Royal Pavilion, Art Gallery and Museums, Brighton).

By mid-March he was in Delhi, making 'Delhineations of the Dehlicate Architecture' (see Cat. 95) and of the Fort of Tughlakabad (Cat. 34*g*), where he drew two views, 'each very remarkable, and characteristic of the eternal squash and harry this land has been devoted to' (I.J., MS., 12.iii.74).

Moving up into the Himalayas he found it bitterly cold, particularly in the early morning when he liked to begin his work. But he set to busily (Cat. 34*h*), 'getting outlines of the hills, clearer than I have yet seen them, and with the plains beyond the first range. Then to the top of Landour, where there is a most sublime view all across the vast horizon of the Snowy Himalayas, a long long range, and *quite unlike* what one saw from Darjeeling, where Kinchinjunga,—a sort of mountain Epic, controls & absorbs every interest' (I.J., MS., 27.iii.74; see Cat. 63) .

In Simla (Cat. 34*i*) he found that 'Size—immensity are the most striking qualities of the Landscape' (I.J., MS., 14.iv.74). 'Without doubt,' he wrote, 'I have never seen any landscape so gorgeous' (I.J., MS., 16.iv.74).

Lear was in Poonah (34*j*) on 10 June, and in the afternoon 'went to various parts of the old city, & drew Temples and street scenes;—the people here are more curious & bothering than elsewhere' (I.J., MS., 10.vi.74).

At Hyderabad (Cat. 34*k*) he climbed 'to a height sufficient for drawing the city and I managed to get a goodish sketch of a very beautiful view, the trees making a fine middle distance, & the City Mosques being very noble objects on the horizon' (I.J., MS., 27.vii.74).

But as he progressed across India in trains and gharries and tongas, often sleeping in Dak bungalows and station waiting rooms and eating unfamiliar food, Lear grew tired. In November he was in Ceylon, but found little to admire beyond the foliage. Yet it was he, rather than the landscape, that was jaded. Giorgio was ill with dysentery, and when Lear strained his back he knew that they had had enough. For a man of his age it had it had been an exhausting, though fascinating, fifteen months. He sailed from Bombay on 12 January 1875, and sitting in his cabin drew 'recollections of Indian scenes, & designs for Enoch Arden', his last important oil painting left unfinished at his death in 1888 (I.J., MS., 12.i.75; see Cat. 43*b*).

The drawings Lear made in India, like his other travel watercolours, were not intended for sale. Because of this, there was no need for him to spend valuable time drawing the figures with care; unlike the landscape, which must give him accurate reference for future work, they were no more than *aides-mémoire*.

PROVENANCE *(a)–(k)* W.B. Osgood Field; The Houghton Library, Harvard University.

EXHIBITIONS *(c)* 1968, London, Gooden and Fox Ltd, *Edward Lear* (no. 93). *(d)* 1968, London, Gooden and Fox Ltd, *Edward Lear* (no. 94). *(e)* 1968, London, Gooden and Fox Ltd, *Edward Lear* (no. 95). *(i)* 1968, London, Gooden and Fox Ltd, *Edward Lear* (no. 99).

REFERENCES *(c)* Murphy 1953, repr. opp. p. 44; Noakes 1968 edn, repr. p. 262. *(e)* Hofer 1967, p. 37, repr. pl. 78; Lehmann 1977, repr. p. 103. *(g)* Murphy 1953, pp. 121–22.

35 Indian Flora

a) *Barrackpore*, 1873 [Col. pl. p. 69

Pencil, sepia ink, watercolour, with notes on paper: 30.5 × 45.6 cm/12 × $17\frac{15}{16}$ in

Inscribed, dated and numbered bl.: *Barrackpore 28. Decbr. 1873 11 AM—1.PM & 29 Decbr. 7.—8 AM (79)*

Numbered on mount in Lear's hand: *49*

Department of Printing and Graphic Arts, The Houghton Library, Harvard University

b) *Kersiong*, 1874 [Col. pl. p. 69

Pencil, sepia ink, watercolour, with extensive notes on paper: 35.6 × 50.8 cm/14 × 20 in

Inscribed, dated and numbered bl.: *at Kersiong 2. to 5 PM. Jan. 15. 1874 128*

Inscribed bl.: *All in shade.*

1. Gt trunk—light bn—gy. / foliage (picture) like chesnut / but rounder. Creeper-like / fern with roots at lower / part. (2) Similar trunk, but with / small leaved creeper (picture) & endless / wires & strings falling from (picture) / (3) thick small foliage, dk Green. / (4—4) ditto darker but greyer / (5.5) very dark. (6.6) Huge / dark trunx—dim confusion / of branch & foliage. / 7. Falling. (8.8 solid mass of / feathery beech = like close foliage / a long way from tree No 1. / 9. dark small foliage. 10 very pale / trunk—large ferny blue green creeper / pale at 10, 10, 10, reflecting blue light.

Numbered on mount in Lear's hand: *237*

Department of Printing and Graphic Arts, The Houghton Library, Harvard University

c) *Simla*, 1874 [Col. pl. p. 68

Pencil, sepia ink, watercolour, with notes on paper: 32.7 × 20.9 cm/$12\frac{7}{8} \times 8\frac{1}{4}$ in

Inscribed, dated and numbered bl.: *Simla. 19. April. 1874 452B Gnattural Sighs*

Numbered on mount in Lear's hand: *304*

Department of Printing and Graphic Arts, The Houghton Library, Harvard University

d) *Teog*, 1874

Mounted with Cat. 35*e* by Lear

Pencil, sepia ink, watercolour, on paper: 3.8 × 19.7 cm/ $1\frac{1}{2} \times 7\frac{3}{4}$ in

Department of Printing and Graphic Arts, The Houghton Library, Harvard University

e) *Teog*, 1874 [Col. pl. p. 68

Pencil, sepia ink, watercolour, with notes on paper: 32.7 × 54.4 cm/$12\frac{7}{8} \times 21\frac{7}{16}$ in

Inscribed, dated and numbered bl.: *Teog. 2d May. 1874 (483)*

Numbered on mount in Lear's hand: *324*

Department of Printing and Graphic Arts, The Houghton Library, Harvard University

f) *Poonah*, 1874

Pencil, sepia ink, watercolour, with notes on paper: 20.9 × 33.8 cm/$8\frac{1}{4} \times 13\frac{5}{16}$ in

Inscribed and dated bl.: *Poonah 18, June. 1874*

Numbered on matt in Lear's hand: *406*

Department of Printing and Graphic Arts, The Houghton Library, Harvard University

From the moment of his arrival in India, Lear had been overwhelmed by the beauty of the flora (see Cat. 34), and during his time there he made numerous studies of trees and flowers.

In Barrackpore on 28 and 29 December he drew a Banyan tree (Cat. 35*a*), and at Kersiong, on 15 January 1874, he was 'so delighted by a singularly magnificent group of grand trees, that I drew again for 2 hours' (I.J., MS., 15.i.74; Cat. 35*b*). In Simla, confronted with the problem of satisfactorily recording the huge landscape, he settled down instead to draw rhododendron flowers (Cat. 35*c*).

On 2 May he was in Teog (Cat. 35*d*, *e*), where he found an 'Exquisite white sort of Creeper, brightening the trees,' and he made 'a drawing of the sort of Clematis Creeper, of which Giorgio brought me in spessimince' (I.J., MS., 2.v.74). In Poonah on 18 June, it was 'the exquisite Gohlmohr tree—(Poinciana regia,)' (I.J., MS., 18.vi.74) that he drew (Cat. 35*f*).

On the day he left India he had begun to plan how he might use these studies. Now, in his loneliness, he thought often of Tennyson's shipwrecked sailor, Enoch Arden, marooned on his desert island. He had already made a reference to the sailor in 1873: 'I am feeling as melancholy as Enoch Arden; the loneliness of Sanremo is becoming difficult to bear when I am unable to work' (Diary, 31.viii.73). In 1881 he embarked on a huge painting of that fanciful tropical place. 'Besides my Tennyson Landscapes, I am going to try to paint one subject more, 15 feet long!!' he wrote. 'Do not laugh . . . I mean,—in this new subject (which is already much backed up by innumerable studies,) to introduce every kind of flower & tree I saw in India & Ceylon &c &c. And if any cricket chirping says 'it is impossible that all those should grow in one place!"—I shall say, "Yes they *do*". "*Where?*" "In Enoch Arden's Island." "And where is that?" "215 miles from the port Enoch's ship was going to." "And where then was that port?"—"Just 215 miles from Enoch Arden's island!"' (Mrs Holman Hunt, 28.viii.81, MS., John Rylands University Library, Manchester).

The unfinished picture was still on his easel when he died, and its whereabouts is unknown. The only indication we have of what the painting was like is no. 200, the last of his Tennyson drawings (see Cat. 43*h*).

PROVENANCE *(a)–(f)* W.B. Osgood Field; The Houghton Library, Harvard University.

EXHIBITION *(f)* 1968, Worcester, Mass., Worcester Art Museum, *Edward Lear, Painter, Poet and Draughtsman* (no. 59).

REFERENCES *(d) (e)* Murphy 1953, pp. 131–32. *(f)* Murphy 1953, pp. 152–53.

95*b*

36 Monte Generoso

Monte Generoso, 1878
Pencil, sepia ink, watercolour on paper: 37.1 × 49.2 cm/ $14\frac{5}{8} \times 19\frac{3}{8}$ in
Inscribed and dated bl.: *Monte Generoso July 24 1878 5 pm & Aug 5 5.30 pm. & Aug 7 4.5 PM*
The Fine Art Society, London

During the last years of his life, Lear no longer returned to England for the summer months, but went to the southern Alps. In 1878 he stayed for the first time at Monte Generoso on the Italian-Swiss border to the west of Como. During his stay he wrote to his nephew: 'The views near the Hotel here are wonderful. There is one point from which you may (perhaps) see all the plains & lakes of Italy, besides the rivers Jordan, Mississippi & Amazon, the whole course of the Nile,—as well as the cities of Pekin, St. Petersburg & Copenhagen, not to speak of the straits of Jamaica & Joppa with the adjacent islands of Cappadocia, Ceylon and Islington' (Charles Street, 27.vii.78, TS.)

He began the drawing exhibited here on July 24, 1878, but the mountains clouded over and he returned twice more 'to colour a previously outlined view of the plain' (Diary, 7.viii.78).

He continued to go to Monte Generoso until 1883, when Giorgio, his faithful old servant, died there. Giorgio was buried at nearby Mendrisio, and Lear never returned.

PROVENANCE R.P. Hinks; Peter Powell; The Fine Art Society, London.

EXHIBITION 1983, London, The Fine Art Society, *The Travels of Edward Lear* (no. 19).

36

STUDIO WATERCOLOURS

37*a*

The pleasure that Lear derived from making drawings on his travels found no parallel in his studio work. 'Grinding aching sorrows burn me—thinking of days of freedom & happy beautiful places,' he wrote in London in 1864 (Diary, 26.vii.64). 'I never can apply to remembering how hours of sedentary life make me boil over when I get away—a steam= force which is let off by walking, but bursts out in rage & violence if it has no natural outlet' (Diary, 14.iii.68). Yet it was in his studio that he had to work in order to produce the paintings from which he made his living—the oils, finished watercolours and what he called his Tyrants, all of which were based on his travel studies.

Lear's finished watercolours were painted either as commissions, or for exhibition and possible sale in his studio. Since they were not intended to be stored in portfolios but framed to hang on walls, they had to be both bold enough in colour and dense enough in medium to hold their own next to oil paintings. In this respect these works, although exhibited at neither the Old Water Colour Society nor the New Water Colour Society, conform to the contemporary tastes for finish and virtuosity in the handling of the medium.

His Tyrants, on the other hand, show less evidence of his accomplishments. Speedily painted and variable in quality, at their worst they lack both the rich texture of his finished watercolours and the spontaneous freedom of his travel work; at their best they display his control of a medium which he understood well. V.N., MA.S

37*f*

37 Finished Watercolours

a) *Constantinople*, 1848 [Repr. p. 123
Pencil, sepia ink, watercolour and bodycolour on paper: max. 9.2 × 16 cm/$3\frac{5}{8} \times 6\frac{5}{16}$ in
Inscribed br.: *Constantinople*; bl.: *E. Lear 1848*
Department of Printing and Graphic Arts, The Houghton Library, Harvard University

b) *Athens*, November 1850 [Col. pl. p. 48
Pencil, sepia ink, watercolour and bodycolour on cream paper: 26.3 × 44 cm/$10\frac{3}{8} \times 17\frac{3}{8}$ in
Inscribed br.: *Athens. June 7. 1848*; bl.: *Edward Lear del. Novr. 1850*
H.M.N. Hollis Esq.

c) *Mount Athos*, 1857 [Col. pl. p. 59
Gum arabic, watercolour and bodycolour over black chalk outline on paper: 30 × 46.6 cm/$11\frac{13}{16} \times 18\frac{3}{8}$ in
Signed, inscribed and dated bl.: *Mt. Athos. / Edward Lear. del/ 1857.*
Inscribed on back of mount: *Mt. Athos Rev: W.G.C. Clark/ Trinity College/Cambridge*
The Syndics of the Fitzwilliam Museum, Cambridge

d) *Jaffa* [1865]
Watercolour, bodycolour and touches of chinese white on paper: 17.1 × 37.6 cm/$6\frac{3}{4} \times 14\frac{13}{16}$ in
Signed with monogram:
Her Majesty The Queen

e) *View from Luxor* [1865] [Col. pl. p. 57
Watercolour, bodycolour on paper: 16.2 × 26 cm/$6\frac{3}{8} \times 10\frac{1}{4}$ in
Signed with monogram:
Her Majesty The Queen

f) *Mount Sinai*, 1869
Watercolour and bodycolour on paper: 17.8 × 37.8 cm/$7 \times 14\frac{7}{8}$ in
Inscribed bl.: *Mount Sinai. 1849*; br.: *E. Lear. 1869*
Department of Printing and Graphic Arts, The Houghton Library, Harvard University

Lear regarded the drawings he did on his travels as studies from which he would prepare more finished watercolours and oil paintings in his studio. This studio work performed two functions. It was either done to commission—a potential purchaser could choose a subject from the studies on which Lear would base a finished watercolour—or prepared by Lear for exhibition and sale in his studio. With a very few exceptions, anyone who bought a Lear watercolour during his lifetime would have owned a finished watercolour; it was not until the late 1920s that the freely handled travel watercolours with which we are now familiar came on to the general market.

From as early as 1837, the date of *Wastwater—Cattle* (see Cat. 13*b*), Lear was preparing studio work, and until the second half of the 1850s the style of such work was generally close to the drawing on which it was based. An example of this is the watercolour of Athens (Cat. 37*b*). Lear gave this finished watercolour to Charles M. Church (see Cat. 20), whom he met again in Athens. The more highly finished watercolours, which employ richer colour and greater detail than the earlier finished works, date from the second half of the 1850s. Sometimes these studio works are signed and dated with both the date of the original drawing and that of the studio watercolour (Cat. 37*b*, *f*); sometimes they are signed and dated with the studio date only (Cat. 37*c*); and later they are usually, though not always, undated and signed only with the monogram (Cat. 37*d*, *e*) which Lear first used in 1858. Due to the misdating by Lady Strachey of a letter to Fortescue, the first use of his monogram has been given as July 1859 (LEL 1907, p. 140). The correct date for this letter is September 1858, thus dating Lear's monogram or 'new assygram' (ibid.) in the earlier year.

The finished watercolours, *Jaffa* and *View from Luxor* (Cat. 37*d*, *e*) from the Royal Collection were chosen by the Prince of Wales in June 1865. Lear had already met the Prince; in 1859 he had visited Lear's studio in Rome (see Diary, 29.iii.59). In his diary for 10 June, 1865, Lear wrote: 'Comes a letter, saying that that [*sic*] HRH Prince of Wales is coming at 4. . . . Waiting—till 4—or 4.30, when the Prince came, attended by Col Keppel & Ld. Newry. His manner is kindly but more manly & hearty than in 1860–&–quâ prince—I suppose no one can be so amiable. He spoke at once of having seen me "last at Corfû"—& "looking at all my Palestine draw-

37*e*

ings at Rome!" & then began to observe the drawings, wh. he did judiciously enough,—both as to Switzerland, & to Italy; but he was more interested in the Palestine & Nile sketches, & fixed on many of them, Hebron, &c,—as well known. Then he said,—"I should like to have—to possess some of them"—& forthwith looked over all the Niles & Palestine sketches—selecting 10—: . . . . I could not but shake hands with him heartily.' Working from the sketches that the Prince had chosen, Lear prepared ten finished watercolours.

PROVENANCE *(a)* W.B. Osgood Field; The Houghton Library, Harvard University. *(b)* Charles M. Church; by family descent. *(c)* Rev. W.G.C. Clark; 1878, bequeathed to Joseph Prior; 1918, bequeathed to the Fitzwilliam Museum, Cambridge. *(d) (e)* H.R.H. The Prince of Wales (later Edward VII), by family descent. *(f)* Frances L. Hofer; The Houghton Library, Harvard University.

EXHIBITIONS *(c)* 1958, London, Arts Council of Great Britain, *Edward Lear* (no. 32); 1968, London, Gooden and Fox Ltd (no. 62). *(f)* Worcester, Mass., Worcester Art Museum, *Edward Lear, Painter, Poet and Draughtsman* (no. 54).

38 Hubert Congreve

San Remo from Villa Congreve, 1870 [Col. pl. p. 71
Watercolour on buff paper: 23 × 36 cm/9 × 14$\frac{3}{16}$ in
Inscribed br.: *Edward Lear at San Remo—Villa Congreve and Villa Emily*
Signed with monogram br.: ℒ
Private Collection

The view of San Remo from the garden of Villa Congreve is unusual in having two identifiable sitters; generally Lear's landscape work is peopled with innominate peasants. These two were Hubert and Arnold Congreve, the young sons of his neighbour in San Remo, Walter Congreve. The presence of the Congreve family was probably one of the deciding factors when Lear was considering building in San Remo, and during his early years there they provided the only consistent companionship he had (see Cat. 110).

For Hubert in particular Lear developed a strong affection. Without sons of his own he projected onto the growing boy the care and ambitions he might have felt for his own child. He gave both boys drawing lessons, and at one time he hoped that Hubert might become a painter. In fact, he left San Remo to go to King's College, London, leaving a gap in Lear's life which was never filled.

Hubert has left an account of his recollections of Lear, including his memory of their first meeting: 'One evening in the early autumn of 1869, when quite a small boy, I ran down the steep path which led up to our house at San Remo to meet my father; I found him accompanied by a tall, heavily-built gentleman, with a large curly beard and wearing well-made but unusually loosely fitting clothes, and what at the time struck me most of all, very large, round spectacles. He at once asked me if I knew who he was, and without waiting for a reply proceeded to tell me a long, nonsense name, compounded of all the languages he knew, and with which he was always quite pat [see Cat. 46]. This completed my discomfiture, and made me feel very awkward and self-conscious. My new acquaintance seemed to perceive this at once, and, laying his hand on my shoulder, said, "I am also the Old Derry Down Derry, who loves to see little folks merry, and I hope we shall be good friends." This was said with a wonderful charm of manner and voice, and accompanied with such a genial, yet quizzical smile, as to put me at my ease at once. This was my first meeting with Edward Lear, who from that day to his death was my dearest and best friend of the older generation, and who for nineteen years stood in almost a paternal relation to me' (LLEL 1911, pp. 17–18).

On Lear's last visit to London, he invited Hubert to dine with him at the Zoological Society: 'It was a beautiful evening in July and we dined in the open and sat under the trees till the gardens closed, he telling me all the story of his boyhood and early struggles, and of his meeting with Lord Derby in those gardens, and the outcome of that meeting—the now famous book, "The Knowsley Menagerie." I never spent a more enjoyable evening with him, and Lear, when at his best, was the most inspiring and delightful of companions. He was then absolutely natural, and we were like youths together, despite the forty and more years that lay between us' (LLEL 1911, pp. 35–36).

Hubert Congreve summed Lear up as: 'a man of versatile and original genius, with great gifts, one of the most interesting, affectionate, and lovable characters it has been my good fortune to know and to love' (LLEL 1911, p. 37).

PROVENANCE Walter Congreve, by family descent.

39 Tyrants

a) *Jerusalem* [Col. pl. p. 58
Watercolour and bodycolour on paper:
17.8×37.5 cm/$7 \times 14\frac{3}{4}$ in
Signed with monogram and dated bl.: *ℒ 1858 1862*
Trustees of the Victoria and Albert Museum

b) *Corfu* [Col. pl. p. 58
Watercolour and bodycolour on paper:
17.8×37.5 cm/$7 \times 14\frac{3}{4}$ in
Signed with monogram and dated bl.: *ℒ 1862*
Trustees of the Victoria and Albert Museum

c) *Catania—Mount Etna*
Watercolour and bodycolour on paper:
16.3×25.9 cm/$6\frac{7}{16} \times 10\frac{3}{16}$ in
The Department of Printing and Graphic Arts, The Houghton Library, Harvard University

d) Letter to Chichester Fortescue, 22 February 1863
Ink on paper: 21.1×26 cm/$8\frac{5}{16} \times 10\frac{1}{4}$ in
Somerset Record Office, Taunton

One of the peculiarities of Lear's working life was the production of what he called his Tyrants, mass-produced watercolours which were made simply for sale. For a man who always struggled for progress and self-improvement, it was a soul-destroying process forced upon him by lack of money.

Lear's first mention of the Tyrants is in his diary for 26 November 1862; in London that summer his large oil painting of the Cedars of Lebanon (see Cat. 26) had again failed to sell, and when he returned to Corfu for the winter he settled at once to his self-appointed task. Two boxes of drawings had been sent out from London, and on 26 November he sorted through them for suitable subjects. He planned to make sixty drawings in two batches of thirty, and he 'began to draw outlines of the drawings "to be made"—to the amount of 30!!!!!!!!!' (Diary, 26.xi.62).

He tells us nothing about his working methods for this first group; for the second group, executed during the winter of 1864–65 he gives some rather confusing details of his methods.

39*c*

Although he seems to have varied the process slightly each time, the details he gives of the preparation of his third group of 120 Tyrants in the first four months of 1873 is typical of his general approach. Having selected the drawings from which he intended to work, he first drew in pencil outlines (first process; Diary, 17.i.73). The following day he went over these outlines in grey watercolour (second process), and when these had dried he rubbed out the pencil (Diary, 18.i.73). On 20 January (he did not work at his Tyrants on 19 January, for it was a Sunday) he laid in a pale blue wash (third process). The next day he painted in red in the morning (fourth process), and yellow in the afternoon (fifth process; Diary, 21.i.73). On 22 January he began to paint in what he described as 'gray details', and 'gray outlining & shadow' (sixth process; Diary, 22 and 23.i.73). This process, working on one Tyrant after another, took several days, and was not finished until 1 February, when he began on the 'ochic process' (seventh process). On 3 February he worked on 'general bits of effect & applications of Indigo & stronger colours' (eighth process), and then on the 'nearly finished distance' (ninth process). By 8 February he was painting in the 'white paint foreground' (tenth process). This was the final process. By 12 April the task was finished; it had taken him seventy-two working days to complete one hundred and twenty watercolours.

Sir Edward Strachey wrote that Lear's method 'seemed to be to dip a brush into a large wide-necked bottle of watercolour, and when he had made one or two touches on the drawing, to carry it to the end of the room and put it on the floor, the performance being repeated till quite a row was arranged across the room' (*Nonsense Songs and Stories*, 1894, 9th edn).

Writing to Fortescue after he had completed his first group of Tyrants (from which Cat. 39*a* and *b* are taken) in 1863, Lear said: 'About the 20th I finished the last of 60 drawings—all of 10 or 12 guineas each a piece—and last week the frames came, and then, after two days' insertion of the drawings, measuring and nail knocking, I have made a really remarkable gallery of water colour works. . . . Among those who most enjoy seeing what I have done, Sir H. Storks is eminent. His delight in looking over the drawings was very marked—and at once he bought one of Jerusalem and one of Corfù . . .

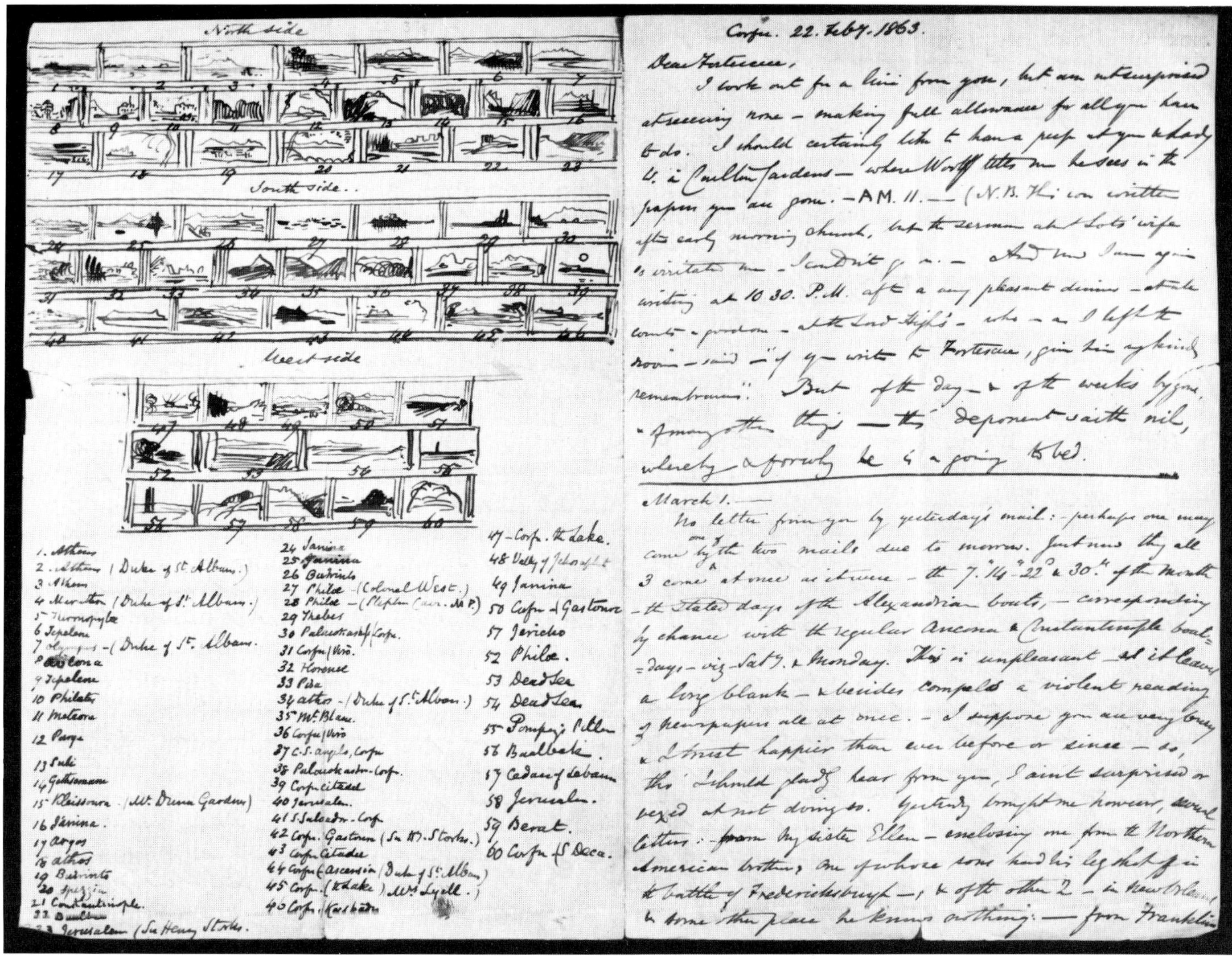

Corfu. 22. Feby. 1863.

Dear Fortescue,

I look out for a line from you, but am not surprised at seeing none – making full allowance for all you have to do. I should certainly like to have a peep at you & Lady W. in Carlton Gardens – where Wolff tells me he sees in the papers you are gone. – AM. 11. — (N.B. This was written after early morning church, but the sermon about Lots' wife so irritated me – I couldn't go on. — And now I am again writing at 10.30. P.M. after a very pleasant dinner – at the [illegible] – at the Lord High's – who – as I left the room – said – "if you write to Fortescue, give him my kind remembrances." But of the day – & of the weeks bygone, & of many other things — this deponent saith nil, whereby & forasmuch he is a going to bed.

March 1. —

No letter from you by yesterday's mail: – perhaps one may come by one of the two mails due tomorrow. Just now they all 3 come at once as it were – the 7. 14. 22 & 30 of the month – the stated days of the Alexandrian boats, – corresponding by chance with the regular Ancona & Constantinople boat-days – viz Saty. & Monday. This is unpleasant as it leaves a long blank – & besides compels a violent reading of newspapers all at once. – I suppose you are very busy & I trust happier than ever before or since – so, tho' I should gladly hear from you, I aint surprised or vexed at not doing so. Yesterday brought me however, several letters: – from my sister Ellen – enclosing one from the Northern American brother, one of whose sons had his leg shot off in the battle of Fredericksburgh – & of the other 2 – in New Orleans & some other place he knows nothing: — from Franklin

39*d*

Others will irritate me—Sir C. Sargent to wit—who saw all 60 drawing in 19 minutes, calling over the names of each and saying "£700! why you must give a ball!" Fool! As yet I have sold £120 worth—but have not received one farthing—for great people generally suppose that artists gnaw their colours and brushes for food' (Fortescue, 1.iii.63, LEL 1907, pp. 273–74).

He then listed the sixty subjects (Fortescue, 1.iii.63, MS., Somerset Record Office, Taunton) and made a drawing to show Fortescue how the pictures were hung (ibid., LEL 1907, p. 274; Cat. 39*d*). The Tyrants of Jerusalem and Corfu exhibited here were those bought by Sir Henry Storks, who was High Commissioner of the Ionian Islands between 1859 and 1863.

Many groups of Tyrants were not dated, and although most are signed with Lear's monogram, this was not always the case. He produced nearly one thousand such watercolours between 1862 and 1884. Although at their worst the Tyrants were remarkably bad and can easily be distinguished as Tyrants, it is sometimes difficult with the better examples to distinguish them from his finished watercolours (see Cat. 37).

This exhibition *en masse* of inferior work, though seen by Lear as a necessity, probably did more harm to his reputation as a painter than anything else; contemporaries commented on his lack of discernment in what he exhibited. Lear himself was aware of their poor quality, but by the time he began to work on his Tyrants he knew that he would not achieve the position that his best work merited; he was working to pay his bills, but one also senses a cynicism about the standards of popular taste and the slavish following of fashion in picture buying which suggests that he felt he was giving the public what it deserved.

PROVENANCE *(a) (b)* Sir H.J.K. Storks; Lt.-Col. H.K. Sadler DSO; 7 December 1961, bequeathed by him to the Victoria and Albert Museum. *(c)* W.B. Osgood Field; The Houghton Library, Harvard University. *(d)* Chichester Fortescue, by family descent to Lord Strachey; deposited with the Somerset Record Office, Taunton.

43*a*

LEAR AND TENNYSON

Lear first met Tennyson in 1851. *Journals of a Landscape Painter in Albania, &c*, published that year, prompted the poet to write 'To E.L., on his Travels in Greece', a compliment from which Lear derived lasting pleasure.

His plan to illustrate Tennyson's poems had been in Lear's mind since before their meeting, but began to take real shape during the summer of 1852 (see Cat. 42). His description of these proposed illustrations as 'Painting = Sympathizations' (n.d., MS., Beinecke Rare Book and Manuscript Library, Yale University), with the sense of loosely defined association rather than pedantic interpretation, was echoed in Tennyson's description of Lear's settings of his songs (Cat. 41): 'They seem to throw a diaphanous veil over the words—nothing more' (Charles Tennyson, *Alfred Tennyson*, 1949, p. 441). Perhaps, thought Lear, Tennyson might write a second poem, this time to his musical settings, so that he could 'wear one on each shoulder, epaulette-wise'. The suggestion came to nothing and neither, during his lifetime, did Lear's proposed publication of the Tennyson illustrations, though he dreamt of selling them for £18,000 and buying 'a chocolate coloured carriage speckled with gold, & driven by a coachman in green vestments and silver spectacles,—wherein, sitting on a lofty cushion composed of muffins & volumes of the Apocrypha, I shall disport myself all about the London parks' (Fortescue, 24.x.80, MS., Somerset Record Office, Taunton).

For Emily, Lear had a particular affection: 'that woman is 10000 angels boiled down,' he wrote—'an essence of goodness' (Diary, 10.ii.72). He thought Hallam and Lionel 'complete little darlings' (Fortescue, 12.vi.59, LEL 1907, p. 138). He dreamt of spending his old age near them, so that he could 'moon cripply cripply about those hills, & sometimes see by turns Hallam & Lionel's children . . . & so slide pleasantly out of life. Alfred, by that time would have written endlessly, & there would be 6 or 8 thick green volumes of poems. I—possibly,—should be in the workhouse, but I know you would all come & see me' (28.x.55, MS., Tennyson Research Centre, Lincoln). Instead, Lear's last days were spent in the loneliness of San Remo, working until the last months of his life on the Tennyson drawings, creating a huge painting of Tennyson's poem, 'Enoch Arden', in which he created a fantasy world of tropical foliage, and occasionally parodying the poet's verse:

'He only said, 'I'm very weary.
The rheumatiz he said.
He said, it's awful dull and dreary
I think I'll go to bed.'

(Fortescue, 10.xii.86, LLEL 1911, p. 353) V.N.

40*e*

40 Tennyson

a) Alfred Tennyson, 'To E.L., on his Travels in Greece', 1851
First published in Alfred Tennyson, *English Idylls and other poems*, 1854
In soft covered notebook: 16.2 × 10.2 cm/$6\frac{3}{8}$ × 4 in
Ink on paper: 16.2 × 10.2 cm/$6\frac{3}{8}$ × 4 in
Department of Printing and Graphic Arts, The Houghton Library, Harvard University, purchased with income from the bequest of Amy Lowell

b) Alphabet [1855]
26 pages in folio, mounted on canvas and edged in dark blue silk
Open at 'H was a hat'
Pencil and ink on paper
Watermarked: 1855
Private Collection

c) *Farringford*, 1864
Pencil and ink on paper: 35 × 48.5 cm/$13\frac{13}{16}$ × $19\frac{1}{4}$ in
Inscribed and dated bl.: '*Φάρριγγφορδ*', *15 October 1864*
Inscribed br.: '*Φάρργγφορδ*'
The Tennyson Research Centre, Lincoln, by kind permission of Lincolnshire Library Service

d) Self-portrait in a letter to Emily Tennyson, 1876
Sepia ink on paper: 20.5 × 13.2 cm/$8\frac{1}{8}$ × $5\frac{3}{16}$ in
Dated: *5 Jan 1876*
The Tennyson Research Centre, Lincoln, by kind permission of Lincolnshire Library Service

e) Letter to Hallam Tennyson, 1885 [Repr. p. 129
Sepia ink on paper 21 × 13.4 cm/$8\frac{1}{4}$ × $5\frac{1}{4}$ in
Dated: *8 Sept 1885*
The Tennyson Research Centre, Lincoln, by kind permission of Lincolnshire Library Service

Lear was introduced to Alfred and Emily Tennyson in 1851 by Franklin Lushington (Cat. 112); Tennyson's sister, Cecilia, was married to Lushington's brother, Edmund (see Cat. 105). Shortly after their meeting, Lear sent the Tennysons a copy of his *Journals of a Landscape Painter in Albania, &c.* (see Cat. 67), and the book inspired Tennyson's poem, 'To E.L., on his Travels in Greece'.

Over the succeeding years the personal affection between Tennyson and Lear waned, although Lear's admiration for Tennyson's poetry remained. Tennyson found Lear's facetiousness trying: when Tennyson followed his poem 'Northern Farmer, Old Style', with 'Norther Farmer, New Style' Lear suggested that if he wrote any more 'he might publish them all in a Farmercopia wh. disgusted him' (Diary, 11.vii.65). Lear, for his part, came to dislike 'the anomaly of high souled & philosophic writings combined with slovenliness, selfishness & morbid folly' (Diary, 17.x.64). 'I would he were as his poems,' he wrote (Diary 11.vii.65). Towards Emily, however, Lear felt no such reservations. 'I should think, computing moderately, that 15 angels, several hundreds of ordinary women, many philosophers, a heap of truly wise & kind mothers, 3 or 4 minor prophets, & a lot of doctors & schoolmistresses, might all be boiled down, & yet their combined essence fall short of what Emily Tennyson really is,' he wrote to Fortescue (12.vi.59, LEL 1907, p. 138).

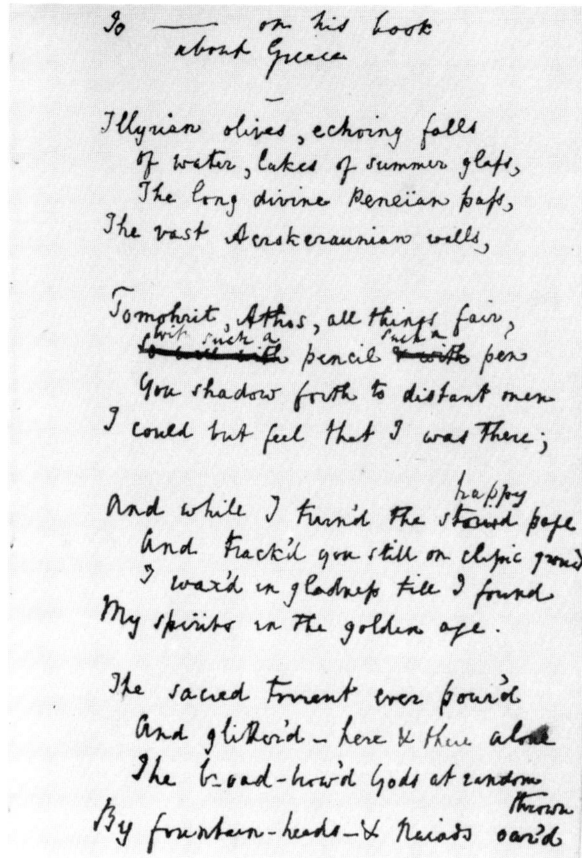
To —— on his book
about Greece

Illyrian olives, echoing falls
Of water, lakes of summer glass,
The long divine Peneïan pass,
The vast Akrokeraunian walls,

Tomohrit, Athos, all things fair,
With such a pencil, such a pen
You shadow forth to distant men
I could but feel that I was there;

And while I turn'd the happy page
And track'd you still on classic ground
I wax'd in gladness till I found
My spirits in the golden age.

The sacred torrent ever pour'd
And glitter'd – here & there alone
The broad-brow'd Gods at random thrown
By fountain-heads – & Naiads oar'd

40a

40b

40*c*

40*d*

Lear stayed frequently at Farringford, the Tennysons' family house on the Isle of Wight, and after one such visit wrote to Emily, '. . . the 3 or 4 days of the 16–20th October/55,—were the best I have passed for many a long day.—If I live to grow old, & can hope to exist in England, I *should* like to be somewhere near you in one's later days' (Emily Tennyson, 28.x.55, MS., Tennyson Research Centre, Lincoln). He was at Farringford in October, 1864 and on the 15th wrote in his diary: 'Perfectly lovely day. Rose shortly after 6—& at 7 drew in the garden—Hallam & Lionel coming now & then' (Cat. 40*c*).

It was for Hallam and Lionel, the Tennyson children, that he prepared the alphabet exhibited here (Cat. 40*b*). Writing to thank Lear, and to explain that the paper sheets had been pasted onto linen, Emily said, 'first I must tell you how grateful we are for those beautiful letters though you do, I hope know this. The pasting and ironing have been by no means so successful as they ought to have been but then I hope you will consider the remarkable fact of the Poet Laureate being seen ironing by nearly the whole household as something of a compensation . . . Hallam made no invidious remarks, such as "Gandy or Eliza would have done this better" but with rapturous delight pronounced all "bootful" and particularly insisted that it was "Mr. Lear's hat"' (Emily Tennyson to Lear, 11.i.[56], MS., Tennyson Research Centre, Lincoln).

Lear's later letters to the Tennysons frequently contained self-portraits (Cat. 40*d*), and that of 8 September 1885 (Cat. 40*e*) also contains a poem which, whilst placing Tennyson below the Bible and Shakespeare, shows that Lear considers his poetry a close third.

PROVENANCE *(a)* 1954, purchased with funds bequeathed by Amy Lowell; The Houghton Library, Harvard University. *(b)* Hallam and Lionel Tennyson, by family descent; 1980, 22 July, Sotheby's London (lot 401); bt by E. Joseph; bt by present owner. *(c)(d)(e)* Alfred Lord Tennyson, by family descent; 1964 deposited by the Tennyson Trustees at the Tennyson Research Centre, Lincoln.

REFERENCES *(a)* C. Ricks, *Tennyson*, 1972, pp. 240–41. *(c)* Lehmann 1977, p. 28; A. Wheatcroft, *The Tennyson Album*, 1980. *(d)* Noakes 1979 edn, p. 314. *(e)* Noakes 1968 edn, p. 297; Lehmann 1977, p. 100; Hyman 1980, p. 86.

41 The Tennyson Settings

a) Printed advertisement announcing the publication of four songs [1853]: 'Flow down, Cold Rivulet', 'Edward Gray', 'Tears, idle tears' and 'Wind of the Western Sea'
Paper: 16.5 × 11.4 cm/$6\frac{1}{2} \times 4\frac{1}{2}$ in
Private Collection

b) Sheet music for settings to poems by Alfred, Lord Tennyson, 1853
Publication containing settings of 4 poems: 'Flow down, Cold Rivulet', 'Edward Gray', 'Tears, idle tears' and 'Wind of the Western Sea', Cramer, Beale and Co. 1853
Paper: 35 × 25.5 cm/$13\frac{3}{4} \times 10$ in
The Tennyson Research Centre, Lincoln, by kind permission of Lincolnshire Library Service

The earliest mention of Lear's musical settings of Tennyson's poems is found in Marianne North's recollections of the summer of 1853 (see Cat. 49, 82), when Lear 'would wander into our sitting-room through the windows at dusk when his work was over, sit down to the piano, and sing Tennyson's songs for hours, composing as he went on, and picking out the accompaniments by ear' (*Recollections of a Happy Life*, 1892, vol. 1, p. 29). Tennyson preferred Lear's settings to any others, for 'they seem to throw a diaphanous veil over the words—nothing more' (C. Tennyson, *Alfred Tennyson*, 1949, p. 441). There are many descriptions of Lear reducing his listeners to tears, and on one occasion Archbishop Tait exclaimed, 'Sir! You ought to have half the Laureateship!' (quoted in Fortescue, 9.xii.82, LLEL 1911, p. 279).

Lear composed by ear, but in 1853 he arranged to have four of his settings to Tennyson poems written down, and in November that year they were published by Cramer, Beale & Co. (Cat. 41*a*,*b*). The four were: 'Flow down, Cold Rivulet' from *A Farewell*, 'Edward Gray', 'Tears, idle tears' and 'Wind of the Western Sea' from *The Princess*. Lear's setting of 'Tears, idle tears' was included in Holman Hunt's painting, *The Awakening Conscience* (1853–54, with subsequent retouchings; Tate Gallery, London).

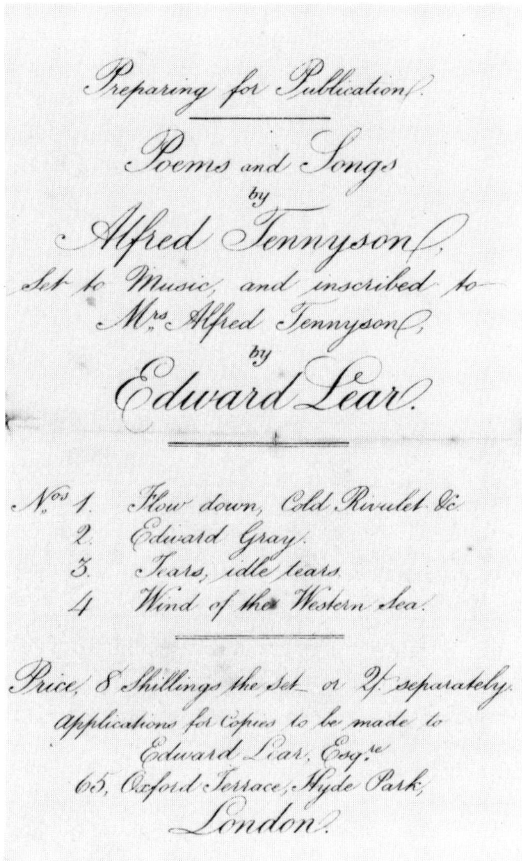
Preparing for Publication.
Poems and Songs
by
Alfred Tennyson,
Set to Music, and inscribed to
Mrs Alfred Tennyson,
by
Edward Lear.

Nos 1. Flow down, Cold Rivulet &c
2. Edward Gray.
3. Tears, idle tears.
4 Wind of the Western Sea.

Price, 8 Shillings the Set or 2/ separately.
Applications for Copies to be made to
Edward Lear, Esqre
65, Oxford Terrace, Hyde Park,
London.

41*a*

Early in 1858 Lear decided to publish more of his Tennyson musical settings. The music was set down for him by Edward Francis Rimbault (1816–76), and in the spring of that year the second collection appeared; it contained the four already published, with an additional five: 'Home they brought her warrior dead' and 'As through the land at eve we went', both from *The Princess*, 'Come not, when I am dead' and 'O let the solid ground not fail' from *Maud*, and 'The time draws near' from *In Memoriam*. Anne Henry Ehrenpreis (1979) suggests that a further three settings, from *Idylls of the King*, were published in 1860, and that there were at least nine other Tennyson settings by Lear. None of these appear to have survived (see Cat. 95*b*). The only other known setting by Lear is 'O world, O life, O time!' from Shelley's *A Lament* (Houghton Library, Harvard University; see Cat. 29; Diary, 7.iii.63).

PROVENANCE *(a)* Rev. George Clark, by family descent. *(b) c.* 1968, deposited anonymously at the Tennyson Research Centre, Lincoln.

LITERATURE *(b)* A. Henry Ehrenpreis, 'Edward Lear Sings Tennyson Songs', *Harvard Literary Bulletin*, vol. XXVII, no. 1, January 1979, pp. 65–85.

42 The Tennyson Illustrations: The Scheme

Lear's list of Tennyson illustrations, 1886
Printed on paper: 27 × 21 cm/$10\frac{5}{8} \times 8\frac{1}{4}$ in
Inscribed tl.: *Correct List Feby 26 1886*
Ruskin Galleries, Bembridge School, Isle of Wight

Although Lear considered illustrating Tennyson's poems before 1852, the first definite idea for such a project came in the summer of 1852 when he and Hunt were together at Clive Vale Farm (see Cat. 49).

Lear felt himself particularly well qualified for the task of preparing such drawings. Tennyson's response to Lear's paintings (see Cat. 40*a*) had been poetic, and Lear was proud when Arthur Stanley (1815–81), Dean of Westminster (see Cat. 13*d*) described him as '"The Painter of Topographical Poetry"' (Lord Derby, 13.iv.81, MS., Public Records Office, Liverpool). 'I can't help thinking,' Lear wrote to Emily Tennyson on 5 October 1852, setting out his plans for the scheme, '"No-one could illustrate Tennyson's landscape lines & feelings more aptly than I could do—but this very modest assertion may after all turn out to be groundless inasmuch as my powers of execution do not at all equal my wishes, or my understanding of the passages I have alluded to' (MS., Private Collection). In the same letter he explains: 'I have latterly extracted & placed in a sort of order all the lines which convey to me in the most decided manner his genius for the perception of the beautiful in Landscape, & I have divided them into "suggestive" & "Positive". . . . By "suggestive" I mean such lines as "vast images in glittering dawn"—"Hateful is the dark blue sky—&c &c &c—which are adaptable to any country or a wide scope of scenery. By "positive"—such as—"The lonely *moated grange*—"They cut away my tallest *pines*— "A huge *crag platform*—"The balmy moon of blessed *Isreal*—&c &c—which indicate perforce certain limits of landscape & wh: I am possibly more than most in my profession able to illustrate—not—pray understand me—from any other reason than that I possess a very remarkable collection of sketches from Nature in such widely separated districts of Europe—not to say Asia & Africa' (MS., Private Collection).

Although Lear had Tennyson's poems in mind as he travelled, he did not immediately carry out his scheme for a series of drawings. Following the publication of Moxon's edition of Tennyson's poems in 1857, whose illustrations, including some by Holman Hunt, had caused Tennyson considerable unease, Lear had no illusions as to the difficulty which his task presented. In an early list of the lines of Tennyson's poems for which Lear planned to make drawings (Beinecke Manuscript and Rare Books Library, Yale University), he says warily, '"Illustrations" is not a word fit for the matter. "Painting = sympathizations" would be better if there were such a phrase.'

PROVENANCE ?John Ruskin; ?Arthur Severn; *c.* 1930, with Haddon C. Adams; Ruskin Galleries, Bembridge School, Isle of Wight.

43 The Tennyson Illustrations: The Drawings

a) *The Capo Sant' Angelo, Amalfi* [Repr. p. 128
Pencil, grey ink and grey wash on paper:
(image) 16.5 × 26.3 cm/$6\frac{1}{2} \times 10\frac{3}{4}$ in;
(sheet) 22.6 × 35.5 cm/$8\frac{7}{8} \times 12\frac{3}{4}$ in
Signed with monogram bl.:
Inscribed in pencil tl.: *6*; tc.: *Z*
Yale Center for British Art, Paul Mellon Collection

b) *Bavella, Corsica*
Pencil, brown ink on paper: (image) 22.9 × 36.9 cm/ $9 \times 14\frac{1}{2}$ in; (sheet) 27.9 × 42.6 cm/$11 \times 16\frac{3}{4}$ in
Inscribed in pencil tl.: *15*
Yale Center for British Art, Paul Mellon Collection

c) *Wady Feiran, Palestine*, for 'A Dream of Fair Women' ('All night the spires of silver shine')
Pencil, sepia ink and wash on paper, pinched along all sides:
(image) 22.2 × 36.8 cm/$8\frac{15}{16} \times 14\frac{7}{16}$ in;
(sheet) 30.3 × 44.9 cm/$11\frac{15}{16} \times 17\frac{11}{16}$ in
Numbered in pencil tl.: *103/37* [crossed out in pencil]
Museum of Art, Rhode Island School of Design, Providence

d) *Mar Sabbas*
Autotype: 17 × 27.5 cm/$6\frac{11}{16} \times 13\frac{13}{16}$ in
Inscribed and dated br.: *Mar Sabbas 1858*; signed with monogram bl.: *N° 48*
Searight Collection

e) *Barrackpore*, for 'Love and Death'
Lightly printed lithographic image with wash and brown ink over pencil on paper: (image) 26 × 52 cm/$10\frac{1}{4} \times 20\frac{1}{2}$ in;
(sheet) 34 × 54.2 cm/$13\frac{3}{8} \times 21\frac{3}{8}$ in
Inscribed and numbered t.: *18/. The tree, stands in the sun, and shadows all beneath. Calcutta. (India)*
Faintly inscribed in pencil t.: *The Tree / 17 / also Deadsea*
Museum of Art, Rhode Island School of Design, Providence

f) *Thebes* [1884–85]
Mounted with Cat. 43*g* by Lear
Pencil, ink and wash on paper: 9.5 × 14.6 cm/$3\frac{3}{4} \times 5\frac{3}{4}$ in
Inscribed bl.: *On some vast plain before a setting sun/ (Guinevere)*; br.: *Plain of Thebes/ Egypt*
Numbered tl.: *199*
Private Collection

43*b*

g) *Enoch Arden* [1884–85]
Pencil, ink and wash on paper: 9.5 × 14.6 cm/$3\frac{3}{4} \times 5\frac{3}{4}$ in
Inscribed bl.: *The Mounted mooded to the Peak (Enoch Arden) Iland* [*sic*]
Numbered tl.: *200*
Private Collection

h) *Civitella* 1885 [Repr. p. 12
Pencil, black and grey wash: 16.8 × 26 cm/$6\frac{5}{8} \times 10\frac{1}{4}$ in
Department of Printing and Graphic Arts, The Houghton Library, Harvard University

43*c*

43*e*

Although Lear found much pleasure in choosing the lines of Tennyson's poems on which to base his 'Painting-=sympathizations' (see Cat. 42), the same cannot be said of his search for a suitable method of reproduction. The search was one of repeated experiment and failure during which Lear made so many groups of Tennyson illustrations that it is now almost impossible to trace the development of his work, or to identify the groups from which individual drawings come.

He began to work on the scheme more than once (eg. February 1862 when he planned 250 illustrations, March 1871 when he planned 100, May 1872 when he planned 120) but it was not until the summer of 1878 when he had come to the end of his Indian commissions (see Cat. 63) that he finally settled to the task. His plan then was to make 250 'good sized finished watercolor drawings' (Lady Wyatt, [29].viii.78, MS., Private Collection). That summer he worked on 30 watercolours as

43d

he would on a group of Tyrants (see Cat. 39). There were fifteen stages in their gestation: '(1) pencil, (2) pale colour outlines; (3) blue; (4) lake; (5) ochre; (6) indigo; (7) double ochre; (8) gamboge; (9) pmadder; (10) detail; (11) washing; (12) rubbing out; (13) opaque white; (14) detail; (15) foreground, generalizing &c.' However, on 19 July 1878 he wrote despairingly in his diary, 'Anything more utterly beastly than the appearance of these wretched drawings just now, can't be imagined.'

He decided to try a different way of working, and in October 1880 told Holman Hunt that as a stage towards '300 large watercolor drawings' (27.x.80, MS., Huntington Library, San Marino) he was making 'detailed monochrome outlines of the full size they are to be' (ibid.).

The first hint of the kind of publication he had in mind for his final selection of 200 illustrations comes in his diary for 1 August, 1882 when he noted: 'I ordered a copy £5.5.0 of the Autotype Reproduction of Turner's Liber Studiorum.' At the end of that month he told Fortescue, 'I work incessantly at the Tennyson Illustrations, which some day or other I hope I may publish in Autotype—after a sort of resemblance to Turner's Liber Studiorum' (MS., Somerset Record Office, Taunton).

He sent a few of his drawings to be autotyped, but was not happy with the results, for the 'drawings are pretty enough, but the effect I made is all lost' adding 'I am now to do very large drawings in Brown monochrome,—very finished, & these they say can be rejuiced all right' (Fortescue, 6.x.82, MS., Somerset Record Office, Taunton). The autotype, Cat. 43*d*, may date from this time, or from later experiments in autotype which he made in 1884 and 1886.

Over the next five years Lear prepared drawings for possible photochromolithography (April 1885), acquatint (June 1885), lithography (October 1885), photography (May 1886 and February 1887), and in May 1887 Platnatype was considered, but all without success.

During the winter of 1884–85 he prepared 200 small wash drawings, '(3 or 4 inches long,) as I calls "Eggs"' (Amelia Edwards, 19.v.85, MS., Somerville College, Oxford). These he mounted on large cards each with 8 drawings. He then ruled lines round each drawing and inscribed the Tennyson quotation beneath. Later in the year he decided that these mounts were 'too unwieldy and unmanageable for practical purposes./ / By 1 PM—all were cut up—now there are 100 smaller sheets, each holding 2 Eggs' (Diary, 14.x.85; Cat. 43*f g*). Until 1980 this set was part of the collection at the Tennyson Research Centre, Lincoln. It has now been further cut up and dispersed. A photographic record of the set, begun when the dispersal was already under way, was made at the instigation of Ruth Pitman of Bristol University, and is now deposited in the University Library at Bristol.

During the summer of 1885 Lear redrew the 200 illustrations in a larger size which he called 'Chrysalisses' (Amelia Edwards, 19.v.85, MS., Somerville College, Oxford). This is

43*f*, *g*

almost certainly the set in the Houghton Library of which Cat. 43*h* is a part. Working from this set, a young artist called Underhill prepared lithographic plates, and Lear was optimistic enough to write a Dedication to Emily Tennyson which he sent to be printed (24.xi.85, MS., Ruskin Museum, Bembridge School). In this he spoke of 'the united musical charm, vivid imagination, terse and descriptive power' of Tennyson's poetry (ibid.), describing his drawings as 'Poetical Topographical Tennysoniana' (ibid.). However, the arrival of the proofs for the Dedication coincided with that of the proofs for the illustrations which were 'absolutely good for nothing' (Diary, 1.iv.86).

Despite this, Lear worked doggedly on, and it was not until the autumn of 1887, a few months before his death in January 1888, that he finally abandoned any hope of the successful outcome of the project. During those years his sight had deteriorated, and he wrote to Holman Hunt, 'being so blind as I am, I am compelled to begin with a forcible dark outline, & that aint easy to get rid of—though without it I could do nothing' (27.x.80, MS., Huntington Library, San Marino). Any assessment of the quality of these drawings must consider the state of the man; what is extraordinary is that he continued to work as he did. But then, in 1862 he had written: 'I have been looking carefully over all Alfred Tennyson's poems, & noting out all the Landscape subjects once more—which in all amount to 250. Sometimes I think I shall make the last effort of my life to illustrate the whole of these by degrees, & finally, having constructed a gallery near London—receive shillings for the sight of my pictures, & expire myself gradually in the middle of my own works—wheeling or being wheeled in a Narm=chair' (Fortescue, 16.ii.62, LEL 1907, pp. 229–30).

PROVENANCE *(a) (b)* Sir Osbert Sitwell; Thomas Agnew and Sons; March 1967, bt by the Yale Center for British Art. *(c) (e)* 1967, Thomas Agnew and Sons; 1971, given anonymously to the Museum of Art, Rhode Island School of Design. *(d)* bt by present owner. *(f) (g)* Alfred, Lord Tennyson, by family descent; 1980, 22 July, Sotheby's, London (lot 400), bt by Thomas Agnew and Sons; purchased by present owner. *(h)* W.B. Osgood Field; The Houghton Library, Harvard University.

EXHIBITIONS *(a)* 1967, London, Thomas Agnew and Sons, *94th Annual Exhibition of Watercolours and Drawings* (no. 92). *(b)* 1967, London, Thomas Agnew and Sons, *94th Annual Exhibition of Watercolours and Drawings* (no. 89). *(c)* 1967, London, Thomas Agnew and Sons, *94th Annual Exhibition of Watercolours and Drawings* (no. 100); 1982, Providence, Rhode Island, Museum of Art, Rhode Island School of Design, *How Pleasant to know Mr Lear: Watercolours by Edward Lear from Rhode Island Collections* (no. 46); 1983, London, The Fine Art Society, *The Travels of Edward Lear* (no. 98*e*). *(d)* 1967, London, Thomas Agnew and Sons, *94th Annual Exhibition of Watercolours and Drawings* (no. 99); 1972, Providence, Rhode Island, Museum of Art, Rhode Island School of Design, *Selection II: British Watercolours and Drawings from the Museum's Collection* (no. 119); 1982, Providence, Rhode Island, Museum of Art, Rhode Island School of Design, *How Pleasant to know Mr. Lear: Watercolours by Edward Lear from Rhode Island Collections* (no. 44); 1983, London, The Fine Art Society, *The Travels of Edward Lear* (no. 98*f*). *(h)* 1968, Worcester, Mass., Worcester Art Museum, *Edward Lear, Painter, Poet and Draughtsman* (no. 69).

REFERENCES *(e)* 'Notes', *Bulletin of Rhode Island School of Design Museum*, April 1972, no. 119 (repr.). *(h)* Osgood Field 1933, pp. 269–70, no. 56.

[The compiler is indebted to Ruth Pitman, who is preparing a work on the Tennyon illustrations, for most generously sharing her ideas.]

44 The Tennyson Illustrations: The Published Book

a) Proofs for the illustrations to Tennyson's poems
3 proof plates from a group of 10
i *Kasr-es-Saad*
Etching with pencil notes by an unidentified hand on paper: 8.6 × 14.6 cm/$3\frac{3}{8} \times 5\frac{3}{4}$ in
Inscribed b.: [*The crag that fronts*]
Etched by Charles O. Murray
Beinecke Rare Book and Manuscript Library, Yale University

ii *Palaiokastritza*
Etching with pencil notes by an unidentified hand on paper: 8.6 × 14.6 cm/$3\frac{3}{8} \times 5\frac{3}{4}$ in
Inscribed b.: *Sweet is the colour of cove*
Etched by Charles O. Murray
Beinecke Rare Book and Manuscript Library, Yale University

iii [*Virò Corfù*]
Etching with pencil notes in an unidentified hand on paper: 9.5 × 14 cm/$3\frac{3}{4} \times 5\frac{1}{2}$ in
Inscribed b.: *And when the lemon grove*
Etched by Francis S. Walker
Beinecke Rare Book and Manuscript Library, Yale University

b) *Poems of Alfred, Lord Tennyson, illustrated by Edward Lear, 1889*
Volume: 32.6 × 25.1 cm/$12\frac{15}{16} \times 9\frac{15}{16}$ in
Published by Boussod, Valadon & Co, London
No. 9 of an edition of 100, all signed by Alfred, Lord Tennyson
Private Collection

'Of course, directly I die, they will (all the 200) be recognized as sublime, poetical and unique: they will all be exquisitely engraved, and endless beastly booksellers and pestiferous publishers will be enriched thereby,' wrote Lear to Emily Tennyson on 20 December, 1883 (MS., Tennyson Research Centre, Lincoln).

In fact, the first serious overture from a publisher came during Lear's lifetime when Dana Estes, from Boston, called to see him on 7 May 1887 (see Cat. 98). Estes planned to publish an illustrated edition of Tennyson's poems, and thought the '200 drawings are very interesting and would add greatly to the interest of our proposed Edition, but some portions are unfinished in details, and would require *very artistic treatment* at the hands of an engraver or etcher. It is very evident that their reproduction and publication are the dearest wish of the old gentleman's heart, but that he almost despairs of the result. . . .I did not make any direct proposals to Mr. Lear for his drawings in such a very uncertain stage of my plan, but took one of them which he entrusted to me to endeavour to see what would be the most practicable form of reproduction in case any arrangement can be ultimately made to go on with the publication' (Dana Estes to Hallam Tennyson, 8.v.87, MS., Tennyson Research Centre, Lincoln).

Nothing came of this plan, and it was not until after Lear's death that a selection of the illustrations, taken from the 1885 set (see Cat. 43) were reproduced in *Poems by Alfred, Lord Tennyson*, Boussod, Valadon & Co, London, 1889). The edition was limited to 100 copies, each signed by Tennyson (Cat. 44*b*).

It contained sixteen full-page reproductions and six vignettes illustrating three poems: 'To E.L. . . .', 'The Palace of Art' and 'The Daisy.'

The proofs of etchings from Lear drawings exhibited here are taken from a set of ten. They may have been trials carried out by Estes (Cat. 44*a*).

PROVENANCE *(a)* Col. E.S.M. Prinsep; 1949, bt by the Beinecke Rare Book and Manuscript Library, Yale University. *(b)* bt from a bookseller by present owner.

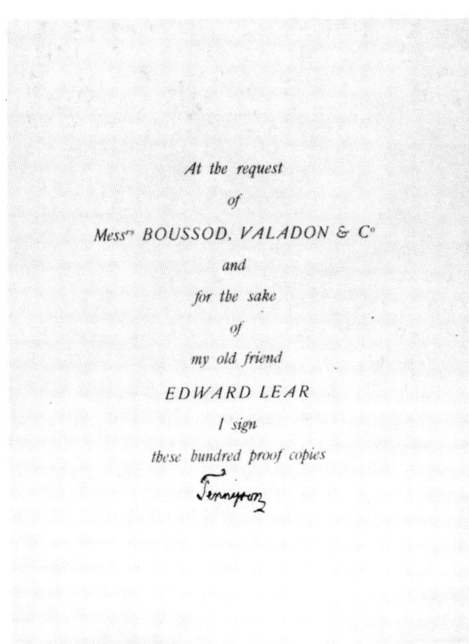
At the request
of
Messrs BOUSSOD, VALADON & Co
and
for the sake
of
my old friend
EDWARD LEAR
I sign
these hundred proof copies
Tennyson

44*b*

OIL PAINTINGS

54

Lear took up oil painting in 1838 (Cat. 45) and his first finished pictures in this medium date from 1840. He subsequently produced some three hundred paintings, many being variants of the same subject. Apart from his brief attempt at adopting the Pre-Raphaelite principle of painting on a large canvas out of doors (Cat. 49–51), Lear's compositions were all created in the studio on the basis of his numerous travel studies. Lear was primarily moved by the beautiful and the dramatic in nature. Both the choice and organisation of his subjects are capable, often within the same picture, of containing references to the traditional landscape conventions of Claude and the Sublime, and an innovatory concern for detail, light and colour. However, his need to conform to the contemporary taste in landscapes and his desire to establish a reputation as a serious poetic landscape painter dictated his choice of subject and required that topographical sites possess an historical element, which would endow them with a deeper, moral dimension. Lear's oil paintings were accepted at the Royal Academy annual exhibitions from 1850 to 1856 and again in 1871 and 1872 and at the British Institution in 1852, 1853, 1855, 1861 and 1863. Most of his oils, however, were painted either from commissions or in anticipation of purchase by one of the artists's wealthy and well-connected friends or acquaintances. MA.S.

[The entries in this section have been written by B.L. and MA.S; relevant Lear material was provided by V.N.]

45 Corpo di Cava

Tree Roots, 1838 [Col. pl. p. 32
Oil on paper mounted on canvas: 25 × 22.5 cm/9⅜ × 8⅜ in
Inscribed and dated br.: *June. 21. 1838 / La Cava*
The Forbes Magazine Collection, New York

45

Lear had originally intended to spend his first summer in Naples with the artist, Thomas Uwins. However, with his characteristic dislike of urban surroundings (see Cat. 59), he found the city crowded, noisy and dirty, and retreated with Uwins after a few days to the tiny, picturesquely sited village of Corpo di Cava, situated in a valley above La Cava, a summer retreat for Neapolitans to the southeast of the city. From there he wrote to Ann: 'Corpo di Cava is perched upon a hill, at the end of a deep valley—all covered with wood . . . Nothing can be so delightful as the quiet of this place after Naples—the birds singing in the morning, & the exquisite air . . . Salvator Rosa studied for many years among the woods of La Cava, & you see numbers of the actual rocks so common in his paintings' (10.vi.38, TS.).

This study of tree roots, made on 21 June 1838, was undertaken above La Cava. The narrow focus on an individual object in nature and the medium of oil on paper suggest that the work is an oil sketch made out of doors, in front of the subject. In a letter to Gould of 1839, Lear stated that 'last summer, I commenced oil painting' (MS., Houghton Library, Harvard University). He then goes on to say that he took up the procedure again in the summer of 1839. In the list of *Pictures Painted* (LEL 1907, pp. 311–18), however, Lear dates his earliest oil paintings to 1840. Thus it would be reasonable to assume that works in oil preceding 1840 were almost certainly oil sketches (see Cat. 46) rather than finished works (see Cat. 47).

It is uncertain as to how Lear became interested in the technique of sketching in oil out of doors. It is possible that both Samuel Palmer (1805–81) and Thomas Uwins (1782–1857) may have been involved. Although Lear may have met Palmer amongst the English artists in Rome before his trip to Naples, since Palmer had arrived in Rome in October 1837, the two artists certainly met for a few days at the Hôtel de la Ville de Rome in Naples in June 1838 (letter from Palmer to Richmond, 3.vi.38, in *The Letters of Samuel Palmer*, ed. R. Lister, 1974, vol. 1, p. 138). They were to stay in the same pensione in June 1839 at Civitella (see Cat. 47). Most of Palmer's work in Italy was confined to drawings and watercolours, but many of these suggest that he had not lost the habit of the close observation of detail in nature (see Linnell, 10.vii.39; ibid., p. 358) which he had already used in his 'visionary' landscape paintings made during his Shoreham years (1824/5–1832). Thomas Uwins, a painter of genre scenes, had already spent the years 1824–31 in Rome; he returned for a second sojourn from 1835 to 1839. In 1810, Uwins had exhibited a picture at the Royal Academy entitled *Gleaners; a sketch from Nature* (no. 444) and he was a close associate of John Linnell, an advocate of sketching out of doors (eg. *Twickenham*, 1806, Private Collection) through the reformed Society of Painters in Watercolour (Mrs Uwins, *A Memoir of Thomas Uwins R.A.*, vol. 1, 1858, p. 32).

Lear's interest in the details of roots and foliage in this study partially refers back to the minute observation of detail demanded in his ornithological and animal studies made in the 1830s (see Cat. 6–12). Further, there is evidence of a continued interest in sketching in oil out of doors in the *Temple of Venus and Rome* (see Cat. 46), in a series of oil studies executed in Sicily in 1847 (eg. Houghton Library, Harvard University; Museum of Art, Rhode Island School of Design) and in a few undated studies, for example one made in Corfu (Victoria and Albert Museum, London).

He continued to demonstrate a concern for detailed foliage and rocks in the foregrounds of large oil paintings such as *Bassae* (Cat. 51) and the *Quarries of Syracuse* (see Cat. 49). However, the procedures followed for recording these details involved their direct transcription on to large canvases in front of the subject itself. MA.S.

PROVENANCE 1983, 16 November, Sotheby's, London (lot 74); bt by the Forbes Magazine Collection.

46 Rome

Temple of Venus in Rome, 1840
Oil on paper mounted on canvas: 24.6 × 34.3 cm/9¾ × 13½ in
Inscribed on a label on the back: *View of the Temple of Venus & Rome / at Rome / painted by in 1840 / Mr Abebika, / Kratoponoko, Prizzikalo / Kattefello / Ablegorabalus / Ableborintophashyph (?—) Or a (?.). / Chakonoton the Cozovex . . . / Dossi / Fossi / Sini / Tomentilla / Coronilla / Polentilla / Batteldore & Shuttlecock / Derry down Derry / DUMPS / otherwise Edward Lear*
Yale Center for British Art, Paul Mellon Fund

The Temple of Venus and Rome was erected by the Emperor Hadrian in AD 135 and lies to the south of the Arch of Titus on the Via Sacra. It was restored by Maxentius in AD 307 after a disastrous fire and was considered one of the most magnificent temples in Rome.

This picture, looking from the southwest towards the buildings of S. Franscesca Romana, is executed in oil on paper. Its broad technique suggests that it was made on the spot, and the emphasis upon the simplification of shapes and the flat blue sky places it within the tradition of oil sketches made by late eighteenth-century landscapists in Rome, namely Valenciennes and Thomas Jones, and early nineteenth-century artists such as Corot.

Lear made a number of watercolour studies of the Temple of Venus and Rome (eg. Tate Gallery, London). In addition, two of the first finished oil paintings dating from 1840 were of Roman subjects (*Rome. Borghese Garden*, LEL 1907, p. 311, no. 3; *Rome. Arco Oscuro*, LEL 1907, p. 311, no. 4). However, Lear does not appear to have used this oil sketch either in these paintings or in any of the other forty pictures listed by Lady Strachey as being of Roman subjects (LEL 1907, pp. 311–18). These pictures include both ancient and modern views. In this respect they suggest that Lear, unlike his eighteenth-century predecessors but in keeping with the taste of both his patrons and potential purchasers and his contemporary artists such as Uwins (see Cat. 45), sought to celebrate the Renaissance city as enthusiastically as that of the emperors (see Mrs Uwins, *A Memoir of Thomas Uwins R.A.*, vol. 1, 1858, p. 229). MA.S.

The inscription on the label attached to the back of the picture is what Lear called his 'long name' (see Cat. 38).

In fact, the name was derived in part from *Aldiborontiphoskyphorniostikos: A Round Game, for Merry Parties*, by R. Stennet published in 1822. In this the players read aloud the tongue-twisting names and descriptions of the characters, and 'Rapidity of utterance, and gesticulation are essential.'

An inscription by Lear in a copy of his *Book of Nonsense* (Private Collection) reads: 'ABLEGORĀBBOLUS, ĀLDEBORONTIFOSKY, FORMIŌS / TICOS, CROHONONTONTHO / LOGOOSE, DŌSSI, FŌSSI, SINY / TÓMENTILLA, CORONILLA, POTENTILLA DERRY DOWN DERRY / DUMPS.' Both versions of the long name have variations of the game's title. In the inscription in the *Book of Nonsense*, 'CROHONONTONTHOLOGOOSE' is a variation on the character 'CHRONONHOTONTHOLOGOS.' 'Derry down Derry' was the name under which Lear published the first two editions of the *Book of Nonsense* (see Cat. 72 and 73). Battledore and Shuttlecock, the child's game, returns as 'battlecock and shuttledoor' in 'The Daddy Long-legs and the Fly.' V.N.

PROVENANCE 1980, 13 March, Sotheby's London (lot 162); bt by Somerville and Simpson, London; 1980, bt by Yale Center for British Art.

REFERENCE M. Cormack, *How pleasant to know Mr. Lear*, Museum of Art, Rhode Island School of Design, 1982, p. 4.

[The compiler is grateful to Thomas V. Lange and H. P. Kraus for information about the *Round Game*.]

46

47

47 Civitella

Civitella di Subiaco, 1847
Oil on canvas: 127 × 193 cm/50 × 76 in
Signed and dated br.: *Edward Lear 1847*
The Clothworkers' Company

Civitella (now Bellegra) is an isolated village perched on the top of a dramatic limestone ridge in the Sabine Hills to the southeast of Tivoli. Lear visited the village for the first time in May 1838, possibly in the company of the artist Penry Williams, and again in June 1839, when he appears to have shared a pensione with Samuel and Hannah Palmer (Hannah Palmer [née Linnell] to John and Mary Ann Linnell, 10.vii.39, in *The Letters of Samuel Palmer*, ed. R. Lister, vol. I, 1974, p. 356). Lear's painting shows a distant view of Civitella, on its outcrop of limestone with the Roman campagna in the distance.

Lear's first enthusiastic impressions of the village and its location were given in a letter to Ann dated 11 May 1838, 'it is piled up on a pyramidal rock, in a beautiful valley full of trees as usual,—& from whatever side you approach it the Cardinal's castle at the top is always very fine. The town itself is built as it were on flights of stairs—you must go up and down always—but a more picturesque place never was' (TS.). This response is echoed in Hannah Palmer's letter to her sister Lizzy written shortly after she and Samuel Palmer had arrived at the village: 'We are perched on a mountain and look down into the most lovely fertile valley bounded on one side by wooded mountain and on the other by rich little hills on whose tops and sides stand other little wild villages and over them you can see the campagna of Rome bounded by more distant mountains and stretching far away the glittering Mediterranean—near rocks and trees also make fine foregrounds to this lovely panorama . . .' (30.vi.39, *The Letters of Samuel Palmer*, ed. R. Lister, vol. I, 1974, p. 352).

Despite the immediacy of his response, Lear has produced a landscape painting which is in large measure dependent upon traditional pictorial conventions. The verticality of the right hand side of the composition and the use of interlocking planes to create depth are reminiscent of the landscapes of Gaspard Dughet, whose more rugged landscapes had appealed to eighteenth-century English landscape painters as alternative to the smoother, more beautiful landscapes of Claude Lorraine.

The peasants in the foreground under the rocky cliff on the right in part provide local colour. While in Rome Lear had been a close friend of Penry Williams, who had arrived there in 1828 and who became the centre of the English community in that city. In 1884 when writing to Lord Aberdare on the penurious condition of Williams, Lear remarked: 'The accuracy of Penry Williams's Italian peasant subjects and the correct beauty of their surroundings, could not indeed be appreciated or even understood by those who have never known Italian scenery or any colour but grey. . . . I owe him most for having introduced me to such places as Civitella, Olevano etc.—as well as to my constant observation of his work' (25.ix.84, MS., Glamorgan Record Office). A painter who specialised in Italian genre scenes, Penry Williams provided three illustrations of Italian peasants for Lear's *Illustrated Excursions in Italy* (1846; see Cat. 65). Lear's peasants in this painting also appear as passive versions of Salvator Rosa's banditti in rugged landscapes. Their attitudes of repose from the labours of the day set the Horation mood of this painting and infer a reference to Arcadia within the Romans campagna.

Lear executed several variants of this subject; in 1840 for Lord Derby (LEL 1907, p. 311, no. 5), and in 1843 for Rev. J. J. Hornby (LEL 1907, p. 312, no. 30). In 1853, Chichester Fortescue commissioned *Civitella di Subiaco Looking South* (LEL 1907, p. 314, no. 99) while two years later William Nevill acquired a *Civitella di Subiaco, Sunrise* (LEL 1907, p. 314, no. 117) a picture which was accompanied by the lines from Tennyson 'Morn broaden'd on the borders of the dark' ('A Dream of Fair Women', 1855). The painting exhibited here, dating from 1847, did not result from any commission, for on 6 February 1847, Lear wrote to Ann stating that he was working on 'a big one of my own fancy; destined for nobody in particular' (TS.). Lear did not exhibit the painting, and eventually sold it on 3 March 1861 for 150 guineas to Sir Francis Goldsmid, Bart. (Diary, 4.iii.61), the first Jew to be called to the English Bar. On its sale, Lear declared: 'so the old brown picture goes at last' (ibid.).

In later life, the beauty of Civitella came to hold a special place in Lear's memory. He looked back to it with a mixture of nostalgia, despair and melancholy. In Corfu in 1862, he confided his sense of sorrow at lost pleasures never again to be experienced: 'There is everywhere a flood of gold & green & blue. This, & the breeze, blowing freshly now & then, remind me of days in many lands before *that* knowledge came which tells us we have so little, & so much conjecture. On Swiss, & Como hills in 1837—in the first years of Roman & Amalfi life /38, /9—the long Civitella sojourns—1839–40. . . I do not now suppose that kind of happiness can ever come back but by unexpected & unsought snatches; so I do not strive after it, nor mourn that I cannot have it' (Diary, 10.v.62). Again: 'The wonderful bright calm of today! And the poignant way in which the shade of singing brings back days of Albania—Abruzzi—& worse—Civitella days of ole—when one sate from noon to 3 in August & July—listening to the songs coming up from the great silent depths below the rock!' (Diary, 16.i.67). MA.S.

PROVENANCE 1861, bt by Sir Francis Goldsmid Bart., MP; the Moore Family; 1961, presented by Mr R. O. Moore to the Clothworkers' Company.

REFERENCE LEL 1907, p. 313, no. 67.

48 Mount Tomorit

Mount Tomohrit, Albania, c. 1849–*c.* 1852, 1872–77
Oil on canvas: 122 × 186 cm/48 × 73¼ in [Col. pl. p. 35;
Signed with monogram bl.: ℒ [repr. p. 19
Private Collection

Lear visited Mount Tomorit during his Albanian tour of 1848 (see Cat. 24). On 16 October he noted in his journal: 'As this day was to be passed on the banks of the Apsus, for the purpose of sketching Tomohr, I awoke and rose at three, and

48

by daylight the mountains sparkled like clear cystal' (*Journals of a Landscape Painter in Albania, &c.*, 1851, p. 195). As he drew 'a gray sirocco had thrown a cloud over all the beauty of colour, yet the form of Tomohrit is in itself a picture, combined with the broad Beratino in its stony channel and cliff banks . . .'.

Lear began work on the picture after his return to England in 1849. A watercolour of the same view, inscribed *Pass of Tyrana, Albania*, is dated 1851 (1983, London, the Fine Art Society, *The Travels of Edward Lear*, no. 62). His meeting with William Holman Hunt in 1852, however, may have caused him to abandon work on a subject for which English landscape could not supply an equivalent from which he could work directly onto the canvas. The painting remained in his possession unfinished. In 1872 it was one of five large oils which he exhibited in his new gallery at Villa Emily (see Cat. 107), although at that time he did not intend to sell them (Fortescue 28.iv.72, LLEL 1911, p. 145). Like the others on exhibition, this painting illustrated lines from Tennyson's poems; in this case, 'To E.L. on his travels in Greece':

'Tomohrit, Athos, all things fair,
With such a pencil, such a pen,
You shadow forth to distant men,
I read and felt that I was there.'

Later in 1872 Lear decided to rework the painting, exclaiming in his diary, 'Dash = smash—crashing glazings over the beech trees of the Tomohr & the lower foreground,—& all with effect' (Diary, 4.xii.72). *Mount Tomohrit* was eventually sold, together with 'And the crag that fronts the Even' (Cat. 62), to Louisa, Lady Ashburton in 1877. The painting's V-shaped composition, formed by the view from the mountain pass plunging to the valley below, with higher mountains in the distance, was repeated by Lear in other paintings, notably *Mount Kinchinjunga* (see Cat. 63). In each picture, natives of the region serve both to add local colour and, by contrast, to emphasise the sublime qualities of the landscape. B.L.

PROVENANCE 1877, Louisa, Lady Ashburton; 1978, 24 October, Sotheby's Belgravia (lot 28); bt by The Fine Art Society, London; bt by present owner.

49 Quarries of Syracuse

The Quarries of Syracuse, 1852
Oil on canvas: 22.9 × 35.6 cm/9 × 14 in
Inscribed on a label on the back: *Given by Edward Lear to Lord Tennyson*
Mr Henry Yordan Obegi

Lear had visited Sicily in 1847 in the company of John Proby (see Cat. 19). They met in Palermo and set off on 11 May to travel round the island. They reached Syracuse on 8 June, to find that the modern city afforded some level of comfort after the deprivations of travel through the western part of the island (Lear to Ann, 22.vii.47, TS.).

In a letter to Emily Tennyson, dated 12 October 1852, Lear refers to the painting exhibited here as 'the little Oil-sketch' which he is sending with this letter as a gift to Emily and

49

Alfred: 'The picture represents the great Quarries at Syracuse where the Athenians were imprisoned after their defeat in the Harbour. You see the City on its peninsula (Ortygia) beyond, with the hills bounding the greater harbour on the horizon. Nearer is the broad green belt of cultivation now occupying the sloping ground of part of the old city—and the Quarries themselves overgrown with weedibilities and stuffed full of foliage—on the foreground. I hope you and Alfred may like the little picture' (MS., Tennyson Research Centre, Lincoln).

The picture is a smaller version of the five-foot canvas, *The city of Syracuse from the ancient quarries where the Athenians were imprisoned*, exhibited at the Royal Academy in 1853 (no. 1062). This was the first painting to be made under the influence of the Pre-Raphaelite William Holman Hunt, and represents a major step in the evolution of Lear's landscape painting. Holman Hunt had been brought to Lear's studio at Stratford Place in June 1852 by Robert Martineau (1826–69). The meeting between the two artists came at a particularly opportune moment in Lear's career. Although he had experimented in sketching in oil out of doors (see Cat. 45 and 46), he had normally taken all his topographical and colour information for his oil paintings from the pencil and watercolour drawings executed during his travels. The preparation of the large version of the *Quarries of Syracuse* had conformed to a similar pattern, derived from his extensive series of watercolour drawings of which one is almost identical in composition (see Cat. 19c). By 1852 however, Lear, according to Hunt, appears to have been troubled by the degree to which a painter could be certain of recording a scene truthfully when working in a studio on the basis of rapid pencil studies done in front of the subject. 'When I was about to take leave he frankly inquired of me what I should do to make use of such materials, whether, in short, I could as Roberts and Stanfield did, realize enough to paint pictures from their pencil sketches. For when I set myself to try', he added, 'I often break down in despair' (W. Holman Hunt, *Pre-Raphaelitism and the Pre-Raphaelite Brotherhood*, 1905, p. 328). Hunt took this opportunity to preach the principles of early Pre-Raphaelitism; he advised Lear that, in the case of the *Quarries of Syracuse*, he could either return to Sicily to paint the limestone rocks and figs directly from nature or he would have to find alternative models in England which could be painted in oil directly onto the large canvas. 'Under the open sky, with the sun shining, you would have little difficulty in giving an air of reality to this part of the scene. For distant fields and the hills again you would easily find nature near at hand, only these would have to be adapted to suit the form given in your outlines. Nature would in summer soon supply clouds and azure firmament for your sky without calling too much on your memory. Now what more do you want? You have indicated the presence of innumerable rocks. These you can easily paint in the open air without leaving England' (ibid., pp. 328–9).

With this encouragement Lear agreed to travel to Fairlight, near Hastings, where Hunt was planning to work on his painting *Our English Coasts (Strayed Sheep)* (1852; Tate Gallery, London).

Lear made good progress on the five-foot canvas. For the background he used the same view as Hunt in *Our English Coasts* and for the fig tree he chose as his model a specimen in Frederick North's garden (see Cat. 41*b*). However, the technical problems posed by painting on a large scale in front of the subject caused Lear such problems that he feared that the *Quarries of Syracuse* would be a failure (Lear to Hunt, 6.ii.53, MS., Huntington Library, San Marino). The larger painting, with its reference to a momentous historical event in ancient history was however accepted at the Royal Academy Summer Exhibition of 1853, when it was selected by Henry Lygon, later Earl of Beauchamp, as the Art Union Prize. The picture was sold for £250. Lear was delighted and requested Hunt to tell 'Millais—and W. Rossetti from me.—I am now going out to hop on one leg all the way to Hastings' (MS., n.d., Huntington Library, San Marino). It indicated his faith in the Pre-Raphaelite belief that truthful representation could only be achieved when working in front of nature, a method which he had also employed in another major oil painting, *Thermopylae* (see Cat. 50), and was to use for the last time in *Bassae* (see Cat. 51). MA.S.

PROVENANCE Alfred Tennyson Esq., later Alfred, Lord Tennyson, by family descent; The Hallam, Lord Tennyson Will Trust; 1974, 18 October, Christie's London (lot 191); bt by Mr H. Yordan Obegi.

REFERENCE LEL 1907, p. 314, no. 96.

50 Thermopylae

The Mountains of Thermopylae, 1852 [Col. pl. p. 37
Oil on canvas: 68.5 × 113.8 cm/26 × 44 in
Signed with monogram and dated br.: *ℒ 1852*
City of Bristol Museum and Art Gallery

Travelling southwards from Lamia on his trip through Euboea and Sterea with Charles Church in July 1848 (see Cat. 67), Lear arrived at 'the celebrated pass of Thermopylae, where the few Spartans withstood so many Persians' (Ann, 19.vii.48, TS.). The view of this painting is probably taken looking southwards across the plain of the Spercheios towards the mountains of Thermopylae; the deep gorge in the centre of the composition is the pass of Thermopylae itself.

During the autumn of 1852, Lear was working on at least four subjects in oils: the *Quarries of Syracuse* (see Cat. 49), *Reg-*

50

gio. Calabria (LEL 1907, p. 314, no. 91; Tate Gallery, London), *Venosa. Apulia* (LEL 1907, p. 313, no. 90; Museum of Art, Toledo, Ohio) and *The Mountains of Thermopylae.* By 19 December, both *Reggio. Calabria* and *Venosa. Apulia* were 'done and in frames' (Holman Hunt, 19.xii.52, MS., Huntington Library, San Marino), and by the end of the year, *The Mountains of Thermopylae* must have been completed (Holman Hunt, 16.i.53, MS., Huntington Library, San Marino).

In the preparation of all these paintings, Lear acknowledged his debt to the advice and instruction which he had received from Holman Hunt during the summer of 1852 (see Cat. 49) and during the ensuing Autumn: 'I really cannnot help again expressing my thanks to you for the progress I have made this Autumn . . .' (19.xii.52, MS.). In the case of the *Mountains of Thermopylae*, Lear was more precise as to the nature of this debt. In a letter to William Michael Rossetti, dated 8 February 1853, after discussing the difficulty of capturing the 'particular character of the mountains,' Lear declared, 'the colouring & its mode of being worked out, though I am equally sure they are in that painting the best I have yet tried at, I have not the conscience to take the credit of, for they are solely and wholly the result of Holman Hunts teaching, without which Mt. Oeta would probably have been done in black & white—the sky & sea grim grey, & all the rest umber—for so much are we creatures of habit that we can hardly refrain from partly imitating what all about us save a few consider the "only right way"' (MS., University of British Columbia).

The main source of such instruction in colour may have come from the questions which Lear had posed to Hunt during the evenings at Fairlight, near Hastings, the previous summer. Lear is known to have recorded these in a notebook entitled 'Ye Booke of Hunte', now lost (see Cat. 104).

Although Lear's use of a brighter palette and a white ground owed much to Holman Hunt, his capacity to capture the peculiarly translucent quality of Greek light may also in part be due to his own watercolour practices. Like Turner, Lear translates the white of paper into a thick white ground on canvas. Upon this, as with watercolour, he lays in smooth, thin glazes, working from light to dark rather than the normal oil procedure of working from dark to light. This method ensures that the white of the ground shines through the glazes and contributes to the luminosity of the painting.

In contrast to the carefully composed landscape of Mount Tomorit (Cat. 48), the composition of the *Mountains of Thermopylae* is organised in horizontal bands, the expanse of the landscape being implied by the extension of the mountains beyond the edges of the canvas. This is a formula for handling views with mountains in the distance which Lear used repeatedly in his later oil paintings (eg. *Mount Parnassus*, bought by Lord Clermont, 1860; LEL 1907, p. 316, no. 172; 1979, London, the Fine Art Society, *The Rediscovery of Greece*, no. 125; see also Cat. 60). In addition, Lear concentrates in the *Mountains of Thermopylae* upon the foreground, with its figures in Greek costume, and on the mountain range in the background. This arrangement leaves the middle ground, with the plain of the Spercheios relatively undefined. In this respect, Lear may have been adopting one of Thomas Uwins's principles of landscape painting (see Cat. 47): 'Take care of the greatest distance, and take care of the nearest, and the middle will take care of itself' (Mrs Uwins, *A Memoir of Thomas Uwins R.A.*, 1858, vol. I, p. 49).

The *Mountains of Thermopylae* was exhibited at the British Institution in spring 1853 (no. 428), where it was not well hung. This did not deter F.G. Stephens from writing to Thomas Woolner: 'Lear has a picture at the R.I. which is capital; he delights to acknowledge his obligations to Hunt for instruction while they were staying at Fairlight together. He goes everywhere saying that Hunt taught him all he knows and he has improved wonderfully' (21.iv.53, quoted in A. Woolner, *Thomas Woolner, R.A., Sculptor and Poet: His Life in Letters*, 1917, pp. 58–59).

Lear painted at least one other version of the subject which was sold to Augustus Harcourt in 1872 (LEL 1907, p. 317, no. 243). MA.S.

PROVENANCE William F. Beadon Esq.; Chichester Fortescue; Lady Strachey, by family descent; 1975, bt by the City of Bristol Museum and Art Gallery (with assistance from Government Grant-in-Aid and H.M. Treasury).

EXHIBITIONS 1853, London, British Institution (no. 428); 1975, Bristol, City Museum and Art Gallery, Swansea, Glyn Vivian Art Gallery, *Victorian and Edwardian Paintings* (no. 5).

REFERENCES LEL 1907, p. 314, no. 92, repr. opp. p. 12; Noakes 1979 edn, pp. 111, 114–15; M. Cormack, 'How Pleasant to know Mr. Lear', Museum of Art, Rhode Island School of Design, 1982, p. 6; *The Travels of Edward Lear*, The Fine Art Society, 1983, 'Introduction', p. 12.

51 Bassae

The Temple of Bassae or Phigaleia, in Arcadia from the Oakwoods of Mt. Cotylium. The Hills of Sparta, Ithome and Navarino in the Distance, 1854 [Col. pl. p. 36
Oil on canvas: 142 × 231 cm/56 × 91 in
Signed with monogram and dated br.: *L 1854–55*
The Syndics of the Fitzwilliam Museum, Cambridge

The Temple of Bassae, built in the fifth century BC, lies between Andritsaina and the Ionian Sea in an isolated part of the mountains amid solitary oaks and scattered rocks. Apollo was worshipped here as the god of health.

Lear had visited Bassae during his tour of the Peloponnese with Franklin Lushington in spring 1849 (see Cat. 20*c*). During this trip, Lear made extensive travel studies, including at least two related to this subject (eg. Ashmolean Museum, Oxford). Lear began to paint *Bassae* in 1853, when he was also working on another large painting, *Windsor Castle*, commissioned by Lord Derby (with Appleby and Son Ltd, London 1964).

The recent success of his painting, the *Mountains of Thermopylae* (Cat. 50), had confirmed Lear's conversion to the early Pre-Raphaelite principle of working on the canvas out of doors in front of the subject (Holman Hunt, 16.i.53, MS., Huntington Library, San Marino). Lear determined to apply this principle to both *Windsor Castle* and *The Temple of Bassae*. However, the limitations of the British weather, the fickleness of the light and the onset of autumn appear to have doomed its application to failure. Lear began work on a smaller version of the *Temple of Bassae*, and in order to paint the rocks in the

51

foreground, he travelled to Leicestershire in September 1853. However, bad light and poor eyesight made the detail of foliage in the foreground a strain to paint. Lear abandoned this smaller picture, ordered a seven-foot canvas from Leicester and 'set to work with outline at once as I did at the Syracuse last year . . . Of course the next day, the 4th,—it poured torrents & did so on the 5th, 6. 7th—& 8th.—all day long each day. I got oak boughs indoors, but did no good by so doing.' His luck changed and he had just over a day of fine weather—but then catastrophe struck: 'instantly it came down in waterspouts, & nobody coming to me I absolutely took the 7 foot canvass on my shoulders—& walked off to the inn—a good half mile & more.—To day it rains al solito. I hate giving anything up—it demoralizes one so. If I could only get the *leaves* done, & one little bit of fern, I could get the branches and rocks easily. But the leaves are falling fast . . . Lord! how I wish I could go back to sloshing & Asphaltism [a reference to Sir Joshua Reynolds]' (Holman Hunt, 12.x.[53], MS., Huntington Library, San Marino).

The *Temple of Bassae* was finally completed one year later in the studio. It was exhibited at the Royal Academy of 1855 (no. 319) and subsequently bought by seventy subscribers 'desirous that Mr. Lear's Picture of the 'Temple of Bassae', should find an appropriate and permanent place in the Museum of a Classical University'; they presented it in 1859 to the Fitzwilliam Museum, Cambridge (LLEL 1911, pp. 380–81).

The story of Lear's tribulations in applying to the *Temple of Bassae* the Pre-Raphaelite principle of painting in front of the subject was similar to that encountered in the preparation of *Windsor Castle* (Holman Hunt, 11.vii.53, MS., Huntington Library, San Marino). Taken together, the experiences confirmed Lear's decision to abandon this method of composition and his subsequent oil paintings, like his finished watercolours (see Cat. 37, 38) and Tyrants (see Cat. 39) were all executed in the studio from travel studies. However, the *Temple of Bassae*, despite its rather yellow tonality, does contain a number of references to Lear's debt to Holman Hunt: the rocky ravine in the foreground places the spectator as precariously within the landscape as in the *Quarries of Syracuse*, where a similar disregard for landscape conventions had been introduced into the composition. Second, despite the framing tree on the right, Lear has emphasised the horizontality of the landscape, a method which he had already applied in the *Mountains of Thermopylae* (Cat. 50) as a more accurate statement of the character of this particular spot. Yet, as with the earlier painting, there are also features in the *Temple of Bassae* which link it firmly to Lear's own artistic past: the rocks and tree roots recall the detailed oil sketch of the same subject which he had executed in 1838 above La Cava (Cat. 45), and the small turtle lumbering across the rocks on the right reflects Lear's early delineation of animals at the Zoological Society Gardens and at Knowsley (see Cat. 6–12).

As with many of Lear's large landscape paintings, it is difficult to gauge the degree to which he endowed this picture with a meaning beyond the mere topographical rendering of the scene. In keeping with *Quarries of Syracuse* (Cat. 49) and *Mountains of Thermopylae* (Cat. 50), however, the reference to either historical events or ancient remains may represent the artist's need to raise his topographical landscapes onto a 'poetical' level in keeping with the tradition of historical landscape painting evolved in the seventeenth century and celebrated so fully by an artist for whom Lear had great admiration, J.M.W. Turner (see p. 20 and Cat. 58). This is reinforced by Lear's exercise of poetic licence in this picture by moving the mountain peaks in the background to create a more pleasing and balanced composition and by omitting the whole of the cella within the colonnade. MA.S.

PROVENANCE 1859, bt by subscription and given to the Fitzwilliam Museum, Cambridge.

EXHIBITIONS 1855, London, Royal Academy (no. 319); 1958, London, Arts Council of Great Britain, *Edward Lear* (no. 3).

REFERENCES LEL 1907, p. 314, no. 112; LLEL 1911, pp. 380–81, repr. opp. p. 306; Davidson 1968 edn, p. 80; Noakes 1968 edn, p. 174; Fitzwilliam Museum, *Catalogue of Paintings*, 1977, no. 460; M. Cormack, *How pleasant to know Mr. Lear*, Museum of Art, Rhode Island School of Design, 1982, p. 6; *The Travels of Mr. Lear*, The Fine Art Society, 1983, 'Introduction', p. 13.

52 Philae

Philae [1855] [Col. pl. p. 38
Oil on canvas: 91 × 145 cm/35¾ × 58¼ in
Signed and dated br.: *E. Lear 1855*
Inscribed on a label on the back: *Philae | Edward Lear 1855 | I will see before I die | The Palms & Temples of the south*
Martin R. Davies Collection

Of all the Pharaonic temples and their scenery which Lear saw on his journey along the Nile in January and February 1854, Philae, lying just above the First Cataract, impressed him the most. It was 'the most romantic & varied, & the most capable of being represented; I have 25 drawings . . . but of its colour I can give no idea . . . I shall never forget the 10 comfortable days I passed in my temple chambers' (Ann, 15.ii.54, TS.).

In an earlier letter to his sister he had written: 'It is impossible to describe the place to you, any further than by saying it is more like a real *fairy-island* than anything else I can compare it to. It is very small, & was formerly all covered with temples, of which the ruins of 5 or 6 now only remain. The great temple of Isis, on the terrace of which I now am writing, is so extremely wonderful that no words can give the least idea of it. The Nile is divided here into several channels, by other rocky islands, & beyond you see the desert & the great granite hills of Assouan' (Ann, 7.ii.54, TS.).

Lear was not alone in finding the island of Philae, sacred to the goddess Isis, the most attractive of Egypt's ancient sites. Its beauty was eulogised by the many other tourists who visited it in the nineteenth century, and it was one of the most painted places in Egypt. He also found the extraordinary clarity of light difficult to translate into colour in both his watercolour drawings (see Cat. 27*b*) and his oil paintings.

As well as innumerable watercolours, Lear painted at least twenty oils of Philae. The present example is from a viewpoint on the rocky bank of the Nile to the south of the island, on which can be seen the first pylon at the southern end of the Ptolomaic Temple of Isis and to its right the later Kiosk of Trajan. Lear's attention, however, focussed primarily on the huge boulders and lush palm trees, has been drawn by the natural phenomena of the island's setting rather than by its antiquities.

Philae is one of the earliest of Lear's oil paintings to be

52

53

linked directly with a Tennysonian theme. He inscribed a slip on the back of the painting: 'Philae—"I will see before I die / The Palms & Temples of the South"' ('You ask me, why, tho' ill at ease' [1842]). In 1855 it was bought, together with *Civitella di Subiaco, Sunrise* (1855; Worcester Art Museum, Mass.; see Cat. 47), which recalled to Lear the Tennyson line, 'Morn broadens on the borders of the Dark' ('A Dream of Fair Women', 1833) by a boyhood friend, William Nevill. Writing to Emily Tennyson on 11 November, he said, 'This is the first of the large "Tennyson Landscapes" I have sold, and being in no end of difficulty just now, I have sold it for a mere nothing' (MS., Private Collection). Despite its literary reference, Lear did not use this particular view of Philae for an illustration to the Tennyson poems.

When William Nevill died in January 1874, mindful perhaps of the price he had paid for the paintings, he bequeathed them to Lear, stating in his will, 'to my friend Edward Lear his pictures "Philae looking north", "I will see before I die the Palms and Temples of the East [*sic*]", and "Civitella di Subiaco Sunrise", "Morn broadens on the borders of the Dark" with their frames and my best thanks for the many years of pleasure their possession has given me'. B.L.

PROVENANCE William Nevill Esq.; Spink and Son, London; 1976, 29 November, bt by Martin R. Davies Esq.

EXHIBITION 1856, London, Royal Academy, (no. 625).

REFERENCES LEL 1907, p. 314, no. 116; Amelia Edwards, *A Thousand Miles up the Nile*, London 1974 edn, repr. in colour (in reverse) on cover.

53 Mount Athos

Mount Athos and the Monastery of Stavroniketes, 1857
Oil on canvas: 24.3 × 54.6 cm/13 × 20½ in
Signed with initials bl.
Dated on the stretcher tc.: *1857*
Yale Center for British Art, Paul Mellon Collection

Two previous attempts, in 1848 and 1849, to visit Mount Athos, had been unsuccessful (see Cat. 22), and Lear eventually arrived there in late summer 1856. Accompanied by Giorgio, he spent three weeks exploring the Holy Mountain and its numerous monasteries. Its scenery was magnificent and he was hospitably received by the monks, but he disliked their way of life. As on many other occasions, he suffered much discomfort for the sake of his art: 'oh, Holy Mountain! what have I not suffered to get drawings of you!—Well, Pantokrátora is on the sea; & so is Stavronikétes, & as they are built on rocks, & look up to the mighty peak of Athos—they make noble scenes, a lonely grandeur one hardly can understand' (Ann, 8.x.56, TS.). He gave a more extended review of his impressions to Fortescue: 'But however wondrous & picturesque the [ex]terior and interior of the monasteries—& however abundantly & exquisitely glorious & stupendous the scenery of the mountain, I would not go again to the 'Αγιος 'Ορος for any money, so gloomy—so shockingly unnatural—so lonely—so lying—so unatonably odious seems to me all the atmosphere of such monkery. That half of our species which it is natural to every man to cherish & love best—ignored prohibited & abhored—all life spent in everlasting repetition of monotonous prayers—no sympathy with one's fellowbeans of any nation class or age—the name of Christ on every garment & at every tongues end, but his maxims trodden under foot—God's world & will turned upside down, maimed & caricatured:—if this I say be Xtianity—let Xtianity be rooted out as soon as possible. More pleasing in the sight of the Almighty I really believe, & more like what Jesus Christ intended man to become—is an honest Turk with 6 wives, or a Jew working hard to feed his little old clo'babbies—than these muttering, miserable, muttonhating, manavoiding, misogynic, morose, & merriment=marring, monotoning, many Mulemaking, mocking, mournful, mincedfish & marmalade masticating Monx. Poor old pigs!—Yet one or two were kind enough in their way—dirty as they were: but it is not them,—it is their system I rail at' (Fortescue, 9.x.56, LEL 1907, pp. 41–42). Lear returned to Corfu in October.

His intentions to publish his Mount Athos drawings never materialised, but he painted at least ten oils of the area and reworked the subject of the oil exhibited, as no. 122 of his illustrations to Tennyson: 'Athos, all things fair' ('To EL. on his travels in Greece'; see Cat. 40). The last oil painting of Mount Athos occupied much of his time in the early 1880s and was described by Lushington as his *magnum opus* (Lushington to Hallam Tennyson, 14.x.86, MS., Tennyson Research Centre, Lincoln). The present example was purchased by Mrs Empson, the wife of the vicar of Romsey.

Given the rugged nature of the area, this is a gentler, less dramatic view than one that Lear might have chosen. Both the tonality and the composition, with plants and rocks in the foreground, broad sea and snow-capped mountains, are characteristic of Lear's landscape paintings of this period (see Cat. 54) and combine to produce an image which essentially celebrates the beauty of the location. However, Lear's knowledge of the long Christian monastic tradition of Mount Athos may also have added in his mind an historical dimension to the scene. B.L.

PROVENANCE Mrs Empson; Spink and Son Ltd, London; 1965, bt by Paul Mellon; 1981, December, given to the Yale Center for British Art.

REFERENCES LEL 1907, p. 315, no. 136; Noakes 1968 edn, repr. pp. 142–43.

54 Corfu

Corfu from below Ascension, *c.* 1857
Oil on canvas: 34.3 × 54.6 cm/13 × 21 in
Signed with monogram bl.: *ℒ*
Yale Center for British Art, Gift of Mr and Mrs Michael Coe, 1979

Lear regarded Corfu, his home for more than six years between 1855 and 1864, as the epitome of landscape beauty. Seeing the island for the first time in 1848, he called it a 'Paradise', and in 1856, shortly after he had returned there to live, he wrote: 'I really think no place on Earth can be lovelier than this:—the olives in their half wild & uncared for semi-culture are so perfectly beautiful—& the views of every part of the Albanian coast so exquisitely majestic' (W. Martin Leake, 22.ii.56, MS., Hertfordshire County Council Record Office).

That spring he began searching for a suitable subject for a large picture. He chose the view from above the village of Ascension, now Analipsis, looking across a promontory to the Citadel of Corfu and the mountains of Albania in the distance. In a letter to Ann he wrote: 'I have some idea of devoting a good bit of time to illustrating this little promontory for it is . . . full of interest, as the old city of Ascension (Coreyra), was built on it, ancient coins and marbles are still found' (29.vi.56, TS.). The present exhibit is a similar view but taken from lower down, below the village, and just above the rocky shore with the ruins of a Hellenistic temple in the foreground. Lear painted at least 15 oils of the view from above or below Ascension, believing that 'the whole scene, in general, & in detail, was so perfectly lovely' (Ann, 3.xii.57, TS.).

In Corfu, Lear found a community who would buy his pictures, although generally with little understanding of them. The society of the British garrison of the island seemed to him tedious and superficial. 'The sort of lonely feeling of having no one who can sympathyze professionally with one's goings on, is very odious at times,' he told Fortescue (19.ii.56, LEL 1907, p. 34). His boredom is reflected in his gossip, as when he told Fortescue: 'Madam Vitalis the Greek Consul's wife has purchased a large red maccaw. Mrs Macfarlane's female domestic has fallen downstairs, by which precipitate act Mrs. M's baby has been killed. Sir Gorgeous Figginson Blowing has had an attack of fever. Colonel Campbell (first cousin of Sir J. Simeon) dined with Mr. Lear the Artist on Thursday. On Friday that accomplished person entertained Mr. Bunsen & Mr. Justice Lushington. Capt. R. has purchased a Cornopeon, & practises on it, (Mrs G invariably calls it a cornicopean.) but it is not heard generally, on account of the superior row made by Mrs. Vitalis' maccaw, Capt. P's howling dogs, & about 400 turkey who live at ease about the terrace and adopt a remarkable gobble at certain periods' (10.i.58, LEL 1907, p. 79). Though depressed by such triviality, he was constantly uplifted by his natural surroundings, writing in his diary the year before he left the island, 'the more I see of this place, so the more I feel that no other spot on earth can be fuller of beauty & variety of beauty' (Diary, 30.iii.63).

The combination of a peaceful, rural scene, rocky shoreline, calm, blue sea and distant snow-capped mountains, suggests an Arcadian landscape reminiscent of Claude. During the 1830s, Lear had compared the landscape around Rome to paintings by Claude and throughout his life he remained aware of this landscape convention. As on several other occasions, he introduces ancient ruins to invest the landscape with an historical dimension. B.L.

PROVENANCE Alfred Seymour Esq.; Mr and Mrs Michael Coe; 1979, given to the Yale Center for British Art.

EXHIBITION 1968, Worcester Mass., Worcester Museum of Art, *Edward Lear: Painter, Poet and Draughtsman* (no. 87).

55 Mount Sinai

Mount Sinai with the Monastery of St. Catherine in the Distance, 1858 [Col. pl. p. 33
Oil on panel: diam. 15 cm/6 in
Signed with monogram and dated bl.: *ℒ 1858*
Private Collection

On 12 January 1849 Lear, in the company of John Cross, whom he had met at Knowsley, left Cairo, intending to travel via Sinai to Beirut (Lord Derby, 12.i.49, MS., Liverpool Public Record Office).

Before setting out, he told Ann of the extensive preparations for their desert journey, adding, 'I have got a capital hat lined with green, & a double umbrella—& a green gauze veil, and an Arab cloak, and a thick Capote' (Ann, 11.i.49, TS.). On 24 January they reached 'El Raha, the great plain which universal tradition has affixed as the site of the Israelites camp below the immense mountain—called Horeb or Sinai. The excessive & wonderful grandeur of the spot is not to be described, though I hope to shew you drawings of it—: the adaptation of the whole scene to that recorded in Scripture is equally astonishing' (Ann, 16.i.49, MS., Private Collection). Lear believed the recent theories questioning the traditional identification of the mountain with that where Moses received the

Tablets of the Law (*Exodus* XX–XXXIV) to be absurd; for him its biblical associations remained inviolable.

In buoyant spirits Lear made several drawings of the peaks surrounding the monastery of St Catherine. He returned to the subject for both oils and watercolours several times during his career (see Cat. 37*f*). One of the last was included in the Tennyson series (no. 183), *On Sinai's peaks* (see Cat. 42).

The composition of this small oil sketch is similar to a larger oil, also circular, dated five years earlier, which was bought by T. Gambier Parry, a friend of Lear's from Roman days. Although unusual in Lear's work, the circular format of *Mount Sinai* is not unique: he used the same format for a watercolour

55

of a view from Ascension on Corfu (collection of Sir Steven Runciman). In addition there is a drawing at Houghton Library, Harvard University, of camels in a desert (pencil, sepia ink and notes on paper: 12.2 × 35.7 cm/$4\frac{13}{16}$ × $14\frac{1}{16}$ in), dated 20 January 1849 and inscribed 'near Wady Gharundel' which, although rectangular, has a circular dotted line around it marked 'AA' and inscribed 'a suggestion for a round picture'.

It is possible that the present exhibit is related to the painting bought by C.A. Knight, with whom Lear had travelled in the Abruzzi (see Cat. 18), in 1872 (LEL 1907, p. 317, no. 246).

Lear and Cross were back in Suez on 4 February and started for Palestine by way of Gaza on the sixth. However the next day the weather changed and Lear became ill. Reluctantly he decided not to continue with the journey and returned to Suez.

B.L.

PROVENANCE 1984, 26 January, Sotheby's, London (lot 272); bt by Mallet; bt by present owner.

56 Jerusalem

Jerusalem from the Mount of Olives, Sunrise, 1859
Oil on canvas: 40 × 60.3 cm/$15\frac{3}{4}$ × $23\frac{3}{4}$ in [Col. pl. p. 41
Signed, inscribed and dated on label on back and on stretcher: *Jerusalem from the Mount of Olives, Sunrise From Drawings made by me in April/May 1858 Painted for Sir James Reid—Edward Lear 1858/9*
Private Collection

Lear's two previous attempts to visit Palestine with John Cross in 1849 (see Cat. 55) and with William Holman Hunt in 1854 had not materialised; instead he travelled there from Corfu in 1858. He arrived in Jerusalem on 27 March and the next day, Palm Sunday, explored the country immediately outside the walls: 'We crossed the Kidron & went up the Mount of Olives—every step bringing fresh beauty to the city uprising behind. At the top, by the Church of Ascension the view is wonderfully beautiful indeed' (Diary, 28.iii.58). Because of the Easter crowds, however, he decided to continue on southwards to Petra. He returned to Jerusalem on 20 April and began work on a painting of Jerusalem at sunset which Lady Waldegrave had commissioned (Ann, 23.iv.58, 28.iv.58, 2.v.58, TS.).

The present exhibit shows Jerusalem from an almost identical viewpoint, but at sunrise. Lear later explained to Lady Waldegrave his difficulties in finding a suitable viewpoint at sunset for her picture: the rays of the setting sun obscured the 'great & splendid prospect of the whole city' from the East, but eventually he 'stumbled on an oblique North-East view, which I mean to paint'. From this point on the Mount of Olives could be seen 'the site of the temple & the 2 domes,—and it shews the ravine of the valley of Jehosaphat, over which the city looks:—and Absalom's pillar—(if so be it is his pillar—), the village of Siloam, part of Aceldama, & Gethsemane are all included in the landscape. And besides this the sun, at sunset, catches the sides of the larger Eastern buildings, while all the upper part of the city is in shadow;—added to all which there is an unlimited foreground of figs, olives, & pomegranates, not to speak of goats, sheep, & huming beings' (Lady Waldegrave, 27.v.58, MS., Somerset Record Office, Taunton).

During a fortnight spent studying this view he 'drew all its details & came to understand its characteristics completely'; he also purchased photographs 'in order that I might do justice exactly to the scene' (ibid.). Lear's thoroughness reflects his serious attitude to landscape painting. He would also have been conscious of the time and care devoted to the representation of Jerusalem by his friends, William Holman Hunt and Thomas Seddon, four years earlier (Seddon had spent four months camped outside the city to work on his painting of the *Valley of Jehoshophat* [Tate Gallery, London]). In his own painting Lear appears to emulate some of the Pre-Raphaelite methods, notably in the high viewpoint, in the diagonal of the hillside, more strongly emphasised in the painting than in the drawings (for example one signed, inscribed and dated 1858, on 13 March 1969 sold at Sotheby's, London [lot 138]) and in the detailed treatment of the plants growing among the rocks in the foreground. However, although both Hunt and Thomas Seddon had admired the view from the Mount of Olives (William Holman Hunt, *Pre-Raphaelitism and the Pre-Raphaelite Brotherhood*, 1905, I, p. 403; John P. Seddon, *Memoir and Letters of the Late Thomas Seddon*, 1858, p. 204), they had chosen different vantage points for their own representations of Jerusalem.

The Mount of Olives, like everywhere else in and around Jerusalem, had strong Biblical associations. Although Lear's reasons for his choice of this viewpoint seem to have been purely pictorial, he was as much aware of the associations of the Holy City and its surroundings as the many other visitors there during the nineteenth century. Nor was he alone in his

56

disgust at the dissent and greed so evident among the various religious factions in the city. In his letter to Lady Waldegrave he expresses a sentiment felt by many: 'And your memories of its interior are but horrid dreams of squalor & filth, clamour & uneasiness, hatred & malice & all uncharitableness. But the outside is full of melancholy glory, exquisite beauty & a world of past history of all ages:—every point forcing you to think on a vastly dim receding past, or a time of Roman war & splendour, (for Ælia Capitolium was a fine city) or a smash of Moslem & Crusader years, with long long dull winter of deep decay through centuries of misrule. The Arab & his sheep are alone the wanderers on the pleasant vallies and breezy hills round Zion:—the file of slow camels all that brings to mind the commerce of Tyre & other bygone merchandize' (27.v.58, LEL 1907, p. 106).

Sir James Reid, for whom the present exhibit was painted, had been Supreme Judge in the Ionian Islands when Lear was living in Corfu before his visit to the Holy Land. Reid had first suggested a painting of Jerusalem in February 1858 but for Sir Moses Montefiore rather than for himself (Lear to Fortescue, 27.ii.58, LEL 1907, p. 88). A year later Lear wrote to Ann from Rome that several of his paintings from his Holy Land trip were well advanced, including Lady Reid's Jerusalem (3.ii.59, TS.), and a *Jerusalem, Sunrise* is recorded in Lady Strachey's list of Lear's paintings for 1859 as acquired by Sir James Reid (no. 148, LEL 1907, p. 315); two further subjects as well as Lady Waldegrave's are also included in this list, at least one, Lord Clermont's, representing the same view. Writing to Lady Waldegrave on 26 March 1859 he protested that he would not paint the scene again, 'for the minute architecture has tried my sight a good deal, & moreover I hold that an Artist loses much of his originality by repetition of his works' (LEL 1907, p. 133). B.L.

PROVENANCE 1859, painted for Sir James Reid; 1980, 29 February, Christie's, London (lot 14), bt by present owner.

EXHIBITIONS 1980, London, The Fine Art Society, *Travellers Beyond the Grand Tour* (no. 3); 1983, London, The Fine Art Society, *The Travels of Edward Lear* (no. 89); 1984, London, Royal Academy, *The Orientalists: Delacroix to Matisse. European Painters in North Africa and the Near East* (no. 83).

REFERENCES LEL 1907, pp. 88, 315, no. 148.

57 Mar Saba

Mar Sabbas, 1860
Oil on canvas: 27.6 × 22.8 cm/$10\frac{13}{16} \times 8\frac{15}{16}$ in
Inscribed on a label on the back: *Monastery of Mar Sabbas on the Kedron between [?] Jerusalem and the Dead Sea. Painted from a Drawing made there in 1858 by Edward Lear. 18[?]60*
Private Collection

From Jerusalem, Lear travelled to Mar Saba which he reached on 30 May, 'a wonderful monastery "all as one cut of a

57

Cheshire cheese" as my man said' (Fortescue, 27.v.58, LEL 1907, p. 108). Writing to Ann, he described its situation 'where the Kedron (when it has water in it) runs steeply down to the Dead Sea between terrific walls of perpendicular rock. Down the sides of this—stuck against it as it were, is the monastery, fortified by immense walls—& oddly differing from my Athos acquaintances in as much as it is all sand colour—all like the desert round it. If it was not for the towers & the white domed church it would hardly seem separate from the rocks . . . the whole place, even on May 1st was so like an oven that I felt as if I should be baked, & came away (after making some good drawings) as early as I could' (Ann, 21.v.58, TS.).

The monastery was built around a cave in the rock inhabited by St Saba, an early Christian hermit, in the fifth and sixth centuries AD. Because of its history, as well as its formidable scenery, it was visited by many European travellers in Palestine: 'In the wild grandeur of its situation, Mar Saba is the most extraordinary building in Palestine' (Murray, *Handbook for Travellers in Syria and Palestine*, 1858, p. 204). A thumbnail sketch for the oil exhibited here appears in Lear's letter to Ann (21.v.58, TS.). In the painting Lear permits the demands of the subject to dictate the shape of his composition, and although he seldom uses a vertical format in his landscapes, he here handles it with assurance.

This appears to be Lear's only oil of the subject, but a slightly different view of the scene was used as no. 48 in his Tennyson series, illustrating the line 'Girt round with blackness' from 'The Palace of Art', 1842 (Cat. 43*a*). B.L.

PROVENANCE Capt. Huish; Fielding and Morley Fletcher Paintings and Drawings; bt by present owner.

EXHIBITION 1968, London, Gooden and Fox Ltd, *Edward Lear* (no. 113).

REFERENCE LEL 1907, p. 316, no. 168.

58 Mont Blanc

Mont Blanc from Pont Pellisier [1862] [Col. pl. p. 34
Oil on canvas: 34.3 × 54 cm/13½ × 21¼ in
Signed with a monogram br.: ℒ
Morton Morris and Company Ltd

Lear's decision to travel to Switzerland in the summer of 1854 (see Cat. 28) was prompted in part by the realisation 'that Swiss views always sell' (Holman Hunt, 11.ix.54, MS., University of British Columbia). 'I really hope some day to paint a Swiss Landscape well,' he told Hunt, 'but I must come again before I can do so, as I feel—as yet at least, that I have not sufficiently studied the characteristics of this astonishing new world. Nevertheless I should far prefer seeing Syria & Asia Minor' (ibid.).

The talk of Syria may well have been prompted by Holman Hunt's protracted stay, from February 1854 to January 1856, in Egypt, the Holy Land, Syria, Lebanon and Constantinople during which he was working on, amongst other compositions, *The Scapegoat* (1854–55, exhibited 1856; Lady Lever Art Gallery, Port Sunlight). Yet Lear may also have been expressing a preference both for the wider, less claustrophobic landscape of open plain and mountain (see Cat. 50, 60) and for landscape with historical associations which Switzerland appeared to lack. Nevertheless, he wrote to Ann from Zermatt that he was 'greatly delighted with what I have seen of Switzerland, though I do not think I can ever paint it; to represent it well, it requires more hard labour than the landscape of any country I am acquainted with,—because, though there are no great distances, yet all around one is as it were on perpendicular & in & out surface,—filled up with innumerable details, to draw which, requires immense study' (23.viii.54, TS.).

It was a study he decided not to pursue, for he did not return to make more drawings in Switzerland. However, he had felt confident enough to paint *The Jungfrau, Interlaken* (1854) after his return (LEL 1907, p. 314, no. 105) and, by 1862, this view of Mont Blanc from Pont Pellissar; it was acquired by Charles Roundell together with a painting of the *Dead Sea* (LEL 1907, p. 317, no. 212). He subsequently painted at least a further five Swiss landscapes, including three other views of Mont Blanc: *Mont Blanc. Col de Baume* (LEL 1907, p. 318, no. 279), *Mont Blanc. Courmayeur* (ibid., p. 318, no. 280) and *Mont Blanc. Mer de Glace* (ibid., p. 318, no. 281).

The Swiss Alps had become a popular subject for artists and collectors from the second half of the eighteenth century, largely through the example of Philippe de Loutherbourg (1740–1812) and A.L.R. Ducros (1748–1810). By the mid-nineteenth century, the Alps had become frequented by geol-

58

ogists and summer tourists alike whose expectations were in part informed by the frequent representation of these sublime landscapes in the paintings of J.M.W. Turner. Lear certainly displays knowledge of Turner's mountain landscapes since in his Indian Journal he records his astonishment in front of the awesome view of Mt Kangchenjunga, comparing the view in the afternoon to 'Turneresque colour & mist & space' (I.J., MS.). Indeed as with *Mt. Kinchinjunga* (and also *Mt. Tomohrit*, Cat. 48), Lear employs a 'v' shaped composition which provides a 'natural' frame for the subject of the painting—the mountain. However, by placing the spectator at ground level rather than on an elevated platform, Lear has benefited from the full effect of the drive up the valley toward Mont Blanc, a device which had been used in a much earlier work by Turner, *Bonneville* (M. Butlin and J. Joll, *The Complete Paintings of J.M.W. Turner*, 1984 edn, no. 50). MA.S.

PROVENANCE S. Roundell Esq.; J. Baskett; 1978, 3 February, Christie's London (lot 202); bt by Morton Morris and Company Ltd.

EXHIBITION 1968, London, Gooden and Fox Ltd, *Edward Lear* (no. 117).

REFERENCE LEL 1907, p. 317, no. 211.

59 Venice

Venice, 1866
Oil on canvas: 67.3 × 114.3 cm/$26\frac{1}{2}$ × 45 in
Inscribed, signed and dated on the verso: *Venice. Painted for Frances Countess Waldegrave, from sketches made by me at Venice, November, 1866. Edward Lear.*
Private Collection

Throughout the nineteenth century Venice remained a popular subject among British artists. In spite of Lear's wish to be associated with the best of such painters, notably Turner, he did not find Venice congenial. Visiting it for the first time in 1857, he wrote to Ann: 'Now, as you will ask me my impressions of Venice, I may as well shock you a good thumping shock at once by saying I don't care a bit for it, & never wish to see it again. Rotterdam & The Hague are 50 times as pretty—(with their green trees & pretty costumes—) barring some of the few buildings here. But those very buildings have been so stuffed & crammed in to my sense since I was a child, that I knew the size, place, colour & effect of all & every one beforehand—& derived not one whit more pleasure from seeing them there, than in any of the many theatre scenes, Diaramas, Panoramas, & all other ramas whatever. Nay—Staupil's—Cooke's & Canalette's pictures please me far better, inasmuch as I cannot in them smell these most stinking canals.—Ugh! A place whose attributes are those (externally) of mere architecture can be completely portrayed & represented to the mind.—Thousands of descriptions & millions of paintings could not do so with Egypt, Sinai, Greece, Sicily, or Switzerland, because the glories & the beauties of nature are in their changes infinite:—here it is wholly otherwise: at least it is so to me' (23.v.57, TS.). Nevertheless, eight years later in 1865, perhaps conscious of the need to paint a traditional subject, he undertook a commission from Lady Waldegrave to make an oil painting of the city. The result is one of the few townscapes Lear ever attempted (another was *Street Scene in Lekhreda*, a town in North Albania, RA 1851 [no. 170]).

Lady Waldegrave does not seem to have specified a location for her painting, and Lear's choice of this canal view seems strange in the light of his antipathy towards urban subjects.

Although on this second visit he had been more impressed by Venice, particularly by the abundance of colour (Diary, 16.xi.65), the components of so many of his oil paintings—trees, rocks and mountains—were missing. He therefore found work on the painting during the winter of 1865–66 (in Malta; Cat. 30) a difficult task. 'These Venetian scenes are no delight to me', he wrote in his diary on 11 January 1866, 'as repeating a life of at best curiosity & interest,—but seldom great pleasure:—never—the poetry of plain or mountains—or woods—or rocks, Man-work—not God work'. Lear was essentially a painter of natural rather than man-made landscape. His unease with his subject is reflected in this painting's lack of individuality.

Lear painted another Venetian scene, *Santa Maria della Salute*, which was bought by Henry Willett in January 1873 (see Cat. 31; exhibited 1981, Thomas Agnew and Sons Ltd, *Life and Landscape in Britain 1670 to 1870* [no. 18]). B.L.

PROVENANCE Frances, Countess Waldegrave, by family descent.

REFERENCES LEL 1907, p. 317, no. 219.

60 Lebanon

Mount Lebanon [1866] [Col. pl. p. 40
Oil on canvas: 36.8 × 67.9 cm/$14\frac{1}{2}$ × $26\frac{3}{4}$ in
Signed with monogram br.:
Inscribed on the original frame: *Mount Lebanon. 1866*
Standard Chartered Bank, London

Lear arrived in Beirut by steamer from Jaffa on 13 May 1858, having spent nearly two arduous but fulfilling months in Palestine. 'This place', he wrote to Ann, 'is quite different from anything in southern Palestine—& reminds me more of Naples by its numerous villas & gardens, & the civil & gay people. I was only looking about me yesterday, but today I shall make a drawing of Mt. Lebanon, & the Bay & town—which are really lovely as a whole . . .' (Ann, 14.v.58, TS.).

However, this subject was no more beautiful than other mountain and coastal scenery he had seen, and it lacked the

59

60

61

comprehensive scriptural and historical associations which had affected him so deeply in Palestine. As with *Kasr-es-Saad* (Cat. 62), remarkable scenery could be an inspiration to Lear for its own sake. The horizontal format of the composition to which the scene lent itself was one with which Lear felt at home (see Cat. 50), and in this case he may have taken certain liberties with the shape of the bay by extending it beyond the left-hand edge of the canvas. This emphasis upon horizontality is reinforced by the placing of the rocky promontory in the foreground and by the laying in of broad, smooth glazes in bands parallel to the sea shore and mountain tops.

Lear painted at least four oils depicting Beirut. In 1866 a friend, Edgar Drummond, expressed some pleasure in the earliest of these, painted in 1860–61, and on 22 September Lear wrote to tell him that he had reduced the price from three hundred guineas to two hundred, adding, 'if you should still wish to possess the Beirut, altho' it might not be convenient to you to do so by paying for it at once, I want you to know that you may have it—(only giving me a note that it was bought for so much,)—& pay for it *at any time that best suits you—in part or at once*' (MS., Private Collection). Drummond bought the picture, but such an approach from Lear was a mistake, contributing to the growing belief in the public mind that he had failed as a painter (see Introduction). B.L.

PROVENANCE Southwark Diocesan Board of Finance; 1977, bt by Hazlitt Gooden and Fox Ltd, London; bt by Standard Chartered Bank.

61 Gizeh

The Pyramids Road, Gizah, 1873 [Col. pl. p. 39
Oil on canvas: 52.1 × 103.2 cm/$20\frac{1}{2} \times 40\frac{5}{8}$ in
Signed with monogram and dated bl.: *Æ 1873*
Inscribed on an old label on the back: *A View of the Pyramids Road at Gizah, with the avenue of Trees planted in 1868 by the Empress Eugenie, at the opening of the SUEZ CANAL*
Private Collection

In a letter to Fortescue, Lear refers to 'two pictures of the Pirrybids' which Lord Northbrook (Cat. 34) had commissioned (LLEL 1911, p. 45). The present exhibit may be one of these. The other is possibly *The Pyramids of Gizeh* (1968, London, Gooden and Fox Ltd [no. 22]). Lear had visited Cairo on four previous occasions but in order to gain fresh inspiration for these paintings he spent a few days there in October 1872. He was on his way to Suez to pick up a boat for India where Lord Northbrook, recently appointed Viceroy, had invited him to stay.

In his diary, Lear commented on the changes which had taken place in Cairo since his last visit, for example, 'Nothing in all life is so amazingly interesting as this new road & avenue—literally all the way to the Pyramids!!!—I could hardly believe my own senses, remembering the place in 1867' (Diary, 13.x.72). So taken was he with the scene that he went out again the next day to draw it: 'The effect of this causeway in the middle of wide waters is singular . . . & were one sure of quiet, there is much of poetry in the scene, but it wants thought and arrangement' (Diary, 14.x.72). Pestered by insects and the local villagers he found drawing hard work: 'I drew again at the head of the great Acacia avenue—but flies made the work *impossible*' (ibid.). At this point a thumbnail sketch of the *Pyramids Road* appears in the margin. Another drawing in pencil is inscribed and dated 'Cairo Oct 14 (1.30. PM) 1872' (Houghton Library, Harvard University).

Shortly before leaving for India, Lear had had a bad fall. He was tired and distraught, and when there was a commotion over his baggage at Suez he impetuously abandoned the Indian journey and returned to Alexandria: 'the landscape painter does not purSuez eastern journey farther' (Fortescue, 24.xi.72, LLEL 1911, p. 151).

Nothing of Lear's irascibility is reflected in his serene painting. It is a highly original variation of the much-painted theme of the Pyramids. By taking a viewpoint at the end of the long avenue of thickly-foliaged acacia trees, planted in 1868, he created a startling composition. Unlike Holman Hunt, who found 'nothing more than antiquarian interest as landscape' (*Pre-Raphaelitism and the Pre-Raphaelite Brotherhood*, 1905, pp. 380–81) in the scenery around Cairo, Lear was intrigued by the juxtaposition of the present and the past (see Cat. 52, 54). He had succeeded in extracting from the scene the poetry of which he wrote. B.L.

PROVENANCE The Earl of Northbrook; The Fine Art Society; bt by the present owner.

EXHIBITION 1983, London, The Fine Art Society, *The Travels of Edward Lear* (no. 80); 1984, London, Royal Academy, *The Orientalists: Delacroix to Matisse. European Painters in North Africa and the Near East* (no. 85); 1984, Washington DC, National Gallery of Art, *The Orientalists: Delacroix to Matisse. The Allure of North Africa and the Near East* (no. 63).

62

62 Kasr-es-Saiyyad

Kasr-es-Saad, 1877 [Col. pl. p. 40
Oil on canvas: 55.9 × 137.2 cm/22 × 54 in
Signed with monogram bl.: ℒ
Private Collection

On his way up the Nile in January 1854 Lear wrote enthusiastically to Ann of the scenery at Kasr-es-Saad (now Kasr-es-Saiyyad): 'Imagine immense cliffs, quite perpendicular about as high as St. Paul's & of yellow stone—rising from the most exquisite meadows all along the river! while below them are villages almost hidden in palms' (Ann, 18.i.54, TS.). The scene suggested to Lear Tennyson's line, 'And the crag that fronts the Even', and is no. 23 in his series of Tennyson illustrations (see Cat. 42). Kasr-es-Saiyyad, near Kena, was not a well-known historical site, but its grandiose scenery of tall cliffs set against the flat water of the Nile, was of the type that often appealed to Lear. As at Philae, it was natural phenomena that inspired him more than ancient ruins. Unlike the famous antiquities along the Nile, this place was not a common subject for artists, but he depicted it in at least four oils.

This late example was purchased, with *Mount Tomohrit* (see Cat. 48), by Lady Ashburton, who had earlier bought his large oil of *The Cedars* (see Cat. 26). Lear's diary reveals that he was working on it in December 1872; he writes that he '"took up" the Crag that fronts the Evening, which I glazed & bebothered all over' (27.ii.72). Despite the use of a white ground and broad smooth glazes of colour, such as he had used in *Corfu* (see Cat. 54) and *Lebanon* (see Cat. 60) this painting had not escaped Lear's tendency in later life to overwork his canvases.

The painting was well received. In 1880 he wrote to Fortescue that he had seen it at Lady Ashburton's 'let into the wall in vast black frame all the room being gilt leather! Never saw anything so fine of my own doing before—& walked afterwards with a Nelevated & superb deportment & a sweet smile on everybody I met' (7.xii.82, LLEL 1911, p. 231). B.L.

PROVENANCE Louisa, Lady Ashburton, by family descent.

EXHIBITION 1968, London, Gooden and Fox Ltd, *Edward Lear* (no. 125).

REFERENCES LEL 1907, p. 318, no. 257; Davidson 1968 edn, p. 251.

63 Kangchenjunga

Kinchinjunga, 1877
Oil on canvas: 118 × 180 cm/46 $\frac{7}{16}$ × 70 $\frac{7}{8}$ in
Signed with monogram and dated br.: ℒ *1877*
Cynon Valley Borough Council

In 1871 Lord Northbrook (see Cat. 114) was appointed Viceroy of India. Within weeks he had invited Lear to go there as his guest so that he might see and draw the country (see Cat. 34).

In the summer of 1872, Lear visited England where he received commissions for Indian paintings. One of these was from Lord Aberdare, who suggested that Lear should choose his own subject for the painting. Writing to Aberdare on 11 September 1872, Lear said 'Thank you for your good wishes, India=wise: and particularly also for your commission—which I will take the greatest pains with. But will you not tell me if you have any special wish for one view more than another. Shall I paint Jingerry Wangerry Bang, or Wizzibizzi-gollyworryboo?' (MS., Glamorgan Record Office).

Lear's first thought was to paint Benares (see Cat. 34*d*), and on 13 December 1873, shortly after he had arrived in India, he made drawings of the great ghat, 'yet it seems to me hardly a possibly subject for Lord Aberdare's view.' (I.J., MS.).

He reached Darjeeling in the middle of January, 1874, and decided that the subject for Lord Aberdare's painting would be Mount Kangchenjunga, one of the highest peaks in the Himalayas. He painted three large oils of this spectacular scene: for Louisa, Lady Ashburton (Private Collection, U.S.A.), for Lord Northbrook (Private Collection, U.S.A.) and the present exhibit.

His response to the mountain scenery was mixed. '*Wonderful wonderful* view of Kinchinjunga !!!!!' he wrote in his diary on 17 January; but the next day he noted that 'Kinchinjunga is not—so it seems to me—a sympathetic mountain; it is so far off, so very god=like & stupendous, & all that great world of dark opal vallies full of misty, hardly to be imagined forms,—besides the all but impossibility of expressing the whole as a scene—make-up a rather distracting and repelling whole.' On 19 January he thought 'Kinchinjunga at sunrise is a glory not to be forgotten; Kinchinjunga PM is apt to become a wonderful hash of Turneresque colour & mist &

63

space but with little claim to forming a picture of grand effect' (I.J., MS.). The flora also impressed him for he wrote to Fortescue that 'the foregrounds of ferns are truly bunderful—only there are no apes & no parrots & no nothing alive—which vexes me' (Lady Waldegrave, 24.i.74, LLEL 1911, p. 170).

On 22 January he went to Doyle's shop, 'where I buy 2 of his & 14 of Shepherd and Bourne's Photographs,' (I.J., MS.) presumably as *aides-mémoire* to the scenery .

Back in San Remo in September 1875, Lear settled to work on his Indian paintings. 'I intend that the "Kinchinjunga" shall be so good a picture' he told Lord Aberdare, 'that nobody will ever be able,—if it is hung in your Dining room—to eat any dinner along of contemplating it,—so that the painting will not only be a desirable, but a highly economical object. And I shall fully trust that all future grandchildren of yours & Lady Aberdare will be Christened Kinchinjunga as an additional appellation' (26.ix.75, MS., Robert Manning Strozier Library, Florida State University).

In December he had some canvases sent out from England. Work on the paintings was soon well advanced, and in May of 1877 the Aberdare and Ashburton *Kinchinjungas* were despatched to London. Writing to Lady Aberdare on 11 August that year he said: 'I hope you will kindly write me a line, when the "Kinchinjunga" arrived at Duffryn, to tell me how you like it. All I beg of you particularly is this,—that if it stands on the ground, you will put up a railing to prevent the children—particularly the twins, from falling over the edge into the Abyss. Any slight wire fence will do' (MS., Glamorgan Record Office).

Lord Aberdare was delighted with his painting, and Lear responded to their thanks: 'I am in a Norfle state of sattlesphaction & delight at your & Lady Aberdare's letters just now derived. I am really immensely pleased that the Venerable the Kinchinjunga is so well placed & so much liked. After all it is better to be the means of giving armless pleasure to a limited number of people, than to be the means of slaughtering indefinite thousands—though I grant the latter function requires the greater ability' (23.viii.1877, MS., Robert Manning Strozier Library, Florida State University).

The awesome Himalayan scenery of Kangchenjunga is a supreme example of the sublime in its traditional (eighteenth-century) sense. Lear's concern, in his use of a dramatic V-shaped format (see also Cat. 48), was to evoke the contrary feelings of attraction and repulsion which such a landscape might inspire in a spectator, and by which he himself had been affected. The main subject, namely the mountain, in the three paintings is substantially the same. But the disposition of such details as the foreground foliage, rock ledge and figures around the Buddhist shrine differs between the Aberdare and Ashburton canvases, and is thus an example of poetic licence with which Lear treated many of his landscapes to gain specific pictorial effect. On several occasions he referred to himself as a 'Painter of Poetical Topography' (for example, Fortescue, 22.viii.81, LLEL 1911, p. 245); his painting of *Mount Kinchinjunga* would seem to justify this claim.

A different view of Kangchenjunga, from Darjeeling, is number 145 in Lear's illustrations of Tennyson's poems (see Cat. 42). B.L.

PROVENANCE 1877, Henry Austin Bruce, 1st Baron Aberdare; early 1920s, given by Lord Aberdare to the Mountain Ash Urban District Council (after 1974, Cynon Valley Borough Council).

REFERENCES LEL 1907, p. 318, no. 275; Davidson 1968 edn, pp. 227–28, 243.

ILLUSTRATED TRAVEL BOOKS

Between 1841 and 1870, Lear published seven books illustrating his travels; of these, four also had a discursive text describing the journeys he made. An additional five or six journals kept on other travels were prepared, but not published by Lear (see Cat. 109).

Two of these without extensive text—*Views in Rome and its Environs* and *Views in the Seven Ionian Islands*—reproduce illustrations of places known to many English people. Those which also contain an account of Lear's travels describe and illustrate places and ways of life little known to the English; they are in some ways the travel equivalents of the books of natural history to which Lear had contributed, where newly discovered species were also described and illustrated. They are not travel guides but accounts of Lear's own journeys, filled with his descriptions of his response to the countryside, the people and the customs, with humorous accounts of the extraordinary situations in which he frequently found himself. Lear described his *Journals of a Landscape Painter in Albania, &c.* (1851) as 'the gleanings of a landscape painter' (introduction, p. 3), and Tennyson's response, 'To E.L., on his travels in Greece', was the highest praise he could have sought.

Illyrian woodlands, echoing falls
Of water, sheets of summer glass,
The long divine Peneian pass,
The vast Akrokeraunian walls,

Tomohrit, Athos, all things fair,
With such a pencil, such a pen,
You shadow forth to distant men,
I read and felt that I was there:

And trust me while I turn'd the page,
And track'd you still on classic ground,
I grew in gladness till I found
My spirits in the golden age.

For me the torrent ever pour'd
And glisten'd—here and there alone
The broad-limb'd Gods at random thrown
By fountain-urns;—and Naiads oar'd

A glimmering shoulder under gloom
Of cavern pillars; on the swell
The silver lily heaved and fell;
And many a slope was rich in bloom

From him that on the mountain lea
By dancing rivulets fed his flocks
To him who sat upon the rocks,
And fluted to the morning sea.

Certainly, the response Lear hoped for was not necessarily conventional. Writing to Lord Aberdare (then Henry Bruce) on 3 July 1868, Lear said:

'I shall examine you with the following parrotgraph, eggstracted from a work on Corsica I am writing. / "The sun, hidden by a cloud, lighted up the depths of the tops of the bottoms of the heights of the Corsican Pinewoods. On their loftiest branches the sky blue moufflon was perched—pouring forth his plaintive but promethean warblings. Far below, myriads of angry Bombyxes pursued the timed flights of Broccio—their natural enemies—through the ambilambiflambient air: while the soft-plumed & rapid Ajaccio strode hastily to & fro in the stillness of nature." / If you can describe the creatures eluded to in these words—well & good. If not, I shall simply pursue the dimpled but dusty path of duty, undismayed by the agonizing efforts of analytic pipkins, the lurid monotony of mulberry tarts—or the succinct suspicions of luminous & obsolete creamcheeses.'

(3.vii.68, MS., Robert Manning Strozier Library, Florida State University) V.N.

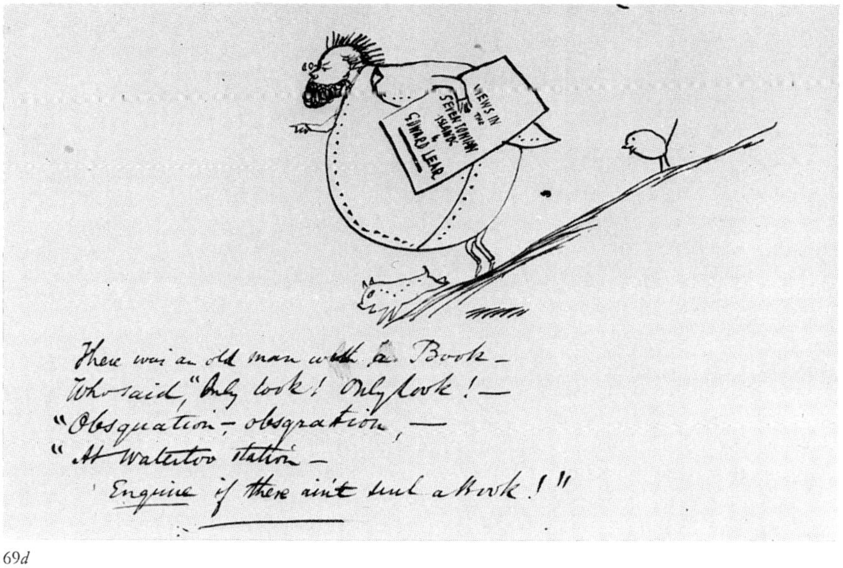

69d

64 Rome

a) Printed advertisement announcing the publication of *Views In Rome and Its Environs*, 1841
Engraving: 19 × 11.4 cm/$7\frac{1}{2} \times 4\frac{1}{2}$ in
W.P. Watson Esq.

b) *Views In Rome And Its Environs; Drawn from Nature and on Stone by Edward Lear*, folio edn, 1841
Published by Thomas McLean, 26 Haymarket, London, and printed by C. Hullmandel
Letterpress with 25 lithographic plates: leaf size 53.3 × 36.8 cm/$21 \times 14\frac{1}{2}$ in
Private Collection

On 14 February 1838 Lear wrote to Lord Derby: 'It is all very beautiful & interesting & wonderful here,—but—it is not England: & I am stupid enough to get into very homesick fits sometimes' (MS., The Public Record Office, Liverpool). It was not until 1841 that he returned to visit England, and he told Gould 'I think of publishing some Lithography on coming to England, to pay expenses &c., but am yet uncertain' (27.ii.41, MS., Houghton Library, Harvard University). This was the first mention of *Views in Rome and its Environs*, the earliest of Lear's six published travel books. It is difficult to be precise about dates at this stage of Lear's life, for there is a gap in his letters to Ann between November 1838 and August 1844, and few other letters have survived. It seems likely, however, that he was in England by May 1841. Certainly he was at Knowsley on 28 August, working on the lithographs for the book, and from there he wrote to Gould, 'my life here is monotonous enough—but such as pleases me more than all the gaiety in the world. Dear Lord Derby is surrounded by his children, grand-children & nephews & nieces & is really happy . . . The lot of things is immense here—birds and beasts &c—: but I am so thoroughly confined by my Lithography as to have little time to see them' (MS., Private Collection).

Views in Rome and its Environs, which contains twenty-five lithographic plates of views in and around Rome, was published by Thomas McLean of 26 Haymarket (see Cat. 65, 69*b*, 72*c*, 111*a*) and printed by Hullmandel, who had printed Lear's Book of Parrots (see Cat. 9*c*). It was available only to subscribers (Cat. 64*b*); the list of subscribers' names is headed by Queen Victoria (see Cat. 66).

PROVENANCE *(a)* bt from Quaritch by present owner. *(b)* bt from a bookseller by present owner.

64*b*

65 Italy

Illustrated Excursions in Italy by Edward Lear, 1846
Published by Thomas McLean, 26 Haymarket, London, and printed by S. & J. Bentley, Wilson, and Fley, Shoe Lane, London
In two volumes
i Volume I
Letterpress with 30 lithographic plates and 40 vignettes on wood printed by Hullmandel & Walton: leaf size 35.5 × 26.7 cm/$14\frac{3}{4} \times 10\frac{1}{2}$ in
ii Volume II
Letterpress with 25 lithographic plates and 13 vignettes on wood printed by Hullmandel & Walton: leaf size 35.5 × 26.7 cm/$14\frac{3}{4} \times 10\frac{1}{2}$ in
Private Collection

Views in Rome and its Environs (Cat. 64) had been a collection of twenty-five lithographic plates; *Illustrated Excursions in Italy*, published in 1846, was a more ambitious work which appeared in two volumes. The first, dated April 1846, is an account of three expeditions made by Lear in the Abruzzi between 26 July and 14 October 1842, on the first of which he was accompanied by Charles Knight (see Cat. 18). The text is illustrated with thirty lithographic plates drawn on stone by Lear, and forty vignettes drawn on wood by Lear and by R. Branston who prepared the architectural vignettes from Lear's drawings. There is a map, a list of the published works read by Lear in preparation for his travels, and the music of four peasant songs recalled by Lear and anonymously set down. The lithographic plates were made by Hullmandel and Walton (see Cat. 67), and the book was published by Thomas McLean of 26, Haymarket (see Cat. 64).

In his Preface, Lear asks 'the indulgence of the Public towards the literary portion of the Work, which I have thought it right to print with little alteration from my journals, written during my rambles, adding only such historical and

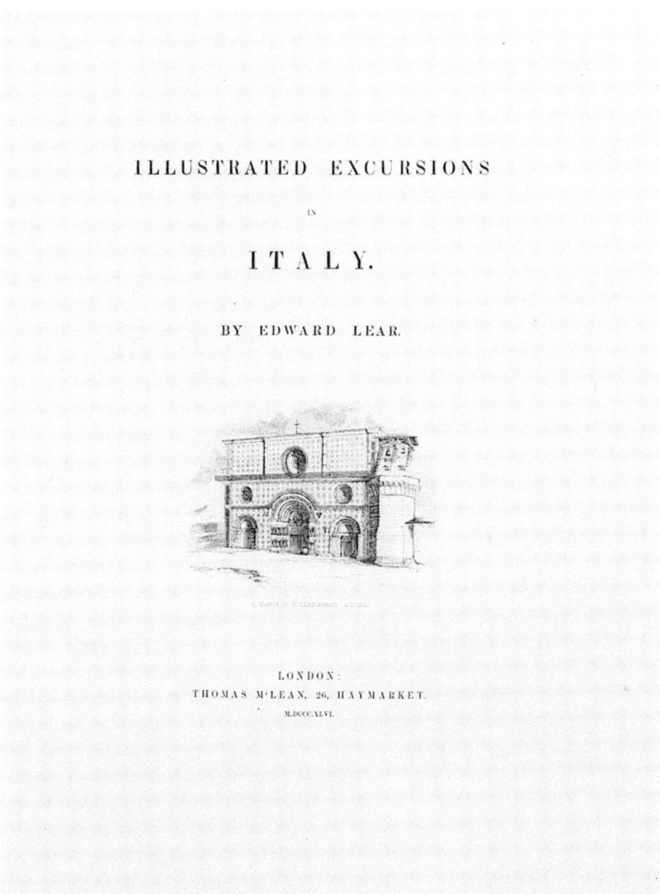
ILLUSTRATED EXCURSIONS

IN

ITALY.

BY EDWARD LEAR.

LONDON:
THOMAS M'LEAN, 26, HAYMARKET.
M.DCCC.XLVI.

65

other information concerning the places listed, as I have' (p. viii), so setting the pattern of personal journals he was to adopt for all his published travel books (see Cat. 109).

'. . . should the present Volume meet with the approbation of the Public,' wrote Lear in the Preface, 'a second series of Excursions may be anticipated at some future period' (p. viii). Approbation came from an unexpected quarter, for it was this book which prompted Queen Victoria to appoint Lear as her drawing master (see Cat. 66).

The second volume was published in August 1846. This time the text was restricted to brief topographical and historical notes to each of the fifteen plates. There was a map and thirteen vignettes drawn on wood by Lear, one from a drawing by Penry Williams (see Cat. 47) and two costume drawings by Williams drawn on wood by R. Branston.

At the back of the book are publisher's announcements, including an unlikely advertisement for *The Book of Nonsense* by Derry down Derry (see Cat. 72*c*), an early clue to the authorship of the anonymously published book which had appeared the previous February.

In Liverpool Public Library are three volumes prepared by Lord Northbrook in which the text and illustrations to *Illustrated Excursions in Italy* are pasted with the related watercolours done on the journeys described (see Cat. 68). In preparing his lithographs, Lear used these watercolours as studies which provided the topographical reference he needed for making new drawings on the lithographic stones.

PROVENANCE bt from a bookseller by present owner.

66 Queen Victoria's Drawing Lessons

a) Modern photograph of a drawing by Queen Victoria copied from Lear, 1846

b) Modern photograph of a drawing by Queen Victoria partly copied from Lear, 1846

c) *Osborne*, 1846
Pencil, chinese white on blue/grey paper: 26.9 × 18.4 cm/ $10\frac{5}{8} \times 7\frac{1}{4}$ in
Inscribed on mount not in Lear's hand: *Osborne, July 1846 E. Lear del.*
Her Majesty The Queen

Queen Victoria was so impressed by the first volume of Lear's *Illustrated Excursions in Italy* (1846; see Cat. 65), to which she had subscribed, that she appointed Lear to give her a series of twelve drawing lessons during the summer of 1846. The Queen, a competent and enthusiastic amateur painter, had already received lessons from Landseer and Leighton Leitch.

The first lessons were at Osborne, and on 15 July 1846 the Queen noted in her journal: 'Had a drawing lesson from Mr Lear, who sketched before me and teaches remarkably well, in landscape painting in water colours.' The next day she wrote: 'Copied one of Mr Lear's drawings and had my lesson downstairs, with him. He was very pleased with my drawing and very encouraging about it.' On 17 July: 'I had another

66*a*

66*b*

66*c*

lesson with Mr Lear, who much praised my 2nd copy. Later in the afternoon I went out and saw a beautiful sketch he had done of the new house.' And on 18 July: 'After luncheon had a drawing lesson, and am, I hope, improving' (Royal Archives, Windsor).

Queen Victoria's own drawings (Cat. 66*a*, *b*), copied from Lear's, are preserved in the Royal Library at Windsor. Beneath that of 18 July she has written 'My copied from Lear July 18. 1846' and beneath that of 20 July 'My copied *partly* from Lear—July—20. 1846.—'.

Lear's drawing of a corner of Osborne House is undated and is one of several done at Osborne House. It is not known whether this is the drawing to which Queen Victoria refers in her journal.

Lear says very little about what must have been an exciting interlude in his life, though we know that he presented his drawings made at Osborne to the Queen and that she had one of them engraved. 'I am really quite pleased with my little engraving,' he wrote to Ann, '. . . you need not however, tell the incident to everybody;—for it would look like boasting upon my part, who have done little enough to deserve so gratifying a notice' (6.ii.47, TS.).

The Queen did not forget her one-time drawing master, and in 1882 when she was staying in nearby Mentone there was talk of her coming to visit Lear in San Remo. In the event, the problems of protocol involved in her crossing the border from France to Italy prevented her coming, and Lear, who had been much complimented by the possibility, wrote to Fortescue, 'I dislike contact with Royalty as you know, being a dirty Landscape painter apt only to speak his thoughts & not to conceal them. The other day when some one said, "why do you keep your garden locked?"—says I,—"to keep out beastly German bands, & odious wandering Germans in general"—Says my friend,—"if the Q. comes to your gallery, you had better not say that sort of thing." Says I, I won't if I can help it' (30.iii.82. LLEL 1911, p. 258). Two years later he summed up his feelings about her: 'I don't know if it is proper to call a sovereign a duck, but I cannot help thinking H.M. a dear and absolute duck' (Fortescue 21.i.84, LLEL 1911, p. 300).

PROVENANCE *(c)* Queen Victoria, by family descent.

67 Albania

Journals Of A Landscape Painter In Albania, &c, By Edward Lear, 1851
Published by Richard Bentley, New Burlington Street, London, and printed by Schulze and Co., 13 Poland Street, London
Letterpress with 20 lithographic plates printed by Hullmandel & Walton: leaf size 25.4 × 15.8 cm/10 × $6\frac{1}{4}$ in
Private Collection

Lear's *Journals Of A Landscape Painter In Albania, &c.* (named on the spine and in advertisements as *Journals of a Landscape Painter in Albania & Illyria*) was the second of his travel journals to have text as well as illustrations (see Cat. 65), and the first of three produced in the smaller format (see Cat. 68, 70). It was published in 1851 by Richard Bentley, and contained twenty lithographic plates prepared by Lear and printed by Hullmandel and Walton (see Cat. 65) and one map.

The *Journals* are an account of Lear's travels between 9 September and 12 November 1848, and 24 April and 9 June 1849 (see Cat. 24). Franklin Lushington states that before Lear visited any country 'he studied every book he could lay hands on that would give him the best information as to its physical characteristics & its history' ('A Leaf from the Journals of a Landscape Painter', *Macmillan's Magazine*, April 1897). Lear pays tribute to others who had already written about Albania (in particular Colonel W. Martin Leake, whose book *A Journey through Albania, &c* was published in 1809–10). His own travels took him to parts of Albania never before visited by a foreigner from western Europe: 'of parts of Acroceraunia—of Króia (the city of Scanderbeg), and of scenes in the neighbourhood of Akhridha—the Lake Lychnitis, the Author believes himself to be the only Englishman who has published any account' (p. 4).

It was in response to this book that Tennyson wrote his poem, 'To E.L. on his travels in Greece' (see Cat. 40*a*).

The copy of the *Journals* exhibited here belonged to Charles M. Church, a friend from Rome whom Lear met again in Athens in June 1848. Church was the nephew of Sir Richard Church (1784–1873) who had commanded the Greek forces during the War of Independence. Lear and Charles Church travelled together in Greece during the summer of 1848 (see Cat. 37*a*), but their journey was abruptly terminated when Lear became ill at Thebes in July 1848 and had to return to Athens. From Athens he went on to Constantinople; from there he set out on 9 September 1848 to meet Church again and travel with him to Mount Athos (see Cat. 22). When he

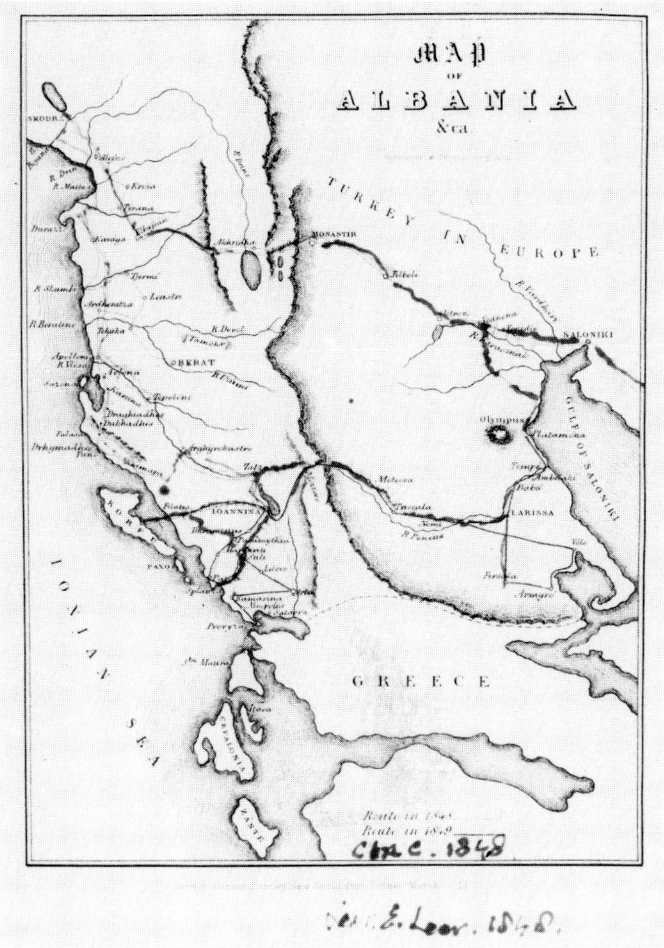

67

reached Salonika he found the city isolated by cholera and was unable to make contact with Church. Instead, he and the manservant whom he engaged for the journey—whose name was Giorgio, but who was not Giorgio Kokali (Cat. 116)—set out to explore Albania. This copy is annotated by Charles Church, and the route of his travels through Greece with Lear is marked on the map in ink.

PROVENANCE Charles M. Church; bt by present owner.

68 Southern Calabria

a) Advertisement for *Journals Of A Landscape Painter In Southern Calabria, &c, by Edward Lear*, 1852
Lithograph on paper: 14 × 8.7 cm/$5\frac{1}{2} \times 3\frac{7}{16}$ in
Vivien Noakes

b) *Journals Of A Landscape Painter In Southern Calabria, &c, by Edward Lear*, 1852
Published by Richard Bentley, New Burlington Street, London, and printed by Bradbury & Evans, Whitefriars, London
Letterpress with 20 lithographic plates printed by Hullmandel & Walton: leaf size 25.4 × 15.5 cm/$10 \times 6\frac{1}{8}$ in
R.A. Farquharson

c) *Journals Of A Landscape Painter in Southern Calabria, &c, by Edward Lear*
Lord Northbrook's paste-up, with original watercolours
Inscribed on title page: *LEAR'S TOPOGRAPHICAL WORKS./ VOL.VII./ JOURNALS OF A LANDSCAPE PAINTER./ PART III./ KINGDOM OF NAPLES*
48.9 × 64 cm/$19\frac{1}{4} \times 25\frac{1}{2}$ in
Liverpool City Libraries

d) 'Ye Poppular author & traveller in Albania & Calabria, keepinge his feete warme'
Sepia ink on paper: 22.9 × 18.4 cm/$9 \times 7\frac{1}{4}$ in
The Pierpont Morgan Library, New York, gift of Mrs Paul G. Pennoyer, 1963

Journals Of A Landscape Painter In Southern Calabria &c. was published by Bentley a year after *Journals Of A Landscape Painter in Albania, &c.* (see Cat. 67). The book follows the same format and uniform binding. It contains twenty lithographic plates and two maps, and a text. The Calabrian *Journals* record Lear's travels between 25 June and 4 October 1847. As in the Albanian *Journals*, he refers to those who have already written on the district, but points out that 'some villages in this, the most southerly portion of the beautiful kingdom of Naples, have, however, hitherto remained unexplored by Englishmen, and others, till now unillustrated by views' (p. vi). William Michael Rossetti helped Lear in correcting the proofs.

In 1887 Lord Northbrook, to whom Lear had given two chests of his travel watercolours, prepared seven volumes in which he mounted the printed text and lithographs of *Illustrated Excursions in Italy* (four volumes; see Cat. 65) and *Journals Of A Landscape Painter In Southern Calabria* (three volumes), together with the original watercolours relating to

83*c*

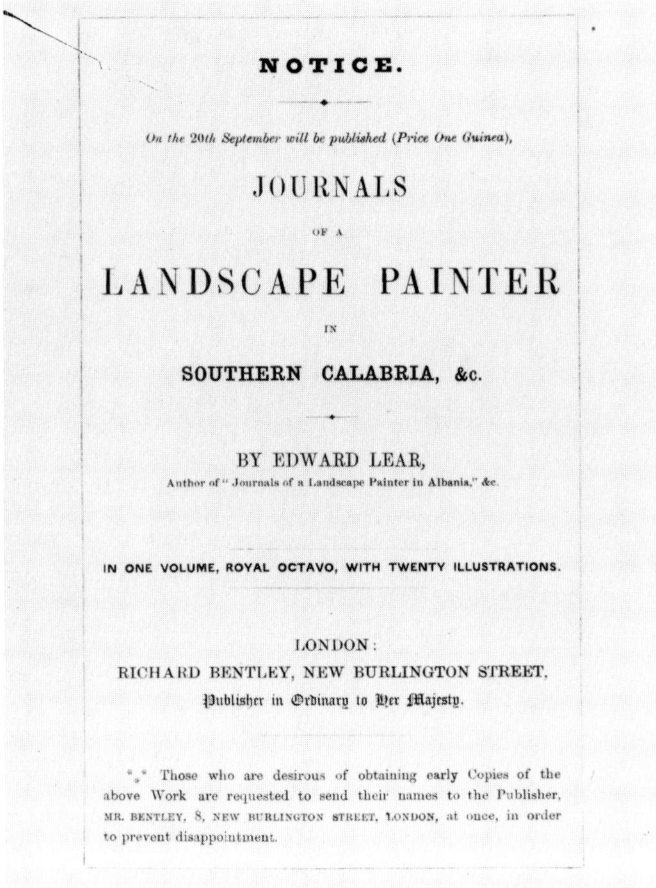

NOTICE.

On the 20th September will be published (Price One Guinea),

JOURNALS

OF A

LANDSCAPE PAINTER

IN

SOUTHERN CALABRIA, &c.

BY EDWARD LEAR,

Author of "Journals of a Landscape Painter in Albania," &c.

IN ONE VOLUME, ROYAL OCTAVO, WITH TWENTY ILLUSTRATIONS.

LONDON:

RICHARD BENTLEY, NEW BURLINGTON STREET,

Publisher in Ordinary to Her Majesty.

_ Those who are desirous of obtaining early Copies of the above Work are requested to send their names to the Publisher, MR. BENTLEY, 8, NEW BURLINGTON STREET, LONDON, at once, in order to prevent disappointment.

68*a*

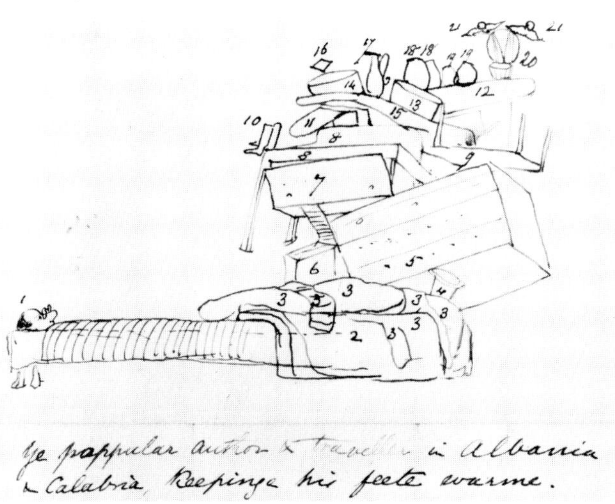

68*c*

the places described. The volume exhibited here is the last of the seven. Lear did not see the volumes, but writing to Lord Northbrook from San Remo he said, 'Your letter about the Abruzzi books greatly delighted me. I think my sketches are highly honoured' (9.ix.87, MS., Liverpool Public Library).

We do not know for whom Lear drew 'Ye poppular author & traveller in Albania & Calabria, keepinge his feete warme' (Cat. 68*d*).

PROVENANCE *(a) c.* 1970, purchased by present owner. *(b)* W.G. Prescott, by family descent. *(c)* Lorth Northbrook; bt by a Liverpool bookseller; 1940, bt by Liverpool City Libraries. *(d)* provenance unknown.

69 The Ionian Islands

a) Advertisement for *Views In The Seven Ionian Islands*, 1863
Verso of letter to Mrs Prescott, 14 November 1863
Lithograph on paper: 18 × 11.4 cm/$7\frac{1}{4} \times 4\frac{1}{2}$ in
J.J.Farquharson

b) *Views In The Seven Ionian Islands, By Edward Lear, Inscribed by His Excellency's Permission To Major Gnl. Sir Henry Knight Storks, K.C.B.G.C.M.G. Lord High Commissioner*, 1863
Published by Edward Lear, 15 Stratford Place, London
Letterpress with 20 lithographic plates printed by Day & Son, London: leaf size 49.2 × 32.7 cm/$19\frac{3}{8} \times 12\frac{7}{8}$ in
Department of Printing and Graphic Arts, The Houghton Library, Harvard University

c) Receipt for *Views In The Seven Ionian Islands*, 1863
Ink on blue paper: 11.3 × 17.8 cm/$4\frac{7}{16} \times 7$ in
Dated: *1. Dec. 63*
Department of Printing and Graphic Arts, The Houghton Library, Harvard University

d) 'There was an old man with a Book' [December 1863]
Sepia ink on paper: 11.9 × 18.6 cm/$4\frac{11}{16} \times 7\frac{5}{16}$ in
J.J. Farquharson [Repr. p. 157

In *Views In The Seven Ionian Islands* Lear returned to a format similar to that used in *Views In Rome and Its Environs*, 1841 (Cat. 64*b*). The book contained twenty lithographic plates with short descriptive texts, but included no account of his own travels there, although at one stage he did plan to publish these also (see Fortescue, 9.viii.63, LEL 1907, p. 283). The lithographic stones were drawn by Lear, and he published the book himself from 15 Stratford Place, Oxford Street (see Cat. 107).

In 1857 Lear talked of having small Corfu sketches lithographed and engraved for sale (Ann, 22.iii.57, TS.), adding, 'I should not do any lithographing myself; it is too eye-wearying, mind-squashing, & tedious.' In 1860 he discussed with Mclean the possibility of his making the lithographs (see Cat. 76), but it was not until the spring of 1863, when the British rule in the Ionian Islands was coming to its end, that Lear made a two-month tour of the islands to build up a collection of drawings from which lithographs could be prepared (see Cat. 21*b*).

Despite his earlier overture to McLean, Lear's eventual plan was to use some other form of reproduction than lithography for this volume. Writing to Fortescue on 9 August 1863 he said, 'All yesterday I tried various materials, charcoal, Lampblack, Pencil, chalk—by which to produce drawings fit for Photography—but all failed' (MS., Somerset Record Office, Taunton). In the Houghton Library there is a drawing of Palaeocastriza probably made for this photographic experi-

69*b*

69*c*

ment (repr. Hofer 1967, pl. 62). Lear listed the twenty proposed views, adding: 'This collection would, you see, have given the beastly public all that was most characteristic of the Islands: and, being *well done*, if at all, would keep up my prestige as a draftsman of Mediterranean scenery—and would, moreover, hold up or pave a way to my more general smaller sized Topography of Greece, to be one day printed with my Journals' (ibid., see Cat. 109).

In the end he returned to lithography, and transferred the drawings on to the stones himself. He found it a wearisome task. '. . . the impossibility of getting any compensation = spiritual from the Views I am drawing, since their being all executed reversed causes them to seem unreal, & without any interest,' he told Fortescue. 'You may ask – then why undertake a task so odious?—The reply to which would be, what else could I do?—The remains of my Watercolor gains could not carry me through the winter, & therefore, as ever the case with Artists who have no settled income,—something else was necessary. And as it would be folly to commence more oil works—those I have done being still unsold,—or to begin more Watercolors when there are none to see them,—the Ionian Book was my only apparent open = door of progress' (Fortescue, 14.ix.63, MS., Somerset Record Office, Taunton).

When the lithography was at last finished, he wrote to Drummond, 'if you hear of my being seen a walking on my head or in any other remarkable mode about town, set my eccentricities down to extreme delight at my work having come to a conclusion' (22.x.63, MS., Private Collection).

With this part of the work complete, Lear then wrote six hundred letters to potential subscribers. These were written on the reverse side of the advertisement for the book (Cat. 69*a*) which he had had printed. (For an example of one such letter, see Lear to Gladstone, British Library, Add. MS. 401.f.10.) The book was published on 1 December 1863. The receipt to F.C.E. Jervoise (Cat. 69*c*) is dated that day; the limerick gives instructions to Mrs Prescott (see Cat. 93) about collecting her copy from the cloakroom at Waterloo Station.

PROVENANCE *(a) (d)* W.G. Prescott, by family descent. *(b)* W.B. Osgood Field; The Houghton Library, Harvard University. *(c)* Frances L. Hofer; The Houghton Library, Harvard University.

REFERENCES *(d)* Noakes 1968 edn, repr. p. 199; Noakes 1979 edn, repr. p. 203.

70 Corsica

Journal Of A Landscape Painter In Corsica, by Edward Lear, 1870

Published by Robert John Bush, 32 Charing Cross, London, and printed by Cassell, Petter and Galpin, London

Letterpress with 40 woodcuts and 40 vignettes: leaf size 26 × 17.6 cm/$10\frac{1}{4} \times 6\frac{15}{16}$ in

Open at the dedication page, inscribed: *Two blots on Corsica!/ O dear, dear dear/Mr Edward Lear./Foss did it*

Department of Printing and Graphic Arts, The Houghton Library, Harvard University

The *Journal Of A Landscape Painter in Corsica* was the last of Lear's travel books. In it he returns to the smaller format, with an account of his travels, which he had used in the Albanian

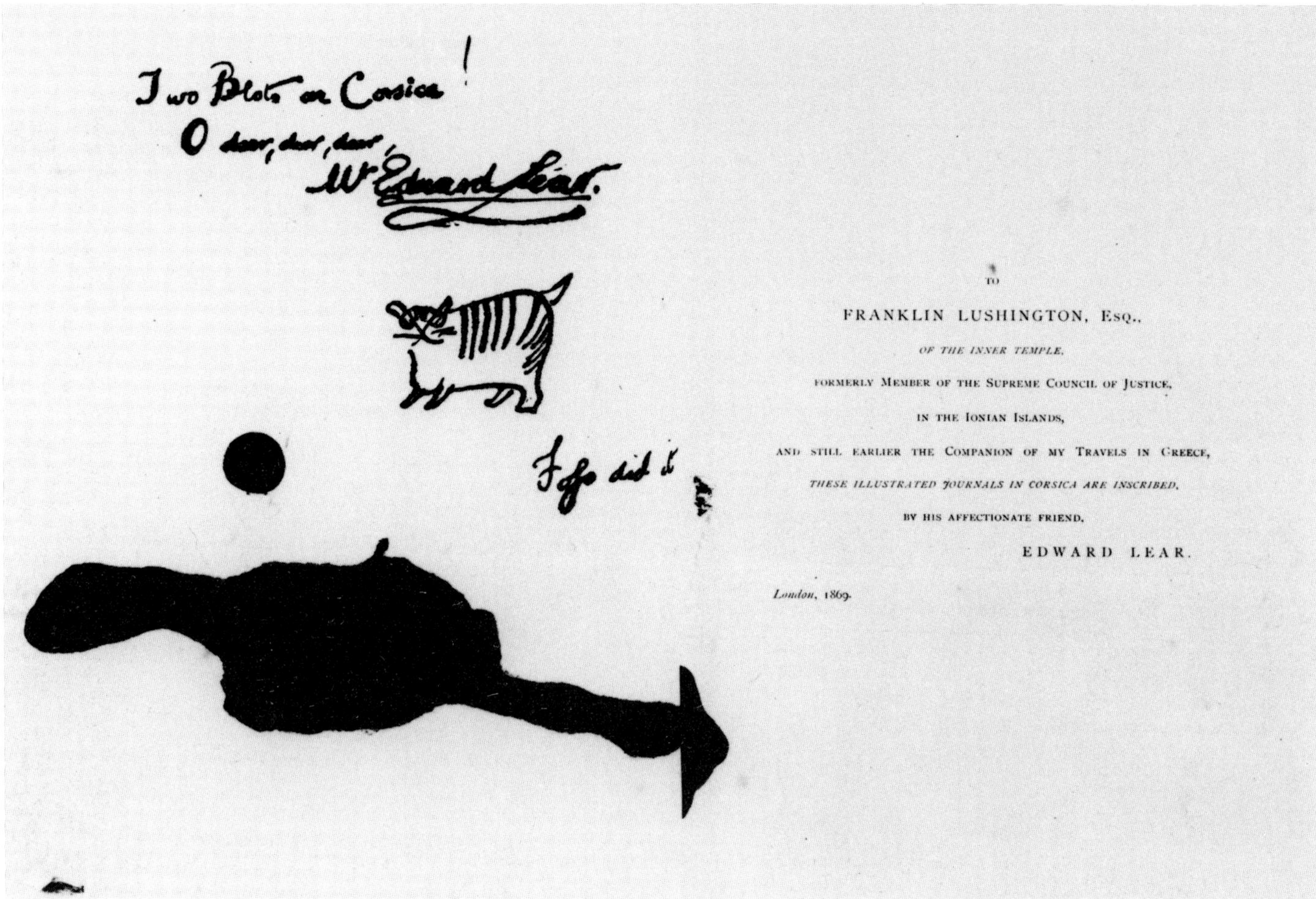

70

and Calabrian *Journals*. There are forty full-page illustrations, forty vignettes and a map. It differs from his other travel journals in two respects: this is the only travel book in which Lear does not use lithography—instead the drawings are reproduced by wood engraving—and there are extensive appendices and footnotes. It was published by Robert John Bush, who went on to publish the rest of Lear's Nonsense books (see Bibliography).

The book describes Lear's travels in Corsica between 8 April and 6 June 1868 (see Cat. 33). In the Preface he explains, somewhat ingenuously, that he had planned to visit Palestine, but finding himself unable to do so had gone instead to Corsica, 'rather perhaps on account of its being a place near at hand and easily reached, than from any particular interest in its history, inhabitants, or scenery' (p. vii). Twenty years separate this journey from the last tour which had provided the basis for a published travel journal, and the excitement of earlier journeys has gone. He says in the Preface: 'A certain monotony of narrative must needs be the result of monotony of travel' (p. x). Now he journeys by carriage rather than on foot or horseback, though 'Many of the illustrations . . . were made in short pedestrian excursions, particularly in the forests, at some distance from the high road' (p. x).

It was Lear's dislike of again preparing lithographic plates as he had done in *Views In the Seven Ionian Islands* (Cat. 69) that made him decide to use wood engraving. But it was not a process of reproduction that was suited to his work. Writing to Wyatt from Paris where many of the blocks were being prepared, he said, 'I firmly believe there is some quality in my drawings untransferable to wood engraving. If they keep the accuracy of form (wh. they do here,) they make the whole hard & hideous: in England they sacrifice that—& with that goes half the value of my stupid style. O that I had been born a pig, or a spider, or a broomstick!' (27.vi.69, MS., Private Collection).

The book was published in December 1869; it cost £1 for subscribers and £1.10.0 to the public. By 1872 the price for non-subscribers had been reduced to £1. At the back of *More Nonsense* (1872) there is a notice stating: 'In order to clear off at once the few remaining copies of the above sumptuous work, the price is now for the first time, reduced to 20s. It was published at 30s., and at that price 1200 Copies were sold.' Although the least successful of Lear's travel books, there was talk in 1884 of its reissue; the plan, however, came to nothing.

PROVENANCE W.B. Osgood Field; The Houghton Library, Harvard University

REFERENCE Hofer 1967, pp. 35–36.

NONSENSE

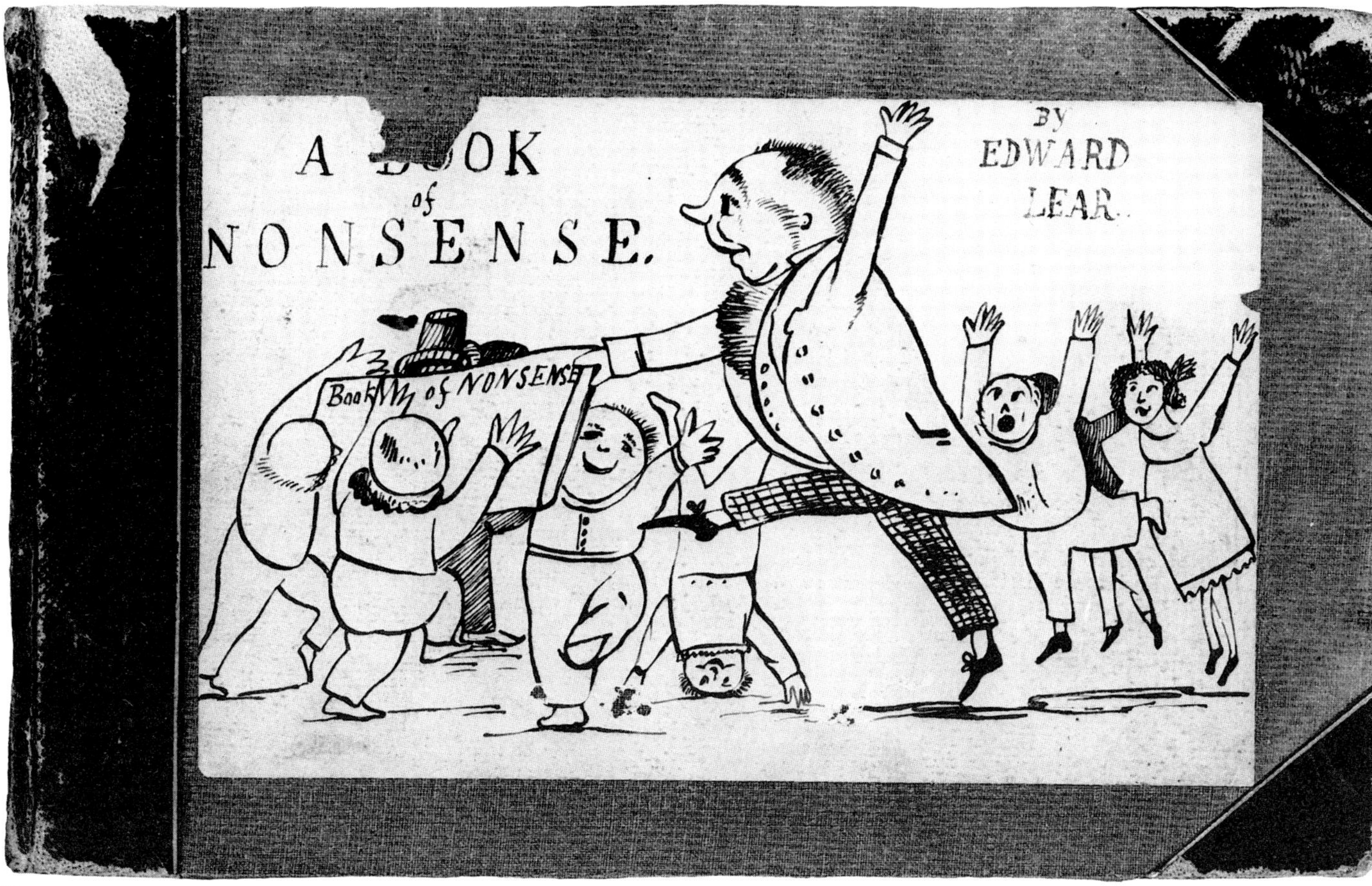

75*a*

Lear 'had the most unquenchable love of the humorous wherever it was found,' wrote Holman Hunt. 'Recognition of what was ridiculous made him a declared enemy to cant and pretension, and an entire disbeliever in posturers and apers of genius whether in mien or in the cut of the coat and affectation of manners' (Holman Hunt, *Pre-Raphaelitism and the Pre-Raphaelite Brotherhood*, 1912). His Nonsense was both a sharing and a defence. It reflected his approach to 'this ludicrously whirligig life which one suffers from first & laughs at afterwards' (Holman Hunt, 7.vii.70, MS., Huntington Library, San Marino), with its zest for living, its creation of merriment and its plea for tolerance (see Introduction, p. 13). It was also a means by which he could speak of the sufferings he both experienced and witnessed, but in such a way that he was protected from closer scrutiny by the absurdity of the genre.

His first steps towards Nonsense came through parody (see Cat. 71); it was, however, the *Book of Nonsense* and its limericks which established the genre of Nonsense writing which took its name from the title of his book. The limericks were written not only for, but with, children who responded with 'uproarious delight and welcome at the appearance of every new absurdity' (Introduction to *More Nonsense*, 1872). 'It is odd, how children like me,' wrote Lear (Diary, 28.ii.62); yet he was neither sanctimonious nor condescending, and they would approach him without fear of hurt (see Cat. 94).

Adults, however, did not always respond so openly to his Nonsense. The Nonsense which appears in his letters (Cat. 95) was only sent to those friends whom Lear could trust to accept his foolishness in the manner in which it was given, with an understanding of the vulnerability and absurdity of the human situation. He assessed instinctively the quality of laughter. '. . . as the crackling of thorns under a pot, so is the laughter of the fool' (*Ecclesiastes,* VII, 6); Lear spoke with dislike of the mocking laughter of unthinking people as 'thorn-under-pot crackling' (Diary, 1.xi.68).

He extended his sharing of a common existence with the animal kingdom, not only to his cat Foss (Cat. 97), but also to the numerous birds and animals which occur particularly in his limericks and later alphabets. Here his knowledge as a natural history draughtsman gives a particular quality to the drawings; indeed, throughout his Nonsense the illustrations, although within a restricted convention, demonstrate his confidence and control as an accomplished draughtsman. V.N.

71 Early Parody

a) Volume containing illustrations to 'Miss Maniac'
Volume: 20.9 × 26 cm/$8\frac{1}{4}$ × $10\frac{1}{4}$ in
Open at pp. 15 and 16
Sepia ink on paper: each 11.4 × 9.2 cm/$4\frac{1}{2}$ × $3\frac{5}{8}$ in
- i Page 15
  Inscribed b.: *Oh—thou who falsely—darkly/lured my frail fond heart/astray,*
- ii Page 16
  Inscribed b.: *Then left me like a broken flower,/alone to waste away,—*

Department of Printing and Graphic Arts, The Houghton Library, Harvard University

b) Volume containing 22 illustrations to 'Auld Robin Gray', *c.* 1836
Volume: 20.3 × 29.2 cm/8 × $11\frac{1}{2}$ in
Open at no. 22
Sepia ink on paper: sheet 12.5 × 20.3 cm/$4\frac{15}{16}$ × 8 in
Signed c. (on horse): *E Lear*
Inscribed b.: *I'll try with all my heart a gude wife to be—For old Robin Gray—is very kind to me.—*
Private Collection

c) 'I slept, and back to my early days'
Sepia ink on 2 sheets of paper: each 23.2 × 19 cm/$9\frac{1}{8}$ × $7\frac{1}{2}$ in
- i Sheet 1, picture 1 (3 pictures on Sheet 1 but none of them numbered)
  Inscribed t.: *I slept: & back to my early days— | Did wandering fancy roam— | When my heart was light | & my Opes vos bright | & my ome a | appy ome.*
- ii Sheet 1, picture 2.
  Inscribed t.: *When I dreamed as I was young & hinnocent—& my art vos free from care | And my Parents smiled on their darling child, & breathed for his* [ ] *a prayer.*
- iii Sheet 1, picture 3.
  Inscribed t.: *Once again I was rising before the sun, for in childhood I was told— | If its early ray on your head should play—it would turn each tress to gold.*
- iv Sheet 2, picture 1.
  Inscribed b.: *Once again I vos roaming through fields & flowers, | & I felt at each step new joys—*
- v Sheet 2, picture 2.
  Inscribed t.: *But I woke with a sigh that memory | should revive what time destroys.*

Pierpont Morgan Library, New York. Gift of Mrs Paul G. Pennoyer, 1963

Lear began his career as a Nonsense writer by parodying the work of others. This he did both verbally in poems which survive largely only in copies, and visually through the illustrations he drew to the heart-rending ballads and songs which were the popular after-dinner entertainment of his day—in particular those of Thomas Moore, the author of *Irish Melodies* (*Lear in the Original*, 1975, pp. 158–59, 163–65, 169–73).

'Auld Robin Gray' (Cat. 71*b*) was written by Lady Anne Lindsay in about 1770. Her family home, Haigh Hall, Wigan, was only a few miles from Knowsley (see Cat. 11), and Lear probably made this series of twenty-two drawings on a visit to the house. Whilst the drawings which accompany both the ballad and 'I slept, and back to my early days' (Cat. 71*c*) show

71*b*

something of the strength of Lear's later Nonsense illustrations, those to the earlier 'Miss Maniac' (Cat. 71*a*) are closer to the work of the illustrator and caricaturist George Cruikshank (1792–1878). The rapid growth of confidence displayed in his Nonsense drawings echoes the extraordinary stylistic development found in Lear's bird drawings (see Cat. 6).

His pleasure in parody remained throughout his life. In September 1873, whilst working on his illustrations to Tennyson's poems (see Cat. 43), he rewrote Tennyson's poem 'To EL . . .' (see Cat. 40*a*). Tennyson's two stanzas:

'Illyrian woodlands, echoing falls
Of water, sheets of summer glass,
The long divine Peneian pass,
And vast Akrokeraunian walls,

Tomohrit, Athos, all things fair,
With such a pencil, such a pen,
You shadow forth to distant men
I read and felt that I was there . . .'

were parodied as:

'Delirious Bulldogs;—echoing, calls
My daughter,—green as summer grass;—
The long supine Plebeian ass,
The nasty crockery boring, falls;—

Tom-Moory Pathos;—all things bare,—
With such a turkey! such a hen!
And scrambling forms of distant men,
O!—ain't you glad you were not there!'
(Fortescue, 12.ix.73, LLEL 1911, p. 161)

The persistence of parody in Lear's work is underlined by mention of 'Tom-Moory Pathos', a reference to the ballads and songs of Thomas Moore which had been one of the sources of his early parody.

PROVENANCE *(a)* W.B. Osgood Field; The Houghton Library, Harvard University. (b) by family descent to present owner. *(c)* James Tregaskis, London; Mrs Paul G. Pennoyer; 1963, given to The Pierpont Morgan Library, New York.

EXHIBITIONS *(a)* 1958, London, Arts Council of Great Britain, *Edward Lear* (no. 27); 1968, London, Gooden and Fox Ltd, *Edward Lear* (no. 12).

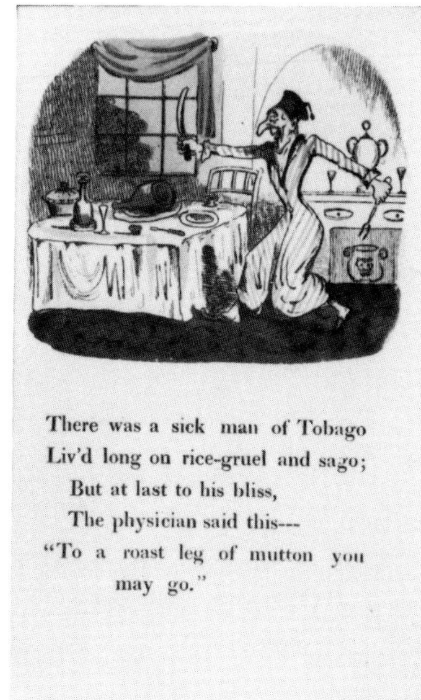

72*a*

72*b*

72 A Book of Nonsense (1st edn)

a) *Anecdotes and Adventures of Fifteen Gentlemen* [?1823]
Published by E. Marshall, London
Volume size 18 × 11 cm/7 × 4⅜ in
Private Collection

b) Illustrations to *Anecdotes and Adventures of Fifteen Gentlemen*
In volume: 48.3 × 33 cm/19 × 13 in
i Drawings nos 7–11 in a numbered series
Sepia ink on paper: av. size of drawings 13.6 × 19.7 cm/5⅜ × 7¾ in
ii Proof for first (1846) edn of *A Book of Nonsense*
Lithograph: 15.2 × 20 cm/6 × 7⅞ in
The Frederick R. Koch Foundation Collection, New York

c) *A Book of Nonsense*, 1846 [Repr. p. 13
Published by Thomas McLean, 62 Haymarket, London
In two volumes
Lithograph: 14.9 × 21.6 cm/5⅞ × 8½ in
Private Collection

Lear's first *Book of Nonsense* was published by Thomas McLean (see Cat. 73, 75) of 26 Haymarket on 10 February 1846. It was in two volumes, each containing thirty-six limericks and a title-page, and each costing 3/6. It was reproduced by lithography. It is not known how many copies were printed. Because of the quality of the binding the pages soon became detached, and few copies are known to have survived. The pages were unnumbered, but the probable order in which they were bound has now been established. In contrast to later editions (see Cat. 73), the limericks in the 1846 edition are printed on five lines and are set in capitals.

Lear published the book anonymously, calling himself 'old Derry down Derry', which was the name of one of the fools in the mummers' plays (see Cat. 84) and recurs in the refrains of some early folk songs. Volume 2 of *Illustrated Excursions in Italy* (see Cat. 65) contains an advertisement for the *Book of Nonsense*, giving an early clue to its authorship, but it was not until the third (1861) edition that Lear claimed the book as his own (see Cat. 75). By then, many people had ascribed authorship to Lord Derby, and even when Lear printed his name on the title-page it was thought that Edward Lear was merely an anagram for Edward Earl.

Although Lord Derby did not write the book, he played a part in its composition, for most of the limericks were composed at Knowsley between 1831 and 1837 (see Cat. 11). 'Long years ago', wrote Lear in his introduction to *More Nonsense* (1871; see Cat. 83), 'in days when much of my time was passed in a country house, where children and mirth abounded, the lines beginning, "There was an Old Man of Tobago," were suggested to me by a valued friend, as a form of verse lending itself to limitless variety for Rhymes and Pictures; and thenceforth the greater part of the original drawings and verses for the first "Book of Nonsense" were struck off with a pen, no assistance ever having been given me in any way but that of uproarious delight and welcome at the appearance of every new absurdity.'

'There was an Old Man of Tobago' had been published in *Anecdotes and Adventures of Fifteen Gentlemen*, which appeared in 1823 (Cat. 72*a*). Lear's own illustrations to the poem have survived (Cat. 72*b*), but although these cannot now be dated they are almost certainly the earliest of Lear's limerick drawings. On the same spread are his illustrations to 'There was an old soldier of Bicester', from the same 1823 book, and the earliest known reproduction of Lear's Nonsense, a proof of 'There was an old person of Sparta' for the first edition of the *Book of Nonsense*. They are pasted into a volume which contains other early Nonsense by Lear made at Knowsley, including parodies, and a later series of drawings of travel adventures made in 1841 (see Cat. 92).

Lear himself never used the word limerick, whose date is given in the Oxford English Dictionary as 1898. Its origins are obscure. Lear called these drawings and verses either his 'Nonsenses' or his 'Old Persons'. For convenience, however, the term has been used here in all descriptions of this verse form.

PROVENANCE *(a) (c)* bt by present owner. *(b)* The Hornby family; 1969, 11 December, Christie's, London (lot 163), bt by H. P. Kraus; bt by present owner and deposited with The Pierpont Morgan Library, New York.

REFERENCES *(b)* H.W. Liebert (ed.), *Lear in the Original*, New York, 1975, drawings 7–9 repr. pp. 53–55, drawings 10–11 repr. pp. 34–35, proof repr. p. 137.

73 A Book of Nonsense (2nd edn)

a) *A Book of Nonsense*, 1855
Proof copy with handwritten alterations:
14.6 × 21.6 cm/$5\frac{3}{4} \times 8\frac{1}{2}$ in
Inscribed on front cover in Lear's hand tr.: *Professor [Nichols] / this congenial tribute / of respect / 'Similis simili gaudato'.*
Liverpool City Libraries

b) *A Book of Nonsense*, 1855
14.3 × 21.6 cm/$5\frac{5}{8} \times 8\frac{1}{2}$ in
Inscribed on cover tr.: *Edward Lear. / 15 Stratford Pl. / W.*
Inscribed on title page tr.: *Franklin Lushington. from Edward Lear. June. 9./56*
Department of Printing and Graphic Arts, The Houghton Library, Harvard University

Little is known about the circumstances of publication of the second edition of the *Book of Nonsense*. Although several presentation copies survive inscribed in Lear's hand, he never speaks of this edition.

It was published in 1855 by Thomas McLean, who also published the first edition. Lithography was again used, but the book was in one volume rather than two. It contained the same limericks, but the text was now arranged on five lines rather than three, and was printed in italics and not capitals. There are also small differences in both text and illustrations, and three substantial differences in illustrations: on the cover and title-page there is a tuft of grass beneath the 'Old Derry Down Derry' (*sic*); 'The Young Lady of Tyre' lacks a feather; and 'The Young Lady of Norway' has acquired a second door.

In both the copies exhibited here the drawings and verses of 'The Old Man of the West' have been confused. In the proof copy (Cat. 73*a*) the drawings and verses of the two limericks—'There was an Old Man of the West / Who wore a plum-coloured vest' and 'There was an Old Man of the West / Who never could get any rest'—are transposed. In the second copy (Cat. 73*b*) the verse 'Who never could get any rest' appears under both drawings. The problem was sorted out however, and in most, though not all, other known copies the verses are beneath the drawings to which they relate (see *The British Museum Quarterly*, vol. XXVIII [1964], pp. 7–8).

The proof copy was given by Lear to Professor Nichols, and is inscribed 'Similis simili gaudato' (Like delights in like). The second (Cat. 73*b*) was Lear's own proof copy which he gave on 9 June 1856 to Franklin Lushington (see Cat. 112).

PROVENANCE *(a)* Prof. Nichols; Liverpool Public Library. *(b)* W.B. Osgood Field; The Houghton Library, Harvard University.

REFERENCE *(b)* Osgood Field 1933, pp. 131–32.

73*b*

74 Lady Duncan's Limericks

Volume of manuscript limerick drawings and verses
No. 31 in a series of 79 drawings
One of two volumes bound in leather and watered silk: 22.9 × 15.2 cm/9 × 6 in
Private Collection

It is difficult to date Lear's individual limericks precisely, for he rarely mentions their composition in either his letters or his diaries.

Lear met Lady Duncan in Rome in the late 1830s, and again in Malta in 1848. The limericks composed for her probably date from the early 1840s before he published the first edition of his *Book of Nonsense* (see Cat. 72*c*). Most of them differ considerably from the published versions: the illustrations seem

74

to have been drawn swiftly, and though many are less resolved than the familiar images, others have a vitality which the published versions lack. This is certainly true of the drawings for 'The Old Lady of Prague'.

This is one of two volumes which were rediscovered in 1981.

PROVENANCE Ada Duncan of Naughton House, Fife, by family descent.
REFERENCE Edward Lear, *Bosh and Nonsense* (facsimile), London, 1982.

75 Albums of Limericks

a) Manuscript for *A Book of Nonsense*, 1861 (3rd edn) [Repr. p. 165
In volume 14.1 × 22.7 cm/$5\frac{9}{16} \times 8\frac{15}{16}$ in; av. size 11.4 × 17.9 cm/$4\frac{1}{2} \times 7\frac{1}{16}$ in
Justin G. Schiller

b) Manuscript for *A Book of Nonsense*, 1861 (3rd edn)
In volume 14 × 24.1 cm/$5\frac{1}{2} \times 9\frac{1}{2}$ in
The Frederick R. Koch Foundation Collection, New York

The problems of dating Lear's limericks are again encountered with these two albums (see Cat. 74).

The Schiller manuscript (Cat. 75*a*) contains limericks published in the first (1846) and second (1855) editions of the *Book of Nonsense*, as well as some of the new limericks which were added to the third (1861) edition (see Cat. 76). Lear's name is on the title-page; this appeared for the first time in the third edition, for until then authorship had been attributed solely to the 'Old Derry down Derry'. These points would suggest that the album was put together some time between 1855 and 1861. However, ownership has been traced back to Sir Samuel Morton Peto. In the catalogue of his library, dated 1854, there appears the entry: 'Edward Lear's Nonsense Mss.' If this does refer to the volume exhibited here, it would date it between the first and second editions, rather than between the second and third. Although the limerick verses are arranged on three lines, a convention adopted in the printing of the first edition only, this in itself gives no positive link to the first edition; a collection of drawings and verses known to have been made in preparation for the third edition (Houghton Library, Harvard University) has both three- and four-line arrangements.

The Pierpont Morgan manuscript (Cat. 75*b*) is a collection of eighty-six drawings possibly taken from the third (1861) edition of the *Book of Nonsense*. They are arranged broadly in the order in which they appear in that edition. Twenty-one limericks published in the first and second editions are omitted (including the three which were dropped after the second edition, see Cat. 73) and eight are omitted from those added to the third edition (Cat. 76). The arrangement of the verses is on three lines.

There is evidence that Lear traced the illustrations from existing drawings, then added the details by hand. If this is the case, he was following a practice he had established in his bird drawing, where the outline of a considered study was traced onto a new sheet and then worked by hand (see Cat. 8). In the present album, however, this has led to some strange misreading of line in, for example, Marseilles and Portugal, where facial outlines differ awkwardly from the published version.

PROVENANCE *(a)* Fletcher and Barlow, King's Lynn; 14 October 1981, Sotheby's London (lot 835); bt by present owner. *(b)* Pickering and Chatto; Justin G. Schiller; bt by the Frederick R. Koch Foundation Collection, New York, on deposit with the Pierpont Morgan Library, New York

76 A Book of Nonsense (3rd edn)

A Book of Nonsense [1861] (Repr. pp. 82, 91, 112
Lear's proof copy with proof of title page on yellow paper.
Volume bound in contemporary mottled blue board: 15.2 × 22.9 cm/6 × 9 in
Signed and dated on proof of title page: *Edward Lear 1861*
On the dedication page, the word *FOOLISH* before *AUTHOR* has been crossed out by Lear
Department of Printing and Graphic Arts, The Houghton Library, Harvard University

It was only in its third edition that the *Book of Nonsense* became a huge popular success, 'originating quite a new class of prose rhymes that for a good twelvemonth were the rage in all societies' (newspaper fragment reviewing a later reprint). It

76

was now that the limerick became witty and sophisticated, so that subsequent generations have tended to find Lear's unexceptional by comparison. This edition contains 112 limericks, with 69 out of the 72 already published ('The Old Sailor of Compton', 'The Old Man of Kildare' and 'The Old Man of New York' are omitted) and 43 additions. It is the first edition to be published with Lear's name on the title-page (see Cat. 75).

The first suggestion that he was thinking of publishing a new edition was on 26 October 1860, when he told Lady Waldegrave, 'I have been making some new nonsenses in my old age' (MS., Somerset Record Office, Taunton). The following February he asked the Dalziel brothers to prepare two sample woodcuts from his drawings, and he then set to work on new limericks. '. . . since I asked people to come & see my pictures, they come,—horridly & disjointedly; sometimes 20 at a time—of all kinds of phases of life: sometimes—for 3 hours no one comes:—so then I partly sleep, & partly draw pages of a new Nonsense book. If I sleep, I wake savagely at some newcomer's entrance, & they go away abashed. If I write nonsense, I am pervaded with smiles, & please the visitors' (Emily Tennyson, 6.iii.61, MS., Tennyson Research Centre, Lincoln).

Lear had decided to use woodcut rather than lithography as it was cheaper, and this time he wanted to sell the book outright to a publisher rather than arrange the publication himself through McLean. In October he suggested 'a Corfû work to Maclean [*sic*]—he to lithograph some 10 or 12 drawings, & pay me so much for the use:—conditional on his giving up ALL rights on the nonsense' (Diary, 10.x.61). He then visited Routledge 'who won't *buy* the Nonsense, but offers to purchase 1000' (Diary, 31.x.61). The next day they discussed the price: '. . . we think 2/6 is too little a price—& 3/6 proper & just.—A wary Scotchman is Routledge' (Diary, 1.xi.61). The next day he arranged that Dalziel should print 1000 copies, and gave them a first payment.

The book was published early in December 1861, and by the following June 4000 copies had been sold with another 2000 printed. Dalziel was pressing for the rest of his payment, but Routledge had given Lear none of the money due to him from the sales. He was finding the book increasingly burdensome, and it was with relief that he finalised the agreement for its outright sale to the 'wary Scotchman' on 1 November 1862.

'I went to the city today,' he told Lady Waldegrave on November 4, 'to put the £125 I got for the "Book of Nonsense" into the funds. It is doubtless a very unusual thing for an artist to put by money, for the whole way from Temple Bar to the Bank was *crowded* with carriages and people,—so immense a sensation did this occurance make' (LEL 1907, p. 255).

The book, which went into nineteen editions in Lear's lifetime, has never been out of print.

PROVENANCE W.B. Osgood Field; The Houghton Library, Harvard University.

EXHIBITION 1968, Worcester, Mass., Worcester Art Museum, *Edward Lear, Painter, Poet and Draughtsman* (no. 95).

REFERENCE Osgood Field 1933, pp. 132–36.

77 A Book of Nonsense (1st American edn)

A Book of Nonsense [1863]
Volume: 15.2 × 23.5 cm/6 × 9¼ in
Thomas V. Lange

The first American edition of Lear's *Book of Nonsense* was published in Philadelphia by Willis P. Hazard in 1863. It was taken from the tenth London edition, and contains the same limericks. However, 'The Young Lady of Clare' is printed on the back cover and not in the body of the book. This fact was not noticed so that subsequent American editions of the *Book of Nonsense* lack the limerick entirely.

The sheets were also distributed in America in the same year by M. Doolady of New York (see Bibliography). This is a stencil-coloured copy of the Doolady issue of the first American *Book of Nonsense*.

Although a reappraisal of Lear's qualities as an artist began with American rather than British collectors, his Nonsense has never had the same popularity in America as it has had in England.

PROVENANCE *c.* 1982, bt from an antiquarian bookseller, New England, U.S.A., by present owner.

78 Nonsense Songs

a) Manuscript for 'The Owl and the Pussy-cat', 1868
Sepia ink on headed writing paper, *PERRYSTONE / ROSS / HEREFORDSHIRE*: 22.2 × 18 cm/8¾ × 7⅛ in
Signed and dated br.: *Oct 19. 1868 Edwd Lear*
Department of Printing and Graphic Arts, The Houghton Library, Harvard University

b) Manuscript for 'The Owl and the Pussy-cat' [1870]
Verse 3 with drawing
Sepia ink on paper: 11.6 × 13.6 cm/4 9/16 × 5⅜ in
Department of Printing and Graphic Arts, The Houghton Library, Harvard University

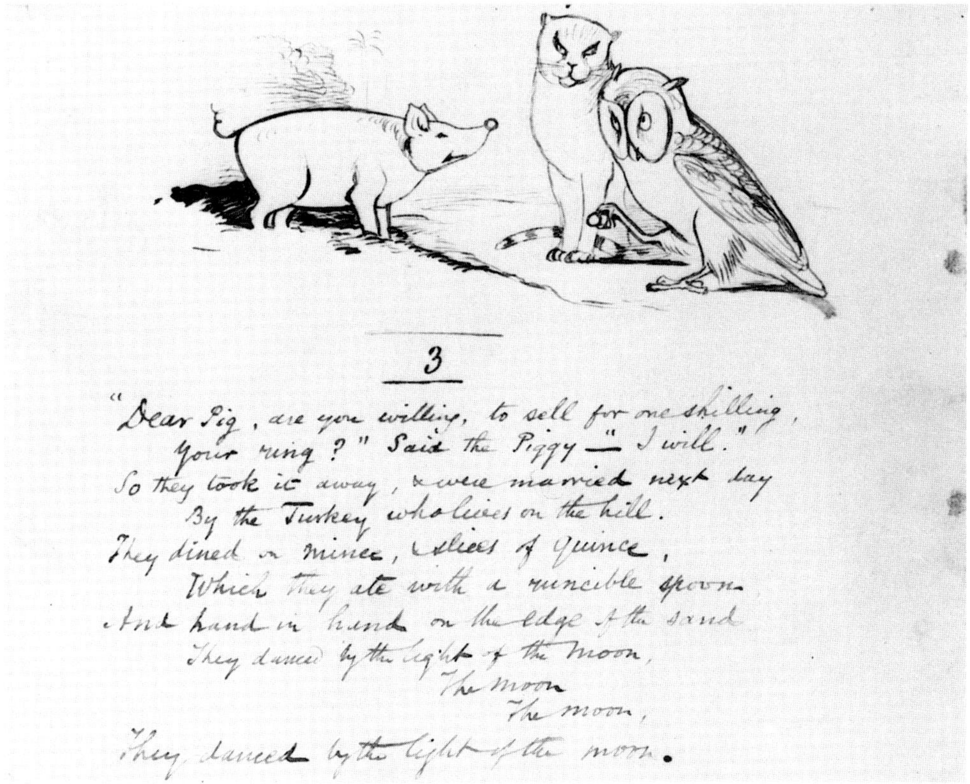

78*b*

c) End drawing for 'The Owl and the Pussy-cat' [1870]
Sepia ink on paper: 7.6 × 13.6 cm/3 × 5⅜ in
Department of Printing and Graphic Arts, The Houghton Library, Havard University

d) Manuscript for 'Calico Pie' [1870] [Repr. p. 16
Pencil and sepia ink on paper: 20.9 × 19.7 cm/8¼ × 7¾ in
Department of Printing and Graphic Arts, The Houghton Library, Harvard University

'The Owl and the Pussy-cat' (Cat. 78*a–c*), the first and perhaps the best-known of Lear's Nonsense songs, was written for Janet Symonds, the daughter of John Addington Symonds and his wife Catherine, daughter of Frederick North, M.P. (see Cat. 49).

On 14 December 1867 Lear noted in his diary, 'Their little girl is unwell—& all is sad.' Four days later he visited them again, taking with him 'a picture poem for little Janet.' The drawings from this first manuscript were published in *Queery Leary Nonsense* (1911), but the whereabouts of the manuscript itself is not known. As was Lear's habit, he made copies of the song to give to others of his friends, and the copy exhibited here (Cat. 78*a*) was made in 1870 for the children of George Clive, whom he had known in Rome in 1846. In variations from the published text, the Bong-tree is here the Phloss tree, and the spoon is muncible. Cat. 78*b* and *c* are probably copies made by Lear in preparation for the publication of the song. By now, the familiar runcible spoon has appeared. 'The Owl and the Pussy-cat' was first published in America in February 1870 (see Bibliography), and the previous November Lear wrote to the publisher, James Fields of Boston, 'will you kindly send, as swiftly as possible, or more swiftly than possible if possible—the name & nature & time or times of your magazine. For, having been just now at Dr Lushington's for some days—where billions of that dear old Gentleman's grand children have been screaming about the songs I sang,—they all want to know the Magazinious nomenclature, that they may order it 4thwith' (18.xi.69, MS., Henry E. Huntington Library, San Marino). By Christmas 1870 it was available to English readers when it was published in *Nonsense Songs, Stories, Botany and Alphabets*.

Lear set 'The Owl and the Pussy-cat' to music, but of that setting no manuscript has survived. Writing in 1907, Lady Strachey recalled a visit she had made to Lear in 1880, when 'though much aged and broken by worries and health, still the same sad and whimsical personality and undefinable charm of the man attracted as ever, and one day to us was literally shown forth, in his singing of an air to which he had set the "Owl and the Pussy Cat." But of this rendering, alas! there is no record, as not knowing music, though a musician by ear, he had been unable to transcribe it to paper, and grudged the £5 he said it would cost to employ another to do so' (LEL 1907, p. xv).

'Calico Pie' (Cat. 78*d*) was written in July 1869, when Lear wrote to Lady Strachey, 'I have been very unpoetical of late, & except one intellectual effusion, "Calico Pie" have made nothing' (24.vii.[69], MS., Somerset Record Office, Taunton). Of all the Lear Nonsense songs, it is perhaps the simplest and most melodious. This fair copy was probably made from earlier drafts when Lear was preparing it for publication.

PROVENANCE *(a)–(d)* Philip Hofer; The Houghton Library, Harvard University.

EXHIBITIONS *(a) (b)* 1962, San Marino, Calif., Henry E. Huntington Library and Art Gallery, *Drawings by Edward Lear* (no. 51); 1968, Worcester, Mass., Worcester Art Museum, *Edward Lear, Painter Poet and Draughtsman* (no. 96a). *(d)* 1962, San Marino, Calif., Henry E. Huntington Library and Art Gallery, *Drawings by Edward Lear* (no. 52); 1968, Worcester, Mass., Worcester Art Museum, *Edward Lear, Painter, Poet and Draughtsman* (no. 96b).

REFERENCE *(d)* Edward Lear, *Calico Pie*, The Harvard College Library, Cambridge, Mass., 1952 (facsimile edn).

79 Nonsense Stories

History of the Seven Families of the Lake Pipple = Popple, 1865
Open at the final page of Chapter 12 and opening page of Chapter 13
Volume: 39.4 × 15.9 cm/$15\frac{1}{2} \times 6\frac{1}{4}$ in
Inscribed on title page: *History of the Seven Families / of the / Lake Pipple = popple / written & illustrated for Lady Charlotte & the Hon*^{bles} */ Hugh & Reginald Wentworth-Fitzwilliam, / by / Derry Down Derry Edward Lear. / Nice. / Feb*^{y} *1865.*
British Library Board

Lear wrote only two sustained pieces of Nonsense prose, apart from the handful of Nonsense letters (see Cat. 91). *The History of the Seven Families of the Lake Pipple-Popple* was written in February 1865, when Lear was in Cannes, for the children of Lord and Lady Fitzwilliam, 'jolly cheerful children!' as Lear

79

described them (Diary, 24.ii.65). On 10 February he had been working on an alphabet for them (also bound into this volume), and three days later he paused in his soulless task of working on a group of 240 Tyrants (see Cat. 39), 'stopping to write a most absurd lot of stories for the little Fs' (Diary, 13.ii.65). It was published in December 1870 in *Nonsense Songs, Stories, Botonay and Alphabets.* The Fitzwilliams were related by marriage to Mrs Wentworth, who had helped Lear at the very start of his career (see Cat. 6).

His other Nonsense story, *The Story of the Four Little Children Who Went Round The World,* was also published in 1870. This had been written in November 1867 for the nephews and nieces of Gussie Bethell (see Cat. 115), but no known manuscript survives.

PROVENANCE 1951, presented by an anonymous gentleman and Messrs W.H. Robinson Ltd to the British Library.

80 Nonsense Botany

a) *Nonsense botanies,* 18 May 1870
4 sheets:
i Multipeoplea Upsidownia
Ink on paper: 19 × 12 cm/$7\frac{1}{2} \times 4\frac{3}{4}$ in
ii Piggiwiggia pyramidalis
Ink on paper: 18 × 11 cm/$7\frac{1}{8} \times 4\frac{1}{2}$ in
iii Cockatooca superba
Ink on paper: 17.9 × 11.4 cm/$7\frac{1}{16} \times 4\frac{1}{2}$ in
iv Bottleforkia Spoonifolia
Ink on paper: 17.9 × 11.7 cm/$7\frac{1}{16} \times 4\frac{5}{8}$ in
Beinecke Rare Book and Manuscript Library, Yale University

b) Letter to Mrs Ker, 19 May 1870
Sepia ink on paper: 13.6 × 15.6 cm/$5\frac{3}{8} \times 6\frac{1}{8}$ in
Beinecke Rare Book and Manuscript Library, Yale University

Wilfrid Blunt (*The Art of Botanical Illustration,* London 1950, pp. 37–41) has suggested that Lear may have been familiar with the fifteenth-century herbal and bestiary, *Ortus Sanitatis,* in which plants believed to have magical and medicinal qualities were fancifully illustrated and described. A copy is known to have been in the library at Knowsley when Lear was working there on the Earl of Derby's menagerie (see Cat. 10). Whatever the source of his drawings, in the classification of newly discovered species Lear was echoing methods with which he had been familiar during his ornithological days.

His earliest known Nonsense Botany dates from 1860, in a letter to Sir George Grove, the musicologist. In this he draws a 'Remarkable Fungus discovered in the woods near the Oatlands Hotel. Supposed to be the Pongchámbinnibóphilos Kakokreasópheros of Naturalists' (15.xi.60, *The Life and Letters of Sir George Grove,* ed. C.L. Graves, 1903), a description which is reminiscent of his long name (Cat. 46). The whereabouts of this manuscript is not known.

There are no further examples of Nonsense Botany until May 1870 (Cat. 80*a*). In an accompanying letter (Cat. 80*b*) Lear wrote: 'Dear Mrs. Ker, / As I know how fond you & Mr Ker are of flowers, I have looked out carefully for any new ones all about the Grasse Hills, & have been fortunate enough to find 9 sorts:—they are all very rare, & only grow about here, & in the Jumbly islands, where I first saw them long ago,—& as there happened to be a Professor of Botany there at that time, I got the Generic & Specific names from him. Unfortunately, the flowers all withered directly after I gathered them, so I made drawings of them on the spot, in order to send you a correct illustration of each. / Yours sincerely, Edward Lear' (19.v.1870, MS., Beinecke Rare Book and Manuscript Library, Yale University). These nine Nonsense botanies, with 'Multipeoplia Upsidownia' being retitled 'Manypeoplia Upsidownia', were published in *Nonsense Songs, Stories, Botany and Alphabets* (London 1871) which also included his Nonsense cookery (no known manuscripts survive). They were introduced by an 'Extract from the *Nonsense Gazette,* for August 1870', in which he states: 'Our readers will be interested in the following communications from our valued and learned contributor, Professor Bosh, whose labours in the field of Culinary and Botanical science, are so

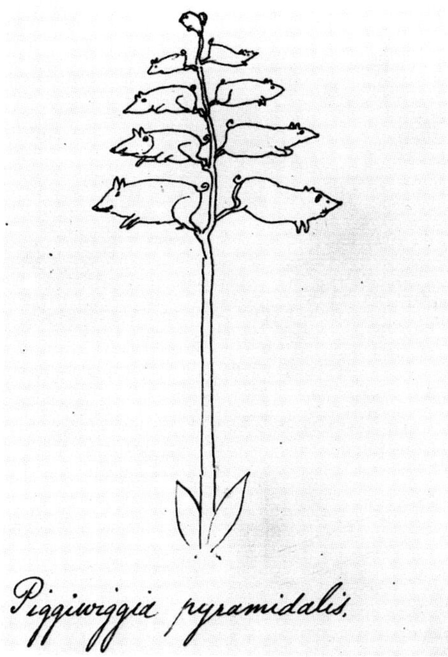

80*a*

well known to all the world . . . we are happy to be able through Dr. Bosh's kindness to present our readers with illustrations of his discoveries. All the new flowers are found in the valley of Verrikwier, near the lake of Oddgrow, and on the summit of the hill Orfeltugg.'

PROVENANCE *(a) (b)* Mrs Ker; Beinecke Rare Book and Manuscript Library, Yale University.

81 Nonsense Alphabets

a) Draft of Prescott alphabet [1860]
One of four sheets: L–R
Blue ink on paper: 18.2 × 11.6 cm/$7\frac{3}{16} \times 4\frac{9}{16}$ in
Department of Printing and Graphic Arts, The Houghton Library, Harvard University

b) Volume containing Prescott alphabet, 22 June 1860
Volume: 90.5 × 20.3 cm/12 × 8 in
Open at the letter P
Blue ink on paper: 30.5 × 20.3 cm/12 × 8 in
Inscribed: *P was a Pig/Who was not very big,/But his tail was too curly/And that made him surly/p!/poor little pig! /*
J. J. Farquarson Esq.

c) Two sheets from *The Absolutely Abstemious Ass* alphabet, 1870
i Sheet for the letter A, pen on paper: 16.8 × 10.9 cm/ $6\frac{5}{8} \times 4\frac{5}{16}$ in
Inscribed tl.: *A*
Inscribed b.: *The Absolutely Abstemious Ass, / who resided in a barrel, and only / lived on Soda Water, and Pickled Cucumbers.*
ii Sheet for the letter Z, pen on paper: 10.4 × 16.8 cm/ $4\frac{1}{8} \times 6\frac{5}{8}$ in
Inscribed tl.: *Z*
Inscribed b.: *The Zigzag Zealous Zebra, who carried five Monkies / on his back all the way to Jellibolee. /*
Department of Printing and Graphic Arts, The Houghton Library, Harvard University

81*c*

d) Alphabet letters A–I from a complete set A–Z, 1880
Ink on paper: each av. 11.43 × 13.97 cm/$4\frac{1}{2} \times 5\frac{1}{2}$
i Inscribed t.: *AaaA*
Inscribed b.: *A was a lovely Apple / which was very red & round / It tumbled off an Apple tree / And fell upon the ground.*
ii Inscribed t.: *BbbB*
Inscribed b.: *B was a lovely Bee, / It flew about a flower / And sung aloud, 'a = buzz', 'a = buzz' / For more than half an hour.*
iii Inscribed t.: *CcCc*
Inscribed b.: *C was a lovely Pussy Cat; / its eyes were large / and pale; / And on its back it had some stripes, / and several on its tale.*
iv Inscribed t.: *DdDd*
Inscribed b.: *D was a beautiful Duck / With spots all over his back. / He swam about in a beautiful pond, / And when he came out, said, Quack.*
v Inscribed t.: *EeEe*
Inscribed b.: *E was a beautiful Eagle, / Whose head was completely white; / He sate and looked at the sun all day, / And was fast asleep all night.*
vi Inscribed t.: *FfFf*
Inscribed b.: *F was a beautiful Fan, / Made of Ivory, feathers and lace, / And was used by a beautiful lady, / To shade her beautiful face.*
vii Inscribed t.: *GgGg*
Inscribed b.: *G was a little old Goose, / Who feeds all day on grass, / And who makes no end of a hissing noise / At all the people who pass.*
viii Inscribed t.: *HhHh*
Inscribed b.: *H was a little old Hat, / Which was neither useful nor pretty, / So they sent it away to an Oldclothes shop / In a street in London City.*
ix Inscribed t.: *IiIi*
Inscribed b.: *I was a little old Inn, / By the side of a dusty road / But very few travellers ever came / To that not very nice abode.*
Trustees of the Victoria and Albert Museum

The alphabet (Cat. 81*a*,*b*) was made for a grandchild of W.G. Prescott (Cat. 93). It was drawn on 22 June 1860 and is typical of the many delightful alphabets which Lear made for children up to 1870; it is unusual in having a surviving draft (Cat. 81*a*). On 8 September 1860 Lear wrote to Mrs Prescott, 'Did I tell you I kept drawing objects for Alphabets in Yorkshre.—& that a domestic nearly fell down with amazement on this order being given him,—"Take a cake, an applepie, an eel, a ham and a lobster into Mr Lear's room,—& afterwards take him to the pump in the courtyard."—' In this alphabet P was a Pig; it was more usually a pump.

The original Absolutely Abstemious Ass alphabet dates from 1870 (Cat. 81*c*). In August of that year, when Lear was staying at Certosa del Pesio, he met two small children whose mother he had known in Rome. One of them later recalled of Lear that 'Something seemed to bubble and sparkle in his talk and his eyes twinkled benignly behind the shining glasses. I had heard of uncles; mine were in America and I had never seen them. I whispered to my mother that I should like to have that gentleman opposite for an uncle. She smiled and did not keep my secret. The delighted old gentleman, who

81*d*

was no other than Edward Lear, glowed, bubbled and twinkled more than ever; he seemed bathed in kindly effulgence. The adoption took place there and then; he became my sworn relative and devoted friend. He took me for walks in chestnut forests; we kicked the chestnut burrs before us, "yonghy bonghy bos", as we called them; he sang to me "The Owl and the Pussycat" to a funny little crooning tune of his own composition; he drew pictures for me.

'I still have a complete nonsense alphabet, beautifully drawn in pen and ink and delicately tinted in watercolours, done on odd scraps of paper, backs of letters, and discarded manuscripts. Every day Arthur and I found a letter of it on our plate at luncheon, and finally a title-page for the collection, with a dedication and a portrait of himself, with his smile and his spectacles, as the "Adopty Duncle"' (Mrs Winthrop Chandler, *Roman Spring*, Boston 1934).

Although this coloured alphabet was still extant in Boston in the 1950s, it has since disappeared. The two sheets exhibited here are pen and ink drawings of this alphabet (see Cat. 81*c*) which were made when Lear was preparing it for publication in *More Nonsense* (1872; see Cat. 83).

All we know of the Pirouet family, for whose son Charles Geffrard Pirouet the fourth of these alphabets (Cat. 81*d*) was drawn in 1880, is that they were in San Remo because of ill health. In his diary Lear records visiting them, but there is no mention of either the alphabet or the coloured birds (Cat. 94).

PROVENANCE *(a) (c)* Philip Hofer; The Houghton Library, Harvard University. *(b)* W.G. Prescott, by family descent. Mrs Agnes A. Corbyn; 1951, bt by The Victoria and Albert Museum. *(d)* Charles Geffrard Pirouet.

EXHIBITION *(d)* 1958, London, Arts Council of Great Britain, *Edward Lear* (nos 62, 63).

REFERENCE *(d)* Edward Lear, *A Nonsense Alphabet*, London, 1952 (facsimile).

82 Nonsense Songs, Stories, Botany and Alphabets [Repr. p. 15, 111

a) *Nonsense Songs, Stories, Botany and Alphabets*, 1871
Volume: 19 × 16.2 cm/7½ × 6⅜ in
Mrs Roger North

b) *Nonsense Songs, Stories, Botany and Alphabets*
(1st American coloured edn), 1882
Volume 19.2 × 16.2 cm/7 9/16 × 6⅜in
Open at pp. 14–15 showing the Jumblies' Stars and Stripes
Justin G. Schiller

Although *Nonsense Songs, Stories, Botany and Alphabets* is dated 1871, it was in the shops in time for Christmas 1870. It was published by Robert John Bush of 32 Charing Cross, who also published *More Nonsense* (see Cat. 83) and *Laughable Lyrics* (see Cat. 87). It went into five editions, but some time after the fifth edition Bush became bankrupt.

These are children's songs—it is arguable that many of those published in *Laughable Lyrics* were written as much for adults as for children—and the recurring theme is one of adventure. Be bold, be daring, Lear says to his young readers;

THE JUMBLIES.

I.

THEY went to sea in a sieve, they did;
In a sieve they went to sea:
In spite of all their friends could say,
On a winter's morn, on a stormy day,
In a sieve they went to sea.
And when the sieve turned round and round,
And every one cried, "You'll all be drowned!"
They called aloud, "Our sieve ain't big:
But we don't care a button; we don't care a fig:
In a sieve we'll go to sea!"
Far and few, far and few,
Are the lands where the Jumblies live:

82*b*

leave the safe world you know and travel to unknown places, for however great the risks you will discover the excitement of new worlds and unfamiliar freedom. It is a lesson he himself knew well.

Lear had intended to dedicate the book to John Addington Symonds (Cat. 33) for whose daughter Janet he had written the first of its songs, 'The Owl and the Pussy-cat' (see Cat. 78), but the book lacks a dedication.

The first of these copies (Cat. 82*a*) was given in 1872 to Marianne North (see Cat. 88), whose sister Catherine was married to John Addington Symonds and after whom the North Galleries at Kew Gardens are named. The letter which accompanied the book reads 'Eye m kwy tat tchor sirvisswen U R eddy Dwor Dleer Eye weight in theorl blo—'.

The first American edition was published in Boston in 1871 by James R. Osgood and Company. In this edition (Cat. 82*b*), issued in Boston by Roberts Brothers in 1882, the illustrations are hand-coloured by stencil, and the Jumblies' 'beautiful pea green veil' has become the stars and stripes (see Bibliography).

PROVENANCE *(a)* Marianne North, by family descent. *(b)* by 1887, John Harper Plaisdell; Justin G. Schiller, New York.

83*b*

83 More Nonsense

a) Draft sheet of limericks
Ink on blue paper: 32.4 × 21 cm/$12\frac{3}{4} \times 8\frac{1}{4}$ in
Department of Printing and Graphic Arts, The Houghton Library, Harvard University

b) Volume of drawings for *More Nonsense, Pictures, Rhymes, Botany, Etc.* [1871]
Volume: 20.9 × 31.5 cm/$8\frac{1}{4}$ × 12 in
Open at sheet numbered 2,3
Pen and ink on paper: 14 × 22 cm/$5\frac{1}{2} \times 8\frac{5}{8}$ in
Inscribed t.l.: *NB / leave out the line / marked A below the / arm.*
Inscribed b.: *There was an old man, who when little / Fell casually into a kettle; / But, growing too stout, He could never get out, So he passed all his life in that kettle.*
Department of Printing and Graphic Arts, The Houghton Library, Harvard University

c) *More Nonsense, Pictures, Rhymes, Botany, Etc.* (1st edn, R.J. Bush, London), 1872 [Repr. p. 161
Volume: 21.4 × 16.2 cm/$8\frac{7}{16} \times 6\frac{3}{8}$ in
Inscribed on cover in ink tc.: *George Cocali*
Autograph leaf inserted at front: *Edward Lear. Villa Tennyson*
Department of Printing and Graphic Arts, The Houghton Library, Harvard University

More Nonsense, dated 1872 but available in time for Christmas 1871, contains a hundred limericks, twelve Nonsense botanies and the alphabet of The Absolutely Abstemious Ass (Cat. 81*c*). This copy (Cat. 83*c*) was given to Giorgio (see Cat. 116) to mark sixteen years in Lear's service.

As far back as 1863 Lear had told Fortescue, 'Nonsense issues from me at times—to make a new book next year' (11.i.63, LEL 1907, p. 267). The sheet (Cat. 83*a*) of draft limericks may date from this time. Four of these—1, Woking; 2, Putney; 3, Brill; 5, Garden—were published in *More Nonsense*. The others, 4, Rhind; 6, Athos; 7, Dunmore—are unpublished. By the end of July his preparations for a new book were complete, and on the 27th he 'Worked at classifying "Nonsenses" till 10' (Diary, 27.vii.66). But neither Warne nor Routledge wanted any more of his Nonsense, 'so all these preparations, wh. I have been carrying on for some time—are a failure' (Diary, 1.viii.66).

Although the following summer he again mentions working on the book, within a few weeks he had written the first of his Nonsense songs, and these appeared first in *Nonsense Songs, Stories, Botany and Alphabets*, 1871 (see Cat. 82). Lear had originally intended that the songs and limericks should be published together, but Bush advised holding the limericks over for separate publication the following year. The album of drawings and verses for *More Nonsense* are probably those prepared for the publisher (Cat. 83*b*).

'Talking of bosh,' Lear wrote to Fortescue, who was then President of the Board of Trade, on 13 September 1871, 'I have done another whole book of it: it is to be called "MORE NONSENSE" Bush brings it out at Xmas. . . . I should like to dedicate it to you, but I thought it was not dignified enough for a Cabinet M.' (LLEL 1911, p. 139).

More Nonsense (Cat. 83*c*) was never as popular as the *Book of Nonsense*, partly because the limerick form which Lear had made so popular had moved on, so that his simple verses now seemed tame, and partly because most of the earlier limericks had been written for the immediate enjoyment of children and only later gathered together for publication. *More Nonsense* was written with publication in mind and the limericks lack some of the exuberant bounce of the earlier verses.

Within days of its publication, Lear was writing from the loneliness of his life in San Remo: 'It is queer (and you would say so if you saw me) that I am the man as is making some three or four thousand people laugh in England all at one time,—to say the least, for I hear 2,000 of the new Nonsense are sold' (Fortescue, 31.xii.71, LLEL 1911, p. 144).

By now Lear too had moved on, and these were the last limericks he wrote.

PROVENANCE *(a)* Philip Hofer; The Houghton Library, Harvard University. *(b) (c)* W.B. Osgood Field; The Houghton Library, Harvard University.

EXHIBITION *(c)* 1958, London, Arts Council of Great Britain, *Edward Lear* (no. 100).

REFERENCES *(b)* Osgood Field 1933, pp. 264–68, repr. p. 145. *(c)* Osgood Field 1933, pp. 168–70.

84 The Yonghy-Bonghy-Bò

a) Manuscript of poem [1871]
Ink on paper: 29×19.4 cm/$11\frac{3}{8} \times 7\frac{5}{8}$ in
Department of Printing and Graphic Arts, The Houghton Library, Harvard University

b) Manuscript music, 1876
Sepia ink on paper: 30.8×24.8 cm/$12\frac{1}{8} \times 9\frac{3}{4}$ in
Department of Printing and Graphic Arts, The Houghton Library, Harvard University

c) Drawing of Yonghy-Bonghy-Bò kneeling, 1876
Sepia ink on paper: 6.7×10.5 cm/$2\frac{5}{8} \times 4\frac{1}{8}$ in
Department of Printing and Graphic Arts, The Houghton Library, Harvard University

d) Proof of drawing, 1876
Wood engraving: 10.5×15.7 cm/$4\frac{1}{8} \times 6\frac{3}{16}$ in
Department of Printing and Graphic Arts, The Houghton Library, Harvard University

The first mention of 'yonghy bonghy bos' is in the summer of 1870 (see Cat. 81*c*). On 11 December 1871 Lear records in his diary, 'Set to work on ( ) [*sic*] Ventimiglia, but bkft & accounts took up time, & later, persistently writing out a foolsong, Yonghy=Bonghy=Bò—eat into morning' The manuscript exhibited here (Cat. 84*a*) is probably the earliest draft of the poem, made on that day.

'The Yonghy-Bonghy-Bò' may be an autobiographical reflection of the failure of Lear's hopes of marriage to Gussie Bethell (see Cat. 115); certainly it echoes Fiddler Wit, the fool of the mummers' plays, just as Derry Down Derry had done (see Cat. 72). In 'The Yonghy-Bonghy-Bò', the fool is Fiddler Wit, with head so large and wits so small:

'Father died the other night
And left me all his riches,
A wooden leg, a feather bed,
And a pair of leather breeches,
A coffee pot without a spout,
A jug without a handle,
A guinea pig without a wig,
And half a farthing candle.'
(R.J.E. Tiddy, *The Mummers' Play*, Oxford 1923, pp. 231)

The turtle on whose back the Yonghy-Bonghy-Bò flees is the Young Chelonia Imbricata, from Bell's *A Monograph of Testudinata* (London 1836), for which Lear made the lithograph (see Bibliography).

84*a*

The musical setting for 'The Yonghy-Bonghy-Bò' (Cat. 84*b*) was composed by Lear, and set down in August 1876 by Signor Pomis, in preparation for its publication in *Laughable Lyrics* (1877). It was a setting with which he used to entertain his friends, and Henry Strachey recalled that 'In the evenings he often sang; the "Yonghy Bonghy Bo" was inimitable.' (*Nonsense Songs and Stories*, 9th edn, 1894). On one occasion, singing to a group of children at a tea party, 'I volunteered to sing "the Owl & the Pussy Cat"—but broke down in the Yonghy Bonghy Bò. I was sorry I could do no more to help the Swarry' (Diary, 26.iv.79).

PROVENANCE *(a)–(d)* Philip Hofer; The Houghton Library, Harvard University.

EXHIBITION *(a)–(d)* 1968, Worcester, Mass., Worcester Art Museum, *Edward Lear, Painter, Poet and Draughtsman* (nos 98a, 98b).

87

85 The Quangle Wangle's Hat

Manuscript for 'The Quangle Wangle's Hat', 1876
Sepia ink on paper: 30.9 × 20.6 cm/$12\frac{3}{16} \times 8\frac{1}{8}$ in
Department of Printing and Graphic Arts, The Houghton Library, Harvard University

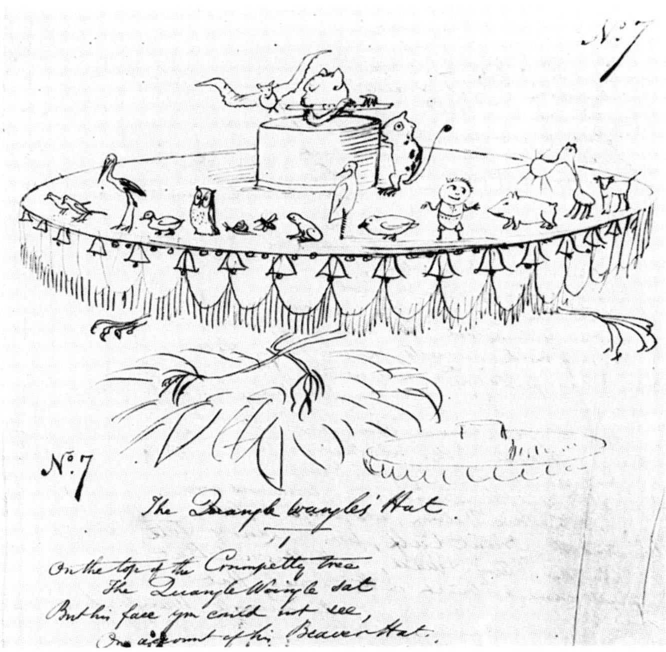

85

Lear's Nonsense world is characterised by width, tolerance and safety. Most often these are found on the Great Gromboolian plain, but here it is the Quangle Wangle's hat (in this manuscript 12 ft wide, but later expanded to 102 ft) which offers joyful sanctuary to all manner of strange creatures who dance together

> 'On the broad green leaves of the Crumpetty Tree,
> And all were as happy as happy could be.'

Lear had introduced the Quangle Wangle as the Clangle Wangle in February 1865, in *The History of the Seven Families of the Lake Pipple-Popple* (Cat. 79). It appeared again, this time as the Quangle Wangle, in November 1867 in *The Story of the Four Little Children who went round the World.* This poem also makes the first mention of the Dong with a luminous nose (Cat. 86) and the Pobble who has no toes, both of whom were later to have songs of their own. (see Cat. 87).

He composed this song during May 1872 for Arthur Buchanan, the son of Lady Kathleen Buchanan who was wintering in San Remo. The whereabouts of that manuscript is unknown, although several later copies are known. This was Lear's own copy, probably made in preparation for its publication in *Laughable Lyrics* (1877).

PROVENANCE Philip Hofer; The Houghton Library, Harvard University.

EXHIBITION 1968, Worcester, Mass., Worcester Art Museum, *Edward Lear, Painter, Poet and Draughtsman* (no. 98c).

86 The Dong with a Luminous Nose

Manuscript for 'The Dong with a Luminous Nose', 1876
Pencil and sepia ink on paper: 29.4 × 19.2 cm/$11\frac{9}{16} \times 7\frac{9}{16}$ in
Department of Printing and Graphic Arts, The Houghton Library, Harvard University

Lear's early Nonsense had included parody of Thomas Moore (see Cat. 71) and in this, the last of his great Nonsense songs, he returns to Moore, echoing his poem, 'The Lake of the Dismal Swamp'. In Moore's poem a young man, deranged by the death of the girl he loves, believes that she is not dead but has gone to the Dismal Swamp:

> 'He saw the Lake, and a meteor bright
> Quick over its surface play'd—
> "Welcome," he said, "my dear one's light!"
> And the dim shore echoed, for many a night,
> The name of the death-cold maid!
>
> . . .
>
> But oft, from the Indian hunter's camp,
> This lover and maid so true
> Are seen, at the hour of midnight damp,
> To cross the lake by a fire-fly lamp
> And paddle their white canoe!'

With the Dong, it is not a 'death-cold maid' but a Jumbly girl whose leaving has caused all the trouble, for

> '. . . the morning came of that hateful day
> When the Jumblies sailed in their sieve away,
> And the Dong was left on the cruel shore
> Gazing—gazing for evermore . . .'

The arrival of the Jumblies in their sieve meant the destruction of the security and immunity from suffering of Lear's Nonsense world.

The first mention of this poem is in August 1876, when Lear 'Wrote out the nonsense poem, "The Dong with a luminous Nose"' (Diary, 22.viii.76). Two days later he had 'quite concluded, "the Dong with a luminous Nose.," & so also ends the new Xmas book' (Diary, 24.viii.76). The manuscript exhibited here is Lear's own copy of the poem, and was a fair copy made in preparation for its publication.

PROVENANCE Philip Hofer; The Houghton Library, Harvard University.

EXHIBITION 1968, London, Gooden and Fox Ltd, *Edward Lear* (no. 30).

86

87 Laughable Lyrics

[Repr. p. 176

a) Lear's proof copy of *Laughable Lyrics*, 1877
Volume bound in red morocco with gilt edges: 21.6×17.8 cm/$8\frac{1}{2} \times 7$ in
Inset in front: proof title page on thick paper with the same design as that of the published volume, reading 'Sage and Onions and other poems by Edward Lear', and contemporary newspaper and periodical reviews mounted on blank sheets
Department of Printing and Graphic Arts, The Houghton Library, Harvard University

b) *Laughable Lyrics*, 1877
Volume: 21.3×17.6 cm/$8\frac{3}{8} \times 6\frac{15}{16}$ in
Open at the last verse of 'Mr and Mrs Discobbolos'
Inscribed: *The Second Part of "Mr and Mrs / Discobbolos" was written by my / old friend Edward Lear at my / suggestion. So far as I know, it / has not yet been published. / Wilkie Collins / 21 July 1888*
Department of Printing and Graphic Arts, The Houghton Library, Harvard University

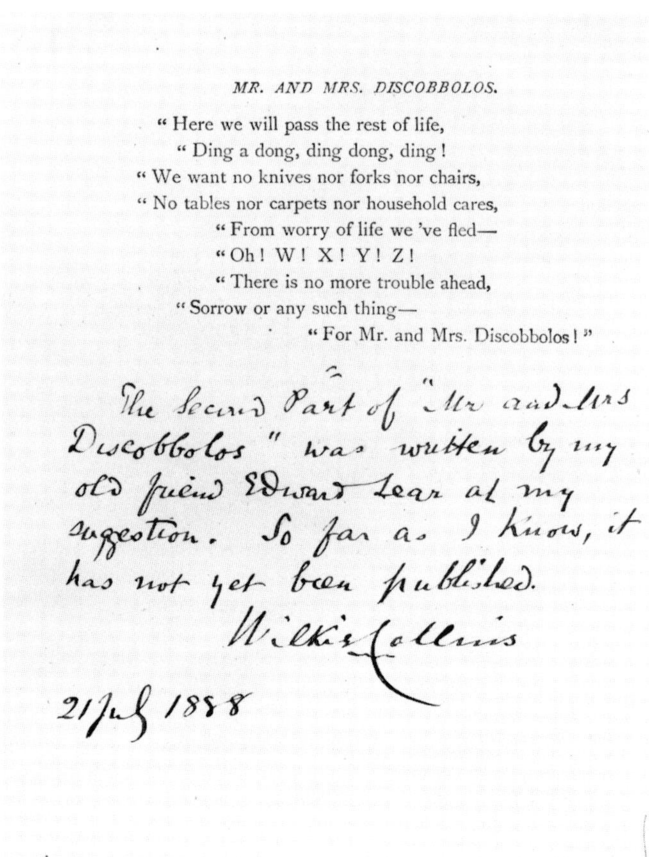
MR. AND MRS. DISCOBBOLOS.

"Here we will pass the rest of life,
"Ding a dong, ding dong, ding!
"We want no knives nor forks nor chairs,
"No tables nor carpets nor household cares,
"From worry of life we 've fled—
"Oh! W! X! Y! Z!
"There is no more trouble ahead,
"Sorrow or any such thing—
"For Mr. and Mrs. Discobbolos!"

The Second Part of "Mr and Mrs Discobbolos" was written by my old friend Edward Lear at my suggestion. So far as I know, it has not yet been published.
Wilkie Collins
21 July 1888

87*b*

Laughable Lyrics was the last book of Nonsense which Lear published. It contains some of his finest—though perhaps his saddest—Nonsense songs, including 'The Dong with a Luminous Nose' (Cat. 86), 'The Pelican Chorus' (see Cat. 101), 'The Courtship of the Yonghy-Bonghy-Bò' (Cat. 84), 'The Pobble who has no Toes', and 'The Quangle Wangle's Hat' (see Cat. 85). It also contains the only two known musical settings by Lear of his Nonsense songs, and the oddity of an alphabet—'A was an Area Arch'—where the illustrations are not his. Lear's own drawings for the alphabet are in the Houghton Library.

He had intended to call this 'Learical Lyrics and Puffles of Prose'; he also considered 'Sage and Onions and Other Poems', and a proof of this title-page is bound into this volume. However, both titles were dropped in favour of *Laughable Lyrics*, giving the *Standard* critic the opportunity to write: 'We should not like to be condemned to read much of this kind of literature. Fortunately, in the present volume there is not much of it. The author must have supposed what he calls his lyrics to be laughable, since he gives them that title. If there is any man or woman whose features would curl, as the novelists might express it, on reading them, we are certain it would not be with a smile' (*The Standard*, 14.xii.76). *The Saturday Review*, however, suggested that 'Mr. Lear's great quality is one which he shares with Milton, and Scott, and Aeschulus. He uses the sonorus names of remote, and indeed undiscovered regions with majestic effect' (9.xii.76).

There was only one edition of the book; shortly after the publication the publisher, Bush, became bankrupt. The volume exhibited here (Cat. 87*a*) is Lear's proof copy with reviews pasted in.

The second copy exhibited (Cat. 87*b*) belonged to Wilkie Collins, the writer of mystery stories including *The Woman in White* (1860) and *The Moonstone* (1888), whom Lear had known since his youth (see Cat. 99*b*). This is open at the last verse of 'Mr and Mrs Discobbolos'.

Lear wrote the second part of 'Mr and Mrs Discobbolos' in October 1879, shortly after building work had begun on the hotel beneath his window at Villa Emily, San Remo (see Cat. 110). In 1866 he had spoken of 'the perpetual misery of all belongings' (Diary, 23.viii.86); all his life he had been cautious of burdening himself with a house and possessions, recalling perhaps the miseries of his own childhood. However, the contentment he felt in his quiet, if lonely, retreat at San Remo from 1870 was echoed in the first part of the song, written a year later. 'From worry of life we've fled,' sang Mr and Mrs Discobbolos, '. . . There is no more trouble ahead, / Sorrow or any such thing . . .'. But Lear, like both the Dong (see Cat. 86) and Mr Discobbolos, discovered that no retreat could guarantee safety or happiness. Within ten years both his home and his peace of mind had been destroyed and for the rest of his life he was burdened with anxiety and despair.

Although Lear records the payment of £5 for this poem by James Fields of Boston (see Cat. 78), it was not published until October 1888, when it appeared in *The Quarterly Review*.

The name of Discobbolos is derived from the classical sculpture of a disc-thrower, a plaster cast which Lear would have known and possibly drawn as a student at the Royal Academy Schools (see Cat. 103).

PROVENANCE *(a)* W.B. Osgood Field; The Houghton Library, Harvard University. *(b)* Wilkie Collins; W.B. Osgood Field; The Houghton Library, Harvard University.

REFERENCES *(a)* Osgood Field 1933, pp. 174–7. *(b)* Osgood Field 1933, p. 92.

88 Nursery Rhymes

'Sing a song of sixpence', 1842
Sepia ink on paper: (i)–(vii) each 13.2 × 19.3 cm/$5\frac{3}{16} \times 7\frac{5}{8}$ in
i Signed and dated bl.: *E. Lear. 22 March. 1842.*
Inscribed b.: *I sing a song of sixpence a bag full of rye.*

ii Signed and dated br.: *E. Lear. 22. March. 1842.*
Inscribed b.: *Four & twenty Blackbirds baked in a pye.*

iii Signed and dated br.: *E. Lear. 22. March. 1842.*
Inscribed b.: *When the Pye was opened the Birds began to sing—*

iv Signed and bated br.: *E. Lear. 22. March. 1842*
Inscribed bc.: *And was not that / a dainty dish to set before a King?—*

v Signed and dated bl.: *Edwd Lear 22. 1842.—Edwd Lear.—*
Inscribed cl.: *The King was in his Countinghouse counting out his money.*

vi Signed and dated bl.: *Edwd Lear 22. March. 1842.*
Inscribed tl.: *The Queen was in her parlour eating bread and honey.*

vii Signed and dated bl.: *22. March. 1842.—E. Lear.*
Inscribed bl.: *The Maid was in the Garden / a hanging out the clothes—*

Sepia ink on paper: 39.8 × 21.6 cm/$15\frac{11}{16} \times 8\frac{1}{2}$ in
viii Inscribed b.: *When down came a blackbird & pecked off her nose.*
Private Collection

Several sets of Lear's illustrations to nursery rhymes have survived. The group from which these drawings are taken was drawn for the children of Archdeacon George Clark, whom

88

Lear knew during his time in Rome (1832–48; see Cat. 15–19). The final drawing (Cat. 88 viii) appears to have been done separately, perhaps to replace a lost drawing. He also illustrated 'Hey Diddle Diddle' and 'Dumpling Dumpling Dee' for the Clark children.

In 1867 Lear illustrated 'Hey Diddle Diddle' and 'Sing a Song of Sixpence' for Janet Symonds (see Cat. 78), drawings which were published in *Queery Leary Nonsense* in 1911. In 1902 George H. Ellis & Co. of Boston published *Sing a Song of Sixpense. Another Lost Legend. By the author of 'Lost Legends of the Nursery Songs' & with eight illustrations by Lear*, but the whereabouts of this manuscript is unknown. There is a further collection in the Houghton Library, including 'Humpty Dumpty', and 'One, two, three, four, five, Once I caught a hare alive'. There are a further four drawings for 'Hey Diddle Diddle', now dispersed.

Marianne North (see Cat. 82) recalls that when Lear was staying in Hastings with Holman Hunt (see Cat. 49), he would 'wander into our sitting room through the windows at dusk when his work was over, sit down to the piano, and sing Tennyson's songs for hours, composing as he went on, and picking out the accompaniments by ear, putting the greatest expression and passion into the most sentimental words. He often set me laughing; then he would say I was not worthy of them, and would continue with intense pathos of expression and gravity of face, while he substituted Hey Diddle Diddle, the Cat and the Fiddle, or some other nonsensical words to the same air' (Marianne North, *Recollections of a Happy Life*, 1892, vol. I, p. 29).

PROVENANCE Rev. George Clark, by family descent.

89 History

The tragical life and death of / Caius Marius—Esqre / late her Majesty's Consul=general / in the Roman States: illustrated / from authentic sauces—by. / Edward Lear. East Sheen—Oct, 30th 1841.—
Volume 11.9 × 18.4 cm/$4\frac{5}{8} \times 7\frac{1}{4}$ in
Open at page 15
Sepia ink on paper: 11.4 × 18.2 cm/$4\frac{1}{2} \times 7\frac{3}{16}$ in
Inscribed b.: *Caius Marius—not feeling himself comfortable, places / himself in the marshes of Minturnum, all among the bull frogs.*
Justin G. Schiller

Only two examples of Lear's personal accounts of historical people and events have so far been discovered. One recounts the adventures of Romulus and Remus, and the other, exhibited here, the life and death of Caius Marius.

In Lear's version of his rise and fall we follow his progress from lowly shepherd to soldier-hero and Consul-General. He marries Miss Julia Caesar, is elected Consul and defeats the Teutons and the Cimbri. His fortunes turn. He quarrels with Mrs Sylla and flees Rome. Pursued by his enemies, he hides in the bullrushes: 'Caius Marius—not feeling himself comfortable, places himself in the Marshes of Minturnum, all among the bull frogs.' Discovered and taken prisoner, he escapes death, is eventually set free and 'flies to Carthage—where he sits among the ruins for a considerable period.' But his days of greatness are not yet over. He returns '& lays seige to Rome, where he cuts off lots of his enemies' heads.' His gesture to the dismembered heads is, to quote Lear's Calabrian journal

89

in a quite different situation, 'not altogether in strict accordance with the...arrangements of polite society.' (J. Cal., pp. 138–39) But now his days are numbered, and although once more elected first Consul, he succumbs to drink and expires.

In this manuscript Lear brings humour to the serious matter of history. As with his parodies (see Cat. 71), it is a familiar combination of affection and leg-pulling with which his contemporaries were not uniformly impressed. Writing to Fortescue in 1862, Lear recounted, 'The Chancellor—(I was there Saturday & Sunday—) was delightful: such an abundance of excellent conversation—with a circle, or with me only—one seldom has the luck of getting. / He,—Speaking of "undique sequaces"— & "sequax",—& saying, "let us remember the line and go & look for the translation" quote the Landscape painter in a fit of absurdity— / "My Lord I can remember it easily by thinking of wild ducks." / —"How of wild Ducks Lear?"—said the Lord C.—"Because they are *sea-quacks*" said I. / "Lear"—said his Lordship "I abominate the forcibly introduction of ridiculous images calculated to distract the mind from what it is contemplating."' (21.x.62, LEL 1907, pp. 252–53). The Lord Chancellor was the father of Gussie Bethell (see Cat. 115).

This volume was made at East Sheen, the home of Edward and Lady Charlotte Penrhyn; Lady Charlotte was the sister of the 13th Earl of Derby.

PROVENANCE Private Collection; 1983, bt through the trade, London; Justin G. Schiller.

90 Zoology

a) *Portraites of the inditchenous beestes of New Olland*
Sepia ink on paper: 18.7 × 11.6 cm/$7\frac{3}{8} \times 4\frac{9}{16}$ in
Inscribed tr.: *Portraites of the inditchenous beestes / of New Olland.*
Inscribed in different places on the sheet:
Ye great Kangaroo. / or Boomer. / 6 feet high
ye. Wallaby / 2 feet high
Ye Bush Kangaroos / 3 feet high.
Ye Kangaroo ratte. / 13 inches high.
Ye Kangaroos—in their propper propperportions
(For ye Bandocootes.)
Ye duck billed Platypuss.
Ye dogge. Ye peculiar or prickly porkyoupine. / Ye possum / up his gum / tree
Ye cowe
his i Ye wombat.
Ye common or Native Catte
Ye sheepe / Ye greate blacke Devil / Ye horse

Pierpont Morgan Library, New York. Gift of Mrs Paul G. Pennoyer, 1963

b) *The animals going into the ark*
Ink on paper: 27.9 × 137.2 cm/11 × 54 in
Inscribed bl.: *Efelant*
Mrs R.E.C. Stileman

c) *Ye Hippopotamouse or Gigantick Rabitte*
Sepia ink on blue paper: 20.3 × 30.4 cm/8 × 12 in
Inscribed b.: *Ye Hippopotamouse or Gigantick Rabitte. This large beaste doth belong to ye familie of Geo. Coombe, Esq., of Preston. It dwelleth in a large boxe and feedeth on lettuce leaves or other salads. Alle day longe he moveth his nose up and down but in other respects he is a harmless beaste. On one side ye picture, to represent one who offerith a bit of domestic spinach for your Hippopotamouse Rabbit, his supper . . .*
David F.M. Stileman Esq.

Lear's *Portraites of the inditchenous beestes of New Olland* were probably inspired by Gould's visit there in 1838 to work on *Birds of Australia*. '. . . the Goulds are going to Van Dieman's Land to catch kangaroos,' he told Ann (29.iii.38, TS.), and the following year he wrote to Gould, 'Do not fancy . . . that I should not be much entertained by an account of your novelties abroad for I still know an Opposum from a Frogon' (17.x.39, MS., Houghton Library, Harvard University).

Both *Ye Hippopotamous or Gigantic Rabbitte* (Cat. 90*c*) and

90*b*

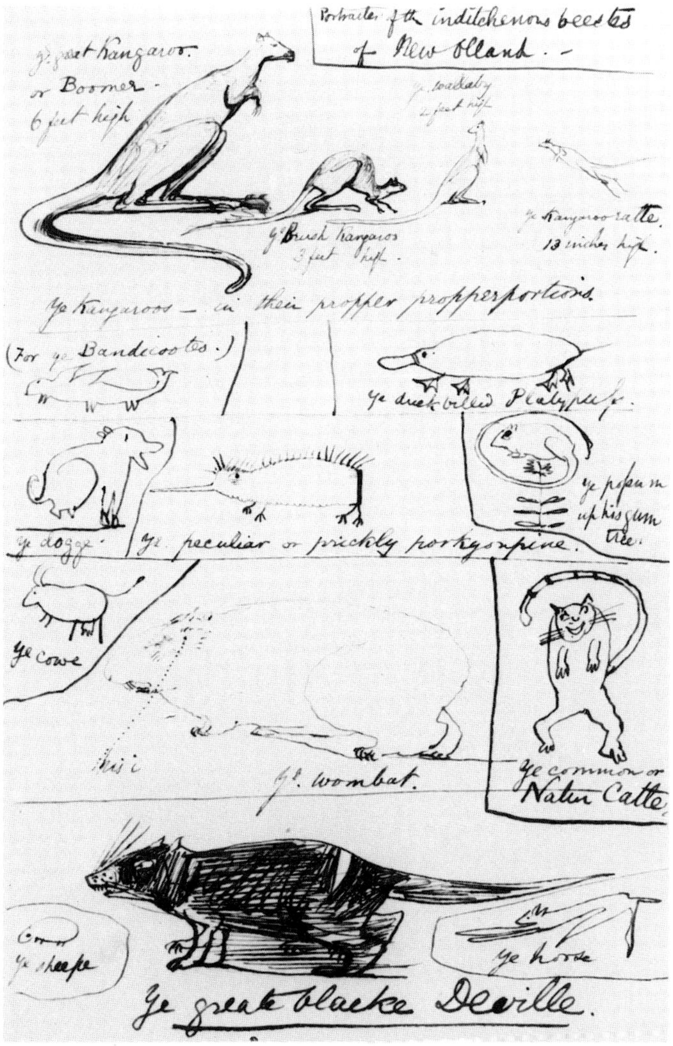

90a

The animals going into the ark (Cat. 90*b*) were drawn for the children of George and Fanny Coombe. Fanny, born Fanny Drewitt, had been a childhood friend of Lear's from Sussex (see p. 73). His earliest Nonsense, most of which now exists only in copies, was done for the Drewitt family. 'My Sussex friends always say that I can do nothing like other people,' he wrote in 1831 (Empson, 1.x.31, MS., Pierpont Morgan Library, New York), and it was probably with them that he first realised that he could make people happy by making them laugh. In 1832 he wrote to George and Fanny's six-month-old daughter, addressing her as 'My dear Niece—par adoption,' and ending the letter, 'Your 3 parts crazy and wholly affectionate Uncle Edward' (Fanny Coombe, n.d. [July 32], MS., The Houghton Library, Harvard University), the first occasion we know when he called himself an 'Adopty Duncle' (see Cat. 81).

PROVENANCE *(a)* James Tregaskis, London; Mrs Paul G. Pennoyer; 1963, given to The Pierpont Morgan Library, New York. *(b) (c)* George and Fanny Coombe, Preston (Brighton); Henry Willett; Mrs Joyce Garrick, by family descent.

REFERENCE *(a)* Noakes 1979 edn, repr. (detail) p. 118.

91 Geography

Lear's moon journey, 26 February 1882
Two drawings contained in a letter to Mrs Stuart Wortley, bound into a volume
Watercolour with bodycolour on paper:
i 5×8.6 cm/$2 \times 3\frac{7}{8}$ in
ii 5.4×8.6 cm/$2\frac{1}{8} \times 3\frac{3}{8}$ in
Both drawings signed with monogram tr.:
Private Collection

Though Lear frequently slipped into Nonsense in otherwise serious letters, examples of sustained Nonsense letters are rare. The letter he wrote to thank Mrs Stuart Wortley for buying a drawing of Monte Generoso was accompanied by two drawings for her—of Simla and Ravenna Forest—and the two exhibited here for her small daughters. 'These are of singular—I may say bingular value,—as they were done in the Moon, to which I lately went one night, returning next morning on a Moonbeam . ! . The first view is of the Jizzdoddle rocks, with 2 of the many remarkable planets which surround the moon rising or riz in the distance; these orangecolourd & peagreen orbs leaving a profound impression of sensational surprise on the mind of the speckletator who first beholds them. The second view represents the Rumbytumby ravine, with the crimson planet Buzz and its 5 Satanites on the horizon. In the foreground on the left is a Blompopp tree, so called from the Blompopp, a gigantic and gorgeous bird which builds on its summit. To the left [right] are the tall Vizzikilly trees, the most common vegetation of the Lunar hummysphere. These trees grow to an immense height, & bloom only once in 15 years, when they produce a large crop of immemorial soapbubbles, submarine suckingpigs, songs of sunrise, & silversixpences,—which last are ground into powder by the Lunar population, & drunk in warm water without any sugar.' He then describes the inhabitants of the moon in a manner reminiscent of the *Adventures of Baron Munchhausen*, a book which Lear would have known from his childhood.

Lear probably first met Mrs Stuart Wortley during his first stay in Rome (1837–48). In 1841 she bought from Lear an oil painting of St Peter's.

PROVENANCE Mrs Stuart Wortley, by family descent.

EXHIBITION 1968, London, Gooden and Fox Ltd, *Edward Lear* (no. 33).

91

92 Travel Adventures

a) *Ye Artist in ye wonderfull bedde*
No. 4 of 8 sheets bound within 1 volume: 20.4 × 29.3 cm/8 × 11½ in
Sepia ink on paper: each 16.8 × 20.9 cm/6½ × 8¼ in
Sheet no. 6 has watermark: *1853*
Inscribed b.: *Ye prospecte is taken from the south side of the beautifulle chamber, with ye Artist / a repoging of himself on the East side of yͤ wonderfull bedde.*

1. *Ye wonderfull bedde.*
2. *Ye artist his head.*
3. *—— his porz.*
4. *—— his Toze.*
5. *Yͤ pillows*
6. *Yͤ long sofa*
7. *Ye artist his garmints.*
8. *Ye chaires*
9. *Ye curtings of ye window*
10. *Ye dressing table.*
11. *Ye Pinnecushing.*
12. *Ye Pinnes.*
13. *Ye curly burlies.*
14. *Ye looking glass.*
15. *Ye distant tree*
16. *Ye cock robin*
17. *Ye hen robbin*
18. *Yͤ little dreames.*
19. *Ye flies on yͤ window pains*
20. *Ye Artist his slippers*

The Syndics of the Fitzwilliam Museum, Cambridge

b) *The Landscape painter perceives the Moufflons on the tops of the/Mountains of Crete*, 1864
Two sheets
i Blue ink on paper: 23 × 18.7 cm/9$\frac{1}{16}$ × 7⅜ in
Plate 1 inscribed b.: *The Landscape painter perceives the Moufflons on the tops of/the Mountains of Crete*
Dated tr.: *July 5 1864*
Plate 2 inscribed b.: *The Landscape painter escapes (with difficulty—) from an/enraged Moufflon.*
ii Blue ink on paper: 20.3 × 13 cm/8 × 5⅛ in
Plate 3 inscribed br.: *The Landscape painter/is enabled to ascend/some of the highest tops/of the mountains of Crete/by sticking on to a/Moufflon's Horns.*
J.J. Farquharson Esq.

From 1841 onwards, Lear would describe graphically the adventures which befell him on his travels (see Cat. 18).

The series of drawings depicting his night in 'ye wonderfull bedde' (Cat. 92*a*) is undated. However, since nos 5 and 6 illustrate his awakening to the sound of musicians beneath his window, playing instruments which look particularly Alpine, the manuscript probably dates from Lear's visit to Switzerland in the summer of 1854 (see Cat. 28). The sixth sheet is watermarked 1853.

Ten years later, when Lear visited Crete (see Cat. 23), he encountered the helpful mountain goats. The moufflon is in fact the wild goat of Corsica and Sardinia; that of Crete is called the agrimi, and is now only found in the region of the Samarian Gorge. These drawings (Cat. 92*b*) were made after Lear's return from Crete, when he was staying with the Prescotts in Roehampton (see Cat. 93).

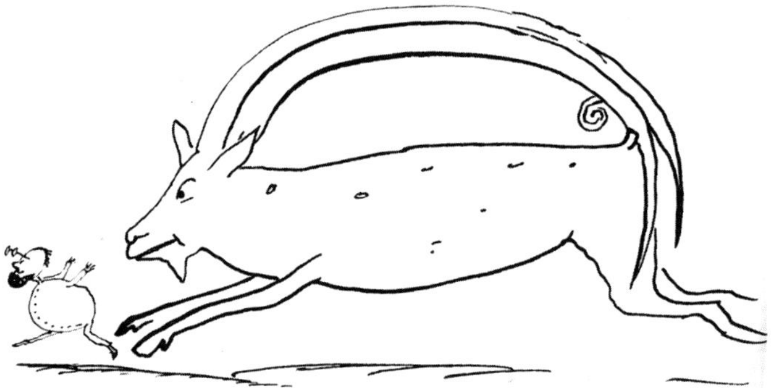

92*b*

PROVENANCE *(a)* W. Barclay Squire; June 1923, presented by him through the National Art-Collections Fund to the Fitzwilliam Museum, Cambridge. *(b)* W. G. Prescott, by family descent.

EXHIBITED *(a)* 1928, London, Victoria and Albert Museum, *The National Art-Collections Fund Exhibition* (no no.).

REFERENCES *(a)* E. Lear, *Ye Long Nite in ye wonderfull Bedde? A Bread-and-Butter Letter with Reservations?*, Fitzwilliam Museum, Cambridge (n.d.). *(b)* Noakes 1968 edn, repr. p. 202; Noakes 1979 edn, repr. p. 206; Fowler 1984, plate 1, repr. p. 72, plate 2, repr. p. 93, plate 3, repr. p. 44.

93 The Object discovered in Beta

a) *Object discovered in Beta*
Wood and ivory: 13.6 × 13.3 × 8.2 cm/5⅜ × 5¼ × 3¼ in
J.J. Farquharson Esq.

b) *Object discovered in Beta*, 1863
Blue ink on paper: 15.4 × 9.8 cm/6$\frac{1}{16}$ × 3⅞ in folded
Dated: *July 11. 1863*
(For inscription see below)
J.J. Farquharson Esq.

Object. Discovered in Beta.
July 11. 1863

We are delighted to acquaint our Readers, (& more especially Harkee! o logical Readers,) that fresh discoveries are on the point of being about to be expected to be supposed to be made at Clarence House Roehampton,—of which the accompanying drawing represents one of the most interesting hitherto offered to the pusillanimous public. The object in question was found in Beta & is of an indescribuble form & indefinable color: and although some idiotic cotemporaries have argued that it is intended to hold pens, there cannot be the smallest doubt that it is the Stand on which the spears of the remarkable & distinguished Beta were kept when she was not using them. For it is well known the Beta never grew to more than 3 feet 1 inch high—& consequently the penlike but warlike instruments above delineated are quite adapted to her size. Moreover their having been discovered in the apartment which for Countless ages has been named after that small but indomitable person, is a parapumphilious proof that requires no other illustration except to the perception of owls, apes, geese, pigs, beetles, or donkies.
Q.E.D.

The Prescott family, who lived at Clarence House, Roehampton (see Cat. 69*a*) named their rooms by the Greek alphabet. As well as this object discovered in Beta, Lear had his own ideas about a wig-stand and a coal skuttle he found in Lambda, and a cloak-stand in Theta.

PROVENANCE *(a) (b)* W.G. Prescott, by family descent.

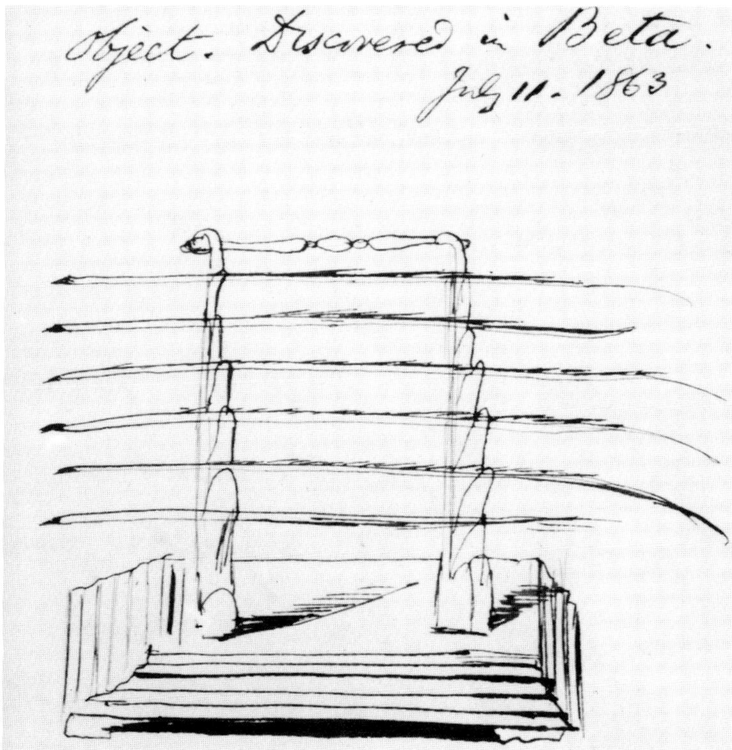

93*b*

94 Coloured Birds

[Col. pl. p. 28; repr. p. 90

A set of sixteen, mounted on three matts, 1880
Sepia and black ink, watercolour: average size
14×11.1 cm/$5\frac{1}{2} \times 4\frac{3}{8}$ in
Arranged in 1 set of 4 images and 2 sets of 6 images
Inscribed: (1) *The Yellow Bird / The Dark=Blue Bird / The Orange—colour Bird / The Lilac Bird*; (2) *The Pink Bird / The Brown Bird / The Gray Bird / The Dark=Green Bird / The Crimson Bird / The Black and White Bird*; (3) *The Black Bird / The Red Bird / The White Bird / The Purple Bird / The Light=Blue Bird / The Light=Green Bird.*
Trustees of The Victoria and Albert Museum

In 1863 Lear made a set of fourteen coloured birds for Mary de Vere, a child whom he knew in Corfu, and on 22 January 1880 he 'made 24 ridiculous drawings of birds for the little Fentons.' (Diary). The whereabouts of both these sets is unknown. Another group of twenty was made in about 1881 for the small son of Evelyn Baring (see Cat. 96*b*). These were published in 1911 in *Queery Leary Nonsense*, and in 1912 in *The Lear Coloured Bird Book for Children*. In his Introduction to *Queery Leary Nonsense*, Lord Cromer said: 'When my eldest son was about three years old, his mother expressed a wish that he should acquire some knowledge of colour. Lear, with his usual kindness, at once sent twenty drawings of birds of various colours—including, of course, his favourite, the Scroobious and the Runcible birds. I had these bound in a book.' The Runcible bird is multi-coloured and the Scroobious bird of an indefinable hue, a demonstration perhaps that not all things in life can be described with convenient certainty. The set exhibited here was made in 1880 for Charles Geffrard Pirouet (see Cat. 81*d*).

94*a*

94*b*

These birds are an example of the way in which Lear instructed children with fun and without patronising them. Those who knew him record that he was on the side of the child, and in his Foreword to *The Lear Coloured Bird Book for Children*, J.St.Loe Strachey wrote: 'I knew he was "safe" and that I was safe and that we were all safe together, and that suspicion might at once be put aside.'

PROVENANCE Charles Geffrard Pirouet; Mrs Agnes A. Corbyn; 1951, bt by The Victoria and Albert Museum.

EXHIBITIONS 1958, London, Arts Council of Great Britain, *Edward Lear* (nos 64–66); 1968, London, Gooden and Fox Ltd, *Edward Lear* (no. 32 [4 birds only]).

REFERENCE Edward Lear, *A Nonsense Alphabet*, London 1952 (facsimile).

95 Nonsense in Letters

a) Letter to Digby Wyatt, 14 November 1863
Sepia ink on paper: 14 × 8.7 cm/$5\frac{1}{2} \times 3\frac{7}{16}$ in
Vivien Noakes

b) Letter to Mrs Richard Ward, 25 August 1873 [Repr. p. 121
Sepia ink on paper: open 27.8 × 21.6 cm/$10\frac{15}{16} \times 8\frac{1}{2}$ in
Inscribed t.: *Morning*
1. Palestrina
2. town of Colonna
3. Alban Hill.
4–4, Volscian Hills.
5. Coriolanus—smoking of a long pipe.
6. 6—site of the Lake of Gabii.
7. site of Corioli.
8. Ghost of Lucretia.
9. Ghost of Tarquin, a eating of a Nomlet & green pease.
Inscribed b.: *(Evening)*
1. Roons of Claudian Acqueduct.
2. Mount Soracte.
3. 4—Horace & Macenas, a playing of Snowball on the top.
5.5.5—the Sabine ills
6 6. Barlams
7. Ghost of an ancient Sabbin.
The Frederick R. Koch Foundation Collection, New York

c) Letter to Lady Wyatt, 16 April 1875
Ink on paper: 23.1 × 18.4 cm/$9\frac{1}{8} \times 7\frac{1}{4}$ in
The Frederick R. Koch Foundation Collection, New York

From his early youth, Lear descended into the absurd in his letters—though only to trusted correspondents; nowhere is the sheer joy that he found in words more clearly seen. An early letter to Ann dated 17 January 1826, for which the manuscript is now lost, consists of 111 lines all ending with words which finish in -ation. His habit of playing with a single word, here *mint* (Cat. 95*c*), is shown in other letters. From Delhi he wrote that he had stayed ten days 'making Delhineations of the Dehlicate architecture as is all impressed on my mind as inDehlibly as the Dehliterious quality of the water of that city' (Fortescue, 24.iv.74, LLEL 1911, p. 171; see Cat. 34*g*).

Digby Wyatt (Cat. 95*a*), whose dinner invitation Lear wished poetically not to refuse, was an architect and writer on art. He had been secretary to the executive committee of the Great Exhibition in 1851, and later became the first Slade Professor of Fine Arts at Cambridge. He was knighted in 1869. Lear and he first met in Rome.

The letter to Mrs Richard Ward (Cat. 95*b*) accompanied two small drawings he was sending as a wedding present. They were *Morning, near the Pinetree of Redicicoli* and *Evening—on the Via Appia*. 'I have made a little scratchibillity just to show you the principal localities,' he wrote in the letter, 'which happen to be interesting . . . I am in such a Norful mess! bricks & mortar & stone—making a terrace, & a back entrance & offices as oughted to have been made long ago. Excavation also,—to keep the Elephants in as I may bring back from Ingy.'

Mrs Richard Ward was the daughter of Sir John Simeon, whom Lear met through the Tennysons. It was after the death of Simeon that Tennyson wrote 'In the Garden of Swainston', one of his poems which Lear set to music but for which no known copy survives (see Cat. 41).

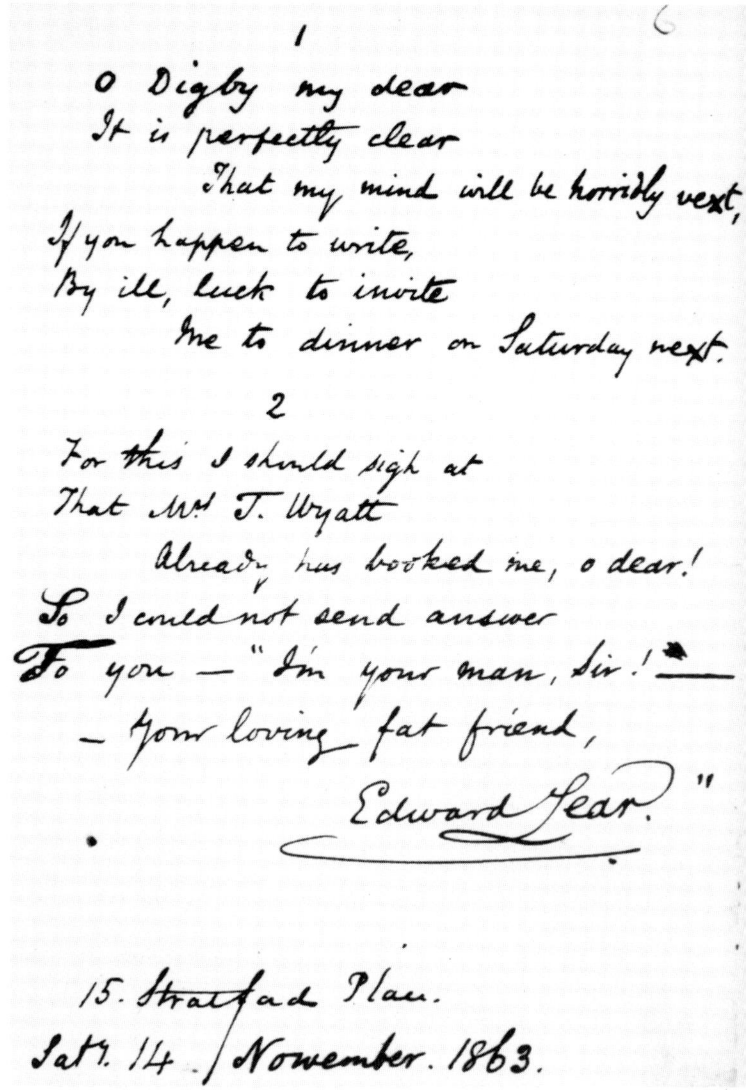
6

1
O Digby my dear
It is perfectly clear
That my mind will be horridly vext,
If you happen to write,
By ill, luck to invite
Me to dinner on Saturday next.

2
For this I should sigh at
That Mrs T. Wyatt
Already has booked me, o dear!
So I could not send answer
To you — "I'm your man, Sir!" —
— Your loving fat friend,
Edward Lear."

15. Stratford Place.
Saty. 14 / November. 1863.

95*a*

PROVENANCE *(a)* Sir Digby Wyatt; by family descent to Dr B.W. Paine; 1980, 16 December, Sotheby's London (lot 327); bt by Vivien Noakes. *(b)* Mrs Richard Ward; 1982, 29 June, Sotheby's London (lot 248); bt by The Frederick R. Koch Foundation Collection, New York, on deposit with The Pierpont Morgan Library, New York. *(c)* Lady Wyatt, by family descent to Dr B.W. Paine; 1980, 16 December, Sotheby's London (lot 339); bt by Bernard Quaritch Ltd; 1982, 15 December, Sotheby's London (lot 144); bt by Richard MacNutt; bt by The Frederick R. Koch Foundation Collection, New York, on deposit with The Pierpont Morgan Library, New York.

96 Self-portraits [Repr. p. 101

a) The artist standing on a bench painting a picture
Letter to Lady Waldegrave, Thursday 26 July 1860
Sepia ink on paper: 18.5 × 23 cm/$7\frac{1}{4}$ × 9 in
Somerset Record Office, Taunton

b) The artist as a bird [Repr. p. 196
Letter to Evelyn Baring, *c.* January 1864
Pen and ink on paper: 14 × 17.5 cm/$5\frac{1}{2}$ × $6\frac{7}{8}$ in
National Portrait Gallery, London

c) The artist and Giorgio on an elephant and the Ahkond of Swat
Letter to Lady Waldegrave, 25 October 1873
Sepia ink on paper: 21.6 × 29.2 cm/$8\frac{1}{2}$ × $11\frac{1}{2}$ in
Somerset Record Office, Taunton

d) The artist riding on the back of a porpoise [Repr. p. 10
Letter to Chichester Fortescue, 26 September 1875
Sepia ink on paper: 17.9 × 10.7 cm/$7\frac{1}{16}$ × $4\frac{7}{16}$ in
Somerset Record Office, Taunton

The earliest known self-portrait of Lear is in a letter dated 1 October 1831 (Pierpont Morgan Library, New York), and shows a straightforward youth with a parrot perched upon his shoulder. It was not until July 1860 (Fortescue, 9.vii.[60], LEL 1907, p. 143) that he first used the 'perfectly spherical' shape to which he refers in 'How Pleasant to Know Mr Lear' (see Cat. 98).

The drawing of Lear standing on a bench painting (Cat. 96*a*) was made seventeen days later on 26 July 1860, and from this date onwards, such caricatures adorned many of his letters. The image of rotundity was inspired by his increasing girth, but is one recalled from his childhood, as when his sister Ann wrote to their brother Fred in 1847: 'Do you remember, dear Fred, what I used to call you many years ago? Your constant increase in *circumference* reminds me again of the *Norfolk Biffin*—what a fine specimen of this rounded fruit you must represent!! I think I see you now how you used to run round the room after me when I compar'd you to the flat *spreading* Norfolk Apple' (Ann to Frederick Lear, 10.ix.47, MS., Private Collection).

The letter to Evelyn Baring (later Lord Cromer) dating from January 1864 (Cat. 96*b*) is one of twelve illustrated letters which Lear sent to Baring in Corfu during the winter of 1863–64. These were published in 1911 (*Queery Leary Nonsense*, pp. 8–17). Lear had met Baring on Corfu in 1863, when the latter was aide-de-camp to the Governor, Sir Henry Storks. He was subsequently private secretary to his cousin, Lord Northbrook, Viceroy of India, a post he held when Lear visited the sub-continent in 1873–75. He later became British Agent and Consul General in Egypt (1883–90).

The self-portrait of Lear on an elephant (Cat. 96*c*) was inspired by his visit to India; he is accompanied by Giorgio (see Cat. 116). *The Times of India* for 18 July 1873 carried a short piece in which 'It is reported from Swat that the Akhoond's son has quarrelled with his father, and left the parental presence with a following of 500 sowars, refusing to listen to the Akhoond's orders to come back.' 'Why, or when, or which, or what / Or who, or where, is the Ahkond of Swat?' asked Lear in a letter to Fortescue (12.ix.73, LLEL 1911,

96*c*

p. 162); his poetic thoughts on the subject were published in *Laughable Lyrics* (1877). Though this particular problem remained unsolved, by 25 October (Cat. 96*c*) he had obviously decided just how the Akhond looked.

On 24 October 1878 Fortescue wrote to Lear: 'I read sometime ago with deep regret the death of the Akhond of Swat—Do you think he knew before he died, that you had made him more famous than any other Indian potentate?' Lear replied sadly, 'The Akhond of Swāt would have left me all his pppropppprty, but he thought I was dead: so didn't. The mistake arose from someone officiously pointing out to him that King Lear died 7 centuries ago, & that the poem referred to one of the Akhond's predecessors' (Fortescue, 28.x.78, LLEL 1911, p. 213).

The picture of Lear on the back of a porpoise (Cat. 96*d*) was in a letter written just before he left England to return to San Remo in September 1875. Writing to Fortescue he said, 'If the sea is very rough I mean to hire a prudent and pussilanimous porpoise, and cross on his bak' (26.ix.75, LEL 1907, p. 185).

PROVENANCE *(a) (c)* Lady Waldegrave; by descent to Lord Strachie; 1973, bequethed by Lord Strachie to the Somerset Record Office, Taunton. *(b)* Evelyn Baring (later 1st Earl of Cromer); by descent to Captain John Hills; 26 February 1964, Sotheby's London (lot 1); bt by Thomas Agnew and Sons on behalf of private collector; resold by Agnews to The National Portrait Gallery. *(d)* Chichester Fortescue (later Lord Carlingford); by family descent to Lord Strachey; on deposit at the Somerset Record Office, Taunton.

EXHIBITION *(b)* 1968, London, Gooden and Fox Ltd, *Edward Lear* (no. 17).

REFERENCES *(a)* LEL 1907, p. 173; Noakes 1968 edn, p. 238; Noakes 1979 edn, p. 148; Hyman 1980, p. 73; Fowler 1984, p. 32. *(b)* Lady Strachey ed., *Queery Leary Nonsense*, London 1911, p. 9; Lehmann 1977, repr. p. 30; *National Portrait Gallery complete illustrated catalogue*, 1981, repr. p. 337. *(c)* LLEL 1911, pp. 166–68; Noakes 1979 edn, repr. p. 271 (detail). *(d)* LLEL 1911, pp. 184–85; Noakes 1979 edn, repr. p. 245.

97 Foss

Ink on paper: 26 × 20.6 cm/$10\frac{1}{4} \times 8\frac{1}{8}$ in
Signed and dated br.: *Edward Lear 15 July, 1875*
Inscribed c.: *PHOS*
Department of Printing and Graphic Arts, the Houghton Library, Harvard University

Foss joined Lear's household as a kitten in November 1872, after the disappearance of his brother Potiphar, 'who has no end of a tail—because it had been cut off' (Fortescue 28.ii.72, LLEL 1911, p. 145). Foss was also tailless; the operation was performed by Giorgio who believed that a cat would not wander from the house in which it had left its tail.

Within days of Foss's arrival he was found tearing Lear's letters to shreds, and was banished to the kitchen. 'Pity,' wrote Lear, 'for he was a sort of companion;—yet being so literally & really alone,—it is perhaps as well to have no sham substitutes for society' (Diary, 31.i.73). But the banishment was short-lived, and for the next seventeen years Foss was Lear's constant and much-loved companion.

97

At one stage Lear had ambitions for the cat's artistic development, for Foss was found each morning sitting beneath the blackbird's cage, and 'we . . . expected eventually to hear poor dear Foss warble effusively. But alas! it has been discovered that there is a hole in the lower part of Merlo's cage, and Foss's attention relates to pieces of biscuit falling through' (Fortescue, 2.v.82, LLEL 1911, p. 263).

As well as appearing in numerous self-portraits by Lear (see Cat. 40), Foss had his own iconography. Lear began on a series of absurd drawings of the cat, but after he had done seven 'he said it was great shame to caricature Foss, and laid aside the pen' (*Nonsense Songs and Stories*, 1894). This series was eventually published as *The Heraldic Blazon of Foss the Cat* (ibid.).

Foss died in September, 1887, and was buried in the garden of Villa Tennyson (see Cat. 117).

PROVENANCE Philip Hofer; The Houghton Library, Harvard University.

EXHIBITIONS 1962, San Marino, Calif., Henry E. Huntington Library and Art Gallery, *Drawings by Edward Lear* (no. 53); 1968, London, Gooden and Fox Ltd, *Edward Lear* (no. 29).

REFERENCE Noakes & Lewsen 1978, repr. (no p. no.).

98 How Pleasant to Know Mr Lear

Manuscript for *How Pleasant to Know Mr Lear*, 14 January 1879
Sepia ink on paper containing a drawing of the artist, the poem and accompanying note:
30.8 × 20.8 cm/$12\frac{1}{8} \times 8\frac{3}{16}$ in
Accompanying note: *Dear Bevan,/I disclose you a Pome, which you may or you may Knott send to the Lady who says "How pleasant to know Mr Lear!"—It may be sung to the air "How cheerful along the gay meade."/Yours sincerely/Edward Lear./Villa Emily. Sanremo/14. January 1879*
The British Library Board

Lear talks of writing out 'my & Miss Bevan's verses of "How Pleasant to know Mr Lear"' (Diary, 9.iv.79), which suggests that this was a joint composition. Certainly it was prompted by the remark of a young lady who was overheard to exclaim, 'How pleasant to know Mr Lear!' Miss Bevan was the daughter of the British Vice-Consul in San Remo.

98

Not everyone found it so pleasant to know Mr Lear, and the disputes which followed the building of the hotel in 1879 in front of the Villa Emily in San Remo brought Lear many enemies there. Although he continued to welcome the many old friends who came to see him, increasingly he cut himself off from contact with local residents, finding in San Remo not 'a single creature here for whom I care the 999th part of the eight thousand = five = hundred = & = sixty = fifth fraction of a hog's bristle' (Fortescue, 12.ii.82, MS., Somerset Record Office, Taunton). As the years went by he became steadily more testy, turning away all chance visitors and on one occasion even sending back flowers sent to him for Easter. When Estes, the American publisher who was considering publishing the Tennyson drawings (see Cat. 44), enquired for Villa Tennyson, the villa built by Lear at San Remo to replace Villa Emily, 'I was warned not to visit it, unless I was a friend of its inmate.' (Estes to Hallam Tennyson, 8.v.87, MS., Tennyson Research Centre, Lincoln).

His old friends, however, knew a different man, and writing to him in January 1886, Emily Tennyson said, 'However solitary your life has, for many years been, you must not forget that to you is given the precious gift of peopling the lives of many not only of this generation but of generations to come with good & beautiful things & thoughts, to say nothing of your own life of which so many think with a loving admiration very precious to them' (22.i.86, MS., Tennyson Research Centre, Lincoln).

PROVENANCE Private collection; 1981, Christies, London (lot 182a); bt by the British Library.

99 Uncle Arly

a) First draft for 'Some incidents in the Life of my Uncle Arly', April 1873
MS. in pencil on front end-papers of *The Letters of Horace Walpole Earl of Orford*, ed. Peter Cunningham, vol. IX, London 1866
Volume: 22.8 × 15 cm/$8\frac{7}{8} \times 5\frac{7}{8}$ in
Inscribed on title page in Lear's hand: *Edward Lear. 1872*
The Beinecke Rare Book and Manuscript Library, Yale University

b) Manuscript for 'Some Incidents in the Life of my Uncle Arly', *1866*
One of at least 13 manuscript copies of the poem
Ink on paper: 22.9 × 10.2 cm/9 × 4 in
Inscribed b.: *Villa Tennyson Sanremo 7. March 1886.*
Department of Printing and Graphic Arts, The Houghton Library, Harvard University

In San Remo during the winter and spring of 1872–73 Lear read the nine volumes of Horace Walpole's letters; Horace Walpole's house, Strawberry Hill, had subsequently become the home of Lady Waldegrave (see Cat. 59). In April 1873, bedridden with bronchitis, he made his first jottings for 'Some Incidents in the Life of my Uncle Arly' in the end-papers of volumes viii and ix (Cat. 99*a*). Nothing more is heard of the poem until April 1885, when he made a further draft on the end-papers of his copy of Addison's *Essays from the Spectator* (Private Collection). The following April he was again ill, 'Kept always in bed—& read—(also writing "my aged Uncle Arley" ——)' (Diary, 22.ii.86). On 1 March he wrote to his doctor's wife, 'I have just written (the last Nonsense I shall ever write,) a history of my "Aged Uncle Arley."—stuff begun years ago for Lady E. Baring.' (Mrs Hassall, 1.iii.86, LLEL 1911, pp. 364–65). Lady Emma Baring was the daughter of Lord Northbrook. However, nothing is known of her part in its composition.

Lear subsequently made copies to send to his friends (in some the name is 'Arley' and in others 'Arly'; it was eventually published as 'Arly'). At least thirteen copies are known to have existed. The manuscipt copy exhibited here (Cat. 99*b*) was made on 7 March for Wilkie Collins (see Cat. 87), to whom Lear wrote '"E'en in our ashes live" &c &c—so,—though I have been in bed some 14 weeks, I have nonetheless written an absurdity which I fancy you may like—whereby I sent it.' (7.iii.86, MS., Pierpont Morgan Library, New York). According to Lear, Wilkie Collins 'thinks it the best of all "my poetry!"' (Selwyn, 19.v.86, MS., Private Collection).

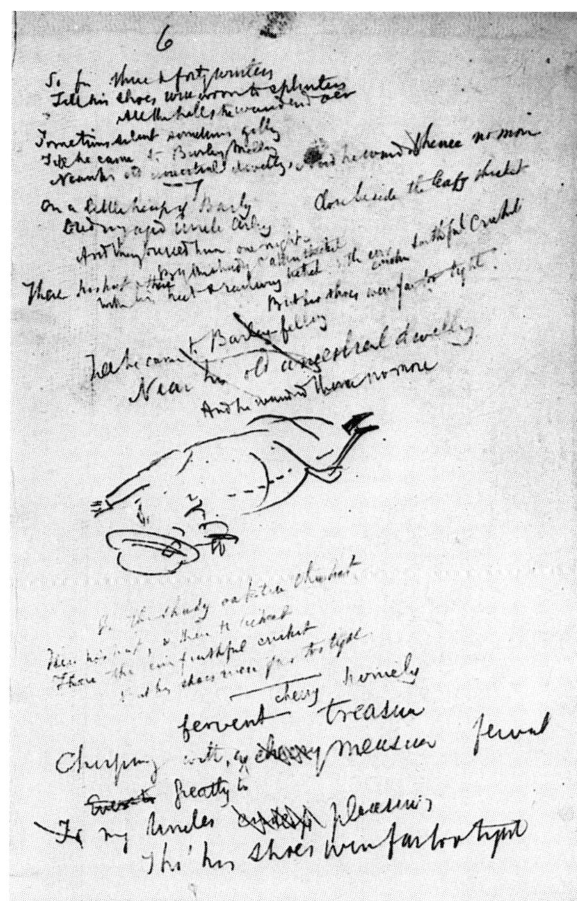

99*a*

Thomas Byrom (*Nonsense and Wonder: The Poems and Cartoons of Edward Lear*, 1977, p. 219) sees 'Lear hiding "unclearly" in "UncLE ARly"'. Certainly, it is an autobiographical study of a man who became the Adopty Duncle to many young friends (see Cat. 81).

PROVENANCE *(a)* Mr and Mrs Robert Blum, given to The Beinecke Rare Book and Manuscript Library, Yale University. *(b)* Wilkie Collins; John H. Fleming; Private Collection; 1980 given to The Houghton Library, Harvard University.

100 Lear and Ruskin

a) 'The Choice of Books / by Mr. John Ruskin', *The Pall Mall Gazette*, Monday 15 February 1886 (vol. XLIII no. 6527)
Newspaper (double spread): each page 38.7 × 26.3 cm/ 15$\frac{1}{4}$ × 10$\frac{3}{8}$ in
Department of Printing and Graphic Arts, The Houghton Library, Harvard University

b) Letter to John Ruskin, 19 February 1886
On headed writing paper, *VILLA TENNYSON SANREMO*: 13.6 × 10.8 cm/5$\frac{3}{8}$ × 4$\frac{1}{4}$ in
Dated on recto tl. (in Lear's hand): *19 Feby. 1886*
Inscribed on recto tl. (in Ruskin's hand): *Answered today/JR*
Department of Printing and Graphic Arts, The Houghton Library, Harvard University

When Ruskin wrote in *The Pall Mall Gazette* for 15 February 1886 (Cat. 100*a*): 'I really don't know any author to whom I am half so grateful, for my idle self, as Edward Lear. I shall put him first of *my* hundred authors,' Lear was delighted. 'I never knew him repeat any story telling against his Nonsense, and Ruskin's praise was very dear to him,' recalled Hubert Congreve in 1910 (LLEL 1911, p. 22).

'This morning's post brings me many duplicates of a letter written by Ruskin on "Choice of Books",' he told Fortescue. 'Naturally it is a matter of pride with me that he places "*Edward Lear*" at the *head of his list* of 100!! (Vy! Vell! No I never did!!!)!!' (19.ii.86, LLEL 1911, p. 350). Forgotten were the days when he had called Ruskin 'Roughskin', and he now promptly wrote (Cat. 100*b*): '19.Feby. 1886 / Dear Mr. Ruskin, / Several friends have sent me/by this last post—(cut from the Pall Mall of Feby 15—) your letter about the "Choice of Books." And I cannot help writing a line to thank you for your most kind mention of my "Nonsense"—& to say how proud & gratified I am by your praise. / I am now (aet 74) nearly always in bed—but can sit up now & then,—& even go on working at my 200 Tennyson illustrations begun in 1849 in Sussex in the days of W Holman Hunt—& Tennyson. I suppose perseverance is a virtue, even if in a foolish cause—: only one can't be sure whether the sequel will be foolishness or not. Most probably I shall die before the 200 are ready to Autotype. / With many and sincere thanks, / believe me Your's, / Edward Lear' (MS., Houghton Library, Harvard University).

On 7 March he made a further copy of Uncle Arly (see Cat. 99), and sent it to Ruskin.

PROVENANCE *(a)* Philip Hofer; The Houghton Library, Harvard University. *(b)* John Ruskin; Philip Hofer; The Houghton Library, Harvard University.
REFERENCE *(a)* Osgood Field 1933, pp. 105–06; Noakes 1979 edn, p. 313.

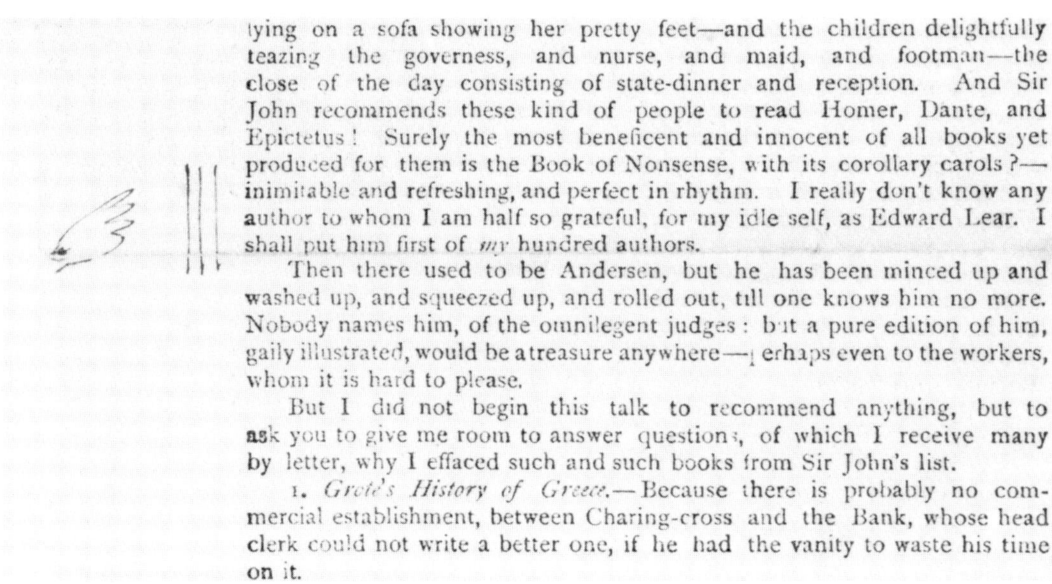
lying on a sofa showing her pretty feet—and the children delightfully teazing the governess, and nurse, and maid, and footman—the close of the day consisting of state-dinner and reception. And Sir John recommends these kind of people to read Homer, Dante, and Epictetus! Surely the most beneficent and innocent of all books yet produced for them is the Book of Nonsense, with its corollary carols?—inimitable and refreshing, and perfect in rhythm. I really don't know any author to whom I am half so grateful, for my idle self, as Edward Lear. I shall put him first of *my* hundred authors.

Then there used to be Andersen, but he has been minced up and washed up, and squeezed up, and rolled out, till one knows him no more. Nobody names him, of the omnilegent judges: but a pure edition of him, gaily illustrated, would be a treasure anywhere—perhaps even to the workers, whom it is hard to please.

But I did not begin this talk to recommend anything, but to ask you to give me room to answer questions, of which I receive many by letter, why I effaced such and such books from Sir John's list.

1. *Grote's History of Greece.*—Because there is probably no commercial establishment, between Charing-cross and the Bank, whose head clerk could not write a better one, if he had the vanity to waste his time on it.

100*a*

THE PELICAN

101*b*

Despite the diversity of Lear's talent, the various threads of his life and creativity interweave and overlap. The approach to life which gave rise to the Nonsense was part of Lear's whole personality, and not restricted to his Nonsense writing alone. In the studies for his parrots he caricatures the visitors to the parrot house (see Cat. 7*a*, *b*), and his Nonsense is filled with drawings of birds and animals (eg. Cat. 94). The Yonghy-Bonghy-Bò (Cat. 84) escapes on the back of a Young *Chelonia imbricata*, a turtle illustrated in one of the plates for which Lear prepared the lithograph in Bell's *A Monograph of Testudinata* (1836).

Absurd drawings appear in otherwise straightforward landscape (see Cat. 17*d*, 18*a*), and landscape in his Nonsense (see Cat. 76). He writes of the failure of a painting about which he felt most deeply, *The Cedars of Lebanon*, in his own particular style: 'sometimes I consider as to the wit of taking my Cedars out of its frame & putting round it a border of rose colored velvet,—embellished with a fringe of yellow worsted with black spots, to protypify the possible proximate propinquity of predatorial panthers,—& then selling the whole lot for floorcloth by auction' (Fortescue, 9.viii.67, LLEL 1911, p. 86).

His observations of the absurd give a particular character to the descriptions of his travels published in his various journals and found in his letters and diaries. In Albania he was the guest of the local, youthful Bey who spoke no English, 'so I drew for him—& amused him immensely by drawing a steam carriage & saying—rattle-attle-attle-attle-attle—& a ship-steamer—saying wishwashsquishsquash—at which the poor boy laughed immensely' (Ann, 21.x.48, TS.).

By taking a single theme—that of the pelican—it is possible to draw together the various threads of Lear's life and creative output—as ornithological draughtsman, traveller, painter, Nonsense writer and illustrator, musician, letter-writer and diarist.

V.N.

101 The Pelican

a) *Pelican*
Pencil, watercolour on paper: 35.8×47.3 cm/ $14\frac{1}{8} \times 18\frac{5}{8}$ in
Department of Printing and Graphic Arts, The Houghton Library, Harvard University

b) *Pelican*
Pl. 405 from John Gould's *The Birds of Europe*, vol. v; printed by C. Hullmandel
Hand-coloured lithograph: sheet size 36.5×53.9 cm/ $14\frac{3}{8} \times 21\frac{1}{4}$ in
Inscribed and signed b.: *PELICAN/Pelecanus Onocrothalus, Linn. E. Lear. del.*
By permission of the Council of the Linnean Society of London

c) *Avlona*, 1848
Pencil, watercolour, sepia ink with notes on paper: 24.8×51 cm/$9\frac{3}{4} \times 20\frac{1}{16}$ in
Inscribed and dated bl.: *Avlona. October 29. 1848. (in haste)*
Inscribed, dated and numbered br.: *Avlona. Oct. 29. 1848 (201) 201*
Department of Printing and Graphic Arts, The Houghton Library, Harvard University

d) *Avlóna*
Pl. 11 from Edward Lear, *Journals of a Landscape Painter in Albania, &c.*, opp. p. 294; published by Richard Bentley, New Burlington Street, 1851
Lithograph: 15.8×25.4 cm/$6\frac{1}{4} \times 10$ in
R.A. Farquharson, Esq.

e) Music for 'The Pelican Chorus'
Ink on paper: 30.5×24.8 cm/$12 \times 9\frac{3}{4}$ in
Department of Printing and Graphic Arts, The Houghton Library, Harvard University

f) Proof of the illustration for 'The Pelican Chorus'
Lithograph: 8.4×10.6 cm/$3\frac{5}{16} \times 4\frac{3}{16}$ in
Department of Printing and Graphic Arts, The Houghton Library, Harvard University

g) *Laughable Lyrics*
Edward Lear, *Laughable Lyrics: A Fourth Book of Nonsense Poems, Songs, Botany, Music, etc.*, 1877
Volume: 20.3×16.5 cm/$8 \times 6\frac{1}{2}$ in
Open at 'The Pelican Chorus'
Private Collection

101*a*

101*c*

The drawing of the pelican (Cat. 101*a*) was made in preparation for the lithograph in Gould's *Birds of Europe* (vol. v, pl. 405; Cat. 101*b* and see Cat. 12). Writing to Lord Derby on 12 January 1849, Lear said: 'When I was in Avlona, (west coast of Albania—) I went across the salt marshes to see a Convent on the shore—&perceiving an innumerable multitude of odd looking white stones (as I thought)—I rode up to them, when lo! they were all pelicans! & away they flew . . . I never was more amused in my life at seeing so many thousand Pelicans all together—& I greatly wished I could have dispatched some to your Lordship' (MS., Liverpool Record Office). Lear described the scene in his *Journals of a Landscape Painter in Albania, &c.* (Cat. 101*d*):

'As we skirted these salt lagunes, I observed an infinite number of what appeared to be large white stones, arranged in rows with great regularity, though yet with something odd in their form not easily to be described. The more I looked at them, the more I felt they were not what they seemed to be. . . so I resolved to examine these mysterious white stones forthwith, and off we went, when—lo! on my near approach, one and all put forth legs, long necks, and great wings, and "stood confessed" so many great pelicans, which, with croakings expressive of great disgust at all such ill-timed interruptions, rose up into the air in a body of five or six hundred, and soared slowly away to the cliffs north of the gulf.

'These birds frequent the coast around Avlóna in great numbers, breeding in the rocky inlets beyond the bay, and living on fish and refuse in the salt lagunes. Pleased with these ornithological novelties, hitherto only seen in zoological gardens, or at Knowsley, I followed the faithful Margiánn (who nearly fell off his horse with laughter at my surprise at the transmutation of the white stones), through levels of deep sand, by tracts of sedge and rushes, and groups of salt-kilns, till we reached the foot of the low hills' (1851, 29.x.48, pp. 294–95).

101*d*

101*e*

The watercolour drawing (Cat. 101*c*) was made at Avlona on that day, and is a preparatory study for the lithographic plate in the Albanian *Journals* (Cat. 101*d*).

Though the Avlona pelicans amused him, it was the pelicans of the Nile who inspired 'The Pelican Chorus'. 'O queer community of birds!' he wrote in his diary. 'On a long sand spit are 4 black storks—one legged: apart.—8 Pelicans—careless foolish. 17 small ducks, cohesive. 23 Herons—watchful variously posed: & 2 or 3 flocks of lovely ivory ibis—(or Paddybirds—) flying all about' (Diary, 9.i.67).

'. . . We live on the Nile. The Nile we love.
By night we sleep on the cliffs above;
By day we fish, and at eve we stand
On long bare islands of yellow sand.
And when the sun sinks slowly down
And the great rock walls grow dark and brown,
Where the purple river rolls fast and dim
And the Ivory Ibis starlike skim,
Wing to wing we dance around,—
Stamping our feet with a flumpy sound,—
Opening our mouths as Pelicans ought,
And this is the song we nightly snort;—
    Ploffskin, Pluffskin, Pelican jee,—
    We think no Birds so happy as we!
    Plumpskin, Ploshkin, Pelican jill,—
    We think so then, and we thought so still.

Last year came out our Daughter, Dell;
And all the Birds received her well.
To do her honour, a feast we made
For every bird that can swim or wade.
Herons and Gulls, and Cormorants black,
Cranes, and Flamingoes with scarlet back,
Plovers and Storks, and Geese in clouds,
Swans and Dilberry Ducks in crowds.
Thousand of Birds in wondrous flight!
They ate and drank and danced all night,
And echoing back from the rocks you heard
Multitude-echoes from Bird and Bird,—
    Ploffskin, Pluffskin, Pelican jee,
    We think no Birds so happy as we!
    Plumpskin, Ploshkin, Pelican jill,
    We think so then, and we thought so still! . . .'

'The Pelican Chorus' was published in *Laughable Lyrics* (1877; Cat. 101*g*), for which the proof (Cat. 101*f*) was prepared. The music (Cat. 101*e*) was composed by Lear, and set down by Monsieur Pomis at his direction.

Writing to Alfred Tennyson in June 1855, Lear said: 'I feel woundily like a spectator,—all through my life—of what goes on amongst those I know: very little as an actor. David's particular Pelican in the Wilderness was a fool to what I have been all my days, whether in a crowd or not—But I suppose it's all right, or will come so bye and bye' (9.vi.[55], Tennyson Research Centre, Lincoln).

PROVENANCE *(a) (c)* W.B. Osgood Field; The Houghton Library, Harvard University. *(b)* The Linnean Society. *(d)* W.G. Prescott, by family descent. *(e) (f)* Philip Hofer; The Houghton Library, Harvard University. *(g)* Given to Mary S. Clark; by family descent.

REFERENCES *(b)* Brian Reade, 'Two Famous Bird Artists' in *The Saturday Book*, no. 9, 1949, repr. opp. p. 29.

101*f*

LATER MEMORABILIA

Lear's choice of Franklin Lushington as his literary executor was unfortunate, for Lushington destroyed many of the carefully arranged papers and memorabilia which Lear left. His task, of course, was not easy. He arrived in San Remo a few days after Lear's death, and had little time to arrange for the preservation of what he found. The real problem, however, was that although Lushington was Lear's closest friend, he had less appreciation than some others of the importance of Lear's artistic contribution. Writing to Emily Tennyson in 1856, Lushington said 'He has been making some very beautiful & careful watercolour drawings of various views in Corfu for 12£ a piece . . . Nevertheless I should say, don't waste your monies on them' (Franklin Lushington-Emily Tennyson, 20.vi.56, MS., Tennyson Research Centre, Lincoln).

Both Fortescue and Northbrook were aware of Lear's importance in a way that Lushington was not. Lady Strachey, Lady Waldegrave's niece, published in 1907 and 1911 Lear's letters to Fortescue and his wife, Lady Waldegrave (*The Letters* and *The Later Letters of Edward Lear*). In 1911 she also published *Queery Leary Nonsense* and in 1912 she edited *The Complete Nonsense*, all at a time when Lear's reputation was at its lowest. Lord Northbrook, to whom Lear had given a collection of his travel watercolours in 1884, arranged for the preparation of seven volumes in which Lear's published travel journals and their related watercolours were arranged (Cat. 68). Had either of these two men been responsible for the preservation of Lear material, it is likely that far more would have survived for a generation at least; had Fortescue been Lear's literary executor, much would have survived until now.

Some family memorabilia was inherited by Lear's niece, Emily Gillies, who lived in New Zealand, and is therefore not available for this exhibition. Others have come down through the descendants of Lear's sisters, Sarah Street, Eleanor Newsom and Mary Boswell.

'I often say,' wrote Lear to his nephew, Charles Street, 'that if I get to heaven, the first question I shall ask will be, "How the deuce did I make & keep so many friends?"—(only of course, I shouldn't say "how the deuce")' (7.ii.79, TS.). Of Lear's friends, those represented here are the three closest—Franklin Lushington, Chichester Fortescue and Lord Northbrook—with Gussie Bethell, whom he thought of marrying, and Giorgio, his manservant for twenty-seven years. Once he had built his house in San Remo Lear made few new friends apart from the Congreve family (see Cat. 38), cutting himself off from all new contacts. 'Here I am absolutely alone,' he wrote to Fortescue on 2 July 1882. '"Do you go much into Society—?" said the snail to the Oyster. "certainly knot"—replied the Oyster' (MS., Somerset Record Office, Taunton). Instead, he derived what pleasure he could from his house and garden. He wrote to Fortescue on 30 April 1885 (LLEL 1911, p. 336):

'And this is certain; if so be
You could just now my garden see,
The aspic of my flowers so bright
Would make you shudder with delight.

And if you voz to see my roziz
As is a boon to all men's noziz,—
You'd fall upon your back & scream—
'O Lawk! O criky! it's a dream!'

When Lear died, Franklin Lushington wrote of him that the love of his friends was 'the best and sweetest of garlands that can in spirit be laid on his tomb' (Franklin Lushington to Hallam Tennyson, 4.ii.88, MS., Tennyson Research Centre, Lincoln).

V.N.

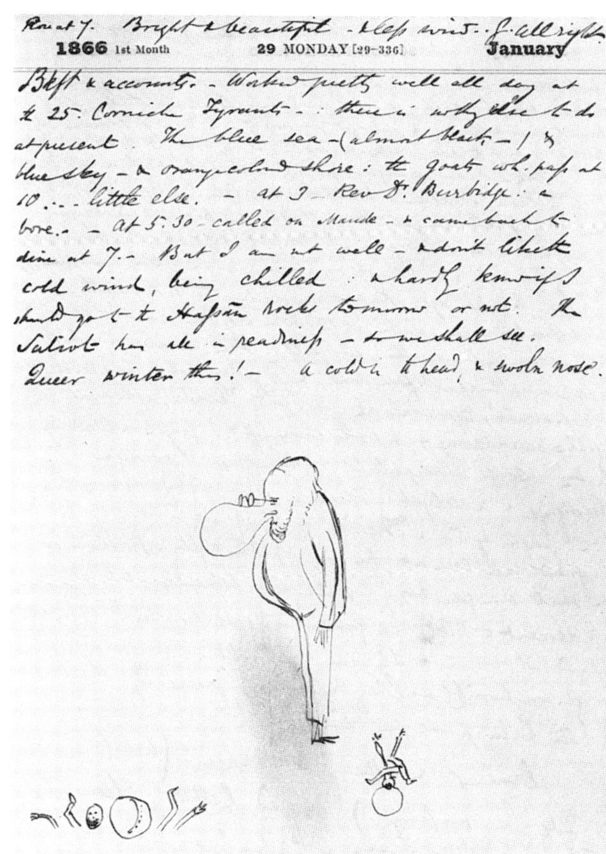
Rose at 7. Bright & beautiful - less wind. - G. all right.
1866 1st Month 29 MONDAY [29-336] January
Bkft & accounts. - Worked pretty well all day at the 25 Corniche Tyrants - : there is nothing else to do at present. The blue sea - (almost black -) & blue sky - & orange coloured shore: the goats wh. pass at 10 ... little else. - at 3 - Rev Dr. Burbidge: a bore. - at 5.30 - called on Maude - & came back to dine at 7. - But I am not well - & don't like the cold wind, being chilled: & hardly know if I should go to the Hafsan rocks tomorrow or not. The Suliot has all in readiness - so we shall see. Queer winter this! - a cold in the head, & swoln nose.

108*a*

102 Lear's Used Sketch Pad, 1836

Green marbled board with leather binding and corners: 34 × 25 cm/13⅜ × 9⅞ in
Inscribed on the cover: *E. Lear. 1836. White 4to No. 3.*
Private Collection

Lear probably used the paper from this emptied sketch pad, dated by him on the cover 1836, during his exploration of the Lake District (see Cat. 13). The paper measured 9⅜ × 12¾ in (23.8 × 32.4 cm), and was made and sold by Roberson & Miller of 51 Long Acre, London.

In making his ornithological drawings, Lear frequently worked on both sides of a sheet of paper or on the back of a lithographic proof in order to save paper. Such economy was rarely practised in his landscape watercolours, but Henry Strachey recalled that when Lear embarked upon his Nonsense drawings for 'The Heraldic Blazons of Foss the Cat' (see Cat. 97), 'he took from a place in his bureau a number of carefully cut-out backs of old envelopes, and on these he drew' (*Nonsense Songs and Stories*, 1894).

PROVENANCE Rev. George Clark, by family descent.

103 Registration as a Student at the Royal Academy Schools

Photograph from the Student Registration Book, 1826–90

Writing to Fortescue in 1848, Lear had exclaimed: 'What to do my dear Fortescue when I return to England!!??¿–¿¡! (expressive of indelible doubt, wonder & ignorance). *London* must be the place—& then comes the choice of two lines:—society—& half day's work—pretty pictures—petitmaitre praise boundless—frequented studio—&c. &c.—wound up with vexation of spirit as age comes on that talents have been thrown away.—or—*hard study* beginning at the root of the matter—the human figure—which to master alone would enable me to carry out the views and feelings of landscape I know to exist within me. Alas! if real art is a *student*, I know no more than a child—an infant—a foetus:—how could I—I have had myself to thank for all education—& a vortex of society hath eaten my time.—So you see I must choose one or other—& with my many friends it will go hard at 36 to retire—please God I live—for 8 to 10 years—*but*—if I did—*wouldn't* the "Lears" sell in your grandchildren's time!' (25.viii.48, LEL 1907, pp. 13–14).

Lear's wish to train as a painter dates back to 1834, when he entered Sass's Drawing Academy, Bloomsbury, where students could prepare for the entrance examination to the Royal Academy Schools. His tuition was cut short by lack of funds, but in 1849 a legacy of £500 enabled him to re-enrol at Sass's. In January 1850, he was accepted at the Royal Academy Schools for the three-month probationary period: 'What fun!—pretty little dear—! he got into the Academy—he did!—Yes—so he did. / You will be pleased to hear that the R. Academy have sate on my drawing from the antique, and I am "probationer"—& on my trial till April, when the 3 drawings I have to make will be again sate on—& I shall be admirtted for 10 years a student—or—rejected.—Verdermo qualo saro. / I tried with 51—little boys—& 19 of us were admitted' (Fortescue, 20.i.[50], MS., Perkins Library, Duke University; repr. LEL 1907, pp. 22–24, where it is misdated as post-August 1851).

On 26 April 1850 Lear was accepted as a full student. Little is known about this period of his life, but he seems to have stayed at the Schools for a year and would have spent most of his time drawing from the antique. By going to the Royal Academy Schools Lear probably derived little more than the fulfillment of a boyhood ambition.

REFERENCE Noakes 1968 edn, p. 106.

104 Holman Hunt

William Holman Hunt, Portrait of Edward Lear, 1857
Crayon and chalk on paper: 61 × 48.7 cm/24⅛ × 19¼ in
Signed with monogram and dated bl.: *WHH Nov 7 1857*
Merseyside County Council, The Walker Art Gallery, Liverpool

Hunt's drawing of Lear was made in 1857, five years after the two artists first met in 1852 (see Cat. 49). They spent some weeks in the summer of 1852 at Clive Vale Farm, near Hastings, where Lear worked on his paintings of *The Quarries of Syracuse* and *Thermopylae* (see Cat. 49, 50) and Hunt on *Our English Coasts (Strayed Sheep)* (1852; Tate Gallery, London).

During those weeks Hunt gave Lear advice about oil painting, whilst Lear gave Hunt Italian lessons. Hunt recalls that Lear would sit after dinner 'writing what he entitled "Ye Booke of Hunte", in which he wrote down my answers to enquiries as to the pigments and system I should use in the different features of a landscape. I hazarded my replies with many protests against their standing as more than the formula of a system, to be modified in every case by conditions and circumstances. Whilst thus satisfying him, he exercised me with funny sentences in Italian of every variety' (W. Holman Hunt, *Pre-Raphaelitism and the Pre-Raphaelite Brotherhood*, 1905, vol. 1, p. 332).

Lear considered himself a second generation Pre-Raphaelite Brother, and he called Holman Hunt 'Daddy'. It was in some ways a surprising friendship for their temperaments were very different, yet they shared many thoughts and ideas. In particular they agreed about the lack of intelligent patronage. Writing in 1878, Hunt recalled the days together at Clive Vale Farm, 'when neither had a gray hair—and there seemed plenty of time for regenerating oneself and the world by display of powers yet unknown. I feel that I might have got nearer than I did—to speak of my own part only but there were the heavy weights to drag me back all the while my life had spring in it, and so the impossibility of thinking of anything but how to get my next quarter's rent. I often wonder that when a young man has done something to prove the possession of talents some of the many people who have more money than they know how to have with satisfaction do not endow him with a hundred or two per annum to give him a better chance of doing his best with his short life' (Holman Hunt to Edward

104

105

Lear, 22.viii.78, MS., John Rylands University Library, Manchester). These were sentiments which echoed Lear's completely. In 1865, Lear summed up his feelings for Hunt: 'Daddy Hunt's head would cut up sufficient for 10 men, & his heart for 200 at least. God bless him' (Diary, 27.v.65).

Though his respect for Hunt as a man did not diminish, Lear regarded his subject-matter with increasing misgivings. After seeing *The Scapegoat* (R.A. 1854–56, Lady Lever Art Gallery, Port Sunlight) Lear wrote to Ann: 'I agree with you in not liking the subject, but, where the skill and genius which Hunt possesses is so immeasurably in advance of that of the mass of painters, we must take when we can get' (31.v.56, TS.).

During their time at Clive Vale Farm, Lear and Hunt made plans to travel together in Egypt and the Holy Land (see Cat. 27). In the event the plans did not materialise.

PROVENANCE 1907, presented to the Walker Art Gallery, Liverpool, by William Holman Hunt.

EXHIBITIONS 1907, Liverpool, Walker Art Gallery, *Pictures and Drawings by William Holman Hunt, OM, DCL* (no. 122); 1907, Glasgow, City Art Gallery, *Pictures and Drawings by William Holman Hunt, OM, DCL* (no. 48); 1947, Birmingham, City Art Gallery, *The Pre-Raphaelite Brotherhood (1848–1862)* (no. 159); 1948, Port Sunlight, Lady Lever Art Gallery, *The Pre-Raphaelites—Their Friends and Followers* (no. 116); 1951, Bournemouth, Russell Cotes Museum, *Paintings and Drawings by the Pre-Raphaelites and their Followers* (no. 106); 1958, London, Arts Council of Great Britain, *Edward Lear* (no. 128); 1969, Liverpool, Walker Art Gallery and London, Victoria and Albert Museum, *William Holman Hunt* (no. 194); 1975, Liverpool, Walker Art Gallery, *Edward Lear and Knowsley* (no. 2).

REFERENCE W. Holman Hunt, *Pre-Raphaelitism & the Pre-Raphaelite Brotherhood*, 1905, vol. I, repr. p. 331; Davidson 1938 edn, pp. 76–82, 103.

105 Drawing on a Visiting Card

Corfu
Sepia ink on verso of a visiting card of Mrs James M. Leigh: 6.3 × 9.5 cm/$2\frac{1}{2} \times 3\frac{3}{4}$ in
Signed bl.: *Edward Lear. del*
Inscribed br.: *Corfu*
Department of Printing and Graphic Arts, The Houghton Library, Harvard University

This is one of Lear's smallest landscapes, and is drawn on the back of a visiting card. It comes from an album put together by Lear as a present for Cecilia Lushington and given to her on 25 May 1855. The album originally contained fifty-four items—birds and animal drawings, landscape, Nonsense and lithographs. Some of the items are dated and come from the years 1851–55; many are earlier. In preparing such an album Lear went through his studio drawers and folios to put together a representative selection. Nothing is known of Mrs Leigh.

Cecilia Lushington was Alfred Tennyson's sister. She was married in 1842 to Edmund Lushington, Franklin's brother (see Cat. 112); their epithalamium forms the epilogue to *In Memoriam*. Although Lear generally prepared such albums for special friends, Cecilia was never a particularly close friend of his. However, this present was made at a time when Lear's affection for Franklin Lushington was at its most intense.

PROVENANCE Cecilia Lushington; W.B. Osgood Field; The Houghton Library, Harvard University.

REFERENCES W.B. Osgood Field 1933, p. 257; Hofer 1967, p. 31, repr. pl. 108b.

106 Memento from Mount Athos

Wooden bread marker:
8.9 × 7 × 3.8 cm/$3\frac{1}{2} \times 2\frac{3}{4} \times 1\frac{1}{2}$ in
Private Collection

As Lear travelled, he collected mementos of the places he visited. For himself he bought local costumes which he could later use for the figures in his studio paintings.

For his sisters, especially for Ann, he gathered all manner of objects. He gave her a scarf and a bead bag from Constantinople, a scarab from Egypt, an amber fish from Sicily, silk dresses from Malta, handspun stockings from Greece, a fish basket, a paper cutter, a spoon and a pair of nut crackers from Switzerland, and many more. Some presents were more welcome than others: 'Should you like me to send you a green frog in the next parcel?' he wrote from Corfu, 'or a tortoise? I won't do so unless you ask me—but perhaps you may have changed your ways of thinking about pets nowadays' (15.xii.56, TS.).

On Mount Athos he bought 'little remembrances of one of the most extraordinary places in the world, & one which I never intend to see again . . . I bought some of the carved wood crosses—& bone crosses—& spoons—& gourd water jars—& wooden things for marking bread—& beads & a monk's dress—to be of use in painting—& above all 3 of what I thought to be salad mixers—very long handled spoons—with little sharp nobs of wood cut in relief on the—(so I believed) bowl of the spoon. Now what do you think these turned out to be? Ma'am—they were flea scratchers!—I thought I must have screamed when an old monk said—these are not spoons—but are for this . . . whereon he began to put it to its proper use' (8.x.56,TS.).

The Mount Athos souvenir exhibited here was given to Lear's sister, Eleanor.

PROVENANCE Eleanor Newsom (née Lear), by family descent.

107 Advertisement for Studio Open Days, *c.* 1858

On verso of a letter to Mrs Mansfield: 18.2 × 11.6 cm/ $7\frac{3}{16} \times 4\frac{9}{16}$ in

Department of Printing and Graphic Arts, The Houghton Library, Harvard University

Although Lear exhibited at the Royal Academy and the British Institution, most of his work was commissioned by people who came to his studio. He had held studio open days in Rome, and in 1848 had written to Ann 'every Wed. you may think of me as being very busy with explorers' (25.i.48, TS.).

The works exhibited in public instititutions were confined to oil paintings and finished watercolours, whereas those exhibited in his studio also included his travel studies. Potential patrons would look through the drawings and commission from them either what Lear himself called finished watercolours or oil paintings. The original travel drawings were not for sale; Lear regarded them as his working capital on which he based further work.

Lear held his studio open days in London, and in Corfu, Malta, Cannes, Nice and eventually in both of his houses in San Remo, where he filled his 'maggrifficent gallery, with 99 watercolor drawings—not to speak of 5 larger oils . . . (In one of which is a big beech tree, at which all intelligent huming beans say—"Beech!"—when they see it. For all that one forlorn ijiot said—"Is that a *Palm*-tree Sir"—"No", replied I quietly, "it is a Peruvian Brocoli".)' (Fortescue, 28.ii.72, LLEL 1911, p. 145).

It was a way of showing his work with which he became increasingly disabused, for it took a great deal of his time and produced less and less. Eventually he handed over the exhibition of his work to Foord & Dickenson in Wardour Street.

PROVENANCE Philip Hofer; The Houghton Library, Harvard University.

96b

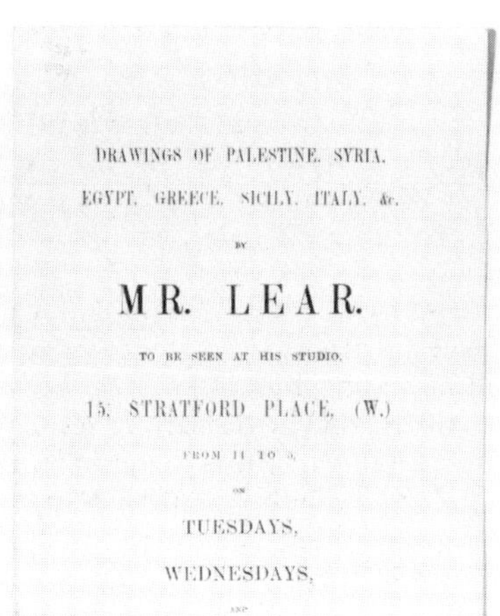

DRAWINGS OF PALESTINE, SYRIA,
EGYPT, GREECE, SICILY, ITALY, &c.
BY
MR. LEAR.
TO BE SEEN AT HIS STUDIO,
15, STRATFORD PLACE, (W.)
FROM 11 TO 5,
ON
TUESDAYS,
WEDNESDAYS,
AND
THURSDAYS.

107

108 Lear's Diaries

a) Diary for 1866 [Repr. p. 193

Volume: 20.2 × 13.3 cm/ $7\frac{15}{16} \times 5\frac{1}{4}$ in

Page size: 19 × 12.1 cm/ $7\frac{1}{2} \times 4\frac{3}{4}$ in

Department of Printing and Graphic Arts, The Houghton Library, Harvard University

b) Diary for 1882

Volume: 20.2 × 13.3 cm/ $7\frac{15}{16} \times 5\frac{1}{4}$ in

Page size: 19 × 12.1 cm/ $7\frac{1}{2} \times 4\frac{3}{4}$ in

Department of Printing and Graphic Arts, The Houghton Library, Harvard University

'I cannot help thinking that my life, letters and diaries would be as interesting . . . as many that are now published,' wrote Lear in 1873 (Fortescue, 12.ix.73, LLEL 1911, pp. 156–57). From his youth he had kept a daily journal, but only those covering the years 1858 to 1887 have survived; they are held by the Houghton Library, Harvard University. In 1840, apparently prompted by discretion, Lear burned the diaries describing his years at Knowsley. At least some of those for the years 1840 to 1857 were in his possession late in his life, but these have now disappeared.

Those diaries that survive record both the minutiae of his daily life—his time of rising, the weather, what he ate, the letters he received and wrote—and also descriptions of his travels, his work and his thoughts. They reveal a secret unknown to even his closest friends, the epilepsy which was the key to so much in his life. On 31 July 1882 (Cat. 108*b*) he writes: 'The day is lovely=glorious—all beautiful without—within depression & vexation. Opposed to my being so utterly at sea mentally & morally, my better health contrasts most curiously. I suppose the ever=presence of the Demon since I was 7 years old would have prevented happiness under any sort of circumstances. It is a most merciful blessing that I have kept up as I have, & have not gone utterly the bad mad sad.' The two crosses at the bottom of the page indicate epileptic attacks; the number 8 indicates the number of days in that month when he has been afflicted. 'Alas! Alas! how fearful a birthright was mine', he confided to his diary in the last year of his life (2.v.87). 'I wonder if others suffer similarly? Yet I dare not ask or endeavour to know.' Not even his closest friend, Franklin Lushington (see Cat. 112), knew of this birthright until after Lear's death when he inherited the diaries. In revealing it at last, albeit posthumously, Lear could expect some understanding of the secret burden he had carried all his life.

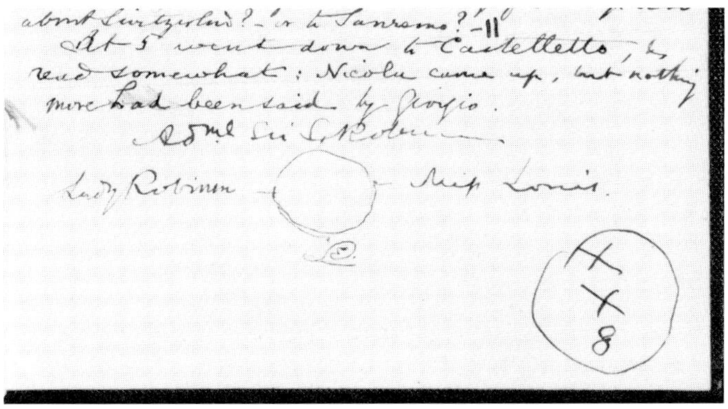

108*b*

The diaries also record his response to beauty, and his happiness. Sometimes they give hints of his first thoughts about particular pieces of Nonsense. The fragmented figure on 29 January 1866 (Cat. 108*a*) was expanded later that year into the 'Adventures of Mr Lear, the Polly and the Pusseybite on their way to the Ritertitle Mountains' (publ. *Teapots and Quails* 1953, pp. 50–54). Seating plans for dinner parties, such as the one in the diary exhibited here, occur frequently.

PROVENANCE *(a) (b)* W.B. Osgood Field; The Houghton Library, Harvard University.

EXHIBITION *(a) (b)* 1958, London, Arts Council of Great Britain, *Edward Lear* (nos 116, 117).

REFERENCES *(a) (b)* Osgood Field 1933, pp. 227–36. *(a)* Osgood Field 1933, repr. p. 234; *(b)* Noakes 1968 edn, detail repr. p. 295; Noakes 1979 edn, repr. p. 240.

109 The Indian Journals, 1873–75

Volume 1 of two volumes, bound in brown leather
Volume: 31.7 × 21.6 cm/$12\frac{1}{2} \times 8\frac{1}{2}$ in
Page Size: 31.1 × 21 cm/$12\frac{1}{4} \times 8\frac{1}{4}$ in
Department of Printing and Graphic Arts, The Houghton Library, Harvard University

'By degrees,' wrote Lear in 1868, 'I want to topographize & typographize all the journeyings of my life—so I shall have been of some use after all to my fellow critters' (Lady Waldegrave, 9.i.68, LLEL 1911, p. 91). He published four descriptive books of travel—about the Abruzzi (see Cat. 65), Albania (see Cat. 67), Southern Calabria (see Cat. 68) and Corsica (see Cat. 70)—and prepared others for publication. These were his journeys describing the Nile, Crete, the Corniche, Petra and India. In addition, he talked of preparing his journals of Mount Athos (Ann, 8.x.56, TS.; see Cat. 22) but does not appear to have done so, and Angus Davidson (1938, p. xi) speaks of Lear's unpublished journals of Greece of which nothing is now known.

In all his published works Lear apologises for the personal nature of his journals; they are not travel guides, but accounts of one man's journeys. In speaking of the possible publication of his Nile journals—for which an advertisement of impending publication appears on the last page of *More Nonsense* (1872; see Cat. 83)—Lear is anxious about this aspect of his work. He wrote to Amelia Edwards, whose volume of Nile travels had been published in 1877—'there is & must be a great drawback in *my* writing wh. your's on a similar subject would not have:—& that is, that whatever *I* write would be *Edward Lear*—egotistical & unmitigated—fanciful—individual—correct or what not—but nevertheless always *Edward Lear*: whereas what *you* write might be written by Mrs Tompkins, or Queen Boadicea, or Lady Jane Grey, or Rizpah of Gibeah, Joan of Arc or anybody else—because "A.B. Edwards" never appears at all' (26.x.85, MS., Somerville College, Oxford).

The copy of the journals exhibited here is the first of two volumes describing Lear's tour of India from 1873 to 1875, and is open to show his description of the Taj Mahal (see Cat. 34*e*). Sending the journals to Lord Northbrook after Lear's death, Lushington cautioned: 'There is a great deal personal about them—& would hardly do to submit to general reading without some excision . . . you will see how like they are to him in the vehement revulsions of feelings & spirits, and the absolute frankness with which he always confided himself to his diaries.' (28.viii.88, MS., Houghton Library, Harvard University). Extracts from the Indian Journals were eventually published in 1953, edited by Ray Murphy. Posthumous publication of Lear's other travel journals have been: *The Journey to Petra—a Leaf from the Journals of a Landscape Painter*, with notes by Franklin Lushington, published in *Macmillans Magazine* in April 1897, and *Edward Lear: The Cretan Journal*, edited by Dr Rowena Fowler and published in 1984.

PROVENANCE W.B. Osgood Field; The Houghton Library, Harvard University.

EXHIBITION 1968, Worcester Mass., Worcester Art Museum, *Edward Lear, Painter, Poet and Draughtsman* (no. 106).

110 Villa Emily and Villa Tennyson, 1870–88

a) Modern copy of a contemporary photograph of Villa Emily

b) Villa Tennyson under construction, 1880
Photograph: 9.4 × 14.6 cm/$3\frac{11}{16} \times 5\frac{3}{4}$ in
Private Collection

c) Villa Tennyson completed [after June 1881]
Photograph: 9.5 × 14.9 cm/$3\frac{3}{4} \times 5\frac{7}{8}$ in
Private Collection

d) View from the garden of Villa Tennyson [after June 1881]
Photograph: 14.8 × 10.5 cm/$5\frac{13}{16} \times 4\frac{1}{8}$ in
Private Collection

For most of his life Lear lived in rented rooms, moving from place to place. It was not until 1869, when he had given up all hope of achieving critical acclaim and financial stability as a painter, that he decided to settle permanently abroad. In early 1870 he chose a plot of land in San Remo on the Italian Riviera, a place 'Neither too much *in*, nor altogether *out* of the world' (Holman Hunt, 7.vii.70, MS., Huntington Library, San Marino), then designed a house and garden in which he could spend the rest of his days painting quietly. Villa Emily, named after a niece in New Zealand, was finished in March 1871. 'I never before had such a painting room' he told Fortescue, '32 feet by 20—& with a light I can work by at all hours, & a clear view S. over the sea. Below it is a room of the same

110*a*

110*b*

110*c*

size, which I now use as a Gallery, & am "at home" in once a week' (24.iv.71, LLEL 1911, p. 133; see Cat. 107). He had saved enough from his writings to be free from financial stress, and he found in Villa Emily 'a certain tranquility of life' (Diary, 22.v.71; Cat. 110*a*).

But the tranquillity did not last. In the autumn of 1878 the land between his house and the sea was cleared of its olive trees, and by the spring of 1879 the foundations were laid for a four-storey hotel. Not only did this block his view to the sea and destroy his peace, but the brilliant whiteness of its walls dazzled his studio light, making it impossible for him to work. In the end he was forced to abandon Villa Emily, buy more land and build again. 'My new land has only the road and the Railway between it and the sea,' he told Emily

110*d*

Tennyson, 'so unless the Fishes begin to build, or Noah's Ark comes to an Anchor below the site, the new Villa Oduardo cannot be spoiled' (16.ii.80, MS., Tennyson Research Centre, Lincoln). The new house, built to the same design as the old so that Foss the cat would know his way about, was called Villa Tennyson (Cat. 110*b–d*). Lear moved into the house in June 1881, and lived there until he died in 1888.

Villa Emily remained unsold until February 1884. Lear had been forced to reduce the price substantially. The financial loss and the three-year period as the owner of two houses, left Lear in debt until almost the last year of his life.

PROVENANCE *(b)–(d)* discovered by present owner.

REFERENCES *(b)* Lehmann 1977, repr. p. 110. *(c)* Noakes 1968 edn, p. 278; Lehmann 1977, repr. p. 111. *(d)* Strachey 1911, repr. opp. p. 136.

111 Photographs of Lear

a) Carte-de-visite, 1862
No. 5838 by McLean, Melhuish & Haes, 26 Haymarket
10.2×6.3 cm/$4 \times 2\frac{1}{2}$ in
Mrs R.E.C. Stileman

b) Carte-de-visite, 1864–65
By Perret, rue Gioffredo, Nice
9.5×6.3 cm/$3\frac{3}{4} \times 2\frac{1}{2}$ in
Mrs R.E.C. Stileman

c) Composite sheet
Sheet: 20.6×26.2 cm/$8\frac{1}{8} \times 10\frac{5}{16}$ in
i Sepia photograph: 14×10.2 cm/$5\frac{1}{2} \times 4$ in
ii Willowk/wail: max. 10.8×11 cm/$4\frac{1}{4} \times 4\frac{5}{16}$ in
iii Manuscript visiting card: 1.6×7.6 cm/$1\frac{9}{16} \times 3$ in
Department of Printing and Graphic Arts, The Houghton Library, Harvard University

'His mind is concrete and fastidious,
His nose is remarkably big;
His visage is more or less hideous,
His beard it resembles a wig.'

111*a*

111*c*

112

This was Lear's own description of himself in 'How Pleasant to Know Mr Lear' (1879, see Cat. 98). 'Tall, not handsome, and rather ungainly in figure, he was very agreeable and genial in manner,' wrote the Canadian painter, Daniel Fowler (*Autobiography or Recollections of an Artist*, ed. F.K. Smith, Ontario), whilst Hubert Congreve recalled that he was a 'tall heavily-built gentleman, with a large curly beard and wearing well-made but unusually loosely fitting clothes, and what at the same time struck me most of all, very large, round spectacles' (LLEL 1911, p. 17).

Although Lear sent many of his friends his own graphic descriptions of how he looked (see Cat. 96), he also sent them cartes-de-visite. The earlier portrait photograph (Cat. 111*a*) was taken in London on 27 October 1862 by McLean, the publisher of his first *Book of Nonsense* (see Cat. 72). The other carte-de-visite exhibited here (Cat. 111*b*) was taken in Nice during the winter of 1864–65.

The composite sheet (Cat. 111*c*) shows the last photograph of Lear, taken on 28 April 1887. A few moments before, Foss had been sitting on Lear's lap; had he stayed, we would have had a record of Lear's favourite feline. When shown this photograph, Lear's servant Guiseppi Orsini, remarked 'O che bel vecchio'. This sheet was put together by the Nicholls family who had lived in San Remo, at the Villa Qualia, in the mid-1870s.

PROVENANCE *(a) (b)* Fanny Coombe, by family descent. *(c)* W. B. Osgood Field; The Houghton Library, Harvard University.

112 Franklin Lushington

Artist unknown, *Portrait of Franklin Lushington*, *c.* 1840
Pencil on paper: 30.5 × 27.9 cm/12 × 11 in
Alan Kenn Esq.

Lear met Franklin Lushington (1823–1901) in Malta in the spring of 1849, where Lear was staying with his elder brother, Henry, then Chief Secretary to the Government in Malta. On 3 March 1849 they embarked for Patras and spent six weeks travelling together in southern Greece (see Cat. 20). These were probably the most carefree weeks of Lear's life, when he found Lushington 'the most merry and kind travelling companion' (Ann, 21.iv.49, TS.), and they established a lasting and important friendship. Lushington, too, looked back on that time with happiness, recalling Lear's 'volatile fun which in his youth was always ready to bubble over. The "Book of Nonsense" is the offspring of an always fresh and fertile humour. I remember one night in Greece when, after scrambling for 15 hours on horse back over the roughest mountain paths, we had dismounted & were waiting in black darkness for our guide to find among a few huts a tolerable weather tight shelter for us to sleep in, Lear, who was thoroughly tired, sat down upon what he supposed to be a bank; but an instant grunt & heave convinced him of error as a dark bovine quadruped suddenly rose up under him & tilted him into the mud. As Lear regained his feet he cheerily burst into song;

"There was an old man who said, "Now,
I'll sit down on the horns of that cow!"'
(*A Leaf from the Journals of a Landscape Painter*, 1897, p. 410)

In 1855 Lushington was appointed Judge to the Supreme Court of Justice in the Ionian Islands, and Lear travelled with him to live in Corfu (see Cat. 21). Lear wintered on the island for the next three years, but saw little of Lushington who had become silent and remote. It was only after Lushington's marriage in 1862 that their relationship moved onto a happier, stronger footing. Lear was godfather to all Lushington's children, and when he died Lushington wrote of him: 'He has always been the most charming & delightful of friends to me; & apart from all his various qualities of genius, I have never known a man who deserved more love for his goodness of heart & his determination to do right; & I don't think any human being knew him better than I did. There never was a more generous or more unselfish soul' (Lushington to Mrs Charles Street, 12.v.88, TS., Private Collection).

Lushington was co-author with his brother Henry Lushington of three collections of verse: *Points of Law* (1854), *Battle*

Pieces (1855) and *Joint Compositions* (undated). Lear appointed him his Literary Executor; this was an unfortunate choice for he destroyed many of Lear's papers, no doubt believing that their preservation would be unwise and indiscrete.

PROVENANCE Sir Franklin Lushington, by family descent.

REFERENCE Noakes 1979 edn, repr. opp. p. 129.

113 Chichester Fortescue

Edward Lear and Chichester Fortescue at Red House, Ardee, September 1857
Collotype: 14.3 × 10.3 cm/5⅝ × 4 in
BBC Hulton Picture Library, London

113

When Fortescue (1823–98) first met Lear in Rome in 1848, he described him as 'a delightful companion, full of *nonsense*, puns, riddles, everything in the shape of fun, and brimming with intense appreciation of nature as well as history . . . I don't know when I have met any one to whom I took so great a liking' (LEL 1907, p. xxv).

Fortescue, who was Member of Parliament for Louth, later became Chief Secretary for Ireland, President of the Board of Trade and Lord Privy Seal. When he was given a barony in 1874, taking the title of Lord Carlingford, Lear wrote to him:

'O! Chichester, my Carlingford!
O! Parkinson, my Sam!
O! SPQ, my Fortes*cue!*
  How awful glad I am!
For now you'll do no more hard work
Because by sudden = pleasing-jerk
  You're all at once a peer, —
Whereby I cry, God bless the Queen!
As was, & is, & still has been,
  Your's ever, Edward Lear.'
(24.iv.74, LLEL 1911, p. 170)

In 1871, Fortescue married Frances, Lady Waldegrave, who commissioned a number of paintings from Lear (Cat. 59). She died in 1879.

The letters which Lear wrote to Fortescue and Lady Waldegrave were published in two volumes in 1907 and 1911 (LEL 1907; LLEL 1911), edited by Lady Strachey, Lady Waldegrave's niece, who in 1911 also edited *Queery Leary Nonsense*. These books appeared at a time when Lear's reputation was at a low ebb, and were a demonstration of the affection and respect that Fortescue's family felt for Lear and for his work.

This photograph was taken in September 1857 when Lear was staying with Fortescue at his home, Red House, Ardee, Ireland.

PROVENANCE not known.

REFERENCE LEL 1907, frontis.; Noakes 1968 edn, repr. opp. p. 240.

114 Lord Northbrook

Modern copy of a photograph
Vivien Noakes

On 12 February 1848 Lear wrote to Fortescue, 'thank you for your introduction to Baring: he is an extremely luminous & amiable brick, and I like him very much, & I suppose he likes me or he wouldn't take the trouble of knocking me up as he does, considering the lot of people he might take to instead' (LEL 1907, p. 6). This was Lear's first mention of Thomas George Baring (1876–1904), later the first Earl of Northbrook. Between 1872 and 1876 he was Viceroy of India, and it was at Northbrook's invitation that Lear visited India and Ceylon between 1873 and 1875 (see Cat. 34, 35).

When Villa Emily at San Remo was ruined by the new hotel (see Cat. 110), Northbrook discussed with Lord Derby how they might best help Lear. 'How extremely queer, 2 Earls talking over this "d---d Landscape = painter's" affairs!)' wrote Lear (Diary, 30.x.79). Northbrook made Lear an interest-free loan of £2,000, whilst Lord Derby commissioned £500 worth

114

of drawings, believing loans to be a mistake. It was six years before Lear was able to repay the money, but it made the move to Villa Tennyson possible.

As Lear lay dying he recalled his closest friends, asking his servant to tell them that 'my last thought was for them, especially the Judge [Lushington] and Lord Northbrook and Lord Carlingford. I cannot find words sufficient to thank my good friends for the good they have always done me' (Lushington to Fortescue, 6.ii.88, quoted in LLEL 1911, p. 362).

REFERENCE Noakes 1968, edn, repr. p. 269.

115 Augusta Bethell

Contemporary photograph: 10.2 × 5.7 cm/4 × $2\frac{1}{4}$ in
Mrs M.B. Koe.

Augusta Bethell (1838–1931), known always as Gussie, was the daughter of Richard Bethell, later Lord Bethell (see Cat. 89). Lear had known her from her childhood.

It was not until 1862, when Lear was fifty and Gussie twenty-four, that he began to take particular notice of her. 'Dear little Gussie, who is absolutely good and sweet & delightful,' he wrote, 'BOTHER!' (Diary, 7.xi.62). By 1866 he was seriously considering the possibility of marriage, and at this time Gussie's family indicated their approval of the match. He returned to England the following year determined

115

to propose. It seems likely that Gussie would have accepted him, but he did not put the question directly to her. Instead he discussed the possibility with her sister, Emma, and discovered that the family no longer found it acceptable. 'Yet after what she said a year ago—her "certainty that now A & I could not live together happily"—seems strange. Anyhow—it *broke up a dream* rudely & sadly' he wrote in his diary (3.xi.67).

In 1874 Gussie married Adamson Parker, an invalid many years her senior who died a few years later, in 1882. In April 1887 she visited Lear in San Remo, and he was 'more or less perplexed as to if I shall or shall not ask Gussie to marry me. Once or twice the crisis nearly came off, yet she went at 5 & nothing occurred beyond her very decidedly showing me how much she cared for me' (Diary, 4.iv.87). In 1890 Gussie married Thomas Nash, uncle of the painter Paul Nash.

PROVENANCE The Hon. Augusta Bethell, by family descent.

116 Giorgio Kokali

Modern copy of a photograph taken in 1881

Giorgio Kokali (also spelt Cocali) became Lear's manservant in Corfu in the spring of 1856, and remained with him until his death at Monte Generoso in August 1883. He was by descent an Albanian Christian from Suli (see Cat. 20), and spoke Greek, Italian and Albanian. Apart from his domestic duties he accompanied Lear on his travels, and on their return would model for figures in Lear's oil paintings, dressed in the peasant costumes that Lear had brought back (see Cat. 106). Lear attempted to teach him English—on one occasion Giorgio's lesson was to read aloud the 'Owl and the Pussy-cat' (see Cat. 78)—and to read and write, but without great success.

After the death of Giorgio's wife in1874, Lear gave a home to his sons; the oldest, Nicola, is buried in the grave beside Lear in San Remo (see Cat. 118).

Lear believed that 'The reason of servants being unsatisfactory 9 times out of 10 is that their hirers consider them as chairs or tables—& take no interest in them as human beings' (Fortescue, 11.i.63, LEL 1907, p. 265), and in Lear's later,

116

lonelier years Giorgio became increasingly a companion. One evening a week, Lear would invite him for a drink and a cigar, and they would reminisce about their travels together. 'My poor dear George was ever a semi-civilized Suliot, much like wild Rob Roy or Highlander,' Lear wrote of him after his death in 1883 (Diary, 18.xi.83). 'I wish I could think that I had merited such a friend' (Emily Tennyson, 18.viii.83, MS., Tennyson Research Centre, Lincoln).

REFERENCE Strachey 1911, repr. opp. p. 232; Noakes 1968 edn, repr. p. 273.

117

117 Foss's Grave

Modern copy of a contemporary photograph

Foss (see Cat. 97) died on 26 November 1887. Writing to Lord Aberdare (Cat. 63) Lear said '. . . whoever has known me for 30 years has known that for all that time my cat Foss has been part of my solitary life. / Foss is dead: & I am glad to say did not suffer at all—having become quite paralyzed on all one side of him. So he was placed in a box yesterday, & buried deep below the Figtree at the end of the Orange walk, & tomorrow there will be a stone placed giving the date of his death & his age (31 years,)—(of which 30 were passed in my house) . . . All those friends who have known my life will understand that I grieve over this loss . . . Salvatore has the stone for Foss, & the Inscription, & I suppose in a day or two all will be as before, except the memory of my poor friend Foss' (29.xi. 87, MS., Glamorgan Record Office).

In fact, Foss had come to live with Lear in 1873 and was fourteen when he died.

REFERENCE LLEL 1911, repr. opp. p. 356.

118 Edward Lear's Grave

Modern copy of a contemporary photograph

Lear died on 29 January 1888 and was buried in the English cemetery in San Remo. It was a bleak funeral, attended only by his servant, and the doctor and his wife. She wrote afterwards, 'I have never forgotten it, it was all so sad, so lonely. After such a life as Mr Lear's had been and the immense number of friends he had, there was not one of them able to be with him at the end' (Mrs Hassall to Lady Strachey, 21.i.1911, LLEL 1911, p. 361).

Lear had asked that his gravestone should carry only his name and the dates of his birth and death. Lushington, however, felt this to be inadequate, and added the inscription LANDSCAPE PAINTER IN MANY LANDS/ DEAR FOR HIS MANY GIFTS TO MANY SOULS, and Tennyson's lines:

'—all things fair,
With such a pencil such a pen,
You shadow'd forth to distant men,
I read and felt that I was there.'

Nicola Kokali (or Cocali, see Cat. 116), Giorgio's son, is buried beside him; this headstone bears a commemorative inscription to Giorgio who had died in 1883 and was buried at Mendrisio in Switzerland.

REFERENCE LLEL 1911, repr. opp. p. 362.

118

EDWARD LEAR

BY W. H. AUDEN

Left by his friend to breakfast alone on the white
Italian shore, his Terrible Demon arose
Over his shoulder ; he wept to himself in the night,
A dirty landscape-painter who hated his nose.

The legions of cruel inquisitive " They "
Were so solid and strong, like dogs ; he was upset
By Germans and boats ; affection was miles away :
But, guided by tears, he successfully reached his
Regret.

His welcome was prodigious : A flower took his hat
And bore him off to introduce him to the tongs ;
The demon's false nose made the table laugh ; a cat
Invited him to dance and shyly squeezed his hand ;
Words pushed him to the piano to sing comic songs.

And children swarmed to him like settlers : He
became a land.

119b

119 W. H. Auden and Lear

a) Manuscript for 'Edward Lear'
Ink on paper: 27.3 × 21.3 cm/$10\frac{3}{4} \times 8\frac{3}{8}$ in
Private Collection

b) Proof for 'Edward Lear' [1939]
Single sheet: 47 × 30.8 cm/$18\frac{1}{2} \times 12\frac{1}{8}$ in
Private Collection

Chronology

[Compiled by Briony Llewellyn]

EVENTS	TRAVELS	GENERAL
1812 12 May, Edward Lear born in Holloway		**1811** George, Prince of Wales, created Prince Regent **1815** Congress of Vienna: end of the Napoleonic Wars Ionian Islands ceded to Britain
1820		
1825 Earliest surviving poem: Eclogue *vide* Collins: 'Hassan—Or the Camel Driver' *c.* **1827** Begins to earn living as an artist, making 'uncommon queer shop-sketches' *c.* **1829** Collaboration with Prideaux Selby on *Illustrations of British Ornithology* (1821–34)		**1820** Accession of George IV **1822** Wilkie's *Chelsea Pensioners reading the Gazette of the Battle of Waterloo* exhibited at Royal Academy **1823** Publication of first known book of limericks: 'Anecdotes and Adventures of Fifteen Gentlemen' **1824** Founding of the National Gallery, London **1829** The Zoological Society of London receives Royal Charter
1830		
1830 June, begins drawing parrots at Zoological Society Gardens, London; meets Lord Stanley, later 13th Earl of Derby November, becomes Associate member of Linnean Society *c.* **1831** Invitation from Lord Stanley to draw birds and animals in menagerie at Knowsley Hall; at Knowsley until 1837 Collaboration with John Gould on *The Birds of Europe* (1837) and other works **1832** Publication of *Illustrations of the Family of Psittacidae, or Parrots* **1837** *The Screes, Wastwater, Cumberland* exhibited at the Society of British Artists (no. 831)	**1831** or **1832** Amsterdam, Rotterdam, Berne, Berlin **1835** July–August, Ireland **1836** August–October, Lake District **1837** June–July, Devon and Cornwall; July–December, Belgium, Luxembourg, Germany, Switzerland, Italy, Rome **1838** Rome. May–August, Bay of Naples **1839** Rome. Summer, walking tour towards Florence	**1830** Accession of William IV **1831** Declaration of Greek Independence **1832–48** Railways established in France, Belgium, Germany, Austria, Italy, Holland, Switzerland and Spain **1834** Palace of Westminster destroyed by fire **1836** Charles Barry wins competition to rebuild Palace of Westminster **1837** Accession of Queen Victoria Death of John Constable **1838** Formation of The Clique (Egg, Dadd, Frith, Phillip, O'Neill, Elmore, Joy, Ward) **1838–39** David Roberts tours the Near East **1839** Turner's *The Fighting Temeraire* exhibited at the Royal Academy
1840		
1841 Publication of *Views in Rome and its Environs* **1844** Death of Lear's mother, Ann **1845** Spring, meets Chichester Fortescue **1846** July–August, drawing lessons for Queen Victoria Publication of *Illustrated Excursions in Italy* (2 vols); publication of *Gleanings from the Menagerie and Aviary at Knowsley Hall*; publication of *A Book of Nonsense* (pseud. Derry down Derry) **1848** February, meets Thomas Baring, later Lord Northbrook **1849** March, meets Franklin Lushington	**1840** Rome. Summer, Subiaco **1841** Rome. Spring, England; September, Scotland; December, Rome **1842** Rome, April–May, Sicily; July–October, Abruzzi **1843** Rome. September–October, Abruzzi **1844** Rome. **1845** Rome. May, England **1846** England. December, Rome **1847** Rome. May–June, Sicily; July–October, the Kingdom of the two Sicilies (including southern Calabria) **1848** Rome. April–June, via Malta to Corfu, Ionian Islands; June, Greece: Athens, Marathon, Thermopylae, Thebes; August, Constantinople; September–December, tour of Greece and Albania; December, Malta **1849** January–February, Cairo, Suez, Sinai; February, Malta; March–June, tour of southern Greece, Yannina, Vale of Tempe, Mount Olympus; July, England	**1840–41** David Wilkie in the Near East; dies at sea on journey home **1840–51** John Frederick Lewis in the Near East **1841** William Henry Fox Talbot's calotype process patented Select Committee appointed for the decoration of the Palace of Westminster **1842–49** Publication of Roberts's *The Holy Land, Syria, Idumea, Arabia, Egypt and Nubia* **1843–60** Publication of Ruskin's *Modern Painters* (5 vols) **1848** Formation of the Pre-Raphaelite Brotherhood Chartist meeting Revolutions in Italy

EVENTS	TRAVELS	GENERAL
1850		1850
1850 Attendance at Royal Academy Schools First exhibit at the Royal Academy: *Claude Lorraine's house on the Tiber* (no. 30)	**1850** London.	**1850** Millais' *Christ in the House of His Parents* exhibited at Royal Academy Lewis's *The Hhareem* exhibited at the Old Water Colour Society
1851 Royal Academy exhibits: *Street scene in Lekhreda, a town in North Albania* (no. 170) and *The Castle of Harytena in Arcadia* (no. 679) Meets Alfred and Emily Tennyson Publication of *Journals Of A Landscape Painter In Albania &c*	**1851** London. July–August, Devon	**1851** Great Exhibition, London Landseer's *The Monarch of the Glen* exhibited at the Royal Academy Death of J.M.W. Turner **1851–76** Lewis exhibiting oriental subjects at the Old Water Colour Society and the Royal Academy
1852 Summer, meets William Holman Hunt; idea of illustrating Tennyson's poems initiated Publication of *Journals Of A Landscape Painter In Southern Calabria, &c.* *The Acropolis of Athens, Sunrise, people assembling on the road to the Piraeus* exhibited at the British Institution (no. 238) *Mount Parnassus, Lake Cephissus, and the plains of Boeotia, Northern Greece*, exhibited at the Royal Academy (no. 569)	**1852** London. July–December, Hastings	**1852** Millais' *Ophelia* exhibited at the Royal Academy
1853 *The Mountains of Thermopylae* exhibited at the British Institution (no. 428) *Prato-lungo, near Rome* and *The city of Syracuse from the ancient quarries where the Athenians were imprisoned, B.C.413* (known as *The Quarries of Syracuse*) exhibited at the Royal Academy (nos 475 and 1062) Publication of musical settings to four of Tennyson's poems, including 'Tears, idle tears'	**1853** January–February, Hastings, London; December, Egypt	**1853** Holman Hunt's *Our English Coasts (Strayed Sheep)* exhibited at the Royal Academy
1854 *Marathon* and *Sparta* exhibited at the Royal Academy (nos 105 and 561)	**1854** January–March, Egypt; April, Malta, Marseilles, England; August–October, Switzerland, England	**1854** Holman Hunt and Seddon in Egypt and Palestine John Martin's three Judgement pictures, *The Great Day of His Wrath*, *The Plains of Heaven*, and *The Last Judgement*, embark on a tour of Britain and the United States **1854–56** Crimean War
1855 *The Temple of Bassae or Phigaleia, in Arcadia* exhibited at the Royal Academy (no. 319) *A Calabrian Ravine, Pentedalo* and *A Devonshire Glen—Lydford* exhibited at the Society of British Artists (nos 214 and 216) *Windsor Castle from St Leonard's Hill* exhibited at the British Institution (no. 317) Publication of second edition of *A Book of Nonsense*	**1855** England. December, Corfu	**1855** Paris Universal Exhibition Leighton's *Cimabue* exhibited at the Royal Academy Seddon's *The Valley of Jehoshaphat* exhibited at Berners Street, London
1856 *The island of Philae, above the first cataract on the Nile, from the South—afternoon* and *Island of Philae, above the first cataract on the Nile—from the Noch Mount* exhibited at the Royal Academy (nos 625 and 993) April, employs Giorgio Kokali as his manservant	**1856** Corfu. April, Albania; August–October, Greece, Mount Athos, Dardanelles, Troy, Corfu	**1856** Holman Hunt's *The Scapegoat* exhibited at the Royal Academy
1857 *The Quarries of Syracuse* in the International Exhibition at Manchester	**1857** Corfu. April, Albania; May, via Venice to London; November, Corfu	**1857** Indian Mutiny Manchester Art Treasures Exhibition
1858 First use of the monogram ℒ Publication of five more musical settings to Tennyson's poems	**1858** Corfu. March, Alexandria, Jaffa, Jerusalem; April, Bethlehem, Hebron, Petra, Dead Sea; May, Beirut; June, Corfu; August, England; November, Rome	**1858** Frith's *Derby Day* exhibited at the Royal Academy
1859 December, *The Temple of Bassae* bought by subscription for the Fitzwilliam Museum, Cambridge	**1859** Rome. May, England; July–November, St Leonards; December, Rome	**1859** War declared between Italy and Austria
		1860
1860 Earliest known piece of Nonsense Botany August, begins work on two large paintings, *The Cedars of Lebanon* and *Masada*	**1860** Rome. May, Bay of Spezia, England; October–December, Weybridge	**1860** Holman Hunt's *The Finding of the Saviour in the Temple* exhibited at the German Gallery, London
1861 March, death of Lear's sister, Ann May, *The Cedars of Lebanon* completed August, *The Cedars of Lebanon* exhibited at Liverpool Institute *The Fortress of Masada, on the Dead Sea* exhibited at the British Institution (no. 349) Publication of third edition of *A Book of Nonsense*	**1861** Weybridge. January, London; May–August, Florence, Switzerland, England; November, Corfu	**1861** Death of Prince Albert Foundation of Morris, Marshall, Faulkner and Company
1862–3 Work on first group of Tyrants	**1862** Corfu. May, via Malta to England; November, Corfu	**1862** International Exhibition, London
1863 Publication of first edition in the United States of *A Book of Nonsense* Publication of *Views in the Seven Ionian Islands*	**1863** Corfu. April–May, Ionian Islands; June, via Italy to England	
	1864 January, Corfu; April, Athens, Crete; June, England; November, Nice; December, The Corniche	**1864** Ionian Islands returned to Greece Death of David Roberts
1865 Writes first Nonsense Story, 'The History of the Seven Families of the Lake Pipple-Popple'	**1865** Nice. April, England; November, Venice; December, Malta	**1865** Publication of Lewis Carroll's *Alice's Adventures in Wonderland*

EVENTS	TRAVELS	GENERAL
1866–67 Seriously contemplating proposal of marriage to Gussie Bethell, daughter of Lord Westbury	**1866** Malta. April, via Corfu, Dalmatian coast, Trieste to England; December, Egypt	**1866** Publication of Richard and Samuel Redgrave's *A Century of Painters of the British School*
1867 Writes first of Nonsense Songs, 'The Owl and the Pussycat' *The Cedars of Lebanon* sold to Lady Ashburton	**1867** Egypt. April, Palestine; May, northern Italy; June, England; November, Cannes	**1867** Paris Universal Exhibition
	1868 Cannes. May–June, Corsica, England; December, Cannes	
	1869 Cannes. June, Paris; July, London; December, Cannes	
1870		
1870 March, buys land in San Remo to build a house *Kasr-es-Saad* and *Valdoniello* exhibited at the Royal Academy (nos 271 and 508) Publication of *Journal of a Landscape Painter in Corsica*	**1870** Cannes. March, San Remo (briefly); June, San Remo; summer, Certosa del Pesio	
1871 March, moves into Villa Emily, San Remo *Cáttaro in Dalmatia*, *On the Nile near Assiot*, *On the Nile, Nagâdeh*, and *On the Nile near Ballâs* exhibited at the Royal Academy (nos 638, 759, 1056, 1059) September, invitation from Lord Northbrook to visit India Publication of *Nonsense Songs, Stories, Botany and Alphabets*	**1871** March, moves into Villa Emily, San Remo; Autumn, Genoa, Rome, Frascati, Bologna, Padua	
1872 *Petra* exhibited at the Royal Academy (no. 942) Arrival of Foss at Villy Emily November, begins work in earnest on the Tennyson drawings Publication of *More Nonsense, Pictures, Rhymes, Botany, etc.*	**1872** Villa Emily. June–October, England; October, sets out to India, but turns back at Suez	**1872** Publication of Lewis Carroll's *Alice Through the Looking Glass*
1873 *The Monastery of Megaspelion in the Morea* exhibited at the Royal Academy (no. 744)	**1873** Villa Emily. October, to India; November, arrives Bombay	
1874 Fortescue given peerage, as Lord Carlingford	**1874** India. November, Ceylon; December, leaves Ceylon for India	
	1875 January, leaves India for San Remo; June–September, England	
	1876 Villa Emily	**1876** Death of J.F. Lewis
1877 Publication of *Laughable Lyrics, A Fourth Book of Nonsense Poems, Songs, Botany, Music, &c.*	**1877** Villa Emily. February, Brindisi, Rome; May–September, England; September, Corfu, San Remo	**1877** Queen Victoria becomes Empress of India Grosvenor Gallery established Whistler's *Nocturne in Black and Gold – The Falling Rocket* exhibited at Grosvenor Gallery
	1878 Villa Emily. Summer, Monte Generoso, Switzerland	**1878** Paris Universal Exhibition
1879 July, death of Lady Waldegrave	**1879** Villa Emily. Summer, Monte Generoso	
1880		
1880 January, buys another piece of land at San Remo to build a new house *c.* May–*c.* August, Lear exhibits watercolours at Lord Northbrook's London house	**1880** Villa Emily. April–August, England; September–October, Varese, Monte Generoso	
1881 June, Villa Tennyson, San Remo completed	**1881** Villa Emily. May, moves out of Villa Emily; summer, Monte Generoso; October, moves into Villa Tennyson, San Remo	
	1882 Villa Tennyson. Summer, Monte Generoso	
1883 August, death of Giorgio Kokali	**1883** Villa Tennyson. Summer, Monte Generoso; September, Perugia, Florence, Pisa, La Spezia, Genoa	
	1884 Villa Tennyson. Summer, Recoaro, Milan	**1884** Foundation of Art Workers Guild
	1885 Villa Tennyson. Summer, Brianza	**1885** Formation of New English Art Club
1886 February, John Ruskin's 'Choice of Books' in the *Pall Mall Gazette*	**1886** Villa Tennyson. Summer, Brianza	
1887 November, death of Foss	**1887** Villa Tennyson. Summer, Andorno	**1887** Queen Victoria's Golden Jubilee
1888 29 January, death of Edward Lear at San Remo Publication of first collected edition of Lear's four nonsense books		
1889 Publication of *Poems of Alfred, Lord Tennyson*, illustrated by Edward Lear		

Bibliographies

GENERAL

[The place of publication is London unless otherwise stated. Works which themselves contain substantial bibliographies are marked with an asterisk.]

Davidson, A., *Edward Lear: Landscape Painter and Nonsense Poet (1812–1888)*, John Murray, 1938; second edn 1968.

Hewett, O. W. (ed.), *And Mr Fortescue*, John Murray, 1958. (Excerpts from the diaries of Chichester Fortescue, Lord Carlingford, 1851–1862.)

Hofer, P., *Edward Lear*, Oxford, New York, 1962.

Holman Hunt, W., *Pre-Raphaelitism and the Pre-Raphaelite Brotherhood*, 2 vols, Macmillan, 1905.

Kelen, E., *Mr. Nonsense: a Life of Edward Lear*, Thomas Nelson, Nashville, 1973.

Lehmann, J., *Edward Lear and his World*, Thames and Hudson, 1977.

Noakes, V., *Edward Lear: the Life of a Wanderer*, Collins, 1968; revised edn Fontana, 1979; revised edn 1985, BBC Publications.

Richardson, J., *Edward Lear*, Writers and their Work, no. 184, Longmans, Green, 1965.

Slade, B. C., (ed.), *Edward Lear on My Shelves* (for W. B. Osgood Field), privately printed, New York, 1933.

Baring, M., 'Edward Lear', *Punch and Judy and Other Essays*, Heinemann, 1924, pp. 255–60.

Richardson, J., 'Edward Lear: man of letters', *Ariel*, 1 (1970), pp. 18–28.

Lear the writer

*Byrom, T., *Nonsense and Wonder: the Poems and Cartoons of Edward Lear*, Dutton, New York, 1977.

Cammaerts, E., *The Poetry of Nonsense*, Routledge, 1925.

Chesterton, G. K., 'Edward Lear', *A Handful of Authors*, Sheed and Ward, 1953.

Ede, L. S., 'The Nonsense Literature of Edward Lear and Lewis Carroll', Ph.D. dissertation, Ohio State University, 1975.

*Hark, I. R., *Edward Lear*, Boston, 1982.

Liebert, H. W., *Lear in the Original: Drawings and Limericks by Edward Lear for his Book of Nonsense*, H. P. Kraus, New York, 1975.

Lyons, A. K., Lyons, T. R., Preston, M. J., *A Concordance to the Complete Nonsense of Edward Lear*, Norwood Editions, Norwood, Pa., 1980.

Parisot, H., *Limericks et Autres Poèmes Ineptes*, Mercure de France, Paris, 1968.

Petzold, D., *Formen und Funktionen der englischen Nonsense-Dichtung im 19. Jahrhundert*, Erlanger Beiträge zür Sprach und Kunstwissenschaft, 44, Hans Carl Verlag, Nuremberg, 1972.

Prickett, S., *Victorian Fantasy*, Harvester Press, Sussex, 1979.

Sewell, E., *The Field of Nonsense*, Chatto and Windus, 1952.

Stewart, S. A., *Nonsense: Aspects of Intertextuality in Folklore and Literature*, John Hopkins University Press, Baltimore, 1979.

Brockway, J. T., 'Edward Lear: Poet', *Fortnightly Review*, n.s. 167 (1950), pp. 334–39.

Croft-Cooke, R., *Feasting with Pantheus: a New Consideration of some Late Victorian Writers*, Allen, 1967, chap. 7.

Hark, I. R., 'Edward Lear: Eccentricity and Victorian *Angst*', *Victorian Poetry*, 16 (1978), pp. 112–22.

Huxley, A., 'Edward Lear', *On the Margin*, Chatto and Windus, 1923, pp. 167–72.

Leimert, E., 'Die Nonsense-Poesie von Edward Lear (Ein Beitrag zür Psychologie des Englischen Humors)', *Neueren Sprache*, 45 (1937), pp. 368–73.

Megnz, R. L., 'The Master of Nonsense', *Cornhill Magazine*, 157, no. 938 (1938), pp. 175–90.

Miller, E., 'Two Approaches to Edward Lear's Nonsense Songs', *Victorian Newsletter*, 44 (1973), pp. 5–8.

Nock, S. A., 'Lacrimae Nugarum: Edward Lear of the Nonsense Verses', *Sewanee Review*, 49 (1941), pp. 68–81.

Orwell, G., 'Nonsense Poetry', *Shooting an Elephant and Other Essays*, Harcourt, Brace, New York, 1945, pp. 187–92.

Quennell, P., 'Edward Lear', *The Singular Preference*, Collins, 1952, pp. 95–101.

Robinson, F. M., 'Nonsense and Sadness in Donal Barthelme and Edward Lear', *South Atlantic Quarterly*, 80 (1981), 164–76.

Thompson, R., Hofer, P., 'The Yonghy-Bonghy-Bò: I. The Poem. II. The Music,' *Harvard Library Bulletin*, 15 (1967), pp. 229–37.

Lear the artist

*Hofer, P., *Edward Lear as a Landscape Draughtsman*, Belknap Press, Cambridge, Mass., 1967; Oxford University Press, 1968.

Hyman, S., *Edward Lear's Birds*, Weidenfeld and Nicolson, 1980.

Jackson, C., *Bird Illustrators: some artists in early lithography*, Witherby, 1975.

Reade, B., *Edward Lear's Parrots*, Duckworth, 1949.

Thorpe, A., *The Birds of Edward Lear*, Ariel Press, 1975.

Tsigakou, F. M., 'Edward Lear in Greece', M. Phil. Thesis, University College, London, 1977.

Bruce, M. R. 'A Portfolio of Monasteries: Edward Lear's Sketches of Mount Athos', *Country Life*, (8 October 1964).

Bury, A., 'Lear at Parnassus', *Connoisseur*, CCI (September 1962), p. 49.

Butler, J. T., 'Edward Lear, painter, poet and draughtsman (the American way with art)', *Connoisseur*, CCXVIII (August 1968), pp. 280–81.

Hardie, M., 'Edward Lear', *Artwork*, no. 22 (summer 1930), pp. 114–18.

'Lear's Indian View', *Connoisseur*, CXLIX (April 1962), pp. 253–54.

Murray, A., 'Corfu by Edward Lear', *Rhode Island Bulletin*, XLIII, no. 2, (December 1956), pp. 9–11.

Neve, C., 'The Loneliness of Edward Lear', *Country Life*, CXLIV (17 October 1978), pp. 958–59.

Lear the musician

Copley, I. A., 'Edward Lear—Composer', *Musical Opinion*, CIV, no. 1236, (October 1980), pp. 8–9, 12, 39.

Ehrenpreis, A. H., 'Edward Lear Sings Tennyson Songs', *Harvard Literary Bulletin*, XXVII, no. 1, (January 1979), pp. 65–85.

ORNITHOLOGY AND NATURAL HISTORY

[Compiled by R. D. Wise. Thanks are due to the Department of Library Services, British Museum (Natural History), and in particular to Ann Datta, Jennifer Jeffrey and Frances Warr of the Zoology Library; also to Gina Douglas, Librarian of the Linnean Society.]

I Books illustrated by Lear

(Gray, John Edward), *Gleanings from the Menagerie and Aviary at Knowsley Hall*. Knowsley: Printed for Private Distribution, 1846. Imperial folio. All 17 coloured plates of animals and birds by Lear. They are unsigned but inscribed *E. Lear, del.*, except plate XVI.

The preface by J. E. Gray, dated 1 August 1846, states: 'The following Plates are selected from the series of Drawings made by Mr. Edward Lear from the living animals in the Right Honourable the Earl of Derby's Menagerie at Knowsley Hall, forming part of a large collection of Zoological Drawings in his Lordship's library. They have been lithographed with great care by Mr. J. W. Moore and coloured by Mr. Bayfield.'

Plates 3 and 14 are dated *Decr. 1838*. All plates are inscribed *J. (or I.) W. Moore lithog* except plate 15, which is inscribed *In Lithotint by D. Mitchell.*

A further volume with the same title, plus Hoofed Quadrupeds, was published in 1850. None of the 59 plates was by Lear.

Lear Edward, *Illustrations of the Family of Psittacidae or Parrots*: the greater part of them species hitherto unfigured, containing forty-two Lithographic Plates, drawn from Life and on Stone, by Edward Lear, A.L.S. London: Published by E. Lear, 61, Albany Street, Regent's Park. 1832. Imperial folio.

All plates are signed *E. Lear* except plate 32 (*Hooded Parrakeet*), which appears to be unsigned. They are inscribed *E. Lear del. et lithog.* Printed by C. Hullmandel.

Originally issued in 12 parts. According to G. M. Matthews (*The Birds of Australia*, London: Witherby, 1925, p . 78), 'this work appears in one volume with the plates arranged in a regular manner, but it was issued in twelve parts from 1830–1832; the contents of each Part I have given in the Austral. Av. Rec. Vol. 1 pp. 23–24, June 2nd 1912 . . . The dates of publication of the parts are: part 1 (3 plates) 1 November 1830; 2 (4 plates) 1 November [probably December] 1830; 3 (3 plates) 1 January 1831; 4 (4 plates) 1 February 1831; 5 (3 plates) 1 May 1831; 6 (4 plates) 1 August 1831; 7 (3 plates) 1 September 1831; 8 (3 plates) 1 October 1831; 9 (4 plates), 10 (4 plates), 11 (3 plates), 12 (4 plates) no date: the title page was issued with the final part.'

The following plates are dated: 6 (27 December 1831); 8 (December 1831); 19 (23 December 1831); 22 (December 1831); 25 (30 December 1831). Following the title page and list of subscribers is a list of plates. The plates follow this order and not as issued in the 12 parts.

II Books to which Lear contributed

[†indicates that, whilst the plate is neither signed by Lear nor inscribed with his name, there is positive evidence that it is based on a drawing made by him. Plate numbers in square brackets are for reference only; in these cases the published plates are unnumbered.]

BEECHEY, CAPT. FRANCIS, *The Zoology of Captain Beechey's Voyage*. Compiled from the collections and notes made by Captain Beechey, the Officers and Naturalist of the Expedition, during a voyage to the Pacific and Behring's Straits performed in His Majesty's Ship Blossom under the command of Captain F. W. Beechey, R.N., F.R.S., etc. etc., in the years 1825, 26, 27, and 28 by J. Richardson; N. H. Vigors; John E. Gray; the Rev. W. Buckland & G. B. Sowerby. London: Henry G. Bohn, 1839. Quarto.

There are, in fact, 44 coloured plates and 3 coloured maps. Of these, plates I to XIV are all inscribed *E. Lear del.* and consist of all 12 birds and 2 mammals. 2 plates were engraved by Thomas Landseer, the rest by Zeitter.

Plate I, *Sciurus colliei*; II, *Pteropus pselaphon*; III, *Sialia caeruleocollis*; IV, i *Troglodytes spilurus*, ii *Sitta pygmaea*; V, *Garrulus californicus*; VI, *Pica beechii*; VII, *Pica colliei*; VIII, *Coccothraustes ferreorostris*; IX, *Colaptes collaris*; X, *Columba monilis*; XI, *Ortyx douglasii*; XII, *Recurvirostra occidentalis*; XIII, *Anas caroliniensis*; XIV, *Anas urophasianus*.

For uncoloured copies (?proofs) of plates IV and IX, see note at end of Jardine and Selby, *Illustrations of Ornithology*.

BELL, THOMAS, *A Monograph of the Testudinata*. London: Printed for Samuel Highley. Sold also by J. B. Baillière, Paris: and F. Fleischer, Leipsig. Richard Taylor, Printer. Folio. N.d. (1836–42).

This work was issued in 8 parts, each containing 5 coloured plates, nearly all drawn by James de C. Sowerby and lithographed by Lear. The work was not completed owing to the failure of the publisher. It was eventually reissued in a greatly enlarged form in 1872 under the title 'Tortoises, Terrapins and Turtles'. The plates are unnumbered. Only 2 plates are signed: plate [1] *Testudo tabulata* (signed *E.L. Lith* and dated *Feb. 1832*); [3] *Testudo carbonaria* (signed *E. Lear*). This would appear to imply that they were both drawn and lithographed by Lear, but this is not clear. Plate [40], *Trionyx labiatus* (skeleton), is inscribed *Jane S. Bell del. E. Lear lithog.*

SOWERBY, JAMES DE CARLE and LEAR, EDWARD, *Tortoises, Terrapins & Turtles*, drawn from Life by James de Carle Sowerby and Edward Lear. London, Paris and Frankfurt: Henry Sotheran, Joseph Baer & Co., 1872.

This is a new and considerably enlarged edn of Bell's *Monograph of the Testudinata*. There are 60 plates in the coloured edn and 61 in the uncoloured. The new text is by J. E. Gray.

The British Museum has 3 copies of the Monograph, including the original drawings by Sowerby, 'pattern plates' for the use of colourists and a set of 'India Proof' lithographs. These cover all the 60 or 61 plates in *Tortoises, Terrapins & Turtles*, plus 4 plates never published, 2 of which are noted as being drawn from life and lithographed by Lear.

BELL, THOMAS, *A History of British Quadrupeds*, including the Cetacea. London: John van Voorst, 1837. Imperial octavo.

†Plate 68, Greater Horseshoe Bat; †76, Hedgehog; †115, Water Shrew, †161, Ferret Weasel.

None of the plates bears Lear's signature, nor any inscription. However, notes in Lear's personal copy, now in the Houghton Library, Harvard University, indicate that he made drawings for the above and possibly a few others.

BENNETT, E. T. (ed.), *The Gardens and Menagerie of the Zoological Society delineated*. In 2 volumes. Vol. I, *Quadrupeds*. Chiswick: Printed by C. Whittingham for the Proprietors. Published by Thomas Tegg, London, and N. Hailes, 1830. Vol. II, *Birds*. Chiswick: Printed by Charles Whittingham. Published by John Sharpe, London, 1831. Octavo. At least one and possibly more drawings are by Lear.

Vol. II, p. 125, Blue and Yellow Macaw. The initials *E.L.* are clearly visible below the head of the lower bird. In vol. I, 2 illustrations of Lemurs on pp. 145 and 299 bear marks which could be construed as initials *E.L.*, but this is conjectural.

Another edn of vol. I was published in 1831 by Charles Tilt and both volumes were republished by Thomas Tegg in 1835.

EYTON, T. C., *A Monograph of the Anatidae, or Duck Tribe*. London: Longman, Orme, Brown, Green & Longman; Shrewsbury: Eddowes, 1838. Quarto. 6 coloured lithographic plates and numerous uncoloured anatomical plates and drawings in the text. Lear did the drawings for the plates and may have done most of the lithographs, all printed by C. Hullmandel. Lear is not mentioned in the text.

Plate [1] *Tadorna castanea* (signed *Edward Lear del.*); [2] *Dafila urophasianus* (unsigned); [3] *Moreca chiloensis* (unsigned); [4] *Moreca castanea* (unsigned); [5] *Nyroca brunnea* (unsigned); [6] i *Oxyura unifasciata*, ii *Oxyura dominica* (signed *E. Lear del. T.C.E. lithog.*).

GOULD, JOHN, *The Birds of Europe*. In 5 volumes. Printed by Richard and John E. Taylor. Published by the Author, 20, Broad Street, Golden Square, [1832–] 1837. Imperial folio.

Preface, p. viii: 'Perhaps I may be allowed to add that, not only by far the greater number of the Plates of this work, but all those of my "Century of Birds", of the "Monograph of the Trogons" and at least three-fourths of the "Monograph of the Toucans" have been drawn and lithographed by Mrs. Gould, from sketches and designs by myself, always taken from nature. The remainder of the drawings have been made by Mr. Lear, whose abilities as an artist are so generally acknowledged that any comments of my own are unnecessary.'

There are a total of 449 plates in the 5 volumes, of which 68 are by Lear. They are, with one exception (plate 215), signed. The signature varies, with abbreviations from *Edward Lear del.* to *E. Lear*. With certain exceptions (noted below against the plates) the are inscribed *E.Lear* (or *Edward Lear*) *del. et lithog.* 4 are inscribed as being drawn and lithographed by the Goulds, although they were drawn and lithographed by Lear; 9 are dated.

Vol. I, *Raptores*: plate 2, *Vultur cinereus* (inscribed *Drawn from Nature & on Stone by J.&E. Gould*); 3, *Neophron perenopterus*; 6, *Aquila chrysaëta* (dated *1833*); 8, *Aquila naevius* (inscribed *E. Lear del.*); 9, *Haliaeëtus albicilla* (inscribed *Drawn from Life and on Stone by E. Lear*); 10, *Haliaeëtus leucocephalus*; 11, *Paudion haliaeëtus* (inscribed *Drawn from Life and on Stone by E. Lear*); 13, *Circaëtus brachydactylus*; 14, *Buteo vulgaris*; 15, *Buteo lagopus*; 20, *Falco lanarius*; 21, *Falco peregrinus* (inscribed *E. Lear del.*); 26, *Falco tinnunculus* (dated *1833*; inscribed *Drawn on Stone by E. Lear*); 28, *Milvus vulgaris* (inscribed *E. Lear del.*); 29, *Milvus ater*; 32, *Circus rufus*; 36, *Strix flammea* (inscribed *Drawn from Life on Stone by J. & E. Gould*); 37, *Bubo maximus* (inscribed *Drawn on Stone by E. Lear*); 38, *Bubo ascalaphus* (dated *1837*); 42, *Strix lapponica* (inscribed *E. Lear del.*); 43, *Strix nyctea*; 46, *Strix nebulosa*; 48, *Strix nudipes*; 49, *Strix tengmalmi*.

Vol. II, *Incessores*: no plates by Lear.

Vol. III, *Incessores*: plate 215, *Garrulus infaustus* (unsigned); 219, *Fregilus graculus* (dated *1833*); 220, *Corvus corax*; 221, *Corvus corone*; 222, *Corvus frugilegus*; 239, *Tichodroma phoenicoptera* (dated *1833*; inscribed *Drawn on Stone by E. Lear*).

Vol. IV, *Rasores. Grallatores*: plate 243, *Columba palumbus*; 247, *Phasianus colchicus*; 248, *Tetrao urogallus*; 250, *Tertrao tetrix*; 254, *Lagopus rupestris*; 256, *Lagopus brachydactylus*; 267, *Otis tarda*; 270, *Grus cinerea*; 271, *Grus leucogeranus* (dated *1837*); 272, *Anthropoïdes virgo*; 273, *Ardea cinerea* (dated *1833*); 274, *Ardea purpurea*; 276, *Ardea alba*; 277, *Ardea garzetta* (dated *1833*); 279, *Nycticorax europaeus*; 281, *Botaurus lentiginosus*; 283, *Ciconia alba*; 284, *Ciconia nigra*; 285, *Ciconia maguari*; 287, *Phoenicopterus ruber*; 338, *Fulica ater*.

Vol. V. *Natatores*: plate 347, *Anser palustris*; 348, *Anser segetum*; 351, *Anser ruficollis*; 352, *Anser brenta*; 353, *Chenalopax aegyptica*; 354, *Cygnus mansuetus*; 355, *Cygnus ferus*; 356, *Cygnus bewickii*; 400, *Alca impennis* (inscribed *Drawn from Nature and on Stone by J. & E. Gould*); 405, *Pelicanus onocrotalus* (inscribed *Drawn from Nature and on Stone by J. & E. Gould*); 406, *Pelicanus crispus*; 411, *Phalacrocorax desmarestii*; 412, *Sula bassana*; 413, *Sula melanura*; 430, *Larus marinus*; 432, *Larus glaucus*; 438, *Larus andouinii* (dated *1837*).

GOULD, JOHN, *A Monograph of the Ramphastidae, or Family of Toucans*. London: published by the Author, 20, Broad Street, Golden Square, 1834. Imperial folio. 1st edn, published in 2 volumes. 34 coloured plates; these are not numbered, but the species (except no. 25) are in the index. The plate numbers given here are consecutive through both volumes; 10 plates are by Lear and are both signed and inscribed *E. Lear, del et lithog.*

Plate [1] *Ramphastes culminatus* (dated *1833*); [3] *Ramphastes cuvieri*; [6] *Ramphastes toco* (dated *1833*); [9] *Ramphastes vitellinus* (dated *April 1833*); [14] *Pteroglossus regalis*; [20] *Pteroglossus bailloni* (dated *1833*); [21] *Pteroglossus viridis* (dated *1833*); [23] *Pteroglossus inscriptus*; [24] *Pteroglossus maculirostris*; [30] *Pteroglossus prasinus*.

GOULD, JOHN, *A Monograph of the Ramphastidae, or Family of Toucans*. London, published by the Author, 20, Broad Street, Golden Square, 1854. 2nd edn. 51 coloured plates. In this edn the plates are redrawn and inscribed below: *Gould & Richter del. et lith.* The Culminated Toucan (plate 1 in the 1st edn, plate 2 in the 2nd) is a direct copy, although redrawn. The others appear to be entirely new or with only a slight resemblance.

There is no acknowledgement to Lear in the text of either edn.

GOULD, JOHN, *The Birds of Australia and the adjacent Islands*. London: Published by the Author, 20, Broad Street, Golden Square. Printed by Richard and John Taylor. Part I, August 1837; part II, February 1838. Imperial folio.

Only 2 parts of the original edns were published. Part I contained 10 coloured plates and part II 10 plates. After these 2 parts were issued, Gould realised that he should produce a major work on this subject, and the production was therefore cancelled.

Part I, plate 6 (*Nymphicus novae-hollandiae*) is unsigned, and inscribed below: *Drawn on stone by J. & E. Gould from a Drawing by Edward Lear.* This is an exact copy of Lear's *Palaeornis novae-hollandiae*, *Illustrations of the Psittacidae* plate 27, except that Lear's signature has been removed. The text says: 'The accompanying plate . . . is copied by permission from a beautiful lithograph by Mr. Lear, whose drawing was made from two living birds in the possession of the Countess of Mount Charles.' In fact, it appears to be a print from the same stone.

Part I: plate 10 (*Phalacrocorax punctatus*). Signed *Edward Lear delt.*; inscribed *E. Lear, del et lithog.* There is no mention of Lear in the text, which states that the specimen came from the collection of the United Services Museum.

Part II: there appear to be no plates by Lear.

GOULD, JOHN, *The Birds of Australia* by John Gould, F.R.S, in Seven Volumes. London: published by the Author, 20, Broad Street, Golden Square, 1840–48. Imperial folio. The 7 volumes contain 602 coloured plates.

Vol. V: plate 45 (*Nymphicus novae-hollandiae*) is a reprint of plate 6 in part I of the original edn, unsigned, and with the same inscription. There is no mention of Lear in the greatly enlarged description.

Vol. VII: plate 71 (*Phalacrocorax punctatus*) is a reprint of plate 10 in part I. The signature is still present and the inscription is the same, but there is still no mention of Lear in the slightly enlarged description.

GOULD, JOHN, *A Monograph of the Trogonidae, or Family of Trogons*. London: printed by Richard and John E. Taylor. Published by the Author, 20, Broad Street, Golden Square, 1838. Imperial folio. 36 coloured plates.

†Plate 28 (*Trogon gigas*) bears no signature but is incribed *Drawn from Nature and on Stone by J. & E. Gould*. The original drawing for this plate, with the colouring unfinished, exists. It is also believed that Lear did the drawings for other plates in this work, and probably assisted with the backgrounds. There is no mention of Lear in the work.

GRAY, GEORGE ROBERT, *The Genera of Birds*: comprising their generic Characters, a Notice of the Habits of each Genus, and an extensive list of Species referred to their several Genera. Illustrated by David William Mitchell, B.A., F.L.S., Secretary to the Zoological Society of London. In 3 volumes. London, 1844–49.

Vol. II: plate 104 (*Psittacus augustus*) is inscribed *From Life by E. Lear. In Lithotint by D.M.*

JARDINE, SIR WILLIAM and SELBY, PRIDEAUX JOHN, *Illustrations of Ornithology*. Edinburgh: Daniel Lizars; London: Longman, Rees, Orme, Brown & Green; London: S. Highley; Dublin: Hodges & McArthur, n.d. (1825–39). In 3 volumes. Quarto. Originally published in parts.

JARDINE, SIR WILLIAM and SELBY, PRIDEAUX JOHN, *Illustrations of Ornithology*. Edinburgh: W. H. Lizars; London: S. Highley; Dublin: W. Curry Junr, n.d. (1836–43). Quarto. This is known as 'New Series' or vol. IV, though the title does not mention this.

Vol. I has 57 coloured plates, vol. II has 53, vol. III has 41 and vol. IV has 53. The plates in vols. I–III are numbered consecutively 1–151; those in vol. IV are numbered separately 1–53. There are 3 plates by Lear in vol. II and 17 in vol. IV. There are numerous references to him in the text accompanying the plates. The plates from 139–151 in vol. III and all plates in vol. IV are dated. The plates by Lear are inscribed *E.Lear* (or *Lear*) *del.* (or *del^t*). They are engraved by Lizars.

Vol. III: plate 147, *Rhynchapsis maculatus*, 1835; 149, *Aegotheles lunulata*, 1835; 151, *Oreopholus totanirostris*, 1835.

Vol. IV: plate 2, *Hypsipetes ganeesa*, 1836; 4, *Ianthocincla squamata*, 1836; 5, *Columba princeps*, 1836; 6, *Crax yarrellii*, 1836; 8, *Bernicla sandvicensis*, 1836; 12, *Phasianus lineatus*, 1836; 13, *Vultur hypocleus*, 1837; 16, *Perdrix fuseus*, 1837; 17, *Ibis spinicollis*, 1837; 24, *Falco australis*, 1838; 29, *Cyanopterus fretensis*, 1838; 32, *Corvus leaconotus*, 1839; 33, *Cereopsis novae-hollandiae*, 1839; 34, *Erythura cheet*, 1839; 37, *Merula nestor*, 1840; 38, *Dicrurus rangoonensis*, 1840; 40, *Anas specularis*, 1840.

In the Zoology Library of the British Museum (Natural History) there is a book of manuscript descriptions and proof plates, etc., of the first series only (vols I–III). It includes proofs of the Lear plates 147, 149 and 151. It also includes an uncoloured plate (marked *Plate IV*) of 1 *Troglodytes spilurus* and 2 *Sitta pygmaea*, and another (marked *Plate IX*) of *Colaptes collaris*, both inscribed *E. Lear del.* These are, in fact, plates from *The Zoology of Capt. Beechey's Voyage*.

JARDINE, SIR WILLIAM (ed.), *The Naturalist's Library*. Edinburgh: W. H. Lizars; London: S. Highley; Dublin: W. Curry, Jnr. Octavo. Dates as below.

Mammalia II: *Felinae* (in 2nd edn, *Lions, Tigers etc.*), Sir William Jardine, 1834. 1 uncoloured and 37 coloured plates. The preface states that 'The drawings were all made by Mr Stewart' but 2 plates are inscribed *Lear delt.*: plate 3*, *Felis leo*; 24*, *Felis himalayus*.

Ornithology V: *Pigeons*, by Prideaux John Selby, 1835. 1 uncoloured and 31 coloured plates. All the plates are by Lear and inscribed *E. Lear delt.*, with 3 exceptions: the frontispiece portrait, title vignette and plate 5. Plate 13 is not inscribed but is presumed to be by Lear.

Ornithology VI: *Parrots*, by Prideaux John Selby, 1836. 1 uncoloured and 31 coloured plates. All the plates are by Lear and inscribed *E. Lear delt.*, with the exception of the frontispiece portrait and title vignette. 11 of the plates illustrate species which appeared in Lear's *Illustrations of the Psittacidae*, but only four bear some resemblance to those plates.

JARDINE, SIR WILLIAM, *Sir William Jardine's Illustrations of the Duck Tribe*. Privately printed at the Expense of the Author. Jardine Hall, Lockerby, Dumfries, N.B., n.d. (?1839). There are 9 black and white engraved plates and no letterpress; 3 plates are from drawings by Lear, all signed *E. Lear*; only plate 3 is dated. The other plates are by Jardine (1), Selby (4) and Stewart (1).

Plate 3, *Rynchapsis maculatus* (inscribed *E.Lear delt. 1835*); 6, *Cyanopterus pretensis* (inscribed *E. Lear delt. W.H. Lizars sc.*); 7, *Anas specularis* (inscribed *E. Lear delt. Lizars sc.*).

SELBY, PRIDEAUX JOHN, *Illustrations of British Ornithology: or Figures of British Birds*. Edinburgh: W. H. Lizars; London: Longman, Rees, Orme, Brown, Green & Longman; Dublin: W. Curry Jnr. Printed for the Proprietors. Published in 19 parts 1821–1834. Subsequently entitled *Plates to Selby's Illustrations of British Ornithology*, 1834, vol. I, *Land Birds*, vol. 2, *Water Birds*.

Vol. 2, †plate 82, Great Auk.

Transactions of the Zoological Society of London. London: Printed for the Society by Richard Taylor. Vol. I, 1833–36; vol. II, 1836–41. Quarto. Originally published in parts. Lear provided 5 illustrations for vol. I and 3 for vol. II.

Vol. I, part I (1833), plates 3 (*Cynictis steadmanii*), 4 (*Lagotis cuvieri*); part 2 (1834), plates 14 (*Cryptoprocta ferox*), 24 (*Felis leo goojratensis*); part 3 (1835), plate 37 (*Macropus parryi*).

Vol. II, part I (1836), plates 6 (*Pteropus whitei*), 16 (*Octodon cumingii*), 17 (*Ctenomys magellanicus*).

All are inscribed *E. Lear del.* or *Lear del.* In addition, the last 2 plates are initialled *E.L.*

III Books with illustrations copied from Lear's plates

BOURJOT SAINT-HILAIRE, A., *Histoire Naturelle des Perroquets*. Les figures lithographiées et coloriées avec soin par M. Werner. Paris: F. G. Levrault, 1837–38. Imperial folio. 'Troisième Volume (supplémentaire) pour faire suite aux deux volumes de Levaillant.'

Preface, p. viii: '(Les figures) . . . très rarement puisées dans d'autres auteurs, à moins que les publications étant très-modernes, telles que celles de Spix, de Gould, de Lear . . .'

A number of plates are direct copies of Lear's *Illustrations of the Psittacidae*, though in some cases reduced and reversed. A few are quite close copies. Lear is sometimes but not always given credit in the text, though reference is always made if the species appears in *Illustrations of Psittacidae*.

MORRIS, BEVERLEY R., *British Game Birds and Waterfowl*. London: Groombridge and Sons, n.d. (1855). Quarto.

9 species in this work were also illustrated by Lear in Gould's *Birds of Europe*. Of these, 1 (the Egyptian Goose) would appear to have been copied from Lear's illustration and 2 others bear a resemblance. No mention of Lear is made in the text, which attributes the illustrations to B. Fawcett. Some are unsigned, of which the Egyptian Goose, is one.

MORRIS, REV. FRANCIS ORPEN, *A History of British Birds*. 6 volumes, London: Groombridge and Sons, 1851–57. Octavo.

11 plates are direct copies, though reduced and usually reversed, of Lear's figures in vols I, III, and IV of Gould's *Birds of Europe*. There are also a number obviously taken from Lear's plates of varying degrees of closeness.

IV Birds named after Lear

i) *Anodorhynchus leari (Bonaparte)*, Lear's Macaw

FORSHAW, JOSEPH M., *Parrots of the World*. Illustrated by William T. Cooper, 2nd edn, Newton Abbot and London: David and Charles, 1978 (1st published Australia 1973). Page 366: '*Lear's Macaw* Anodorhynchus leari. Bonaparte. Exact range unknown but probably north-eastern Brazil in the States of Pernambuco and Bahia. Lear's Macaw is a mysterious bird known only from specimens held in captivity. Voous (1965) suggests that it could be a hybrid . . . but this I cannot accept . . . Sick (1969) points out that the species must be regarded as rare, though there is a possibility that further populations may be discovered.'

L'Oiseau et la Revue Française d'Ornithologie, vol. 35, 1965. Page 153, Specimens of Lear's Macaw in the Zoological Museum of Amsterdam, by K. H. Voous: 'The present scanty knowledge about this large and conspicuous bird makes it unlikely, though not impossible, that it represents an independent species.'

NAUMANIA, *Journal für die Ornithologie*, Dessau, 1856. Appendix (folding plate and list): 'Conspectus psittacorum by Prince C-L. Bonaparte. Anodorhynchus leari. Bp. (M. hyacinthus, Lear).'

SALVADORI, T., *Catalogue of Birds in the British Museum*, vol. XX, London, 1891. Sclater collection. Page 148: 'Anodorhynchus leari. Synon. Ara leari. Sittace leari. (and other synons. excluding the name Lear, including Macrocercus hyacinthus, Viell. under which name it appears in Illustrations of Psittacidae Plate 9).'

SOUANCÉ, CHARLES DE, *Iconographie des Perroquets*, Paris, 1857. Plate 1, *Anodorhynchus leari. Bp. L'Anodorhynque de Lear. etc.* (distinguishes *A. leari* as a separate species from *A. glauca*).

ii) *Lopochroa leari (Bonaparte)*, Lear's Cockatoo

GRAY, GEORGE ROBERT, *Hand-list of Genera and Species of Birds . . . in the British Museum*, part II, p. 176: 'Cacatua ducorpsii. Syn. leari. Finsch.' (Note: Forshaw, *Parrots of the World*, does not mention *syn. Lopochroa leari* under *Cacatua ducorpsi*.)

Nederlandohe Tijdschift voor de Dierkunde, Amsterdam, 1863, p. xxiii: 'Cacatua. Lopochroa leari, Bonaparte—nieuwe soort. "Lear's Kakatoe". 1 exampl . . . Ter eere van den Heer Lear genoemd.'

SALVADORI, T., *Catalogue of Birds in the British Museum*, vol. XX, pp. 129–30; 'Cacatua ducorpsi (Solomon Is.). Syn Lopochroa leari Bp.'

iii) *Pyrrhulopsis tabuensis*, Tabuan Parrot

GRAY, GEORGE ROBERT, *Hand-list of Genera and Species of Birds . . . in the British Museum*, part II, p. 139: 'Pyrrhulopsis tabuensis. Syn. leari bp.' (Note this bird is '*Pyrrhulopsis tabuensis* in *Illustrations of Psittacidae*. Forshaw, *Parrots of the World*, does not mention *syn. leari*).

SALVADORI, T., *Catalogue of Birds in the British Museum*, p. 499: 'P. tabuensis—Tabuan Parrot (Fiji). Syn. Platycercus leari.'

TRAVEL BOOKS

Views in Rome and its Environs: Drawn from Nature & on Stone by Edward Lear. London: T. M'Lean, 26, Haymarket. Printed by C. Hullmandel, 1841. Folio. Title with tinted lithographed view and 25 tinted lithographed plates.

Illustrated Excursions in Italy. London: Thomas M'Lean, 26, Haymarket, 1846. Quarto. 2 volumes.

Vol. I: title as above, with 30 tinted lithographed plates, a hand-coloured engraved map and 40 engraved vignettes, including 1 on the title page. Published April 1846.

Vol. II: title as above, with 'Volume II' added. On the front cover and spine the words 'Second Series' have been added. It contains 25 lithographed plates and 15 vignettes, including that on the title-page. Published August 1846.

Journals of a Landscape Painter in Albania, &c. London: Richard Bentley. Publisher in Ordinary to Her Majesty. 1851. Octavo. Map and 20 lithographed plates. 2nd edn, 1852. Title on spine is *Journal of a Landscape Painter in Albania & Illyria*. Reprinted as *Edward Lear in Greece: Journals of a Landscape Painter in Greece and Albania*, William Kimber, 1965.

Journals of a Landscape Painter in Southern Calabria, &c. (London): Richard Bentley. New Burlington Street. Publisher in Ordinary to Her Majesty. 1852. Octavo. 2 maps and 20 lithographed plates.

The second part of the book, with a separate half-title, is *Journals of a Landscape Painter. Kingdom of Naples*. Title on spine is *Journals of a Landscape Painter in Calabria*. Reprinted as *Edward Lear in Southern Calabria and the Kingdom of Naples*, William Kimber, 1964.

Views in the Seven Ionian Islands. Inscribed by His Excellency's permission to Major Genl. Sir Henry Storks, K.C.B., G.C.M.G., Lord High Commissioner. Drawn from Nature by Edward Lear. London: Published by Edward Lear, 15 Stratford Place, Oxford Street. December 1st 1863. Folio. Tinted lithographed title page and 20 other tinted lithographed plates.

Facsimile edn published by Hugh Broadbent, Oldham, 1979, limited to 1,000 copies.

Journal of a Landscape Painter in Corsica. London: Robert John Bush, 32, Charing Cross. 1870. Octavo. 40 plates and 40 vignettes.

A note at the end of the preface, p.x., says: 'With the exception of six of the large plates and ten of the vignettes, the whole of the eighty illustrations have been drawn on wood by myself, from my original sketches. And I gladly take this opportunity of thanking M.M. Pibaraud, Pégard, Pannemaker, Badoureau and Mr. J. D. Cooper, for the care and accuracy with which they have engraved the drawings submitted to their care.'

All the plates bear the monogram *E.L.*, and it is not possible to distinguish the above exceptions. The title on the spine is *Journal of a Landscape Painter in Corsica, 1868*.

Reprinted as *Edward Lear in Corsica: The Journal of a Landscape Painter*, William Kimber, 1966.

Travel books published after Lear's death

'The Journey to Petra—a leaf from the Journals of a Landscape Painter', with notes by Franklin Lushington. *Macmillans Magazine*, April 1897.

PROBY, GRANVILLE, *Lear in Sicily*: Twenty Line Drawings by Edward Lear illustrating a Tour made in May–July 1847, in the company of John Joshua Proby with a Coloured Frontispiece signed by both the Travellers and a full Introduction by Granville Proby. London: Duckworth, 1938. Small oblong quarto.

These are Nonsense drawings illustrating Lear's adventures in Sicily.

Edward Lear's Journals: A Selection, ed. H. Van Thal, Arthur Barker, 1952.

Edward Lear's Indian Journal: Watercolours and extracts from the diary of Edward Lear (1873–75), ed. Ray Murphy. Jarrolds, 1953. Octavo.

Illustrated with 9 coloured and 12 half-tone reproductions of watercolours and sketches by Lear.

Lear's Corfu: An Anthology drawn from the Painter's Letters. With a preface by Lawrence Durrell. Corfu Travel, Corfu 1965.

Illustrated with 9 lithographed plates taken from *Views in the Seven Ionian Islands*.

Edward Lear. The Cretan Journal, ed. Rowena Fowler. Denise Harvey and Company, Athens—Dedham, 1984.

Illustrated with 2 maps, 14 coloured reproductions of watercolours by Lear tipped in, 22 black and white illustrations by Lear and others.

NONSENSE

[A selective checklist of rhymes and stories, arranged chronologically. Compiled by Justin G. Schiller with the assistance of Brian Alderson, Dr Richard E. Buenger, Margaret N. Coughlin (Library of Congress), Eleanor M. Garvey (Department of Printing and Graphic Arts, The Houghton Library, Harvard University), Michael Joseph (New York Historical Society), Thomas V. Lange (The Huntington Library, San Marino), Vivien Noakes and Mrs Carl Shirley.]

A Book of Nonsense, by Derry down Derry. Thos. McLean, London, 10 February 1846. Two separate parts, each with 36 lithographed designs and verse captions in three elongated lines and the same pictorial title-leaf ('There was an old Derry down Derry,' etc) captioned in five lines. First printing of Lear's 73 limericks.

A Book of Nonsense, by Derry down Derry. T. McLean, London, 1855. 2nd edn, the 73 limericks printed together in one volume from new lithographic stones with all verse captions now relettered in the familiar five-line limerick format.

A Book of Nonsense. Routledge, Warne & Routledge, London [1861/2]. 3rd edn, newly enlarged with 43 additional limericks (totalling now 113); three verses have been omitted: the 'Old Man of New York', the 'Old Sailor of Compton' and the 'Old Man of Kildare'. This version is also the first printed with letterpress text and wood-engraved by the Brothers Dalziel, acknowledging Edward Lear as the author, and dedicated to 'the great-grandchildren, grand-nephews, and grand-nieces of Edward, 13th Earl of Derby'. Although the book appeared in 1861, and a copy was deposited in the British Museum in that year, the dedication is dated 1862. A proof copy survives with its dedication dated one year earlier.

A Book of Nonsense. Willis P. Hazard, Philadelphia [1863]. 1st American printing 'from the Tenth London Edition', with 113 limericks as above; the final leaf about the 'Young Lady of Clare' occurs only on the rear cover of the original binding. These same sheets were also apparently distributed with the imprint 'New York: M. Doolady, agent' [1863], its original title-leaf cancelled.

A Book of Nonsense. Frederick Warne, London; Scribner Welford, London [1870]. First quarto edn, the earlier versions (up to at least the 20th) printed as small oblong octavo, and the first with illustrations colour-printed from woodblocks; some earlier octavo edns were also issued with hand-coloured designs.

Nonsense Songs, Stories, Botany, and Alphabets. Robert John Bush, New York, 1871. 1st edn of Lear's second book of Nonsense, including three Nonsense alphabets and several of his most familiar poems: 'The Owl and the Pussy-cat', 'The Duck and the Kangaroo', 'The Daddy Long-legs and the Fly', etc.; these three poems were previously first printed in the American children's magazine *Our Young Folks* (February, March, April 1870 respectively) with different illustrations. The entire book was itself reprinted in America (James R. Osgood, Boston, 1871; deposited at Library of Congress on 22 June 1871) and there is also a version in slightly reduced format (Roberts Brothers, Boston, 1882) with the illustrations hand-coloured by stencil, as such the only known coloured edn of this title issued during Lear's lifetime.

The Owl and the Pussy Cat and other Nonsense Songs. [Joseph] Cundall, London, 1872. Illustrated by Lord Ralph Kerr, reproduced as 12 mounted photographs with inset letterpress text. Also includes Lear's 'The Duck & the Kangaroo' and an anonymous poem, 'How the Beasts got into the Ark'. Issued with permission of the publisher Bush, but most probably unauthorized and unkown to Lear.

Songs for Children: No. 5. *The Owl & the Pussy-Cat*; No. 7. *The Duck & the Kangaroo*. Music by Mrs J. Worthington Bliss (Miss Lindsay). J. B. Cramer, London, *c.* 1870s. 2 Lear poems from a miscellaneous series of 10 nursery songs, each with a fine colour-lithographed pictorial cover.

Nonsense Drolleries. Frederick Warne, London, 1889. Newly illustrated versions of 'The Owl & the Pussy Cat' and 'The Duck & the Kangaroo' by William Foster, the first of many re-illustrated versions published after Lear's death.

Calico Pie. For Philip Hofer, Cambridge, Mass. 1952; limited to 500 copies. Reproduces an original holograph text with ink sketches.

A Drawing Book Alphabet. Harvard College Library, Cambridge, Mass. [1954]. Facsimile of an original manuscript to the 2nd Nonsense alphabet (reproduced in the 1871 *Nonsense Songs*) with holograph text and drawings by Lear, introduction by Philip Hofer; limited to 1000 copies.

The Duck and the Kangaroo. Harvard College Library, Cambridge, Mass. 1956. Facsimile of an original manuscript with pen drawings at the Houghton Library, Harvard University. With an introduction by Philip Hofer; limited to 500 copies.

The Broom, the Shovel, the Poker and the Tongs. Foreword by Philip Hofer. Four Winds Press, [New York], 1977; limited to 150 copies. Facsimile of an original manuscript at the Houghton Library, Harvard University.

More Nonsense, Pictures, Rhymes, Botany etc. Robert John Bush, London, 1872.

1st edn of Lear's 3rd *Book of Nonsense*, including 100 new limerick verses and drawings, a new botany series and a 4th Nonsense alphabet.

Laughable Lyrics: A Fourth Book of Nonsense Poems, Songs, Botany, Music, &c. Robert John Bush, London, 1877. 1st edn thus, comprising 'The Dong with a Luminous Nose', 'The Pelican Chorus', 'The Pobble who has no Toes', 'The Quangle Wangle's Hat', etc., besides another comic botany series and 2 more Nonsense alphabets.

The Quangle Wangle's Hat. For Hugh Sharp, Edinburgh, 1933; limited to 50 copies. A Christmas keepsake reproducing Lear's holograph text and ink sketches, originally prepared for Gertrude Lushington.

The Pobble. For Hugh Sharp, Edinburgh, 1934; limited to 50 copies. As above, a Christmas keepsake reproducing an original Lear manuscript prepared for Gertrude Lushington.

Nonsense Books. Roberts Brothers, Boston, 1888. 1st Collected edn of Lear's 4 Nonsense books (deposited at Library of Congress, 15 September 1888); apparently the last two volumes were not separately published in America. The portrait frontispiece reproduces the last photograph taken of Edward Lear by Roncarolo (San Remo, 1887); the introduction reprints a short biographical account from *The London Saturday Review* (4 February, 1888) and an article in *The London Spectator* (September 1887); and it apparently includes the earliest printing of the Envoi ('How Pleasant to Know Mr. Lear'). A British issue appeared bound from American sheets, distributed by Fisher Unwin (London), and from Frederick Warne.

A Nonsense Birthday Book. Compiled from 'The Book of Nonsense' and 'More Nonsense'. Frederick Warne, London [1894]. 1st edn thus.

Nonsense Songs and Stories. Frederick Warne, London, 1895. Newly expanded with additional songs and an introduction by Sir Edward Strachey: including the Second Part of 'Mr. and Mrs. Discobbolos' (previously printed in *The Quarterly Review*, October 1888) and the autobiographical 'Incidents in the Life of Uncle Arly' (from *The Atlantic Monthly*, May 1894).

Sing a Song of Sixpence. Another Lost Legend, by the author of 'Lost Legends of the Nursery Songs' (?W.H. Hughes). George H. Ellis, Boston, 1902. A curious work with eight sketches by Lear hitherto unpublished.

Queery Leary Nonsense, ed. Lady [Constance (Braham)] Strachey, with an introduction by the Earl of Cromer. Mills & Boon, London [1911]. First printing of 'Drawings for Mother Goose', 3 additional illustrations for 'The Owl and the Pussy-cat', a series of coloured Nonsense birds, etc.

Facsimile of a Nonsense Alphabet. Frederick Warne, London [1926]. First printing of this new Lear manuscript, originally prepared about 1849 for T.E. Tatton; limited to 1000 numbered copies.

Edward Lear On My Shelves [William B. Osgood Field]. Privately Printed at the Bremer Presse, Munich, 1933. The primary bibliographical reference on Lear based on a remarkable private collection, now preserved intact at The Houghton Library, Harvard University. It reproduces many original drawings and holograph texts (Nonsense and otherwise) previously unpublished; limited to 155 numbered copies.

Nonsense Songs & Laughable Lyrics with 2 unfinished poems. Ed. Philip Hofer. Peter Pauper Press, Mt. Vernon, 1935; issued in a variety of limited versions. Includes 'The Scroobious Pip' and 'The Little Mouse'.

The Complete Nonsense of Edward Lear. Ed. and introduced by Holbrook Jackson. Faber & Faber, London [1947]. 1st edn thus.

A Nonsense Alphabet. Victoria & Albert Museum, Small Picture Book no. 32. London, 1952. Facsimile of their Pirouet manuscript plus a selection from 16 watercolours of comic birds.

Teapots and Quails, and other New Nonsenses. Ed. and introduced by Angus Davidson and Philip Hofer. Harvard University Press, Cambridge Mass. [1953]; limited to 155 copies. Besides the title sequence and some limericks, this includes a new 'Flora Nonsensica' and 'The Adventures of Mr. Lear, the Polly and the Pusseybite'.

Lear Alphabet ABC. McGraw-Hill, New York; Constable Young, London, [1965]. Facsimile of a previously unknown Nonsense alphabet, acquired 10 February 1964 (Sotheby's) by Theodore Besterman.

Rhymes of Nonsense: An Alphabet. Bertram Rota, London [1968]. Facsimile of the R. C. Blencowe manuscript, also from the Besterman collection; limited to 500 copies.

Ye Long Nite in ye Wonderfull Bedde: A Bread-and-butter Letter with Reservations? Friends of the Fitzwilliam Museum, Cambridge [1972]. Facsimile of a sequence of captioned drawings (watermarked 1853), hitherto unpublished.

St. Kiven and the Gentle Kathleen. New Haven, 1973. Facsimile of an original manuscript with pen drawings on 8 sheets. With an introduction by Donald Gallup; limited to 500 copies.

A Book of Bosh chosen by Brian Alderson. Puffin Books [Harmondsworth, 1975]. Includes a selective glossary of Lear's 'wurbl inwentions' besides a few 'eggstrax' from unpublished material.

Lear in the Original. With an introduction and notes by Herman W. Leibert. H. P. Kraus, New York, 1975. First printing of the Hornby manuscript with 109 Nonsense drawings by Lear prepared 1835–41, including 48 drawings and verse captions to 45 limericks (38 of them used in the 1846 *Book of Nonsense*); also comprising versions of 'Goosy goosy gander', 'Auld Robin Gray', 'Adventures of Daniel O'Rourke', 'The Ostrich & the Kangaroo', etc.

For Lovers of Birds, For Lovers of Cats, For Lovers of Flowers & Gardens, For Lovers of Food & Drink. Compiled by Vivien Noakes and Charles Lewsen. London: Collins, 1978. Include unpublished Nonsense from Lear's letters.

Bosh and Nonsense. Allen Lane (Penguin Books), London, 1982. Original printing of two Nonsense sketchbooks prepared by Lear for Ada Duncan, including several limerick verses and drawings hitherto unrecorded.

The Tragical Life and Death of Caius Marius Esq. . . . from authentic sauces. [For Justin G. Schiller, New York, 1983.] Facsimile of this hitherto unrecorded manuscript by Lear, amongst the earliest of his Nonsense stories composed in 1841; limited to 100 copies.

[Only those publications which contain previously unpublished material have been listed. A few published works attributed to Edward Lear, but which in the opinion of J.S. and V.N. are not by him, have been omitted. V.N.]

EXHIBITIONS

Edward Lear, 1812–1888, London, Redfern Gallery, March–April 1942.

Watercolour drawings of the Ionian Islands by Edward Lear, London, Adams Gallery, November–December 1946.

Mediterranean Views by Edward Lear, London, Leger Gallery, February–March 1950.

Edward Lear: Water-colours of Greece: A Loan Exhibition, London, Walkers Gallery, 1951.

Edward Lear, New Haven, Conn., Jonathan Edward College, Yale University, 1951.

Edward Lear 1812–1888: An Exhibition of Oil Paintings, Water-colours and Drawings, Books and Prints, Manuscripts, Photographs and Records, London, Arts Council of Great Britain, July 1958.

Drawings by Edward Lear, San Marino, Calif., Henry E. Huntington Library and Art Gallery, November–December 1962.

Corfu (Ionian Islands): Greece, London, The British Council, May–June 1964.

Edward Lear: Drawings from a Greek Tour, Sheffield, The Graves Art Gallery, 1964.

Edward Lear: Painter, Poet and Draughtsman: An Exhibition of Drawings, Water-colours, Oils, Nonsense and Travel Books, Worcester, Mass., Worcester Art Museum, 1968.

Edward Lear, London, Gooden and Fox Ltd, 1968.

English Watercolours in the Collection of C.F.J. Beausire, Liverpool, Walker Art Gallery, 1970.

Edward Lear in Greece: A Loan Exhibition from the Gennadius Library, Athens, Washington, D.C., International Exhibitions Foundation, 1971–72.

Edward Lear and Knowsley, Liverpool, Walker Art Gallery, 1975.

How Pleasant to Know Mr. Lear: Water-colours by Edward Lear from Rhode Island Collections, Providence, R.I., Museum of Art, Rhode Island School of Design, 1982.

The Travels of Edward Lear, London, The Fine Art Society, 1983.

Index

[References to colour plates are in bold type]

Royal Academy Trust

The Trustees and Appeal Committee of the Royal Academy Trust wish to express their gratitude to the many companies and individuals who have already given their support to the appeal. Among many others they would like to extend their thanks to:

H.M. The Queen
H.R.H. Princess Alexandra
The Hon. Angus Ogilvy
Craigie Aitchison, ARA
Akai
Allied-Lyons PLC
American Associates of the R.A. Trust
American Express Europe Limited
The Arthur Andersen Foundation
Mrs John W. Anderson II
Anglia Television Limited
Arbuthnot Latham Bank Limited
James Archibald
Associated British Foods
The Bank of England
Bankers Trust Company
Barclays Bank PLC
The Baring Foundation
B.A.T. Industries p.l.c.
Tom Bendhem
The Benham Charitable Settlement
James Benson
BICC plc
In Memoriam Ida Rose Biggs
Blue Circle Industries plc
The BOC Group
Bollinger Champagne
C.T. Bowring & Co. Limited
Peter Bowring
British Airways
British American Arts Association Inc.
The British Electric Traction Company PLC
British Gas Corporation
British Olivetti Limited
The British Petroleum Company PLC
Britoil plc
Brooke Bond Group
Bunzl PLC
Burmah Oil
C & A Charitable Trust
Chapman Charitable Trust
The Chase Charity
Christie's
CIBA-GEIGY PLC
The Cleary Foundation
The Trustees of the Clore Foundation
The Clothworkers' Company
Cocoa Merchants Limited
The John S. Cohen Foundation
Commercial Union Assurance Company plc
Consolidated Goldfields PLC
Coopers & Lybrand
Coutts & Co.
Raymond Cowern, RA
Basil de Ferranti
Roger de Grey, PRA
The De La Rue Company plc
The Leopold de Rothschild Charitable Trust
The Distillers' Company
Sir Philip Dowson, ARA
The Drapers' Company
Alfred Dunhill Limited
Eagle Star Insurance Group
The Ells Will Trust
Esso UK plc
Esmee Fairbairn Charitable Trust
Finance for Industry plc
The Fishmongers' Company
J. B. Flanagan
Forbes Magazine
The Gordon Fraser Charitable Trust
Mrs W. K. French
Dr Kenzo Fujii
Gallaher Limited
The Garfield Weston Foundation
General Accident Fire & Life Assurance Corporation
The General Electric Company plc
The late Sir Frederick Gibberd, CBE, RA
Simon Gibson Charitable Trust
Gill & Duffus Group Limited
Anthony T. Gillings
Glaxo (1972) Charity Trust
The Jack Goldhill Charitable Trust
The Goldsmiths' Company
Frederick Gore, RA
Her Majesty's Government
Grabar Investments Ltd
The Grocers' Company
Guardian Royal Exchange Assurance plc
Guest, Keen and Nettlefolds plc
Calouste Gulbenkian Foundation
The Haberdashers' Company
Dr and Mrs Armand Hammer
Mrs Sue Hammerson, OBE
The Hammerson Group of Companies
The Lord Hanson
L. G. Harris and Company Limited
Haslemere DFAS
The Hayward Foundation
Hayward Tyler
The Hedley Foundation
H. J. Heinz Charitable Trust
Brian L. Hercules
Herring Son & Daw
Hill Samuel Group PLC
David Hockney BBC Radio 4 Appeal
Hogg Robinson Group
Hongkong Bank
IBM United Kingdom Group
IC Gas
The Idlewild Trust
Imperial Chemical Industries PLC
Imperial Tobacco Limited
Inchcape Charitable Trust
International Thomson Organisation
Princess Esra Jah of Hyderabad
The Kaye Organisation
Kleinwort, Benson Ltd.
Maurice Laing Foundation
Roland P. Lay
Lazard Brothers & Co. Limited
Miss R. A. Le Bas, RE, NEAC
The Leche Trust
Lord Leverhulme's Charitable Trust
Kenneth Levy
John Lewis Partnership plc
Lex Services P.L.C.
Lloyds Bank PLC
The Corporation and Members of Lloyds and Lloyd's Brokers
London Clubs Limited
London & Scottish Marine Oil PLC
London Weekend Television Limited
Sir Jack and Lady Lyons
McCann Erickson Advertising Limited
The Manifold Trust
Leonard Manesseh, OBE, RA
The Manor Charitable Trust
Marks and Spencer p.l.c.
Miss A. W. Martinet
Matheson & Co. Limited
Paul Mellon, KBE
The Anthony and Elizabeth Mellows Charitable Trust
The Mercers' Company
The Merchant Taylors' Company
Metal Box p.l.c.
Midland Bank plc
The Miller and Tiley Charitable Trust
The Peter Minet Trust
Trustees of D.W. Mitchell Charitable Trust
Mobil Oil Company Limited
The Moorgate Trust Fund
Morgan Grenfell & Co. Ltd.
Morgan Guaranty Trust Company of New York
Mount Trust
National Westminster Bank PLC
News International p.l.c.
Stavros S. Niarchos
The Normanby Charitable Trust
Northern Foods PLC
Norwich Union Insurance Group
Sir Duncan Oppenheim
The Ormonde Foundation
The Orrin Trust
Ove Arup Partnership
H. R. Owen Limited
The Paragon Trust
P & O Steam Navigation Company
S. Pearson and Son plc
Peat, Marwick, Mitchell & Co.
Peerless Pump
P. F. Charitable Trust
Michael C. S. Philip
The Pilgrim Trust
R. V. Pitchforth, RA
The Plessey Company plc
Mr and Mrs Greville Poke
Prudential Assurance Company Limited
The Rank Organisation plc
Ranks Hovis McDougall PLC
Rank Xerox Limited
The Rayne Foundation
Reed International PLC
Ivor Roberts-Jones, CBE, RA
The Ronson Charitable Foundation
The Jacob Rothschild Charitable Trust
Rowntree Mackintosh
The Royal Bank of Scotland
Royal Insurance p.l.c.
Royal Oak Foundation, Inc., New York
RTZ Services Limited
Russell Reynolds Associates
The Sainsbury Family Charitable Trusts
Save & Prosper
J. Henry Schroder Wagg & Co. Ltd.
William Scott, CBE, RA
Sea Containers Limited
Shell UK Limited
The late Sir Richard Sheppard, CBE, RA
Sheppard Robson Architects
Harry & Abe Sherman Foundation
Dr Francis Singer, DSC
The Skinners' Company
Slough Estates plc
Edward Speelman Limited
Standard Chartered Bank
Standard Telephones & Cables PLC
Mr and Mrs Dennis C. Stanfill
Sterling Guarantee Trust PLC
Sun Alliance & London Insurance Group
The Bernard Sunley Charitable Foundation
John Swire & Sons Limited
Tate & Lyle plc
Taylor Woodrow Charitable Trust
Technical Indexes Limited
Thames Television Limited
Sir Jules Thorn Charitable Trust
THORN EMI plc
Thomas Tilling plc
Tozer Kemsley & Millbourn (Holdings) Ltd
Trafalgar House Public Limited Company
The Trehaven Trust Limited
The Triangle Trust (1949) Fund
Trident Television plc
Trustee Savings Bank (Holdings) Limited
The Twenty Seven Foundation
Unilever PLC
The Verdon-Smith Family Trust
A. F. Wallace Charitable Trust
S. G. Warburg & Company Limited
Wartski
The Weinberg Family Charitable Trust
Whitbread and Company PLC
Wilde Sapte
Wilkinson Sword Group Limited
H. H. Wingate Charitable Foundation
Winsor and Newton (part of the Reckitt and Colman Group)
The Wolfson Foundation
Sir John Woolf
Egon Zehnder International

The Friends of the Royal Academy

BENEFACTORS

Mrs M. G. T. Askew
Mrs Hilda Benham
Lady Brinton
Sir Nigel & Lady Broackes
Keith Bromley Esq.
The John S. Cohen Foundation
The Colby Trust
Michael E. Flintoff Esq.
The Lady Gibson
Jack Goldhill Esq., FRICS
Mrs Mary Graves
D. J. Hoare Esq.
Sir Anthony Hornby
Irene and Hyman Kreitman
The Landmark Trust
Roland Lay Esq.
The Trustees of the Leach Fourteenth Trust
Hugh Leggatt Esq.
Mr and Mrs M. S. Lipworth
Sir Jack Lyons, CBE
The Manor Charitable Trustees
Lieutenant-Colonel L. S. Michael, OBE
Jan Mitchell Esq.
The Lord Moyne
The Lady Moyne
Mrs Sylvia Mulcahy
G. R. Nicholas Esq.
Lieutenant-Colonel Vincent Paravicini
Mrs Vincent Paravicini
Richard Park Esq.
Phillips Fine Art Auctioneers
Mrs Denise Rapp
Mrs Adrianne Reed
Mrs Basil Samuel
Sir Eric Sharp, CBE
The Revd Prebendary E. F. Shotter
Dr Francis Singer
Lady Daphne Straight
Mrs Pamela Synge
Harry Teacher Esq.
Henry Vyner Charitable Trust
Charles Wollaston Esq.

CORPORATE SPONSORS

American Express Europe Ltd
Bankers Trust Company
Barclays Bank International Limited
Bourne Leisure Group Limited
The British Petroleum Company Limited
Brixton Estate PLC
Christie Manson and Woods Limited
Christ's Hospital
Citibank
P & D Colnaghi & Co Ltd
Consolidated Safeguards Limited
Courage Charitable Trust
Coutts & Co.
Delta Group PLC
Esso Petroleum Company Limited
Ford Motor Company Limited
The General Electric Co. PLC
The Granada Group
Arthur Guiness and Sons PLC
Guiness Peat Group
Alexander Howden Underwriting Limited
IBM United Kingdom Limited
Imperial Chemical Industries PLC
Investment Company of North Atlantic
Johnson Wax Limited
Lex Service Group PLC
London Weekend Television Ltd
Marks and Spencer PLC
Mars Limited
Martini & Rossi Limited
Worshipful Company of Mercers
The Néstle Charitable Trust
Ocean Transport and Trading Limited
(P. H. Holt Trust)
Ove Arup Partnership
The Rio Tinto-Zinc Corporation PLC
Rowe and Pitman
The Royal Bank of Scotland PLC
Save & Prosper Educational Trust
J. Henry Schroder Wagg and Company Limited
Seascape Insurance Holdings Ltd
Shell UK Limited
W. H. Smith & Son Limited
Sotheby & Co
The Spencer Wills Trust
Thames Television Limited
J. Walter Thompson Company Limited
Ultramar PLC
United Biscuits (UK) Limited
Vacuum Instruments & Products Ltd

INDIVIDUAL SPONSORS

Abdullah Ben Saad Al-Saud
Ian Fife Campbell Anstruther Esq.
Mrs Ann Appelbe
Dwight W. Arundale Esq.
Edgar Astaire Esq.
W. M. Ballantyne Esq.
Miss Margaret Louise Band
P. G. Bird Esq.
Mrs C. W. T. Blackwell
Godfrey Bonsack Esq.
Peter Bowring Esq.
Mrs Susan Bradman
Vagn Bremerskov Esq.
Cornelius Broere Esq.
Jeremy Brown Esq.
Mr and Mrs R. Cadbury
W. J. Chapman Esq.
Major A. J. Chrystal
Citicorp International Private Bank
Henry M. Cohen Esq.
Mrs N. S. Conrad
Mrs Elizabeth Corob
Raymond de Prudhoe Esq.
The Marquess of Douro
Mrs Gilbert Edgar
Aidan Ellis Esq.
Miss Rosemary Farmer
Robert S. Ferguson Esq.
Dr Gert-Rudolf Flick
Graham Gauld Esq.
Victor Gauntlett Esq.
Lady Gibberd
Peter George Goulandris Esq.
Gavin Graham Esq.
J. A. Hadjipateras Esq.
Mrs S. Halliday
Miss J. Hazandras
Mrs Penelope Heseltine
Mrs Mark Hoffman
C. Howard Esq.
Norman J. Hyams Esq.
Mrs Manya Igel
J. P. Jacobs Esq.
Mrs Christopher James
Alan Jeavons Esq.
Irwin Joffe Esq.
S. D. M. Kahan Esq.
Mr & Mrs S. H. Karmel
Peter W. Kininmonth Esq.
S. J. Leonard Esq.
Mrs R. W. Levy
D. J. Lewis Esq.
Owen Luder Esq.
Mrs Graham Lyons
Mrs J. G. McCarthy
Ciarán MacGonigal Esq.
Mrs S. McGreevy
Peter McMean Esq.
Dr Abraham Marcus
Mrs P. C. Maresi
José Martin Esq.
M. H. Meissner Esq.
Mrs V. Mercer
Princess Helena Moutafian, MBE
The P. A. Charitable Trust
Raymond A. Parkin Esq.
Hon. Mrs E. H. Pearson
Mrs Olive Pettit
Mrs M. C. S. Philip
Miss Laura Lee Randall
Cyril Ray Esq.
Mrs Margaret Reeves
Miss Lucy Roland-Smith
The Rt. Hon Lord Rootes
J. A. Rosenblatt Esq.
The Hon Sir Steven Runciman, CH
The Master, the Worshipful Company of Saddlers
Sir Robert Sainsbury
Christopher Selmes Esq.
Claude Sere Esq.
R. J. Simia Esq.
Mrs D. Spalding
Thomas Stainton Esq.
Cyril Stein Esq.
James Q. Stringer Esq.
Mrs A. Susman
Robin Symes Esq.
Dr M. G. Walker
The Hon Mrs Quentin Wallop
J. B. Watton Esq.
Sidney S. Wayne Esq.
Frank S. Wenstrom Esq.
David Whitehead Esq.
David Wolfers Esq. MC
Brian Gordon Wolfson Esq.
Lawrence Wood Esq.
F. Worms Esq.

There are also anonymous Benefactors and Sponsors